Collins

Caribbean Social Sciences 1

Lisa Greenstein, Daphne Paizee & Bruce Nicholson
Series Editor: **Cherril Barrett-Field**

William Collins' dream of knowledge for all began with the publication of his first book in 1819. A self-educated mill worker, he not only enriched millions of lives, but also founded a flourishing publishing house. Today, staying true to this spirit, Collins books are packed with inspiration, innovation and practical expertise. They place you at the centre of a world of possibility and give you exactly what you need to explore it.

Collins. Freedom to teach.

Published by Collins
An imprint of HarperCollins*Publishers*
The News Building
1 London Bridge Street
London SE1 9GF

HarperCollins Publishers
Macken House
39/40 Mayor Street Upper
Dublin 1
D01 C9W8
Ireland

Browse the complete Collins catalogue at
www.collins.co.uk

10 9 8 7 6 5 4

ISBN 978-0-00-849709-5

British Library Cataloguing in Publication Data
A catalogue record for this publication is available from the British Library.

Authors: Lisa Greenstein, Daphne Paizee, Bruce Nicholson, Barbara Arrindell, Actillia Arthur, Nicole Phillip-Dowe, Carolyn Forde, & Dave Ramsingh
Series editor: Cherril Barrett-Field
Publisher: Dr Elaine Higgleton
Commissioning editor: Bruce Nicholson
In-house senior editor: Julianna Dunn
Project manager: Claire Parkyns, QBS Learning
Copyeditor: Tania Pattison
Proofreader: Helen Bleck
Indexer, Illustrator, Photo researcher: QBS Learning
Cover designer: Gordon MacGilp
Cover photo: Ritu Manoj Jthani/Shutterstock
Series designer: Kevin Robbins
Typesetter: QBS Learning
Production controller: Rachel Weaver
Printed and bound by: Ashford Colour Press Ltd

See also page 319 for photograph acknowledgements

This book contains FSC™ certified paper and other controlled sources to ensure responsible forest management.

For more information visit: www.harpercollins.co.uk/green

Contents

How to use this book

These learning objectives tell you what you will be learning about in the lesson.

Unit 3: History

The history of my school

We are learning to:

- trace the history of my sources
- collect information through interviews and observations
- work collaboratively to produce a history of our school.

Each topic is divided into headings

Tracing the history of my school

Each topic has colourful photographs and illustrations to add context and meaning.

Many schools in the Caribbean have long, proud traditions. Your own school may be new or it may have started years ago. The people who started the school will have set out their **vision** for it and considered questions like these:

- What type of school is it and who will attend?
- What will be taught at the school (the **curriculum**)?
- Will the students wear a **uniform** and what will that be? How many students will be admitted?
- Where will the lessons take place? Who will teach the students?
- Will there be **extra-curricular** and sports activities?
- Who will lead the school?

School children in Barbuda.

Activity features allow you to do practical activities related to the topic.

Case study

The Far Hills High School is a landmark in its community. The school was **established** in 1953 and its **rationale** was to empower boys and girls of all religions and races to achieve academic success. The school provided education for children who lived in the area, who had previously had to travel far to attend school.

The school opened with 43 students in four classrooms. The school offered a full academic programme, as well as extra-curricular activities such as sports, music and drama. Students from the school have distinguished themselves in many walks of life.

Over the years the school has grown. New classrooms have been added and there are now 450 students.

Activity

Working in pairs, study the photograph of the old school classroom opposite. Compare this classroom with your own classroom.

Try these questions to check your understanding of each topic.

Questions

1. Why was the Far Hills School set up?
2. Do you think all children in the community were welcomed at this school?
3. Has the Far Hills School been successful in serving its community? Explain your answer.

Discussion

What do you know about the history of your own school? Discuss the history of your school with your teacher.

82 Lower Secondary Social Sciences: The history of my school

Discussion features allow you to work in pairs, in a group or as a class to explore the topic further.

Gathering information about your school

3.5

When researching the history of your school, you will need to think about:

- why it was set up and when
- the vision, **mission** and extra-curricular activities
- uniforms, buildings, sports and awards
- the legacy of the school, head teacher, teachers, students
- customs and traditions of the school.

There are many different ways of finding out about the history of your own school. You can start by observing your school buildings and sources of information at your school. Your school library may have information like this:

- primary sources such as photographs that show the school at different times
- copies of old school magazines with photographs and articles about school life during a specific year
- trophies and honour rolls that record the achievements of students over the years.

Older members of the community can provide interesting information about daily life at school. You can set up interviews with some people. Draw up a questionnaire with questions similar to these:

- Did you attend this school?
- Which subjects did you study?
- Did you do any extra-curricular activities?
- Were you punished if you did not obey rules? How?
- What were your best memories of the school?

Secondary sources such as articles in magazines and newspapers can also provide valuable information about schools. You can search the websites of local newspapers for articles.

Schoolchildren during a lesson in Port-au-Prince, Haiti.

Topics have some fascinating extra facts.

Key vocabulary

vision
curriculum (curricula)
uniform
extra-curricular
established
rationale
mission

These are the most important new social sciences words in the topic. You can check their meanings in the Glossary at the end of the book.

Project

Working in groups, and then as a class, produce a booklet about the history of your school. To do this you will need to do some careful planning and then work cooperatively. Everyone in the class should make a contribution.

The information that you collect should come from interviews and other primary and secondary sources. You should also compile a bibliography to acknowledge the sources you have used and create a timeline to show the major events in the school's history.

83

Project features allow you to work on your own or in groups to explore the topic further and present your findings to your class or your teacher.

This page gives a summary of the exciting new ideas you will be learning about in the unit.

These lists at the end of a unit act as a checklist of the key ideas of the unit.

This is the topic covered in the unit, which links to the syllabus.

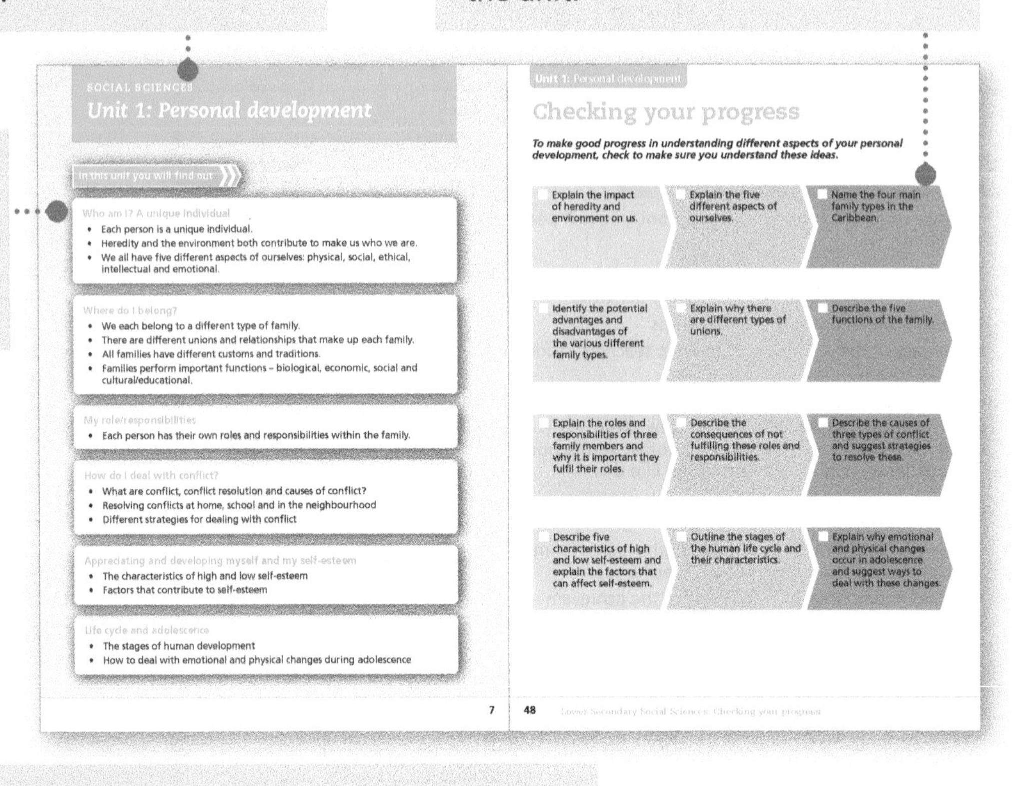

SOCIAL SCIENCES

Unit 1: Personal development

In this unit you will find out

Who am I? A unique individual
- Each person is a unique individual.
- Heredity and the environment both contribute to make us who we are.
- We all have five different aspects of ourselves: physical, social, ethical, intellectual and emotional.

Where do I belong?
- We each belong to a different type of family.
- There are different unions and relationships that make up each family.
- All families have different customs and traditions.
- Families perform important functions – biological, economic, social and cultural/educational.

My role/responsibilities
- Each person has their own roles and responsibilities within the family.

How do I deal with conflict?
- What are conflict, conflict resolution and causes of conflict?
- Resolving conflicts at home, school and in the neighbourhood
- Different strategies for dealing with conflict

Appreciating and developing myself and my self-esteem
- The characteristics of high and low self-esteem
- Factors that contribute to self-esteem

Life cycle and adolescence
- The stages of human development
- How to deal with emotional and physical changes during adolescence

7

Unit 1: Personal development

Checking your progress

To make good progress in understanding different aspects of your personal development, check to make sure you understand these ideas.

- Explain the impact of heredity and environment on us.
- Explain the five different aspects of ourselves.
- Name the four main family types in the Caribbean.
- Identify the potential advantages and disadvantages of the various different family types.
- Explain why there are different types of unions.
- Describe the five functions of the family.
- Explain the roles and responsibilities of three family members and why it is important they fulfil their roles.
- Describe the consequences of not fulfilling these roles and responsibilities.
- Describe the causes of three types of conflict and suggest strategies to resolve these.
- Describe five characteristics of high and low self-esteem and explain the factors that can affect self-esteem.
- Outline the stages of the human life cycle and their characteristics.
- Explain why emotional and physical changes occur in adolescence and suggest ways to deal with these changes.

48 Lower Secondary Social Sciences: Checking your progress

These end-of-unit questions allow you and your teacher to check that you have understood the ideas in unit 1, and that you can explain social sciences using the skills and knowledge you have gained.

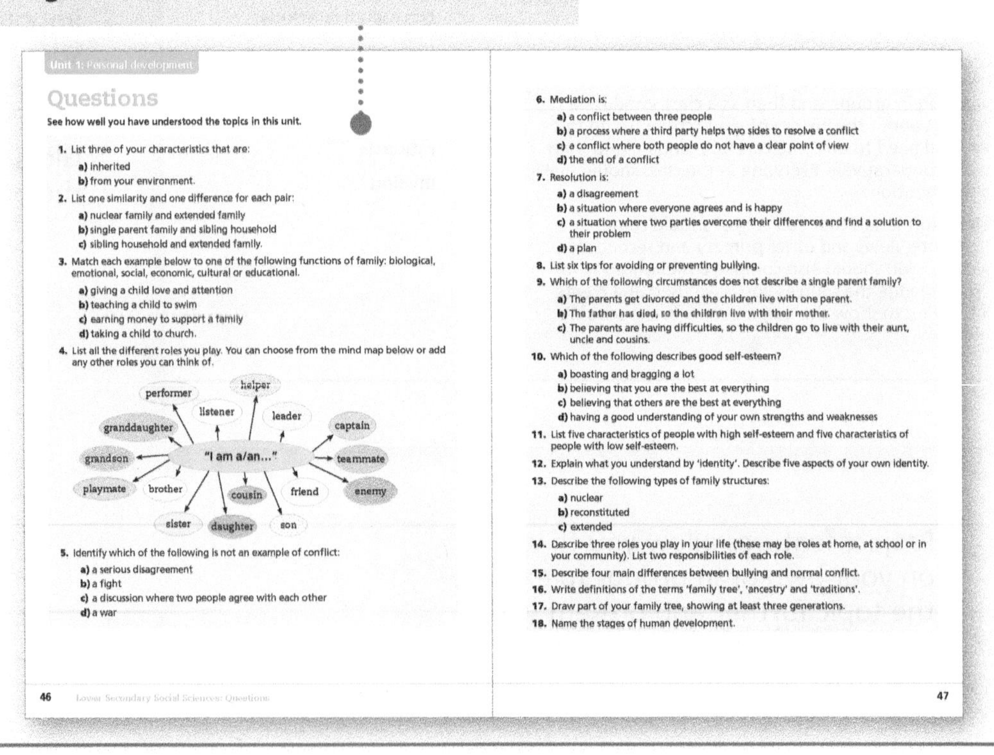

Unit 1: Personal development

Questions

See how well you have understood the topics in this unit.

1. List three of your characteristics that are:
   a) inherited
   b) from your environment.
2. List one similarity and one difference for each pair:
   a) nuclear family and extended family
   b) single parent family and sibling household
   c) sibling household and extended family.
3. Match each example below to one of the following functions of family: biological, emotional, social, economic, cultural or educational.
   a) giving a child love and attention
   b) teaching a child to swim
   c) earning money to support a family
   d) taking a child to church.
4. List all the different roles you play. You can choose from the mind map below or add any other roles you can think of.

5. Identify which of the following is not an example of conflict:
   a) a serious disagreement
   b) a fight
   c) a discussion where two people agree with each other
   d) a war
6. Mediation is:
   a) a conflict between three people
   b) a process where a third party helps two sides to resolve a conflict
   c) a conflict where both people do not have a clear point of view
   d) the end of a conflict
7. Resolution is:
   a) a disagreement
   b) a situation where everyone agrees and is happy
   c) a situation where two parties overcome their differences and find a solution to their problem
   d) a plan
8. List six tips for avoiding or preventing bullying.
9. Which of the following circumstances does not describe a single parent family?
   a) The parents get divorced and the children live with one parent.
   b) The father has died, so the children live with their mother.
   c) The parents are having difficulties, so the children go to live with their aunt, uncle and cousins.
10. Which of the following describes good self-esteem?
    a) boasting and bragging a lot
    b) believing that you are the best at everything
    c) believing that others are the best at everything
    d) having a good understanding of your own strengths and weaknesses
11. List five characteristics of people with high self-esteem and five characteristics of people with low self-esteem.
12. Explain what you understand by 'identity'. Describe five aspects of your own identity.
13. Describe the following types of family structures:
    a) nuclear
    b) reconstituted
    c) extended
14. Describe three roles you play in your life (these may be roles at home, at school or in your community). List two responsibilities of each role.
15. Describe four main differences between bullying and normal conflict.
16. Write definitions of the terms 'family tree', 'ancestry' and 'traditions'.
17. Draw part of your family tree, showing at least three generations.
18. Name the stages of human development.

46 Lower Secondary Social Sciences: Questions

47

Unit 1: Personal development

In this unit you will find out 

Who am I? A unique individual

- Each person is a unique individual.
- Heredity and the environment both contribute to make us who we are.
- We all have five different aspects of ourselves: physical, social, ethical, intellectual and emotional.

Where do I belong?

- We each belong to a different type of family.
- There are different unions and relationships that make up each family.
- All families have different customs and traditions.
- Families perform important functions – biological, economic, social and cultural/educational.

My role/responsibilities

- Each person has their own roles and responsibilities within the family.

How do I deal with conflict?

- What are conflict, conflict resolution and causes of conflict?
- Resolving conflicts at home, school and in the neighbourhood
- Different strategies for dealing with conflict

Appreciating and developing myself and my self-esteem

- The characteristics of high and low self-esteem
- Factors that contribute to self-esteem

Life cycle and adolescence

- The stages of human development
- How to deal with emotional and physical changes during adolescence

Who am I? A unique individual

We are learning to:

- define and use correctly the terms unique, individuality, characteristic and individual differences
- recognise ourselves and others as unique individuals.

Each person is a unique individual

No two **individuals** are exactly alike. Even twins have **individual differences.** Your **identity** is who you are and the **characteristics** that define you.

Each person is **unique**, meaning we are special and different from everyone else. **Individuality** is what makes you different from others. Yet we all have similarities that relate us to other people, such as the colour of our eyes or our sense of humour.

Your individuality comes from your personal characteristics. These may be characteristics on the outside of your body like your size and shape, your appearance and your physical abilities. On the inside, each person has their own thoughts and ideas, interests, hopes and fears. These are your actions, attitudes and behaviours.

We also have our own values (what we believe is important in life) and **ethics** (what we consider to be the right and wrong things to do).

You may look and sound similar to other people in your family and in your community, but no one is exactly like you. Our shared characteristics help us to belong and fit in.

We each have characteristics that make us similar to and different from others.

Exercise

1. Trace the outline of your hand. Fill in the outline with characteristics that make you unique. Write one characteristic in each finger.
2. Compare your hand with a friend's. What is similar? What is different?
3. Look at the photograph above. In pairs, list characteristics about each person:
   a) two similar characteristics
   b) two different characteristics

Did you know...?

No two people have the same fingerprint. Just like your fingerprint, your identity is unique. There is no one exactly like you.

Recognising ourselves as unique individuals

Look at the picture on page 8. You can see the differences between the two people. However, the picture only shows their physical characteristics. It cannot tell us what they like doing, how they treat others or what their interests are.

Each person has their own personal characteristics that determine their **personality**. Your personality is the combination of personal characteristics that make up your character. These characteristics determine how people behave in different situations.

To recognise people as unique individuals, we need to notice their:

- actions – what kinds of things they do
- attitudes – how they approach their actions, and how they view themselves and others
- behaviours – patterns in what they do and how they do it.

Exercise

4. a) Choose five words from the word cloud above to describe yourself.

   b) Why did you choose those words?

5. a) Which words do you think your family and friends would use to describe you?

   b) How accurate do you think other people's descriptions of you are?

6. What three words would you like to use to describe yourself in 10 years' time?

7. Draw a picture of yourself. Divide the area around the picture into five areas. Fill each area with words describing your personality.

Discussion

What would happen if everyone were identical? What problems might we face? How does it benefit the community and the country to be made up of people with so many different talents and skills?

Project

Brainstorm words that describe who you are – your interests, beliefs, values and **personal qualities.**

Cut out words from magazines and newspapers to make your own 'word cloud'.

Key vocabulary

individual

individual differences

identity

characteristic

unique

individuality

ethics

personality

personal qualities

Heredity and the environment

We are learning to:

- define and use correctly the terms heredity, environment and genes
- explain the impact of heredity and environment on us.

Have you ever wondered why we share characteristics with our **parents** and **siblings**? What you look like depends a lot on what your parents look like and the genes you inherit from them.

The characteristics that **children** inherit through **genes** from their parents is called **heredity**. Genes are like a set of instructions for your body and are the reason that you probably bear a resemblance to others in your family. You might inherit the same colour eyes, hair and so on.

What you look like depends on what your parents, or other members of your family, look like.

The environment

How we interact with the **environment** – the world around us – helps to produce our personal characteristics. A person's environment is more than just their physical location. Your environment includes:

- your family
- your peers
- society
- culture and media
- your school
- your home.

All of these help to shape your physical appearance, personality, behaviour, attitudes and beliefs.

Exercise

1. Draw mind maps to illustrate what you understand by:
   a) heredity
   b) environment
2. Give one characteristic of yourself that is only determined by heredity and one characteristic that is only determined by environment. Explain your choices.
3. True or false: every characteristic is the result of either heredity or environment. Give a reason for your answer.
4. Describe characteristics that make you similar to or different from other members of your family.

Discussion

Have a class discussion about the term 'environment' and what you understand by it.

How does the environment and what we inherit from our parents affect us? It can affect our physical appearance, personality, behaviour, attitudes and beliefs.

Physical appearance

Heredity determines physical **traits**, such as eye colour or blood type. The environment can affect physical appearance. For example, a light-skinned person who lives in a sunny environment may develop freckles from the sun.

Personality

Your **social environment** has a strong impact on your personality. This is the world made up of the people around you: home, family, siblings, neighbours, peers, teachers and other people. The development of a child's personality can also be determined by such factors as moving to a new country or school, the loss of a parent, their parents' divorce or a conflict in the family.

Behaviour

Some behaviours come naturally and do not require any teaching. For example, a newborn baby knows how to suckle milk from its mother. However, a lot of our behaviour is learned from our social environment, especially from our family and peers.

Attitudes and beliefs

Your **attitude** is the way you approach people and events in your life. Someone with a positive attitude may be optimistic and expect things to go well. Someone with a negative attitude may be pessimistic and expect things to go badly. In general, attitudes and beliefs come from your environment.

Exercise

5. For each of the following characteristics, say whether it is determined by genes, the environment or both. Give reasons for your answers.

a) the colour of your eyes

b) the sound of your voice

c) the language you speak

d) the music you like listening to

6. In groups create dramatised stories of two characters who grew up in different environments. Show the impact of each environment on their characteristics.

Here are some ideas of different environments: wartime; a loving family home; a family-run hotel. Or you can choose your own.

Identical twins have all the same genes, so their physical characteristics are very similar. However, they may have very different personalities.

Activity

In groups, write a story about a child who grew up in a particular environment (you choose) and the impact the environment had on the child's characteristics.

Key vocabulary

parents
siblings
children
genes
heredity
environment
trait
social environment
attitude

Aspects of ourselves

We are learning to:

- identify and describe different aspects of ourselves
- define and use correctly the terms tolerance, appreciation and respect
- develop an appreciation for the differences in others.

Aspects of ourselves

We all have **aspects** of ourselves. We each have five different aspects: **physical, social, ethical, intellectual** and **emotional**.

Characteristics are qualities that we all have, such as being honest, patient, kind and so on, and are part of our five aspects.

Your physical self is everything to do with your physical body, including your appearance, health, physical strengths and weaknesses.

Your social self is who you are in relation to others, your relationships and the way you interact with others.

Your ethical self is made up of your beliefs and principles about what is right and wrong, how you treat others and the choices you make when facing a moral dilemma.

Your emotional self is made up of your feelings and how you express them. What makes you feel happy, sad, afraid, angry or disappointed? How do you express these **emotions**?

Your intellectual self is made up of your thoughts, ideas and reasoning, and the way you understand and make sense of the world.

Exercise

1. Draw a mind map called 'Five aspects of me'. For each aspect, show at least six characteristics that make up that aspect of you.
2. Which aspect of yourself determines what you do in each of the following scenarios? Describe what you would do and explain how it might differ from what someone else might do.
   a) You have a very tough mathematical problem for homework.
   b) You see a friend cheating on a test.
   c) A friend makes a comment that makes you feel angry.

Tolerance, appreciation and respect

In order to function well with other people, we need to develop an **appreciation** of differences in others. It is easy to **appreciate** the differences that you like or enjoy.

However, some differences may be things that you do not like. For example, you may not agree with a friend's views or beliefs. You may notice someone dresses differently from you or mixes with different friends. In these situations you have to learn to be tolerant.

Tolerance is the willingness to accept behaviour and beliefs that are different from your own, although you might not agree with or approve of them.

Respect for others is the quality of giving others the regard they deserve. Mocking others, making fun of them or attacking their beliefs are all forms of disrespect. It is possible to disagree or hold different views without being disrespectful.

"Compassion and tolerance are not a sign of weakness, but a sign of strength."
– Dalai Lama

Exercise

3. Write your own definitions of:
   a) appreciation **b)** respect **c)** tolerance
4. Work in groups to create a poster entitled 'Ways in which I can show appreciation of others'.
5. Read the quote from the Dalai Lama. Write a paragraph about what you understand from it.
6. Brainstorm different aspects of yourself – your ethical, emotional and intellectual self. Use these ideas to make an identity collage. Cut out pictures and words from magazines to represent aspects of your identity.

Activity

Write a paragraph on the different aspects of yourself and the effects of these on your behaviour.

Project

Role-play a situation in which two people deal with their differences without respect or tolerance. Then replay the role-play showing how the situation changes when both sides show respect, tolerance and appreciation for differences.

Key vocabulary

aspect
physical
social
ethical
intellectual
emotional
emotions
appreciation
appreciate
tolerance
respect

Where do I belong?

We are learning to:

- define and use correctly the terms family and kinship
- identify and describe the different types of families in our society
- compare the different family types.

Different types of families

A **family** is a group of individuals, usually living together and related by blood, marriage or some type of union, such as adoption.

The adults in a family usually take responsibility for caring for the children. There are different types of families, but there is no wrong or right type of family.

Kinship is the most basic form of human relationship or connection. Your kinship to others comes from either:

- **blood ties**, which trace your descent from common **ancestors**
- unions such as marriage, adoption or other connections.

The four main family types in the Caribbean are **nuclear**, **extended**, **sibling** and **single parent** families. There are also **reconstituted** families.

Discussion

Have a class discussion about the term 'family'. What makes a family? Let each student identify their main family members, and suggest which type of family they belong to.

Nuclear family

A mother, father and their children living together in one household.

Extended family

A larger family, with additional family members such as grandparents or married siblings.

Reconstituted family

A family where one or both parents have children from a previous relationship.

Single parent

One parent living with his or her children.

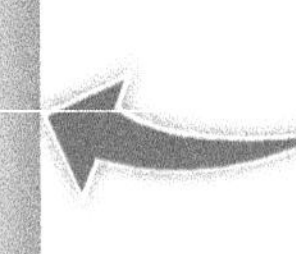

Sibling household

A household in which the parents are absent, so the older brothers and sisters take care of younger siblings.

Exercise

1. Define the terms 'nuclear family' and 'extended family'.
2. Describe your own family type.

Case study

Three different families

A. Michael and Joanne were classmates. During their studies, they began dating. After two years of **courtship**, followed by a six-month engagement, they got married. They have two children, David and Rebecca. They work to support their family, and they also dedicate a lot of time and attention to their children's education and growth.

B. Goodman and Rianna met each other on holiday in Jamaica. After a whirlwind three-month romance, they got married. Soon, Rianna was pregnant with their son, Daniel. When Daniel was two, however, Goodman and Rianna realised the relationship was not working. They got divorced. Rianna lives with Daniel in Georgetown.

C. Kayla (16), Anisha (11) and Benjamin (9) are three children who live alone since their parents died and they became orphans. Kayla takes care of the younger two. They do not have income, so they rely on help from neighbours and from social workers.

Questions

1. Which case study describes:

- **a)** a nuclear family?
- **b)** a single parent family?
- **c)** a sibling household?

2. Describe the challenges you think may be faced by Family B and Family C.

3. Define the words:

- **a)** courtship
- **b)** engagement
- **c)** divorce

4. How can courtship and engagement contribute to a happy family life? Write a paragraph for your answer.

An example of an extended family, here showing three generations of the same family.

Project

Collect data on the different family types in your class.

Complete a tally table with the numbers of each family type and then represent your data on a bar graph.

Key vocabulary

family
kinship
ancestor
blood ties
nuclear family
extended family
sibling household
single parent family
reconstituted family
courtship

Unions and relationships

We are learning to:

- identify potential advantages and disadvantages of various different family types
- define and use correctly the terms union, common-law marriage, visiting relationship and marriage
- identify and describe the different types of unions in our society.

Advantages and disadvantages of different family types

The four main different types of families have advantages and disadvantages for the members of the family.

	Advantages	Disadvantages
Nuclear	• Parents support each other and share responsibilities • Two role models to teach appropriate behaviour • More financially secure; stable and caring environment • Caring home environment helps good self-esteem	• Can be isolated from other relatives • Parents may lack support of extended family • Children have less experience of a range of opinions and views • Less opportunity for problem solving
Extended	• Strong support network • Children learn to cooperate and work with others • Strong sense of belonging • Family members share what they have and protect each other	• There can be disagreements and conflicts • There may be a traditional hierarchy where older men have most power • Sometimes older members of the family may abuse younger or more vulnerable members
Sibling	• Siblings do not get split up if their parents are not available • Strong bonds of love and affection between siblings • Strong development of responsibility	• Children may be too young to look after siblings • Children may leave school to look after siblings and remain uneducated • No source of income, adult guidance or help • Children may be vulnerable to abuse
Single parent	• No fighting between parents • Children take more responsibility to help parents • Children have more independence • Strong communication between parent and child • Smaller family to support	• One parent takes all the responsibilities: very tiring • Less supervision • Child may spend more time alone or with peers • Difficult for one parent to discipline children • Only one income

Different types of unions

Most families form when two people form a **union**. There are three different types of unions:

- **Marriage** – a legally or formally recognised union.
- **Common-law marriage** – a couple who live together as husband and wife without getting married, but who are considered to be married for social and legal purposes.
- **Visiting relationship** – a long-term partnership where the partners do not live together, but one visits the other from time to time; they may have children.

A wedding party at Scarborough, Tobago.

Case study

A. Brandon and Emma met while they were studying. At first they were just classmates, but then they developed stronger feelings for one another. They dated for two years and then they decided to move in together. That was six years ago. They never got married, but they have a baby girl together and they live together as a family.

B. Jenelle still lives with her parents. She has been in a relationship with her boyfriend, Leroy, since she was 18 and he was 24. Now she is 22 and has two children. Her parents help her take care of the children as Leroy still lives with his family.

Questions

1. Describe the types of union in the examples above.
2. Do you think Brandon and Emma should get married? Suggest advantages or disadvantages to support your answer.
3. Why would Jenelle choose to continue living with her parents? Suggest two possible reasons.

Discussion

The nuclear family is usually considered the ideal family type. Do you agree? Which family type would you prefer to be in?

Exercise

1. In your own words, define the terms 'marriage', 'common-law marriage' and 'visiting relationship'.
2. Describe the advantages and disadvantages of each family type.
3. What types of unions do you have in your family?

Key vocabulary

union

marriage

common-law marriage

visiting relationship

Family history

We are learning to:

- define and use correctly the terms family tree, origins, ancestry, customs and traditions
- develop an awareness of our family histories
- construct a family tree.

Family customs and traditions

Your **origins** are where you come from. In a family with records that go back several generations, it is possible to trace your **ancestry**. This is the line of relatives starting with your parents and **grandparents**, and going back in time to each generation's parents and grandparents. Within your family you are linked to your origins through your family's **customs** and **traditions**.

Customs and traditions are thoughts, actions or behaviours that a group of people do and have done for a long time, which help to identify them as part of that group. Read the examples of family traditions opposite.

Once a week, we have a family meal together.

Our family tradition is an annual holiday with all our cousins.

One of our family traditions is walking to church each Sunday. It gives us all a chance to spend some time together without any distractions.

We always say grace and take a moment for thankfulness before meals.

Exercise

1. What do all the family customs above have in common?
2. Does your family have any of these family customs? Which ones? If not, why not?
3. Describe a tradition that you do not have, but that you would like to have in your family. Explain why.

Family histories

Each person has some awareness of their family history from their personal experience of their own family. In addition to this, we each hear stories about older family members and ancestors from the previous generations.

A more formal way of finding out about family histories is by interviewing elders. Family records, such as photographs and old birth and death certificates, can tell us more about our families.

A family tree

An awareness of family history helps a person to understand who they are and where they come from. A **family tree** is a **genealogical** diagram that shows a person's ancestors and how that person is related to each of their ancestors and siblings.

Project

Construct your own family tree showing at least three generations. Present your family tree as a project on a large piece of card.

In other words, your family tree shows how you are related to your parents, grandparents, siblings, **aunts**, **uncles** and cousins.

A family line (also called lineage) is a line of descent that you can trace to a common ancestor. A matriarchal family tree shows the lineage on the mother's side of the family. A patriarchal family tree shows the lineage on the father's side. A family tree showing both sides of the family is bilineal. Family trees also reveal parts of your family's history: which family members got married, and when, and dates on which children were born.

Look at this old family tree and answer the questions that follow.

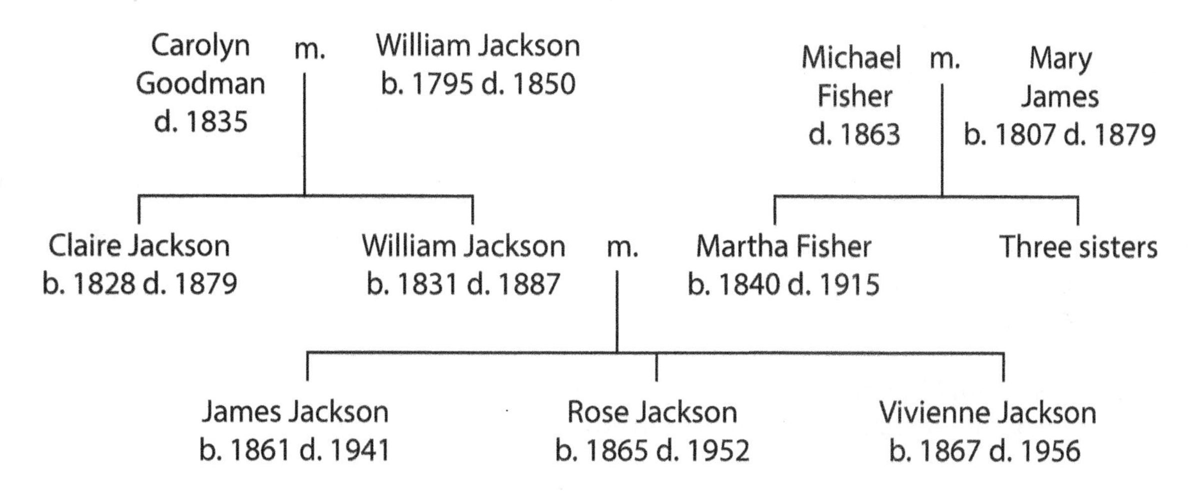

Exercise

4. What do the letters b., d. and m. stand for on the family tree?
5. Why do some people only have one date under their name?
6. How many children did Martha have?
7. Name Rose Jackson's grandfathers.
8. Name Vivienne's aunt on her father's side.

Research

Create a questionnaire for the elder members of your family. Research some stories in your family's history. Give a three-minute oral presentation with some of the most interesting details you found out.

Activity

In groups, compose a song, poem or picture entitled 'My family'. Include any aspects that make your family history special or unique.

Key vocabulary

origins

ancestry

grandparents

customs

traditions

family tree

genealogical

aunts and uncles

Functions of the family

We are learning to:

- explain the relationships that exist within families
- describe the functions of the family.

Family relationships

A family relationship describes the way two people are connected to each other within a family. It may describe the blood tie or the union that connects the people. The family tree below shows the **relationships** that can exist within families.

Grandparents: the parents of your parents are your grandparents. Your mother's parents are your maternal grandparents. Your father's parents are your paternal grandparents.

Parents: mothers and fathers are responsible for taking care of their children.

Children/siblings: from birth to 18 years, a person is considered a child. **Siblings** are children born to the same parents. Your brothers and sisters are your siblings. Half-brothers and half-sisters are siblings who share one parent rather than both.

Aunts, uncles and cousins: your parents' brothers and sisters, and their spouses, are your aunts and uncles. Their children are your cousins.

Nephews and nieces: when your brothers and sisters have children of their own you become an aunt or uncle. Your siblings' daughters are your **nieces**. Your siblings' sons are your **nephews**.

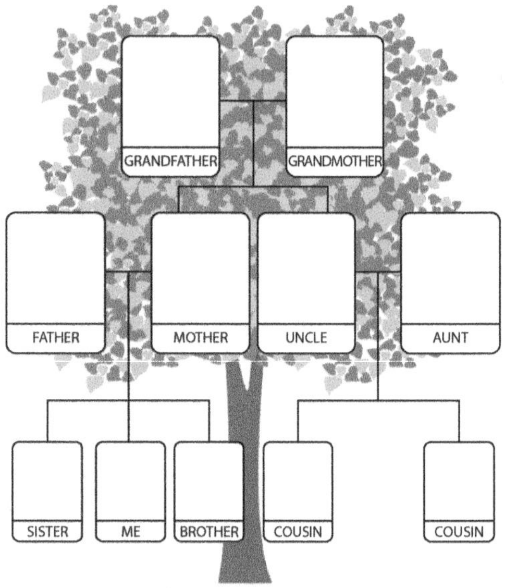

Exercise

1. Identify each family relationship:
   - **a)** Your mother's parents are your ________.
   - **b)** Your parents' other children are your ________ and ________.
   - **c)** When your brothers and sisters have children, they are your ________ and ________.
   - **d)** Cousins are the ________ of your parents' ________.

Discussion

Discuss the functions of the family in groups. Collect photographs to show each of these functions and make a collage to show to the rest of the class.

The five functions of the family

There are five broad functions of the family:

FUNCTIONS OF THE FAMILY

BIOLOGICAL: having children is the biological function of families. Most families begin with a marriage or partnership that results in one or more children.

ECONOMIC: every individual has basic needs for food, shelter, security and clothing. The economic function of the family requires that some members of the family work or have some way of bringing in income for the family's needs.

CULTURAL/ EDUCATIONAL: within a family, a child acquires knowledge, skills, values and attitudes that form part of their education. Beliefs and traditions, morals and values all form part of the cultural function of families.

SOCIAL: in the family, children learn how to interact and communicate with others and how to form relationships. This is known as socialisation.

EMOTIONAL: human beings need love, attention and support as much as they need basic things like food, water and shelter. Part of the family's function is to provide for the emotional needs of its members.

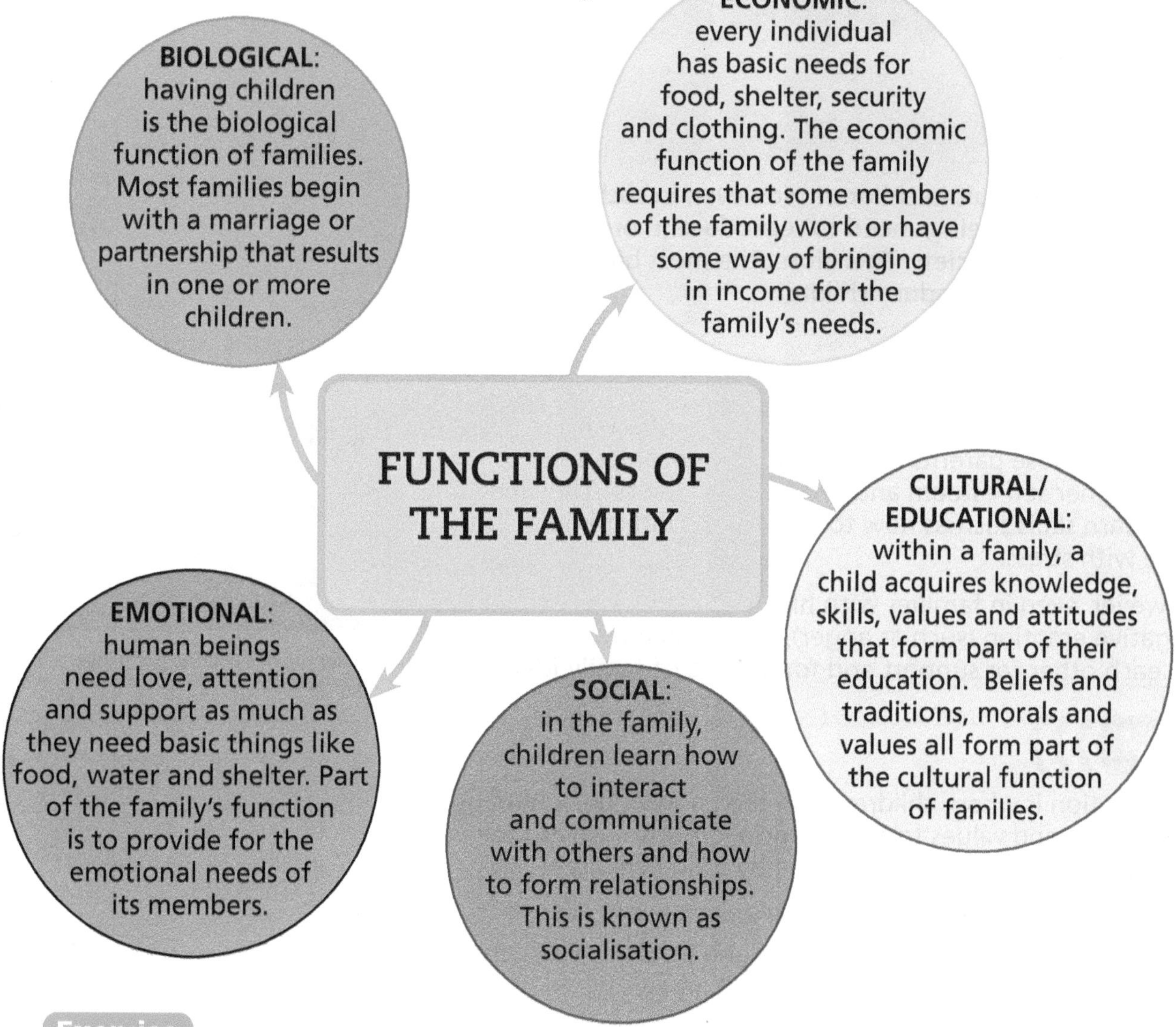

Exercise

2. Into which of the five functions does each of the following fit?
   a) comforting a younger sibling when they are upset
   b) a parent showing a child how to prepare for Christmas celebrations
   c) a couple planning to have a child
   d) grandparents explaining to a child when to say please and thank you
   e) an aunt paying for her niece's school fees
3. In your opinion, which is the most important and least important of the family functions? Write a one-page essay, or present a one-minute oral presentation, explaining your opinion.

Key vocabulary

relationships

siblings

nephews and nieces

biological function

economic function

emotional function

social function

cultural/educational function

The five functions of the family

We are learning to:

- describe the five functions of the family.

Biological

Not all unions result in children. However, in society as a whole, human beings need to reproduce in order to continue human society. Therefore, the most basic function of the family is to produce children.

Emotional

Families provide love, affection, support and attention. Children whose parents have loving relationships tend to have higher self-esteem and greater confidence. They may also learn skills such as how to deal with conflict and how to cope with stress.

However, even in families with high levels of conflict and negative emotion (such as anger), family members still rely on each other for support and for a sense of family identity.

Families provide children with love and affection.

Social

Socialisation is where children gain the knowledge, language, **social skills** and values to fit into social groups, such as their family and community. This is done by giving children:

- a sense of who they are and where they belong
- guidance about how to behave and interact with others
- a sense of their roles and responsibilities
- guidance on how to form and sustain relationships.

Language is a big part of socialisation. Children learn to speak a language and they also learn what kinds of language are appropriate in different settings. For example, you might use language differently when you speak to your parents than when you speak to your peers.

Discussion

Your teacher will show you pictures representing the different functions of the family. Discuss what each picture represents.

Exercise

1. Suggest a family structure that does not have a biological function.
2. Look at the picture above. Which family functions can you see suggested in the picture?
3. How do the family functions you have read about on this page overlap with each other?

Economic

Everyone has basic needs, and families are structures that provide for these needs. In order to provide these, a household needs the following to survive:

- Income: money to pay for goods and services. The person who earns the greatest proportion of money for the family is the **breadwinner**.
- Domestic work: this includes cooking, cleaning and laundry. This may be shared out among the family.
- Childcare: in many families both parents work, so another relative may look after the children or the family may pay for childcare services.
- Care of the elderly or disabled: elderly or disabled members of the family may need care. This may be provided by a relative or by a paid service provider.

A happy family smiling for their portrait.

Cultural and educational

The educational function is to teach children information and skills they will need throughout their lives. Children are highly **impressionable** and develop much of their understanding and knowledge about the world from their family home.

Part of socialisation and education involves teaching family members about their culture. This may include:

- religious beliefs and traditions
- language, accent and style of speaking
- beliefs, morals and values
- customs and heritage.

Most families participate in culture that reflects the groups they belong to within their community. For example, if you are born into a Dominican family, you will grow up familiar with the Dominican accent and way of speaking, popular Dominican dishes and the celebrations of your community.

Activity

Describe three important functions of the family in approximately 250 words.

Exercise

4. How many members of your family work? Who is the main breadwinner?
5. Who does the domestic work in your home? Is this work shared equally between family members? If not, who is responsible for it?
6. Who looks after the children or elderly in your family?

Key vocabulary

social skills

breadwinner

impressionable

My roles and responsibilities

We are learning to:

- define and use correctly the terms role and responsibility
- describe the roles of an individual
- describe the responsibilities of each role
- describe the roles, relationships and responsibilities of family members
- examine the consequences of not fulfilling responsibilities.

Roles and responsibilities

Each member of a family plays their own **role**. A role is a pattern of behaviour that comes from your position in the family. For example, a parent's role is to take care of the children and make decisions for the household. Along with this role may come several **responsibilities** – the things we are expected to do as part of our role – such as providing food, paying rent, buying clothes and so on.

As an individual, your role may change depending on where you are and who you are with. For example, at home you may be a son, an older brother to one of your siblings, a younger brother to another sibling and a grandchild to your grandparents.

Exercise

1. Identify two different roles you play in your family and explain two responsibilities for each role. Write these in your portfolio.
2. In your own words define 'roles' and 'responsibilities'.

Discussion

Discuss which individual in your family takes on each responsibility listed in the mind map.

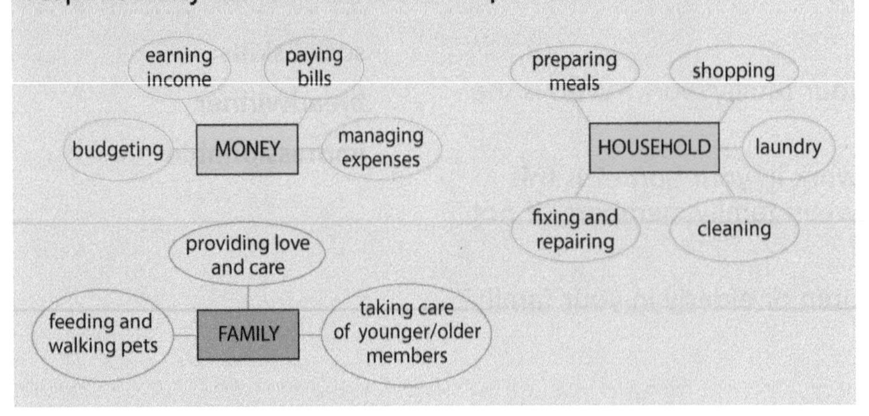

Grandparents

- provide support for parents
- help with looking after the children
- provide financial assistance if they are able to
- help the child's social and emotional growth
- pass on customs, traditions and family history.

Parents

- meet basic economic needs
- provide emotional support, love and affection
- socialise children
- educate children
- pass on traditions and customs.

Continued opposite

Traditional roles and responsibilities

In traditional societies, men were breadwinners and the head of the house, responsible for making decisions. Women took care of the children, doing the housework and preparing meals. Girls helped their mother with the housework and looking after the children. Boys might help with work such as cleaning and gardening.

Today, women and men may both work and spend equal amounts of time earning money for the family. They are also more likely to share equal responsibility for decisions such as how money is spent and how children are disciplined. Today there is greater awareness of women's and girls' **rights** to **equality**. However, some families still expect members to follow more traditional roles.

Children

- show respect for their parents
- help with household chores
- care for siblings and elderly family members
- attend school and take responsibility for their studies
- ensure that they do not waste family money or possessions.

Consequences of not fulfilling roles and responsibilities

If one person fails to fulfil their responsibility in a family, this can cause the whole family to suffer. It may mean that someone else has to take responsibility for a role that is not rightfully theirs. This can lead to anger, jealousy, resentment or depression. Sometimes one family member is unable to fulfil their role, perhaps as the result of sickness or even death.

Case study

"We are a family of four – my mother, my oldest brother, my grandmother and me. My dad died a few years ago, so my oldest brother started working to help my mother support us. With my mother and brother working, my grandmother looked after me most of the time. But she is very old. I worry about something happening to her. Then I would be on my own at home during the day." James

Questions

1. Identify the responsibilities that each person in James' family takes on.
2. List the consequences that follow if no one in the family can:

   a) earn money to support the family

   b) stay at home to look after the children

   c) take care of housework
3. Write on the subject "Have I been fulfilling my responsibilities in my various roles?" Aim for 250 words.

Activity

Role-play the different roles and responsibilities of individual family members. Use the flow chart on pages 24 and 25 to help.

Key vocabulary

role

responsibilities

rights

equality

How do I deal with conflict?

We are learning to:

- define and use correctly the terms conflict, conflict resolution and mediation
- identify the causes of conflict in the home, school and neighbourhood.

What is conflict?

A serious disagreement or clash between two or more people is known as a **conflict**. Conflicts can give us an opportunity to build our negotiation skills.

Conflicts arise from differences of opinions, views, ideas or needs. The differences may not look serious to someone outside the conflict.

However, conflict can trigger very strong feelings. Behind every conflict are powerful needs – the need to feel safe, the need to feel respected, recognised or loved, or the need for closeness and connection.

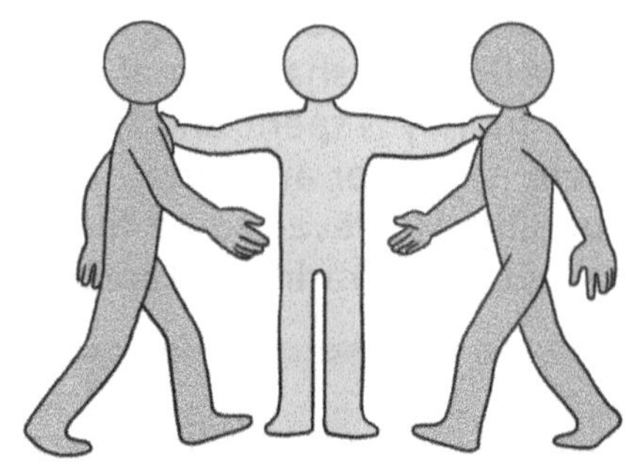

A mediator is someone who can help guide two sides to reach an understanding.

Conflict resolution

The process of ending a conflict and finding a peaceful way forward is known as **conflict resolution**. Conflict resolution involves several steps (see opposite).

One way to **resolve** conflict is through **mediation**. A mediator is a person who is not involved in the conflict, who can help guide the two sides to reach an understanding.

Case study

"Keep that music down! There are people trying to sleep."

"I don't want to come to church today. I want to go to the beach with my friends."

"That crowd is a bad influence. What's wrong with your old school friends?"

Questions

For each statement above, identify:

1. Which issue you think is causing the conflict.
2. Who is making the statement (parent or child).

Acknowledging or admitting the problem

↓

Committing to the process of finding a solution

↓

Expressing oneself clearly and calmly

↓

Listening to and understanding each other

↓

Acknowledgement and forgiveness

↓

Working together to find ideas to prevent the problem from happening again

Causes of conflict

Conflicts are very common and may occur at home, at school and in the neighbourhood. Some causes include:

- Generation gap – when people of different ages have different views.
- Different views of parents and children – sometimes parents and children disagree.
- Choice of friends – when parents do not like or approve of their child's friends.
- Problems with authority – teenagers want to make their own choices. This can lead to conflicts with restrictions such as school rules, dress codes and demanding school work.
- Doing schoolwork – sometimes children spend less time on schoolwork than parents think they should.
- Sibling rivalry – disagreements between brothers and sisters.
- Lack of finance – when a family does not have enough money.
- Drug use and abuse – drug abuse can lead to many other problems, including verbal and emotional abuse.
- Bullying – when an individual or group tries to intimidate others through physical or verbal abuse.
- Extortion – forcing someone to pay money, usually by threats.
- Playing loud music – this can cause conflict between neighbours, or between teenagers and parents.

Discussion

Discuss ways that you would handle the conflicts described on this page. Which ways would prevent the conflict from happening again?

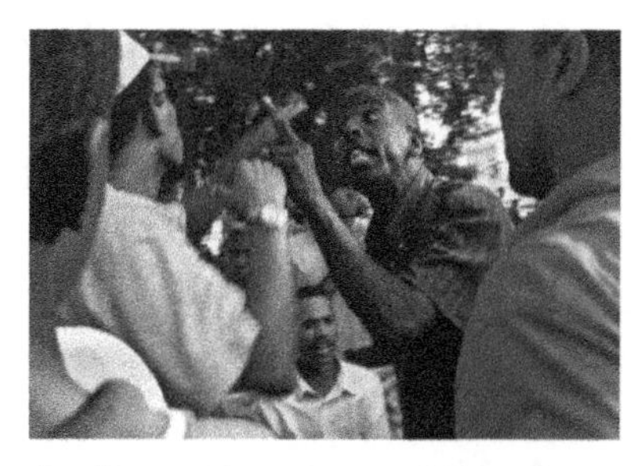

Conflicts can happen anywhere – these men are disagreeing about a sports result.

Exercise

1. Write your own definitions of:

   a) conflict **b)** conflict resolution **c)** mediation
2. Come up with statements of your own to demonstrate conflict situations caused by:

   a) sibling rivalry **b)** bullying
3. Present role-plays to show how conflicts arise. Some groups should present conflicts at home, and others should present conflicts at school and in the neighbourhood.
4. Look at the list of causes of conflict. Sort the conflicts into those that occur at home, at school and in the neighbourhood.

Key vocabulary

conflict

conflict resolution

resolve/resolution

mediation

Resolving conflict

We are learning to:

- resolve conflict.

Resolving conflicts at home

Conflict resolution is a process that two or more conflicting individuals or groups can use to find a peaceful solution to their disagreements.

When conflicts arise at home, they can bring up very strong emotions, such as anger, frustration, disappointment and hurt. These feelings may be particularly strong in conflicts at home as our relationships with family are our closest.

Different families deal with conflict differently. Strategies for dealing with conflict at home include:

- sorting it out before the family goes to sleep
- 'sleeping on it and sorting it out tomorrow'
- taking time to 'cool off' alone
- calling a family meeting
- writing a letter or note
- doing something special as a family.

Sometimes doing something special together as a family can help overcome negative feelings caused by conflicts.

Case study

Conflict at home

A. My youngest sister always takes my clothes and stationery without asking. If I complain, she goes crying to Mother, who says I mustn't upset her. We end up yelling at each other until my parents send us to our rooms. Then the storm passes, at least 'til the next time.

B. My siblings and I used to have raging fights. Then one day our parents got us to sit down and write a list of what we really like and appreciate about each other. Now, when my sisters are driving me crazy, it's easier to remember that I actually like them.

Questions

1. Which issues are causing the conflicts in A and B?
2. What strategy has each family used to deal with the conflict?
3. List four different home conflicts that might be solved by one of these strategies.

Discussion

What is a peer mediator programme? Do you have one at your school? If so, what does it do? If not, how do you think a peer mediator programme could help resolve conflicts at school?

Resolving conflicts at school and in the neighbourhood

Some of the main conflicts at school are caused by: peer pressure, **bullying**, extortion, clashes with authority, a generation gap. In the neighbourhood alcohol use, drug use and crime can cause serious conflicts.

To resolve conflicts at school, you usually need to work with a friend, a teacher or even your whole class or whole school. School is a more formal environment than home. Sometimes this makes it easier to put formal strategies in place to resolve conflicts. Some examples of formal conflict resolution strategies are:

- peer mediator programmes
- anti-bullying programmes
- class meetings
- counselling and guidance.

Conflicts in the neighbourhood can be more serious. They may require community meetings. In some cases, they may require the involvement of the police.

Case study

Conflict at school and the neighbourhood

A. We had a problem with older students extorting money from the younger ones. The class came up with an idea for an anonymous tip-off box. Anyone could post a note about what was happening.

B. I used to bully other students. I didn't really know how to stop, so I made a deal with a friend – that she would step in if she saw me starting to get irritable and do my bullying thing. I also went quietly to those I'd bullied, and apologised. I don't think they trusted me or forgave me straight away, but I felt better about myself.

Questions

1. Which issues caused the conflicts in each story above?
2. Identify the strategy used to resolve the conflict in each story above.
3. In groups, choose one of the stories above. Brainstorm at least two other strategies you could use to resolve the issue.
4. What types of conflicts do alcohol and drug use introduce in a community? In groups, brainstorm your ideas and present them in a poster.

Project

As a group, discuss and plan an anti-bullying programme for your school. Include strategies that offer opportunities for both victims and bullies to ask for help. Present your work as a project, with aims, guidelines and an action plan.

Activity

In groups, talk about the advantages and disadvantages of the strategies mentioned here. Does your family have any other strategies for dealing with conflict? What are they?

Key vocabulary

conflict resolution

bullying

Strategies to deal with conflict

We are learning to:

- explore strategies to deal with conflict.

Guidelines for conflict resolution

There are some general **principles** for dealing with conflict. You can apply these principles to any conflict resolution situation, at home, at school or in your neighbourhood.

In a conflict situation, you may feel stressed, worried, uncomfortable, disappointed or hurt. **Unhealthy responses** lead to further conflict. The most common unhealthy responses are avoidance of conflict out of fear.

Healthy responses lead to understanding and resolution. They are characterised by:

- recognising the importance of the issue to the other person
- a willingness to listen
- the ability to hear another person's perspective
- showing patience and kindness
- the belief that it is possible to reach a resolution that benefits both sides.

The guidelines opposite can help you to deal with conflicts.

Exercise

1. What is the main difference between healthy and unhealthy responses to conflict?
2. Why do you think it is important to remain calm in conflict situations?
3. Give an example of a conflict situation caused by intolerance for other people's differences.
4. **a)** Give three examples of 'I' statements.

   b) Why do you think it is more useful to use 'I' statements than statements starting with 'you'?
5. Choose any of the causes of conflict from page 27 and in groups role-play. At least one group must choose home conflict and other groups must choose conflicts at school or in the neighbourhood. Brainstorm strategies for dealing with the conflict. Then present a rap, poem or song showing your ideas.

1. Stay calm – if you are upset, calm down and cool off before attempting to resolve the conflict.
2. Control your own emotions and behaviour. Do not threaten, frighten or punish others.
3. Identify the cause of the conflict (see the list on page 27).
4. Responses that start with "I ..." help to explain the situation without blaming or attacking the other person.
5. Give each person a chance to say what they have heard: "It sounds like you are saying..." Restating what we have heard shows that we are listening to the other person.
6. Take responsibility – look at your own role in the situation. What could you do differently?
7. Be creative – try to think of different ways you could solve the problem.
8. Give affirmation and offer **forgiveness** or thanks.

Strategies for conflict resolution

Different types of conflicts require different **strategies**. Here are some suggested strategies for conflict resolution.

Conflict	Strategies
Conflicts between parents and children (e.g. differing views; generation gap; application to school work)	• discussions where all parties identify the problems and make suggestions • finding compromises where both sides make allowances for each other
Sibling rivalry	• discussion to develop jointly agreed household rules • siblings could sit down and each write lists of what they like and appreciate about each other
Bullying	• practising funny and clever replies for bullies • practising walking in a confident, assertive way • sticking together with friends • setting up a bullying reporting box at school • anti-bullying guidelines at school • mentor programmes
Extortion	• keeping a record of times, places and details of incidents • reporting incidents to police
Drug use and abuse	• contacting counsellors and social workers • inviting rehabilitated drug addicts to address school

There are guidelines to help you deal with conflict.

Activity

In groups, create a poster entitled 'Guidelines for resolving conflicts'. The poster can either be a general guide, or it can show guidelines for conflict at home, school or in your neigbourhood. Remember to show the steps in conflict resolution (see page 26).

Exercise

6. Why is it important to stay calm when you try to resolve a conflict?
7. Which of the following strategies would be useful for resolving these conflicts: a conflict at home, school or in the neighbourhood?

   a) a police report **b)** a family meeting
   c) a meeting with a guidance counsellor

Key vocabulary

principles
unhealthy response
healthy response
forgiveness
strategy

Self-esteem

We are learning to:

- define and use correctly the term self-esteem
- define and outline the characteristics of high and low self-esteem.

High and low self-esteem

self → to do with yourself

esteem → sense of importance, specialness or value

↓

self-esteem = how much you like and value yourself, and believe you have importance

Having **high self-esteem** is about viewing yourself in a positive, realistic way, appreciating your own abilities and achievements. Someone with high self-esteem recognises and understands their strengths, as well as their weaknesses. High self-esteem means feeling good about yourself.

Low self-esteem is the mistaken belief that we are not as successful or worthy as others. People with low self-esteem have negative feelings and thoughts about themselves. When we allow our self-esteem to get low, we may feel that life is very unfair and we are victims of this unfairness.

Characteristics of people with high self-esteem	Characteristics of people with low self-esteem
• Confidence in own abilities • Can say what they want or need • Communicate effectively with others • Strong motivation to succeed, even if they fail or experience disappointment • Comfortable with change • Able to have healthy relationships • Can set and reach goals • Able to laugh at themselves and accept their own mistakes • Take care of their physical, emotional and mental health.	• Do not have confidence in own abilities • Unable to say what they want or need • Unable to communicate well, often from fear of being judged • Afraid of failure • Afraid of change • May have problems in relationships • Do not set goals • Take themselves very seriously; easily hurt if others notice their mistakes or weaknesses • May neglect their own health.

Exercise

1. Which of the following does not describe someone with high self-esteem?
   a) sets goals and is motivated to succeed
   b) able to see their own weaknesses
   c) does not have any weaknesses or flaws
   d) sees value in themselves and others
2. True or false: Someone with low self-esteem has no skills or abilities. Write a paragraph explaining your answer.

A self-esteem checklist

You can measure how high or low your self-esteem is by checking how you feel about yourself. Copy out each statement below and tick A (always), N (never) or S (sometimes). Then, count up your answers.

	A	N	S
I believe I am a worthy person.	☐	☐	☐
I know I am important.	☐	☐	☐
I accept my weaknesses, as well as my strengths.	☐	☐	☐
It is OK for me to make mistakes.	☐	☐	☐
I have respect for myself.	☐	☐	☐
I cope well with new or difficult situations.	☐	☐	☐
I mix well with other people my own age.	☐	☐	☐
I ask questions when I do not understand.	☐	☐	☐
I do not worry too much about making mistakes.	☐	☐	☐
I cooperate with others when I work in groups.	☐	☐	☐
I can concentrate on new tasks.	☐	☐	☐
I can manage a frustrating task without giving up.	☐	☐	☐
I am involved in activities I enjoy.	☐	☐	☐
I recognise my own achievements.	☐	☐	☐
I accept my past difficulties and move forward.	☐	☐	☐
I can talk about my worries and problems.	☐	☐	☐
I feel loved and appreciated.	☐	☐	☐
I can accept praise without feeling uncomfortable.	☐	☐	☐

Mostly 'always': You have high self-esteem! Congratulations. Follow the guidelines on the next few pages to maintain your healthy self-esteem.

Mostly 'sometimes': You have ups and downs. Work on appreciating your strengths and abilities in order to boost your self-esteem.

Mostly 'never': You may be struggling to appreciate your own strengths and abilities. You can change the way you view yourself by noticing your critical inner voice and changing the messages you tell yourself. Follow the guidelines on the next two pages to boost your self-esteem.

Activity

Create a role-play showing behaviour associated with low self-esteem. Then discuss your role-plays in groups and change them to reflect behaviour associated with high self-esteem.

Activity

Write a reflective journal article called 'How I feel about myself'.

Key vocabulary

self-esteem

high self-esteem

low self-esteem

Factors of self-esteem

We are learning to:

- examine the factors that contribute to self-esteem
- improve self-esteem.

Factors that contribute to self-esteem

Your experiences as a baby and a child help to form your self-esteem. The factors that contribute to your self-esteem are shown in the table below.

Family life is the most important factor. Positive self-esteem develops when parents: • listen to their children • respond to their needs for food, warmth, comfort, attention, love • speak respectfully to their children • provide appropriate affection, love, attention • recognise achievements • acknowledge and accept failures or mistakes.	Your *relationships with peers/neighbours* help you to develop self-esteem by providing: • appreciation from others about your strengths • feedback about your weaknesses and the opportunity to work on them • opportunities to build rewarding relationships • encouragement to try again when you fail.
At *school*, you have opportunities to develop self-esteem by: • completing projects • learning new skills • improving in areas that were previously difficult • seeing the fruit of your effort.	*Extra-curricular* activities offer you opportunities to: • get involved in activities you enjoy • develop talents • achieve personal goals.

Exercise

1. True or false? Give reasons for your answers.
   a) Someone with good self-esteem thinks they are perfect.
   b) Not everyone can have good self-esteem.
   c) Other people can affect your self-esteem.
   d) Some people never face setbacks to their self-esteem.
2. Describe three factors that contribute towards:
   a) high self-esteem **b)** low self-esteem

Activity

Use your ideas to create a chart or poster about factors that contribute to self-esteem.

Discussion

If someone boasts and brags a lot, does that mean they have high self-esteem? How can bragging and boasting also show evidence of low self-esteem?

Self-esteem setbacks

Some people may develop poor self-esteem if they experience:

- physical, sexual or emotional abuse
- instability, conflict or anger at home
- being ignored, mocked, teased, shamed or criticised
- too much emphasis on being perfect.

Some people have good self-esteem, but something happens that changes it. Examples may be:

- moving to a new area where they do not know anyone
- experiencing a divorce
- experiencing a failure at something they thought was very important, such as an important set of exams.

Healthy self-esteem can make you feel good in yourself.

Case study

Dear Amanda,

I really don't feel good about myself. I am very shy and overweight. I'm not sporty like my sister, who is a talented netball player. My mother often criticises me and tells me I am not as talented or attractive as my sister. Sometimes I really feel like I hate myself. I have two close friends at school, but I feel like sooner or later they will realise what a failure I am and then they will drop me. When I get home from school I just want to hide in my room, eat chocolate and write in my diary by myself.

All alone

Dear All alone,

It sounds like you are suffering from some very low self-esteem. Let's talk about how to improve it.

It's not OK for your mother to compare you to your sister. Talk with her and ask her to help you work on ways to feel better about yourself.

It's also not OK for you to compare yourself to your sister! She may be good at netball, but it doesn't sound like that interests you at all. You like writing in your diary – how about joining a creative writing group and exploring something that you enjoy?

It's also time to notice and appreciate your friends. Read some of my tips for ways to improve self-esteem.

Best wishes, Amanda

Amanda's tips for improving self-esteem

- Love the unique person that you are.
- Stop comparing yourself to others.
- Find your own interests.
- Take pride in your own achievements.
- Each day, remind yourself about aspects of yourself you really like.
- Get involved in activities and hobbies that you enjoy. The more you do things you enjoy, the better you will get at them, and the better you will feel about your talents and abilities.

Questions

1. Which two statements tell us that 'All alone' does not value herself?
2. Which statement tells us that 'All alone' does not feel worthy of love or friendship?
3. Choose the top three pieces of advice for 'All alone' to improve her self-esteem. Write a sentence assessing why you think this is an important way to improve self-esteem.

Stages of human development

We are learning to:

- define and use correctly the terms infancy, childhood, adolescence/ puberty, adulthood, senescence
- identify the stages of human development and physical characteristics of each stage.

Stages of development

Humans grow and develop throughout their lives. This is their life cycle. After birth, there are five main stages of development in a human life: infancy, childhood, adolescence/ puberty, adulthood and senescence. It is important to realise that these stages are approximate. Some people start or finish a particular stage earlier or later than others.

Infancy (birth to 1 year)/toddler (1 to 3 years)

During **infancy**, the baby depends on others to provide food and care. Gradually, the baby develops enough strength to hold up its own head, to roll over on its own, and later to sit, to crawl and eventually to walk. After about one year, a baby becomes a toddler (1 to 3 years), walking and exploring the world.

Childhood (3 to 12 years)

Childhood is a period of steady physical and mental growth and development, from birth to just before the teenage years begin. We usually refer to the first three years of childhood as infancy and toddler years. We can divide childhood into early childhood (3 to 6 years), middle childhood (6 to 9 years) and late childhood (9 to 12 years). The child continues to become more and more independent.

Adolescence and puberty (about 12 to 18 years)

Adolescence is the period in which the child changes to become an adult. During this stage there is a growth spurt, accompanied by **puberty**. At the same time, the young adult develops mentally and emotionally.

Adulthood and senescence (about 18 years to death)

Adulthood is the period from about 18 years onwards, when a person is fully grown. Most adults are at their peak strength and fitness from 18 until about 30 years of age. Adult bodies gradually begin ageing and weakening in a process called **senescence**. If a person does not die of other causes, such as accident or illness, they will eventually die as a result of the ageing process.

Exercise

1. What is the name of the stage of growth that an 11–12 year old is in?
   a) infancy **b)** adulthood **c)** childhood

Activity

Draw a timeline showing your own development from birth to the present. Use photographs or drawings to illustrate your timeline.

Development characteristics

The stages of development are characterised by:

Stage	Physical characteristics
Infancy	• Smallest, weakest physical stage • Main method of communication is crying • A newborn doubles its weight in a few months (from 3 kg) • Newborn infants are unable to digest solid food • Top of the baby's head is very soft and vulnerable • Later the baby develops the strength to roll over, sit and crawl
Toddler years	• Gradual increase in length and weight; unsteady walking gait • Gradual acquisition of language; mostly non-verbal communication
Childhood	• Gain of strength, agility and coordination; bones and muscles lengthen
Adolescence	• Body grows to adult height; face lengthens; sexual characteristics start to form; hormones can cause mood and behaviour changes • Girls: breasts develop; hips widen; menstruation begins; pubic hair grows under arms and between legs • Boys: body hair increases, including facial hair and hair around genitals and under arms; penis lengthens; chest widens; voice drops
Adulthood	• Body is fully grown; period of greatest strength and coordination between 18 and 30 • After age 30, there is a gradual loss of skin elasticity, and a slower recovery time from injuries and illness; skin may start developing wrinkles; eyesight and hearing may deteriorate
Senescence	• Weakening of muscles and bones; body may get stiffer • Skin may appear heavily wrinkled; hair starts losing its colour; eyesight and hearing may deteriorate further • Person may need assistance and support

Exercise

2. Which is the longest stage of growth and development?

a) infancy
b) adulthood
c) adolescence

3. What is the name of the process that begins in adulthood and eventually causes death?

a) growth
b) puberty
c) ageing

Key vocabulary

infancy
childhood
adolescence
puberty
adulthood
senescence

Adolescence – physical changes

We are learning to:

- explain the physical changes that occur in adolescence.

Physical changes

Puberty usually starts between ages 8 and 13 in girls, and between 10 and 15 in boys. Some people start a bit earlier or a bit later. That is why some of your friends may look more like children and some look more like adults.

During puberty, your body is rapidly producing hormones, which cause the development of your sexual characteristics. They also have many other physical effects.

Did you know...?

A teenager can grow as much as 10 cm in a year at this time!

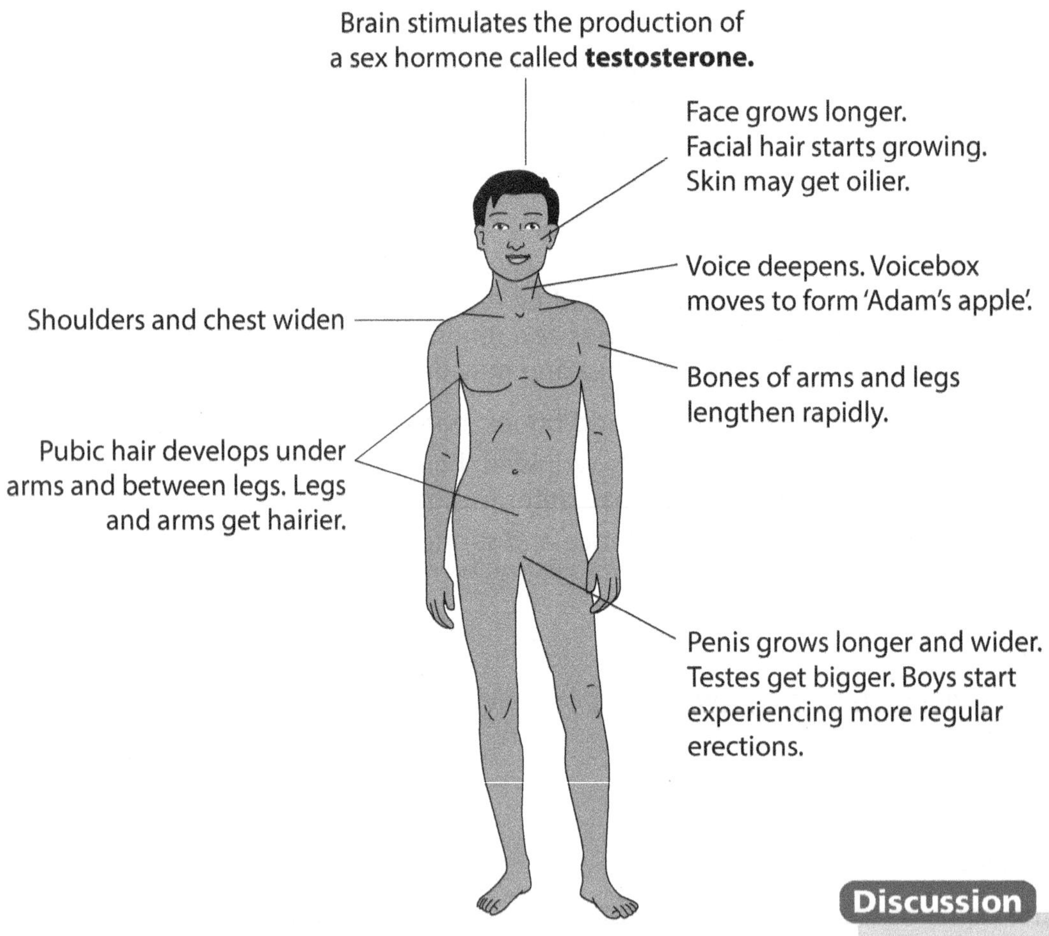

Brain stimulates the production of a sex hormone called **testosterone.**

Face grows longer. Facial hair starts growing. Skin may get oilier.

Voice deepens. Voicebox moves to form 'Adam's apple'.

Shoulders and chest widen

Bones of arms and legs lengthen rapidly.

Pubic hair develops under arms and between legs. Legs and arms get hairier.

Penis grows longer and wider. Testes get bigger. Boys start experiencing more regular erections.

Discussion

Have a class discussion about the physical changes that we have in adolescence.

Exercise

1. **a)** What is puberty?

   b) When does it start?

2. Describe three physical changes that happen during adolescence for boys and girls.

3. True or false? If false, explain why.

   a) Everyone goes through puberty.

   b) During puberty, your body is rapidly producing hormones.

   c) If you start puberty very early or very late, it means there is something wrong with you.

Project

Work in groups to create a dramatic piece on how physical changes in adolescence can affect you both physically and emotionally. Use the words 'upset', 'calm', 'nervous', 'excite', 'embarrassed', 'shy' and 'frustrated', and present your piece to the rest of the class.

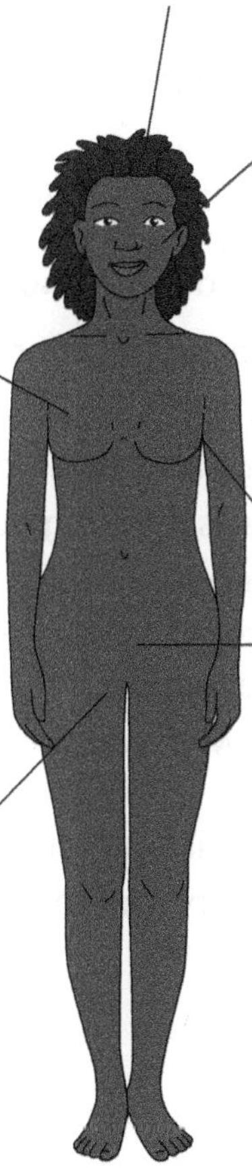

Brain stimulates the production of a sex hormone called **oestrogen.**

Face grows longer. Skin may get oilier.

Breasts change shape. The nipple and breast start sticking out and the areola gets larger. Inside the breast, there are milk ducts developing to help the woman feed her baby or babies in the future.

Pubic hair develops under arms and between legs. Legs and arms get hairier, though not as hairy as for boys.

Hips grow wider. Fat develops on hips, thighs and buttocks. The menstrual cycle begins. Girls start menstruating (bleeding) each month for around five to seven days.

Key vocabulary

puberty

testosterone

oestrogen

Adolescence – emotional changes

We are learning to:

- explain the emotional changes that occur in adolescence.

Emotional changes

Adolescence is the stage in a person's life that begins with puberty and ends when they are fully developed as an adult. Adolescence lasts from about 12 to around 18 years of age.

During adolescence you will experience many physical changes (changes in your body), as well as emotional changes (changes in your feelings and your thoughts). This is all part of your body and mind preparing for life as an adult.

Your body is starting to produce sex hormones, which cause many physical changes to the way your body feels, looks and how it works.

These same sex **hormones** cause many other changes – changes to how you feel, how you think and how you relate to others. Before you start the **physical changes**, you may notice **emotional changes**.

Adults sometimes see adolescents as moody. Teenagers seem to have very strong emotions – happiness, sadness, worry, excitement, embarrassment, anger and many more.

These mood swings come about because of other emotional and personal changes:

- learning about your own feelings and those of others
- establishing your **independence** as a young adult
- balancing your desire for independence with still being a child and having to listen to parents and teachers
- becoming aware of your own sexuality
- developing your own identity – who you are and who you want to be
- relating to others and valuing their opinions
- developing a sense of responsibility and making decisions based on morals and values.

This young girl has just started her adolescence.

Happiness	🙂
Sadness	☹
Worry	😕
Excitement	😃
Embarrassment	😊
Anger	😠

Exercise

1. Write your own definitions of the following terms:
   a) adolescence
   b) puberty
   c) hormones
   d) independence

Sexual feelings and crushes

In addition, you will start noticing strong **sexual feelings**. You may begin to notice parts of your body that are very sensitive, especially your **genitals**.

Sexual feelings may make you want to be very close to someone who attracts you. You may find yourself experiencing **sexual attraction** to someone of the opposite sex.

You may get warm, shivery or tingly feelings when you think about that person or when they are near to you. You may get excited about having a girlfriend or boyfriend.

Sometimes you may get a 'crush' on someone you find really attractive or interesting. Having a 'crush' means that you can't stop thinking about that person. You may even feel that you are in love with him or her. You may feel embarrassed or shy when your crush is around.

Both girls and boys have crushes. Your crush may be someone at your school, someone from your community, someone younger or older than you. Having crushes is a normal part of growing up, and developing sexually and emotionally.

As you get older, you may start to notice that you are attracted to someone of the opposite sex.

Exercise

2. Look at the emotion icons. Can you think of any other emotions teenagers may have? Create an emotion icon for each one. Show them to your partner.
3. Match each term to the best definition.

a) moody	**i)** a strong interest and attraction to someone
b) hormone	**ii)** to do with feelings
c) physical	**iii)** swinging from one mood to another
d) emotional	**iv)** type of chemical that causes development of sexual characteristics
e) crush	**v)** to do with the body

4. Choose five different feelings. Suggest how the experiences of adolescence may lead to these feelings for a teenager.

Discussion

Have a class discussion on ways of dealing with the emotional changes of adolescence.

Key vocabulary

adolescence

hormone

physical changes

emotional changes

independence

sexual feelings

genitals

sexual attraction

Dealing with emotional changes

We are learning to:

- understand ways of dealing with changes during adolescence.

Dealing with changes

Change takes place whenever something starts, stops, increases or decreases. Examples might be:

- starting at a new school
- stopping (or ending) a friendship
- increasing your responsibilities
- decreasing the time you spend on a hobby.

Change can be exciting, but it can also be scary, tiring, disappointing or stressful. Adolescence is a time of many changes.

Your body is changing and becoming sexually mature in preparation for life as an adult. Your childhood is coming to an end. You are not yet an adult, but you are no longer a child. Your feelings, your role in your family, your relationships – everything is changing.

Teenage boys in Trinidad in 1956. Changes during adolescence have always been the same, no matter when you were born.

Activity

In pairs, create a song or poem to show the emotional changes of teenagers and how to deal with them.

Understanding change

One way of dealing with change is to understand it. The points below will help you to understand some important aspects of big life changes.

Change brings a need for new information

Information helps you to understand what is going on. You will need to find out more about the physical changes in your body, exercise and diet, sex and sexuality, and many other topics.

TIP: Find books and websites about being a teenager. Find an adult you can talk to.

Even when you change, you are still the same person

Do you fear some of the changes of adolescence? Do you feel like no one understands you?

TIP: Remember that no matter how much you change, you are still your own unique self.

Change can bring risks

Your peers may want you to try activities such as drinking, smoking and drugs. They may promise that you will feel more grown-up and confident. However, these activities carry **risks**.

Take care
Sexual relationships are very exciting and pleasurable, but require a great deal of care. Entering carelessly into sexual relationships can carry health risks and emotional risks.

TIP: Before you decide to do something, weigh up the benefits and the risks.

Change takes courage
Sometimes you may feel anxious, scared or worried. These feelings are normal, but it is important to face your fears, not avoid them.

TIP: Ask yourself: What would I do if I wasn't afraid?

Change may bring loss as well as freedom
As you get older, you will lose some parts of your childhood self. Some interests and activities will no longer interest you. Some of your friendships or relationships may end.

TIP: Remember the saying 'When one door closes, another one opens'.

Exercise

1. Write down five examples of changes from your own life.
2. For each change you listed, work out whether it was something stopping or ending, starting, increasing or decreasing. Explain what happened.
3. Did the change feel good or bad to you at the time? Did your feelings about it change afterwards?
4. Read the sayings below. Explain what you understand by each one.

"Don't be afraid of change. You might lose something good, but you'll gain something better."

– Unknown

"Happiness is not the absence of problems; it's the ability to deal with them."

– Dr Steve Maraboli

"You can't change the direction of the wind, but you can adjust the sails to reach your destination."

– LifeTastesWell.com

Activity

Use the magazine articles to help you. Suggest four ways of dealing with the changes experienced in adolescence. Write half a page on each of these four ways. Compile your work for your portfolio.

Key vocabulary

change

risk

Dealing with changes

We are learning to:

- deal with changes during adolescence.

Tips to cope with change

Your **hormones** affect the way your brain works. The high levels of hormones in your bloodstream intensify all your emotions. You may find that you over-react when you experience pain, disappointment or upsetting situations. Some of the following tips may help you to cope.

Exercise regularly

Exercise is a great way to regulate the mood swings of adolescence.

It strengthens the body and focuses the mind, and it is also a good way to let off steam when you are feeling stressed, angry, upset or just bored.

Get enough sleep

Adolescents need eight to nine hours of sleep each night.

If you get too little sleep, you may feel irritable and sleepy during the day, and you may find it difficult to concentrate at school.

Melatonin is a hormone that helps to regulate your sleep cycles.

During the teenage years, your body produces melatonin later at night.

This may make you want to stay up later and sleep later in the morning.

Eat a balanced diet

The food you eat affects how you feel.

Skipping meals and eating junk food can have a negative effect on both your body and your mind.

Try to make sure you eat breakfast, lunch and supper each day, with plenty of fresh fruit and vegetables in your diet.

Avoid too many sugary or fatty snacks.

Drink water and fruit juices rather than fizzy or sugary drinks.

Keep a journal

Writing down your thoughts and ideas can help you to express them.

Alternatively, you can do this through drawings and sketches.

Sit quietly and take some deep breaths

Deep breathing and meditation are techniques that can relieve stress, and relax your body and mind. Sit in a quiet place and close your eyes. Breathe in slowly to a count of four and breathe out slowly to a count of six.

Repeat this at least 10 times. With each breath out, imagine that you are letting go of all your anger, sadness or any other negative emotions.

Let off steam

There will be times that you are very angry or upset. You may need to find a private place where you can cry or even scream loudly.

Whether you like playing the drums loudly, tearing up a pile of old paper, going for a walk or run, or dancing to loud music in your room, you can find a way to let off steam to vent your feelings in ways that will not hurt or upset others.

Talk to someone you trust

Sometimes it can help just to talk to someone who cares about you and understands. This may be a friend, relative or trusted adult.

Case study

Dear Amanda

I feel really lucky to be part of the coolest group at my school. The only problem is, at all of their parties there is always a lot of beer and wine, and everyone expects me to drink. I don't really want to, but if I say no, they'll realise I'm not really cool enough to be part of their group. Recently, my friends were talking about getting some 'party pills' for their next party. I don't know which drugs they mean, but I am nervous I will have to try them.

Peer Pressure Patrick

Meditation is a good way to relieve stress, and relax your body and mind.

Questions

1. Do you agree with Patrick that he is part of the coolest group at the school? Why or why not?
2. What is causing Patrick's problem?
3. Identify another change in Patrick's social group.
4. In pairs, come up with a reply to Patrick's letter, with advice for how he can deal with this situation.

Exercise

1. Which of the tips on these pages have you tried? Which do you think works best for you? Why?
2. What else do you try to do?
3. Do you think these are good tips? Why? Why not?

Key vocabulary

hormones

Questions

See how well you have understood the topics in this unit.

1. List three of your characteristics that are:
   a) inherited
   b) from your environment.
2. List one similarity and one difference for each pair:
   a) nuclear family and extended family
   b) single parent family and sibling household
   c) sibling household and extended family.
3. Match each example below to one of the following functions of family: biological, emotional, social, economic, cultural or educational.
   a) giving a child love and attention
   b) teaching a child to swim
   c) earning money to support a family
   d) taking a child to church.
4. List all the different roles you play. You can choose from the mind map below or add any other roles you can think of.

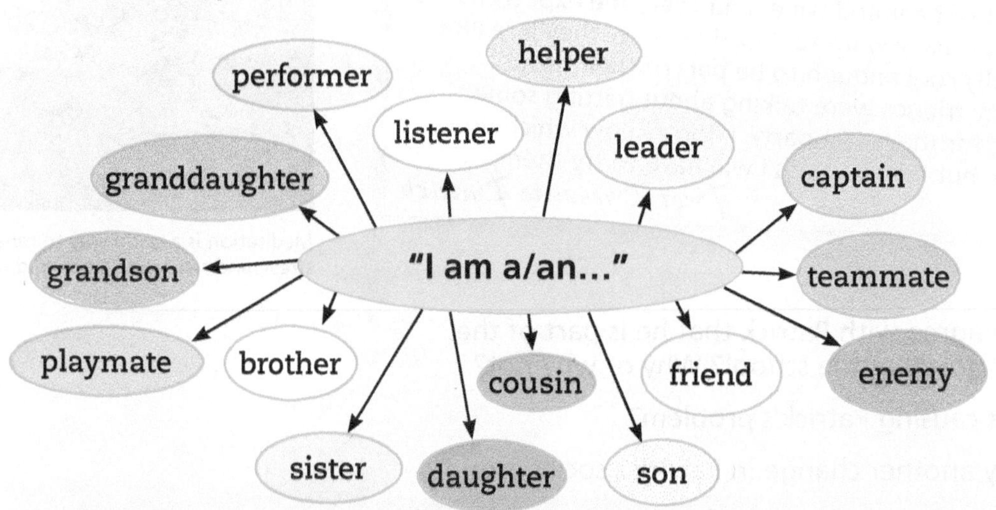

5. Identify which of the following is not an example of conflict:
   a) a serious disagreement
   b) a fight
   c) a discussion where two people agree with each other
   d) a war

6. Mediation is:
    a) a conflict between three people
    b) a process where a third party helps two sides to resolve a conflict
    c) a conflict where both people do not have a clear point of view
    d) the end of a conflict
7. Resolution is:
    a) a disagreement
    b) a situation where everyone agrees and is happy
    c) a situation where two parties overcome their differences and find a solution to their problem
    d) a plan
8. List six tips for avoiding or preventing bullying.
9. Which of the following circumstances does not describe a single parent family?
    a) The parents get divorced and the children live with one parent.
    b) The father has died, so the children live with their mother.
    c) The parents are having difficulties, so the children go to live with their aunt, uncle and cousins.
10. Which of the following describes good self-esteem?
    a) boasting and bragging a lot
    b) believing that you are the best at everything
    c) believing that others are the best at everything
    d) having a good understanding of your own strengths and weaknesses
11. List five characteristics of people with high self-esteem and five characteristics of people with low self-esteem.
12. Explain what you understand by 'identity'. Describe five aspects of your own identity.
13. Describe the following types of family structures:
    a) nuclear
    b) reconstituted
    c) extended
14. Describe three roles you play in your life (these may be roles at home, at school or in your community). List two responsibilities of each role.
15. Describe four main differences between bullying and normal conflict.
16. Write definitions of the terms 'family tree', 'ancestry' and 'traditions'.
17. Draw part of your family tree, showing at least three generations.
18. Name the stages of human development.

Checking your progress

To make good progress in understanding different aspects of your personal development, check to make sure you understand these ideas.

- [ ] Explain the impact of heredity and environment on us.
- [ ] Explain the five different aspects of ourselves.
- [ ] Name the four main family types in the Caribbean.
- [ ] Identify the potential advantages and disadvantages of the various different family types.
- [ ] Explain why there are different types of unions.
- [ ] Describe the five functions of the family.
- [ ] Explain the roles and responsibilities of three family members and why it is important they fulfil their roles.
- [ ] Describe the consequences of not fulfilling these roles and responsibilities.
- [ ] Describe the causes of three types of conflict and suggest strategies to resolve these.
- [ ] Describe five characteristics of high and low self-esteem and explain the factors that can affect self-esteem.
- [ ] Outline the stages of the human life cycle and their characteristics.
- [ ] Explain why emotional and physical changes occur in adolescence and suggest ways to deal with these changes.

Unit 2: Economic growth and development

In this unit you will find out 

Developing human resources

- The difference between human resources and physical resources
- The characteristics of human resources

Factors influencing human resources

- The factors that influence human resources:
  - quality
  - quantity
  - composition
  - skills development
  - creativity

The importance of human resources to the economy

- The importance of human resources to a country's economic development:
  - variety of skills
  - innovation
  - manufacturing and agricultural practices
  - creativity
  - high levels of production

The role of education in the development of human resources

- The importance of education in developing human resources
- Building your nation

The role of health in the development of human resources

- Health benefits and concerns
- How health issues affect the workplace
- Lifestyle diseases
- How health issues can be addressed

What are human resources?

We are learning to:

- define and use correctly the terms resource, human resource, human capital, physical resources, skills, talent, knowledge, ability
- look at the characteristics of human resources
- explain the difference between human and physical resources.

Developing human resources

An **economy** is made up of businesses that provide **goods** and **services** to meet people's needs. In order to provide goods and services, we use **capital**.

Traditionally, there were three kinds of capital: **resources,** land (or natural resources) and **labour**.

- A resource is defined as anything natural or physical that can be used to create wealth or improve the standard of living of people. For example, people use land to grow crops or to mine metals and minerals.
- Natural resources come from the natural environment, for example, wood, water and soil. **Physical resources** are other tangible resources made by people, such as buildings and equipment.
- **Human resources** are people and their various **skills, talents** and **abilities**. People such as teachers, doctors, farmers, office workers, engineers, scientists and shop keepers all have skills that they use to provide goods or services.

The ball is a physical resource. The player, his talent and his skill are all human resources.

Characteristics of human resources

Human resources (HR) has several meanings:

- workers or employees who work for an employer
- talents, skills, **knowledge** and experience that can only be found in people.

Training and education are aspects of human resource development.

Activity

For each of the following, brainstorm the physical and human resources that it requires:

a) a school

b) a restaurant

HUMAN RESOURCES

Similarities and differences

Today, economists talk about two kinds of capital – **physical capital** (including land, which is a physical resource) and **human capital**.

- Physical capital, including land, is a physical resource that cannot make or provide anything by itself. Physical capital refers to assets that have been made or found that we use to produce goods and services.
- Human capital refers to people, skills, training, experience, education and knowledge. It can only be found in people.

An economy needs human capital and physical capital to run smoothly. Skills are special abilities people have. They have been learned or developed.

Project

Create a concept map to show how skills, talent, knowledge and ability relate to human resources.

Choose a working person you know. Collect and present information about the person's skills, talents, knowledge and ability.

Who makes up a country's human resources?

Think about the population of your country. The young and old people in the country are not able to work. Children and teenagers are still at school.

The working-age population is made up of people between the ages of around 17 or 18 up to about 65.

However, younger people are part of the next generation's human resources. For this reason, education is also considered an important part of human resources.

Exercise

1. Choose the correct term to complete each sentence.

resource	human	natural	skill

   a) A ____________ is something that we use.
   b) Wood is an example of a ____________ resource that we use to make different products.
   c) Someone who has a special ____________ for music or dance may go on to become an artist.
   d) The ____________ resources of a country lie in its people.

2. List two main differences between human and physical resources.
3. Look at the picture of the people making up the word 'resources' on the opposite page. What does this picture tell you about human resources?

Key vocabulary

economy
goods
services
capital
resources
labour
physical resources
human resources
skill
talent
ability
knowledge
physical capital
human capital

Factors influencing human resources

We are learning to:

- explain factors that influence the development of human resources.

There are several factors that influence the development of human resources:

- quality
- quantity
- composition
- skills development/enhancement
- creativity.

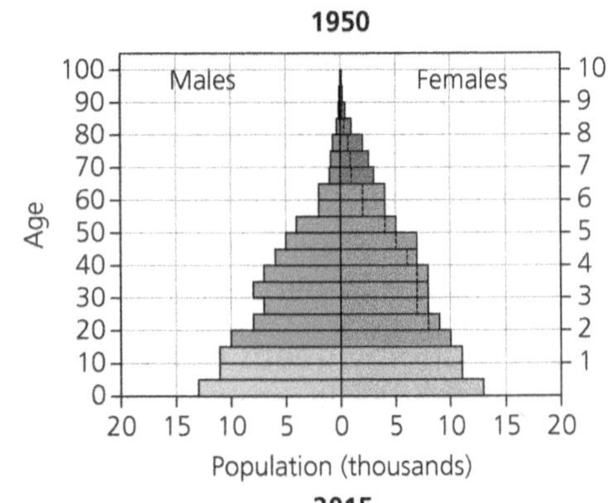

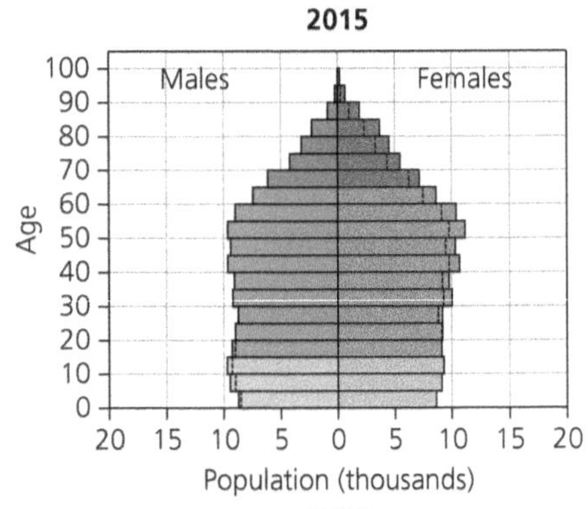

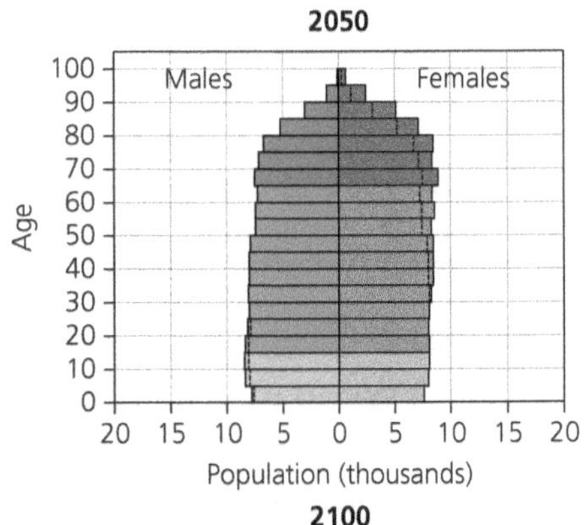

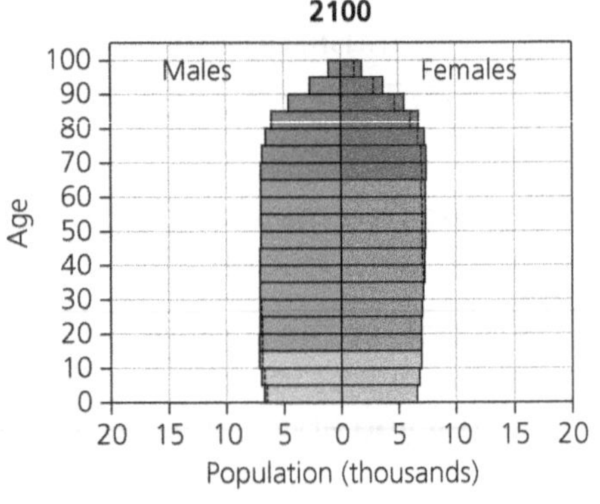

Barbados age distribution graphs 1950–2100

Quality

Quality is a measure of excellence. The quality of a country's human resources is directly linked to its skills development and education. Education includes schools, colleges, universities, training centres and programmes that help adults increase their skills.

Quantity

In a very small country with a very small population, there is likely to be a smaller **quantity** of people making up its human resources. A bigger country is likely to have a bigger pool of human resources.

Composition

Population **composition** refers to the make-up or characteristics of people in a population, such as **gender**, age, ethnicity, occupation or religion.

A **population pyramid** shows the age and sex distribution of a population. The x-axis (along the bottom) gives us population numbers in thousands and is numbered in both directions from the middle. The y-axis (up the side) is divided into age groups.

Age pyramids change over time. As a population becomes more educated, the younger population gets smaller. With more health care available, the older population increases.

These age pyramids show how the population of Barbados has changed over time and how researchers expect it to change in the future.

Skills development/enhancement

A skill is an area of expertise or an ability to carry out activities or job functions involving ideas, things and/or people.

Skills development is where a country, economy or firm provides education and training for its workers so they can improve their existing skills and develop new ones. We also talk about **skills enhancement**, which is the improvement of existing skills.

- **Unskilled** workers are people who want work, but they do not have any special skills. Their job options are limited to work such as cleaning or labourer jobs.
- **Semi-skilled** workers have some training in using tools or machinery. For example, a labourer who has learned to drive a tractor is a semi-skilled worker.
- A **skilled** worker has some training in a particular field and can work independently.
- **Highly skilled** workers have very specialised skills and knowledge, and can also usually supervise others.

If the people in a country are constantly developing their skills, the human resources of the country get stronger and more able to provide goods and services for the country's population.

Creativity

Creativity is a person's capacity to use their imagination to come up with original or new ideas and solutions. We often associate creativity with artistic work such as drawing, painting, music or dance. However, people may be creative in the ways they solve problems, from real-life problems to maths and science.

Exercise

1. Why do all the pyramids get narrower at the top?
2. Look at the graphs on page 52. Which age group made up the biggest part of the population in 2015? How will this change in 2050?
3. Describe the main changes to the population over time, from 1950 to 2100.
4. For each of the following jobs, say whether it is unskilled, semi-skilled, skilled or highly skilled. Give reasons for your answers.

a) doctor	**d)** farm labourer
b) secretary	**e)** machinist
c) pilot	**f)** painter

Research

Choose one of the factors from these pages. Research a product, or industry, in your country and find out how that factor influences the development of human resources in that product/industry.

Activity

Create a mind map showing the factors that influence the development of a country's human resources. Add to the mind map using the information on these pages.

Key vocabulary

quality
quantity
composition
gender
population pyramid
skills development
skills enhancement
unskilled
semi-skilled
skilled
highly skilled
creativity

Human resources and economic development

We are learning to:

- discuss the term economic development
- assess the importance of human resources to a country's economic development.

Human resources and economic development

Economic development is the activity of improving a country's **standard of living** by creating jobs, supporting **innovation** and new ideas, creating **wealth** or making improvements to people's **quality of life**.

When a country has a high standard of education and training, with investment in human resources, there are many benefits to the economy. Skilled, educated people can offer:

- a **variety of skills**, which in turn offer a range of goods and services
- creative innovations
- expertise that can lead to better planning and use of resources
- new **manufacturing** and **agricultural practices**, which can provide for the country's needs more efficiently
- an increase in the wealth generated for the country
- improved **creativity**, allowing people to solve problems facing the country
- increased levels of **production** so that more goods and services become available
- improved standard of living
- more jobs and opportunities
- drops in poverty and crime levels.

The Neal and Massy car assembly plant in Arima, Trinidad, helps to provide employment and economic development to the country.

Exercise

1. Write your own definition of economic development.
2. Using your definition, research the types of economic development that you can find in your country.
3. Brainstorm ways that human resources are important to the development of a country.
4. Outline five benefits to a country's economy that skilled people can offer.

Activity

Write two paragraphs of approximately 250 words on what skilled and educated people can give to a country's economy.

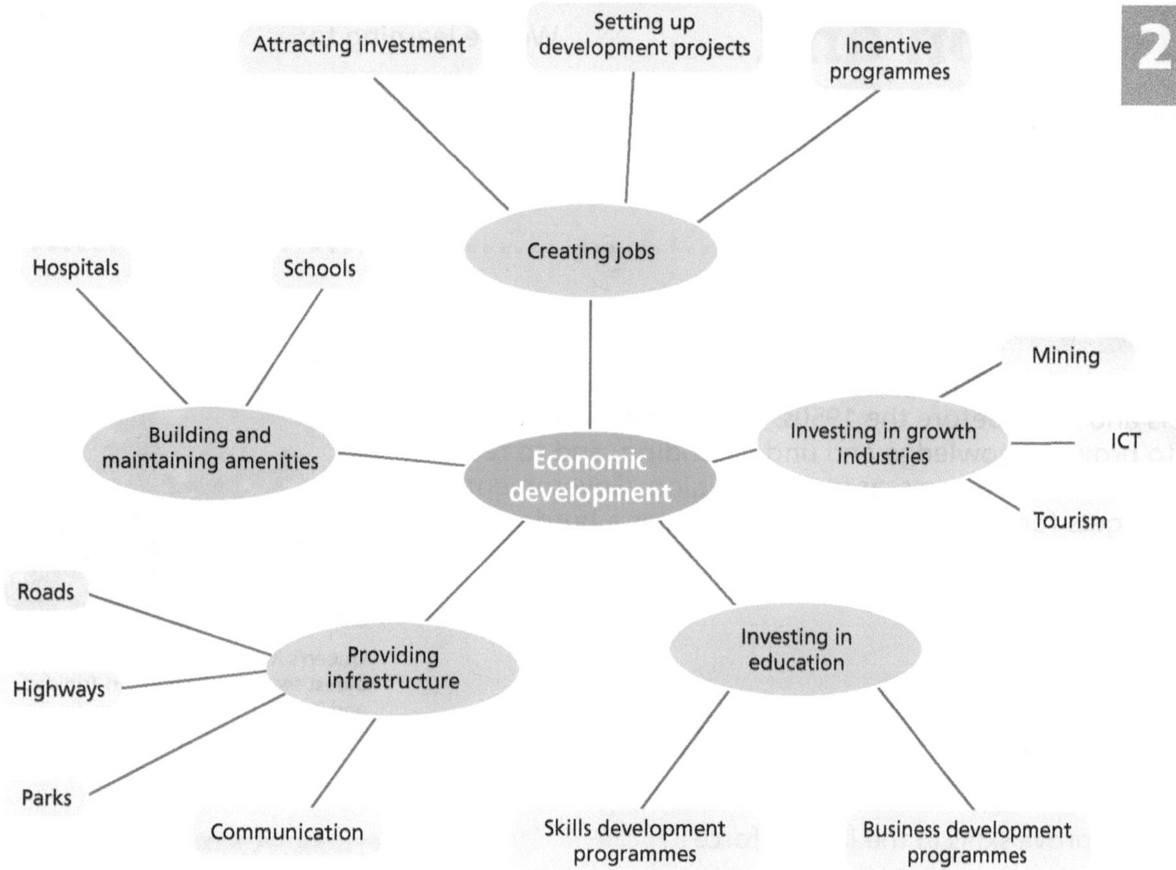

Activities that typically form part of economic development in a country.

Exercise

5. Look at the mind map on this page. For each of the following aspects of economic development, list at least five skilled jobs it involves:

a) building a hospital

b) establishing a school

c) providing communication infrastructure

6. How do you think each of the following could help economic development?

a) A government offers a free computer training course for 500 school-leavers.

b) A business offers internships to 20 students.

c) A bank offers training bursaries for students studying economics and finance, on condition that the students work at the bank for at least one year after qualifying.

Key vocabulary

economic development
standard of living
innovation
wealth
quality of life
skills (variety)
manufacturing practices
agricultural practices
creativity
production

Education and human resources

We are learning to:

- define and use correctly the term education
- examine the importance of education in developing our human resources.

Education and the labour force

Education is the teaching of **knowledge**, ideas, opinions, beliefs and skills. Before the 1950s, the purpose of education was to provide knowledge and understanding, and to teach social values and customs, as well as religion. Governments had budgets for education, but it was seen as a burden on the state.

Queen's Royal College is one of the oldest secondary schools in Trinidad and Tobago.

Case study

For countries like Trinidad and Tobago this was an important change. Today, education is seen as an investment to:

- improve skills in the labour force
- produce knowledge and expertise to create new products
- create new markets and opportunities
- pass on cultural values and traditions
- transform the political landscape.

In the past, Trinidad and Tobago's workforce had a shortage of highly skilled workers. This slowed down economic development. Companies who needed more highly skilled workers had to employ people from other countries. In 2015, the government of Trinidad and Tobago allocated $10.126 billion to education and training. Some of this money went towards free transport for students, book rental programmes and scholarships, as well as towards building schools and training teachers.

Discussion

In groups, define the term 'education' and discuss the importance of education in developing our human resources. Brainstorm your ideas and write them up in a large mind map.

Activity

Take the ideas from your discussion. Use them to create a poem, song or poster showing how education benefits the nation.

However, in the 1950s and 1960s governments began to see education differently. They thought that the more educated the population, the more beneficial they could be in the economy. Education became part of economic development.

Training

The term **human resource development** (HRD) is used when we talk about **employees** developing their personal and professional skills, knowledge and abilities. It focuses on developing the best labour force possible, so that the company and its employees can achieve their work goals and deliver excellent service to customers or clients.

Training can start earlier. Once a student has graduated from secondary school, they can do further training in institutions such as:

- colleges and technical colleges
- universities
- online colleges or training websites.

People who go on to do further training after school may have a wider choice of careers open to them. They can also earn more money.

Once a person is employed, it is still important that they continue to develop their skills and abilities. Some companies and **employers** may offer:

- **on-the-job training** – training whilst working, to help develop skills within a job
- **mentorship** (or coaching) – a more experienced employee gives advice and support to someone less experienced
- **succession training** – where the employee's skills and abilities are developed to prepare them for promotion
- **tuition assistance** – an employee can go on additional training courses to help build up their knowledge and skills.

A pottery in Chaguanas, the largest municipality and fastest-growing town in Trinidad and Tobago.

Did you know...?

"The future of the nation lies in the schoolbags of the children."

Dr Eric Williams, first Prime Minister of Trinidad and Tobago

Exercise

1. Give three reasons why education is seen as an important investment in Trinidad and Tobago.
2. How has the view of education in the Caribbean changed since the 1950s?
3. Define the term 'education'.
4. Why do you think people choose to spend the time and money on further study? Give at least two reasons.
5. Why would employers choose to offer training to their employees?
6. Write a sentence about the role of education in HR for:

   a) companies **b)** employees **c)** the country

   (Hint: What does education do for the human resources in each of these categories?)

Key vocabulary

education

knowledge

human resource development

employee

employer

on-the-job training

mentorship

succession training

tuition assistance

Building our nation

We are learning to:

- define and use correctly the terms responsibility, patriotism and nation building
- explore the contribution individuals can make to a country's development.

Our contribution to our nation

It is the **responsibility** of all citizens to take part in **nation building**. The feeling of belonging, pride and responsibility that citizens feel towards their country is known as **patriotism**.

The national flag of Saint Kitts and Nevis.

The significance of independence

Knowing about our national heroes gives us a sense of joy and pride because they helped to pave the way for the future. They become our role models and create the way for new history. They show us things like courage, honour and justice. Our heroes are symbols for all of us, with qualities we all would like to have.

Dr Simeon Daniel

Dr Simeon Daniel, known as the 'Father of Modern Nevis' made a huge contribution to the **nation** of Nevis. Some of his achievements include the following:

- He was one of the founding members of the Nevis Reformation Party in 1970.
- He established the Nevis Sixth Form College in 1981.
- He was the first Premier of Nevis 1983–1992.
- He founded the Bank of Nevis in 1985.

During his time as Premier he helped to improve the quality of services for Nevisians:

- He set up the Nevis Housing and Land Development Corporation (NHLDC), which allowed Nevisians to own their own land.
- He built new infrastructure, including improvements in housing, healthcare and electricity.
- He created job opportunities in tourism with the establishment of the world-renowned Four Seasons Resort.

As a result of his achievements, Nevis began to play a greater part in the governing of the twin island state of Saint Kitts and Nevis. He had a major role in framing the Independence Constitution of Saint Kitts and Nevis in 1983.

The Bank of Nevis Ltd building, founded by Dr Simeon Daniel in 1985.

Discussion

Discuss why it is important to take part in the building of your nation.

Case study

Sir John Compton

John Compton was born on Canouan, Saint Vincent and the Grenadines in 1925, but moved to Saint Lucia when he was 13 years old. He became the first (and only) Premier of Saint Lucia in 1967 while it was still a colony and led the country to Associated Statehood and Independence in 1979. Following this he became Saint Lucia's first Prime Minister in 1979.

He was deeply committed to regional unity. He is well-known for his role in the establishment of CARICOM, the Caribbean Development Bank, the Organisation of Eastern Caribbean States (OECS) and the Eastern Caribbean Common Market (ECCM).

Like all Caribbean leaders emerging out of the colonial era, Sir John Compton fought strenuously for the rights of the working classes and the poor. He is credited with modernising his adopted homeland. He introduced bananas as the main income earner to assist with the development of Saint Lucia.

Sir John Compton became the first Prime Minister of Saint Lucia in 1979.

Questions

1. What contributions did Sir John Compton make to his adopted country?
2. Create a list of the major Caribbean institutions that Sir John Compton helped to establish.

Exercise

1. What contributions did Dr Daniel make to the island of Nevis?
2. Why do you think this earned him the title of 'Father of Modern Nevis'?
3. Research the following terms:
   a) responsibility **b)** patriotism **c)** nation building
4. Find at least three different definitions of each term. Discuss which definitions make the most sense to you. Write a paragraph explaining each of the terms in your own words.
5. As a citizen of your country, why is it important that you help to build it? Should the development of your country be the responsibility of the government?

Activity

Write two paragraphs of approximately 250 words on how you can contribute to nation building.

Key vocabulary

responsibility

nation building

patriotism

nation

Health and health concerns

We are learning to:

- define and use correctly the terms health, health concerns, health indicator
- examine health issues faced by human resources – maternal care.

Health benefits and concerns

When a population takes care of its **health**, there are many benefits for the country as a whole:

- Working-age adults can work, be **productive** and support their families.
- People live longer and enjoy a better quality of life.
- The economy does not lose many days or hours of work because workers are ill.
- Working people have the strength and energy to be creative and proactive.
- Government reduces spending on treatments.

There are a wide range of factors relating to each other that affect the health of individuals and communities. Problems or lack of any of these factors can lead to **health concerns** for people in that community.

Health indicators

Health indicators are data measures that help researchers to understand the levels of health of a population and what that population's health concerns are. In any country, the main health indicators are:

- **life expectancy** – the average number of years that people in a country are expected to live
- **maternal care** – care available for mothers during pregnancy, childbirth and while they are caring for a newborn
- **infant mortality rate (IMR)** – the number of deaths per thousand infants under the age of one in a given year.

alcohol and drug use
smoking
diet
BEHAVIOURS AND PRACTICES
sexual behaviour
violence
breast feeding
physical activity

Although our IMR has come down in the Caribbean, it is still high in comparison with other industrialised countries. In addition to these three indicators, each country faces its own specific health issues.

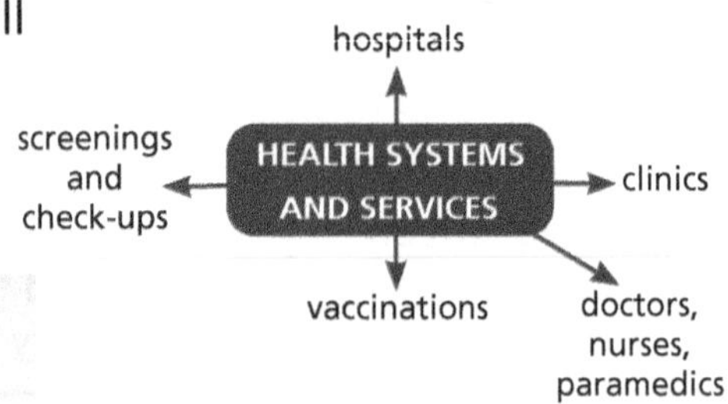

Exercise

1. Give three reasons why it is important for your country that we take care of our health.

Maternal and infant mortality rates

The rates of maternal and infant deaths decrease noticeably in countries where:

- there is continuous prenatal care available
- mothers stop smoking and drinking alcohol while pregnant
- programmes offer information, counselling, testing and medication for HIV/AIDS
- mothers eat a well-balanced diet, which can reduce the chances of birth defects
- mothers breastfeed their babies for the first six months, when a baby's body is not ready to digest other foods
- babies and children receive immunisations against common vaccine-preventable diseases.

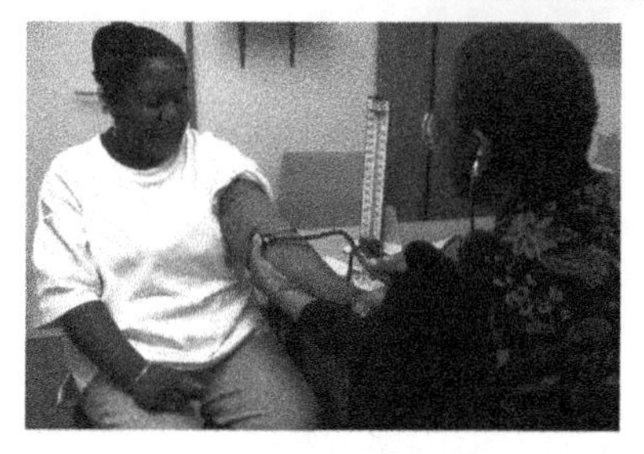

A health visitor taking the blood pressure of a pregnant woman.

Case study

Letitia is a 28-year-old woman who is pregnant with her first child. She works as a clerk at an accounting firm. Letitia applies for time off from work to visit the clinic for prenatal visits.

Questions

1. Letitia applies for time off from work to visit the clinic for prenatal visits. Why is it necessary for her to miss work for these visits?
2. Which is more important – the needs of the company or the needs of the mother? Why?
3. Explain some ways in which the health of pregnant mothers and young babies is important for the future of a country.

Discussion

Read the list of health concerns that follows. Which of these affect people at your school the most?

- tuberculosis
- arthritis
- diabetes
- malnutrition
- colds and flu.

How do you think the rating might be different in a much older group of people?

Exercise

2. Write a sentence explaining the relationship between these health factors:
   a) safe food and the immune system
   b) education level and diet
   c) employment and alcohol/drug abuse
   d) any other pair of factors
3. In your own words, explain what are the main health indicators of a country.
4. "The life expectancy in Guyana is 70 years. That means everyone in Guyana will live to at least 70." Is this statement correct? Why or why not?

Key vocabulary

health

productive

health concerns

health indicators

life expectancy

maternal care

infant mortality rate (IMR)

Health and the workplace

We are learning to:

- define and use correctly the term health care
- examine health issues faced by human resources in the workplace
- explain the importance of health care in HR development.

A healthy workforce

It is important to have a healthy workforce. Each member of the workforce provides income, supports their family and contributes to the country's economy. A healthier workforce means:

- Fewer hours are lost to illness.
- Workers are able to work more productively.
- The country's everyday needs are supplied.
- The economy stays strong.
- There is increased **life expectancy**.

The General Hospital in Port of Spain, Trinidad.

Health care

Health care is the provision of medical services such as clinics, hospitals and pharmacies. There are two levels of health care:

- **primary (preventive)** health care, which aims to keep people healthy and prevent disease
- **secondary (curative)** health care, which aims to address existing health problems.

Health issues affect people at a personal level and also affect the workplace.

The individual

There are four ways that a person can be affected by disease or illness in the workplace: physically, mentally, socially and financially. The table outlines the effects of these illnesses and some examples.

Effects of illness	Example
Physical (on the body)	Pain, fever, tiredness, vomiting, diarrhoea
Mental (on the mind)	Depression, loss of memory, confusion, inability to concentrate
Social (on friends and community)	Isolation, lack of connection with other people
Financial (to do with money)	Loss of income as a result of missing work; lack of money as a result of medical bills

Exercise

1. Why is it important to have a healthy workforce?
2. Write your own definitions of **a)** health care, **b)** primary health care, **c)** secondary health care.
3. Describe three ways that a person can be affected by disease or illness in the workplace.

When a worker is sick, it may be necessary for them to stay at home. This is partly in order not to pass on communicable diseases, and partly in order to recover. Absenteeism is a major cause of **loss of productivity** in companies.

Some diseases are highly contagious and a worker may pass them on to other employees before they realise they are ill. Diseases such as tuberculosis (TB) and flu can cause workplace epidemics. This may cause a huge loss of productivity within a company.

When someone gets a cold, or the flu, germs are spread very easily – this picture shows what it looks like when someone sneezes.

Case study

Illness in the workplace

A. Imagine a company that has 20 employees. One employee gets the flu. He decides to go to work, even though he is sneezing and feverish. The next day he is too ill to come to work, but by then three of his colleagues have developed the same symptoms. They each miss the next two days of work.

B. HIV is a virus that affects the **immune system** – this is the system that helps the body fight diseases and infections.

Most people who get sick from HIV are of working age. High levels of HIV can cause serious shortages of human resources as people may no longer be able to work.

They may also need constant care. This means that in many families not only do they lose the main breadwinner, but other family members are unable to go out and work as they need to stay at home to look after the ill person.

Questions

1. In Example A above, how many man-hours of work have been missed? (A man-hour is one hour of one person's work, so if two people each miss one hour, that's two man-hours lost.)
2. Why is HIV a particular health concern for human resources?
3. How does HIV impact:
   a) families **b)** the workplace?
4. Write 250 words on the importance of health care in the development of human resources.

Discussion

Discuss why health care is important to the nation.

Key vocabulary

life expectancy

health care

primary (preventive) health care

secondary (curative) health care

loss of productivity

immune system

Ageing population and mental health

We are learning to:

- examine health concerns – ageing, mental health
- describe ways of addressing health issues.

An ageing population

Look back at the population pyramids on page 52. In Barbados between 1950 and 2015:

- The number of children under the age of 15 has declined.
- The number of adults over the age of 60 has increased.

This population distribution means that Barbados has an **ageing** population. Ageing populations are a trend worldwide, as **life expectancy** has increased. Life expectancy increases with economic development, partly because people can receive medical care and enjoy a higher standard of living.

Life expectancy has increased in Barbados – people are living longer.

One of the consequences of living with an ageing population is that there is a greater need for people who can care for the elderly. The elderly may rely on relatives and service providers to help them meet their everyday needs.

Elderly people often suffer from loneliness if their younger relatives do not have enough time to spend with them. Loneliness can lead to other problems such as depression, alcohol abuse and unwillingness to eat well or exercise. All of these factors can worsen the health of the elderly.

There are some ways of overcoming the challenges of living with an ageing population. These include:

- educating people about the benefits of living with an extended family
- incentives for students wishing to study nursing and social work, particularly for the elderly
- school initiatives that involve the elderly in the community.

Exercise

1. What do you understand by the term 'ageing population'?
2. Suggest three challenges of living with an ageing population.
3. Name three factors that can worsen the health of the elderly.

The World Health Organization (WHO) defines mental health as follows:

A state of well-being in which every individual realises his or her own potential, can cope with the normal stresses of life, can work productively and fruitfully, and is able to make a contribution to his or her community.

Mental health

A healthy body is only one aspect of human health. The World Health Organisation (WHO) defines health as follows:

> *Health is a state of complete physical, mental and social well-being and not merely the absence of disease or infirmity.*

'Mental' means relating to the mind. Mental health includes how we feel about ourselves and others, and how we are able to meet the demands of our lives.

People who suffer from poor mental health may suffer from disturbances such as poor concentration, mood swings and interrupted sleep. Mental illnesses include disorders such as depression, schizophrenia, bipolar disorders and anxiety.

Depression in particular is one of the most widespread mental health problems affecting adolescents. There are many possible causes, including:

- physical health problems such as HIV or cancer
- trauma such as violence or assault
- childhood abuse or neglect
- genetics and stress levels.

Happy school girls in Castries, Saint Lucia.

Leading causes of death for specific age groups

Age group	Main cause of death
5 years and under	Infectious and parasitic diseases and respiratory infections
5 years to 44 years	External causes – accidents and injuries
45 years and older	Heart disease

Discussion

In groups, discuss the importance of looking after the elderly. Think about ways that you can help in your family and community.

Exercise

4. Discuss the difference, in your opinion, between poor mental health and mental illness.
5. Read the WHO definitions of health. Write a paragraph about why mental health is as important for the labour force as physical health.
6. **a)** Look at the table. Which are the main causes of death in our working population?

   b) Suggest three behaviours that might be directly linked to these causes of death.

Key vocabulary

ageing

life expectancy

Lifestyle diseases

We are learning to:

- define and use correctly the terms lifestyle disease, diet and exercise
- examine unhealthy lifestyles
- describe ways of addressing health issues.

Unhealthy lifestyles

Lifestyle diseases are diseases that may be caused by the way people live, especially by eating too much sugar and fat in the **diet**, and by doing too little **exercise**. Some of these diseases include diabetes, heart disease and cancer.

Think about the many differences between your lifestyle and the life of your ancestors 200 years ago.

	200 years ago	Today
Diet	Fresh meat, fish, fruits and vegetables	Prepared and processed foods, too much fat and sugar
Transport	Walking; riding horses; canoes	Cars, buses; very easy but it does not give any exercise
Home	Collect wood for cooking and light; hunt and prepare food	Switch on a light; buy food from shops
Work	Mostly physical work	Mostly work at computers
Entertainment	Storytelling, dancing	TV, tablets, mobile phones, computers

Diabetes

Diabetes is one of the most common lifestyle diseases in the Caribbean. For example, scientists estimate that in Trinidad and Tobago, more than 1 in every 10 adults has diabetes. The main causes of diabetes are physical inactivity, unhealthy diet (too much sugar and fat, and too little fresh fruit and vegetables), smoking and alcohol abuse.

Most lifestyle diseases today in the Caribbean are caused by diet, low levels of physical activity, stress, smoking, alcohol and drug abuse.

Substance abuse

In the Caribbean, abuse of alcohol and drugs among young people is increasing. Substance abuse is linked to road accidents, violence, stress and mental illness.

Exercise

1. Was our lifestyle 200 years ago better or worse for our health than it is today? Give three reasons for your answer.

Health and diet

Your diet affects your health. It is important to eat a balanced diet, and only eat moderate amounts of sugary and fatty foods. People gain weight when they:

- eat too many energy-rich foods high in fat and sugar
- get too little physical exercise.

Being overweight can lead to serious health problems. Your **body mass index** (BMI) is calculated by dividing your weight (in kilograms) by your height (in metres) and then squaring the resulting number. People with a BMI under 18.5 are considered underweight, and those with a BMI over 25 are considered obese.

Obesity is linked to other problems such as heart disease, cancers, hypertension, back pain, blood clots and diabetes.

In addition, people who eat too much sugary or processed food may suffer from diseases of the mouth and teeth. The most common oral diseases are tooth decay and gum disease. These are extremely common but are easily prevented.

No smoking
Company policy

Many companies have signs like these at work banning people from smoking.

Discussion

Have a classroom discussion on how lifestyle diseases affect people and how the workplace may be affected.

Cancer

Although there are many causes of cancers, there are several lifestyle choices that can increase the risk of cancer:

- smoking increases the risk of lung cancer
- poor diet and obesity are linked to higher rates of cancers such as colon cancer, breast cancer and prostate cancer
- exposure to the sun increases risks of skin cancer.

Accidents and injuries

The leading causes of death in the Caribbean are accidents and injuries. This includes injuries from road accidents, violence, poisoning and suicide. The Caribbean Public Health Agency (CARPHA) has calculated that for each year in the period 2007–2012, 11.5% of all deaths in the Caribbean were due to accidents and injuries.

Project

Keep a diary of what you eat for three days. Make sure you note everything that passes your lips – meals, snacks and drinks.

Write a report where you assess how healthy or balanced your diet is and what you could do to improve it.

Draw up a three-day balanced eating plan.

Exercise

2. What do you understand by the term 'lifestyle disease'?
3. List five factors that contribute to the incidence of lifestyle diseases.
4. Draw a mindmap showing how the different lifestyle diseases relate to each other.

Key vocabulary

lifestyle diseases

diet

exercise

body mass index (BMI)

Dealing with health issues

We are learning to:

- describe how health issues can be addressed by the government and the individual.

Addressing health issues

Healthy lifestyles have many benefits for individuals, companies and for the country. For individuals:

- Exercise and eating healthily make you look and feel good, and increase your life expectancy.
- Many forms of exercise are **sociable** – they bring people together with friends.
- Healthy lifestyle choices make it less likely that you will develop serious diseases later in life.
- A healthy adult is able to work and support their family.

For companies:

- Companies benefit because employees are more productive and there are lower levels of absenteeism.

For the country:

- A healthy workforce is more productive.
- High levels of disease are very costly for the government. High costs of health care use up money that could go towards meeting other needs.

Exercise is a good way to keep healthy. This couple is cycling near Mount Nevis Hotel in Saint Kitts and Nevis.

Activity

Invite a resource person to address your class about the importance of diet, exercise and lifestyle on your health. This could be a doctor, nurse or nutritionist.

Improving our health

The responsibility for citizens' health is a shared responsibility between ourselves, governments and companies. There are several ways to address our health issues:

- Follow a **balanced diet** and exercise regularly.
- Go for regular medical check-ups, especially if you are at risk for specific diseases.
- Avoid smoking and substance abuse.
- Governments allocate money for clinics and hospitals.
- Health-care providers give information and raise awareness about health issues through campaigns and programmes.
- Voluntary organisations, such as the Diabetes Association, work to promote awareness of and education about illnesses such as diabetes.
- Companies support healthy choices for their employees, for example, by paying for medical insurance, providing paid maternity leave or even setting up exercise facilities.

Why do people neglect health issues?

Sometimes people make poor lifestyle choices. It may be easier to snack on junk food than to stick to a healthy diet. A regular exercise plan takes discipline and effort. Sometimes, even though people know they should be taking better care of themselves, they don't do it. There are several reasons for this:

- Effort – healthier choices may take more effort, such as exercising regularly.
- Time – when people are busy, they may feel they don't have time to spend on exercise or check-ups.
- Money – medical check-ups, sports equipment or memberships and healthy foods may cost more than simply staying at home and watching TV.

Discussion

Where would you go for treatment or advice if you were sick? Discuss which places are available to help you if you:

a) get injured in a car accident

b) feel weak and feverish

c) feel anxious and depressed all the time

Education and public awareness

Many people do not realise the importance of a healthy lifestyle until it is too late and they are already suffering from the ill effects of an unhealthy lifestyle. Educating people about the risks of lifestyle diseases and the benefits of a healthy lifestyle helps to motivate individuals to take responsibility for their own health. Education and awareness can help us to make changes to our lifestyles to prevent lifestyle diseases.

How the government provides health support

In order to help the population stay healthy, governments use many resources to provide health-care services, including:

- building and maintaining hospitals, clinics and other health-care institutions, and sports and recreation facilities
- providing programmes for vaccinations
- educational programmes related to health issues
- funding research for cures for diseases such as cancer
- sanitation services, including waste collection and disposal, and the provision of clean water.

Project

Create a three-step plan for increasing awareness of healthy eating among students in your school by making a poster, flyer or newsletter.

Exercise

1. Give two ways that good health benefits:
   a) individuals **b)** companies **c)** the country
2. Whose responsibility should it be to ensure that people understand the importance of a healthy lifestyle?
3. Look back at previous pages. Suggest three things that can help to prevent:
   a) HIV **b)** diabetes **c)** lung cancer
4. Explain three ways lifestyle diseases can be prevented or treated.

Key vocabulary

sociable

balanced diet

Questions

See how well you have understood the topics in this unit.

1. What are the main differences between human and physical resources?
2. Give an example of each of the following types of workers:
   a) unskilled
   b) semi-skilled
   c) skilled
   d) highly skilled
3. Choose the correct term to complete each sentence.

   human capital   physical capital

   __________ refers to assets that have been made or found that we use to produce goods and services.

   _________ refers to people, skills, training, experience, education and knowledge. It can only be found in people.
4. The several factors that influence the development of human resources are:
   a) quality, quantity, composition, skills development/enhancement, creativity
   b) quality, quantity, skills development/enhancement, creativity
   c) quantity, composition, skills development/enhancement, creativity
   d) quality, quantity, composition, skills development/enhancement
5. True or false: nation building is something that only politicians can do.
6. Which of the following is NEVER a lifestyle disease?
   a) tuberculosis
   b) diabetes
   c) stroke
   d) cancer.
7. The three main health indicators for any country are:
   a) infant mortality rate, life expectancy and maternal care
   b) life expectancy, incidence of HIV/AIDS and population distribution
   c) employment rates, vaccination rates and maternal care
   d) population distribution, infant mortality rates and carbon emissions
8. For each of the groups below list two benefits when a population takes care of its health:
   - socio-economic factors
   - environmental factors
   - behaviours and practices
   - health systems and services

9. Make a sentence using each of the following terms to show its meaning:
   - **a)** human resource
   - **b)** capital
   - **c)** physical resource
   - **d)** skills
   - **e)** talent
   - **f)** knowledge
   - **g)** ability
   - **h)** physical capital
10. Imagine you are designing a crossword puzzle. Make up clues for the following words:
   - **a)** quality
   - **b)** quantity
   - **c)** composition
   - **d)** skills enhancement
   - **e)** creativity
11. Draw a mind map to show how human resources contribute to a country's economic development.
12. Write a definition of the word 'education'.
13. Explain the difference between skills development and skills enhancement.
14. Give a brief explanation of the five factors that influence the development of human resources.
15. What is the main difference between on-the-job training, mentorship and succession training?
16. Your country is running a campaign for improving the country's workforce. Its slogan is 'Health is wealth'. Which of the following would support the campaign?
   - **a)** sedentary lifestyles
   - **b)** regular drug and alcohol consumption
   - **c)** a balanced diet and regular exercise
   - **d)** extended leaves of absence
17. What are three challenges of living with an ageing population?
18. What are the main causes of diabetes?
19. Explain three ways an identified health issue (e.g. diabetes) can be prevented or cured.
20. Write three guidelines for avoiding lifestyle diseases.
21. Name five benefits that skilled people can offer a country's economy.

Checking your progress

To make good progress in understanding economic growth and development, check that you understand these ideas.

- [ ] Explain and use correctly the term 'human resources'.
- [ ] Describe the characteristics of human resources.
- [ ] Explain the difference between human resources and physical resources.

- [ ] Name and describe the factors that influence human resources.
- [ ] Explain the importance of human resources to a country's economic development.
- [ ] Name the activities that form part of the economic development of a country.

- [ ] Explain the importance of education in developing our human resources.
- [ ] Define the terms 'patriotism' and 'nation building'.
- [ ] Describe the contribution of an individual to a country's development.

- [ ] Name three benefits to the country if its citizens take care of their health.
- [ ] Explain why it is important to have a healthy workforce.
- [ ] Examine one health issue faced by human resources and describe how this health issue can be addressed.

Unit 3: History

In this unit you will find out 

The value and relevance of history

- Why is history important to me?
  - Past, present and future
- The value and relevance of history
- How we study history
  - Primary sources, secondary sources, bibliographies, conventions for referencing

My personal history

- Finding out about my history
  - Using primary and secondary sources, family trees, documents
  - Place of birth, ancestral lineage, kinship, religion, customs
- Comparing and contrasting lives
  - Compare our lives with those of our parents and grandparents
  - Our community

The history of my school

- Tracing the history of my school
  - Using primary and secondary sources, interviews and questionnaires
  - School life at different times
- The role and legacy of my school
  - The role of teachers and students
  - The legacy of my school to future generations

The contribution of individuals to the Caribbean

- Ronald Webster
- Dame Georgiana Ellen Robinson
- Sir George F. L. Charles
- Dame Ruth Nita Barrow
- Sir Eric Matthew Gairy

The value and relevance of history

We are learning to:

- define and use correctly the terms past, present, future, decade, century, generation
- describe the value and relevance of history to myself and my country.

Why is history important to me?

History is the study of the past. Most of us are so involved with our modern world that we forget to stop and think about the past. Yet, how can we really understand who we are if we do not value our past?

Our understanding of history helps us to understand the present, and to understand and find answers for problems that we may face in the present.

Workers harvesting cocoa beans on a cacao plantation in Grenada, 1934.

Past, present and future

When we talk about history, we are really talking about time – the **past**, the **present** and the **future**. When we talk about the past we are talking about the history of a person or a place, or events that happened before the present time.

The present is what is happening now and the future is what might or will happen in a time that is still to come.

A **century** is a period of 100 years. We are currently living in the 21st century. A **decade** is a period of 10 years. So, for example, the year 2000 was the first year of the first decade of the 21st century. The year 2010 was the first year of the second decade, and so on.

A **generation** is the time that it takes for children to grow up, become adults and start their own families. A generation is usually considered to be between 25 and 30 years. People of the same generation are people who grow up at around the same time.

Research

Create a large poster or collage showing photographs, charts and maps of your country from times past.

Exercise

1. In which century did each of these events occur?
   - **a)** 1979 Saint Lucia gains independence.
   - **b)** 1780 The Great Hurricane becomes the deadliest hurricane on record.
   - **c)** 1980 Dame Eugenia Charles is elected Prime Minister of Dominica, the first woman to hold the office in the Caribbean.
2. In your own words define: 'past', 'present', 'future', 'century', 'decade' and 'generation'.

The value and relevance of history

We need to know what we can learn from the past and what we need to cherish from the past. We need to know what is special about our nation and ourselves. Here are some ideas about why history is valuable in our lives:

- History helps us to understand who we are. It is part of our identity or collective memory.
- History encourages us to express our own points of view on matters of personal, family and national concern.
- History is interesting and helps to explain why things have happened: for example, why there are so many people of African, East Indian and Chinese ancestry in the Caribbean.
- History teaches us that we need to respect our cultural heritage.
- History teaches us to reflect on events and lives. Why, for example, was Eric Williams respected as leader of Trinidad and Tobago?
- History teaches us to look at both sides of a problem – there are always two sides to a story. This is a useful skill to apply when we face practical problems in our everyday lives.

Project

Make a timeline of important dates in the history of your country. Here are examples from Saint Kitts and Nevis:

- 1493 Christopher Columbus spotted Saint Kitts and Nevis.
- 1538 The first French settlers arrived on Saint Kitts.
- 1623 The first English settlers arrived on the island.
- 1783 British rule was finally established with the Treaty of Versailles.
- 1834 Slavery was abolished throughout the British Empire.
- 2005 The sugar industry closed down.

When you have done your timeline, discuss the value and relevance of these events in your own life today.

Exercise

3. Define 'history' in your own words.

4. Give three reasons why history is important in our personal lives.

5. What else do you learn about in history besides dates and names?

Discussion

Work in groups or as a class. With your teacher, discuss the value and relevance of history, and why history is important in your lives today.

Key vocabulary

history

past

present

future

century

decade

generation

How we study history

We are learning to:

- identify primary and secondary sources
- tell the difference between primary and secondary sources.

History is the study of the past. We learn about history from written texts and other documents called **sources**. We also learn from **oral sources** when people recount their experiences.

Primary sources

A **primary source** is a document or physical object that was written or created at the time. It provides direct or first-hand evidence about an event, object, person or work of art.

Primary sources are usually found in museums and libraries. Examples of primary sources include:

- autobiographies, memoirs, literature, works of art and music
- artefacts (coins, clothing, tools, furniture, fossils)
- photographs, drawings and posters
- audio recordings
- DVD and video recordings
- diaries, letters, newspaper articles, emails, the internet
- official documents (birth certificates, wills)
- government documents (reports, bills, proclamations, hearings, etc.), research data and reports.

A documentary film photograph of an event can be a primary source.

Objects that people use, such as clothes, pots, ships and swords, are primary sources.

If you want to find out what life was like in the past, you can study the clothes people wore and the types of transport that they used.

This painting showing a Carib family on Saint Vincent in 1794 is an example of a primary source. Paintings can help us to understand what life was like in the past.

Exercise

1. Write your own definition of 'primary source' to make sure you understand what it means.
2. How many examples of a primary source can you find in your school?

Activity

Write a short journal entry. Choose any time in the past that you think has significance in your life today. Write about something you did on one day or something that happened in your country on that day.

Secondary sources

A **secondary source** is a book or document that provides information that was compiled after an event took place. It describes, discusses, interprets, comments upon, analyses, evaluates, summarises and processes primary sources. Secondary sources usually interpret and analyse events that took place in the past. They also add to information from primary sources. Examples of secondary sources include:

- textbooks, bibliographies and biographical works
- reference books such as dictionaries, encyclopedias and atlases
- articles from journals, magazines and newspapers
- books published after events have occurred
- history books.

Books, such as textbooks or dictionaries, are examples of a secondary source of information.

Bibliographies

A **bibliography** is a list of the sources (usually secondary sources) that you consult when you are doing research. It is important to show the reader where you have used someone else's ideas or words. The sources are written in alphabetical order according to the surname of the person who wrote the book.

You give the title of the book as well as the name of the publisher and the date when the book was published. For example:

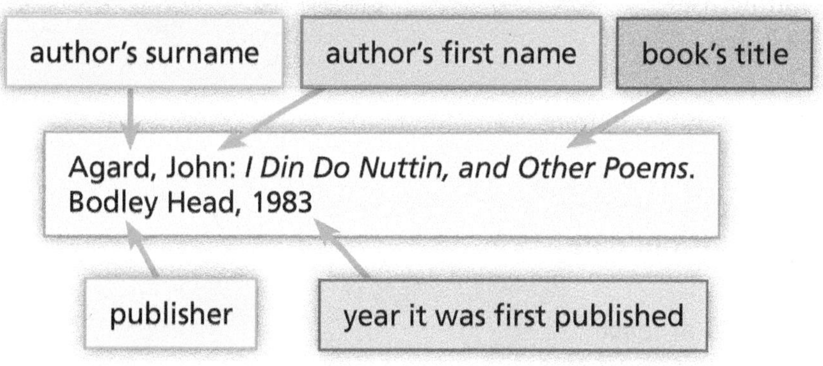

Activity

Using the example given as a guide, choose one of your favourite books and write out its details as if you are putting it into a bibliography.

Exercise

3. Write your own definition of 'secondary source' to make sure you understand what it means.
4. How many examples of a secondary source can you find in your school?
5. Who wrote *I Din Do Nuttin, and Other Poems*? Who published the book? When was it written?

Key vocabulary

sources

oral source

primary source

secondary source

bibliography

My personal history

We are learning to:

- trace the history of our families using primary and secondary sources
- do interviews and make observations to collect information about our early lives.

Finding out about my history

There are several things that you can do to trace or find out more about your own life and family history. You can look at primary sources first.

- Look for original documents – birth and death certificates or family photographs.
- One of your ancestors may have written a diary about their experiences.
- You can interview older members of your family, perhaps your grandparents.

Then you can consult secondary sources.

- Find novels and stories written about the times when your parents or grandparents were young.
- Perhaps someone in your family has written an article or a brochure about earlier members of your family.
- You could also study your family tree if you have one, or you can create your own family tree.

A good place to look for secondary sources is your local library or the school library.

Research project

This project has several parts. Your teacher will give you further guidelines.

1. Create a timeline of the eight most important events in your life so far. Start with your date and place of birth.
2. Create your own family tree. Show at least three generations of your family. To collect this information you can interview members of your family and you can use primary sources like birth, marriage and death certificates.
3. Collect photographs of your family if you can and make a poster of your family tree. Use this poster to make a presentation to the rest of the class. Explain the **kinship** between the family members and explain how you collected your information.

Did you know...?

Your **next of kin** are the members of your immediate family – your mother, father, brothers and sisters.

My personal history

Your **personal history** is the history of the people from whom you are descended (your ancestors) and the people to whom you are related.

What do you know about your personal history?

- **Place of birth** – Where were you born? Were your parents and grandparents born in the same place?
- **Ancestral lineage** – Who were your grandparents, your great-grandparents and your great-great grandparents?
- **Kinship** – Do you know all of the people who are related to you by descent, not marriage?
- **Religion** – Do you and all members of your family follow the same religion?
- **Customs** – Where do your family customs come from?
- **Documents** – What information do family birth certificates or marriage certificates provide?
- **Family tree** – A diagram that shows the generations of a family and how they are related to each other.

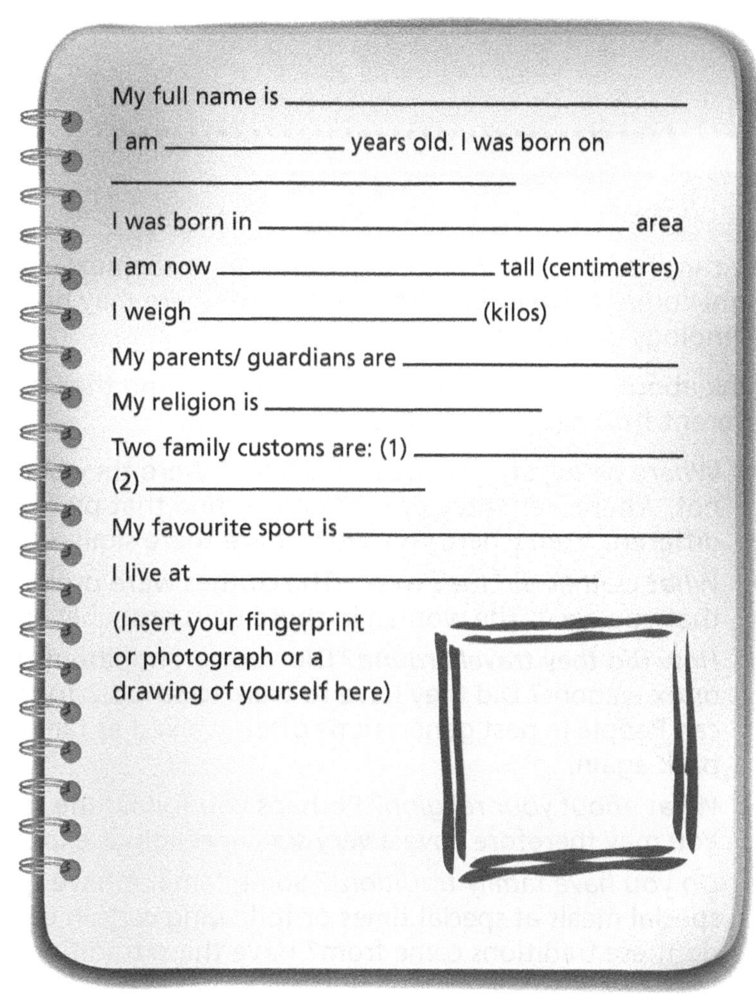

My full name is ____________________

I am ________ years old. I was born on ____________________

I was born in ____________________ area

I am now ________________ tall (centimetres)

I weigh ________________ (kilos)

My parents/ guardians are ____________________

My religion is ____________________

Two family customs are: (1) ________________ (2) ________________

My favourite sport is ____________________

I live at ____________________

(Insert your fingerprint or photograph or a drawing of yourself here)

Exercise

1. Give an example of two documents that are primary sources of information.
2. What could you create to show your kinship relations?
3. Name two items of information that you could include in your personal history.
4. Compile a personal history form (see an example above).

Key vocabulary

next of kin/kinship
personal history
place of birth
ancestral lineage
religion
customs
documents
family tree

Comparing lives

We are learning to:

- compare and contrast our lives with the lives of our parents and grandparents
- appreciate that we are part of a community and that we share goals and principles.

Comparing and contrasting lives

Life can change a lot from one generation to the next. New people with different cultures might come to live in the **community**, and there may be other changes as a result of technology or perhaps political events.

Think about your grandparents, for example, and the ways in which your experiences are different from or similar to their experiences.

- *Where were your grandparents born?* Were they born in the same country as you? If not, where were they born? Can you find that place on a map? Is that country very different from where you live? Or are there similarities?
- *What clothes did they wear?* The clothes were probably very different from the clothes that you wear. The women in those days probably only wore long dresses, for example.
- *How did they travel around?* Did your grandparents have cars? Did they use carriages or ox wagons? Did they have to walk to school? Today we usually go to school by bus or car. People in past generations often walked as far as 20 km a day to get to school and back again.
- *What about your religion?* Perhaps you follow the same religion as your grandparents. You may therefore have a very similar religious experience to that of your grandparents.
- *Do you have family traditions?* Some families have special traditions, such as eating special meals at special times or following certain careers or sporting activities. Where do these traditions come from? Have these traditions changed as times have changed?

Project

Compile a table similar to this one with areas to compare and contrast. You can discuss and add ideas of your own. Other areas to compare could be games played, dress, manners, communication, transport or technology.

Areas to compare and contrast	Grandparents	Parents	Children today
Work expected to do as children			
Rights of women			
Religious practices			
Festivals enjoyed			
Stories enjoyed			

Our community

Most communities in the Caribbean are diverse because people from many different cultures and ancestries live and work there. Families in communities may share **principles**, goals and **traditions** despite coming from different cultural backgrounds. For example, people may share the principle of respecting elders, they may share a goal like wanting their children to get a good education, and they may all enjoy and share a traditional festival or carnival.

In peaceful communities people work together despite their differences. People respect and accept their differences. We learn about each other's values, customs, religions and foods. We share our knowledge and exchange ideas. Our communities are richer and stronger because of this diversity.

A street in St John's, capital of Antigua and Barbuda, circa 1965. Can you find a picture from the 1960s of a street or town in your country? How has the street or town changed?

Research

Working in groups, create a brochure of information about the beliefs, customs, ceremonies and traditions of different families in your community.

a) Use primary and secondary sources to collect information.

b) Compare these beliefs and say how they are similar or different.

c) Include a bibliography with your brochure to show which sources you have consulted.

d) Draw up a timeline of events in your community. Your teacher will help you to decide in what year the timeline should start.

e) Present your work to the rest of the class.

Discussion

As a class, discuss the changes that have taken place in your community in the last two generations. To prepare for this discussion, interview some older members of your community, and look for photographs and documents with relevant information.

Exercise

1. Write down two suggestions about how people can live together peacefully in a community despite having different ancestry.
2. Give an example of a tradition that you share with other members of your class.
3. Give an example of a principle that you share with other members of your community.

Project

Imagine that you went to school 100 years ago. Write a journal entry about a day in your life.

a) Would you have walked to school?

b) What clothes would you have worn?

c) How would you have done your homework?

d) What would you have done in the afternoon and evening?

Key vocabulary

community

principles

traditions

The history of my school

We are learning to:

- trace the history of my sources
- collect information through interviews and observations
- work collaboratively to produce a history of our school.

Tracing the history of my school

Many schools in the Caribbean have long, proud traditions. Your own school may be new or it may have started years ago. The people who started the school will have set out their **vision** for it and considered questions like these:

- What type of school is it and who will attend?
- What will be taught at the school (the **curriculum**)?
- Will the students wear a **uniform** and what will that be? How many students will be admitted?
- Where will the lessons take place? Who will teach the students?
- Will there be **extra-curricular** and sports activities?
- Who will lead the school?

School children in Barbuda.

Case study

The Far Hills High School is a landmark in its community. The school was **established** in 1953 and its **rationale** was to empower boys and girls of all religions and races to achieve academic success. The school provided education for children who lived in the area, who had previously had to travel far to attend school.

The school opened with 43 students in four classrooms. The school offered a full academic programme, as well as extra-curricular activities such as sports, music and drama. Students from the school have distinguished themselves in many walks of life.

Over the years the school has grown. New classrooms have been added and there are now 450 students.

Questions

1. Why was the Far Hills School set up?
2. Do you think all children in the community were welcomed at this school?
3. Has the Far Hills School been successful in serving its community? Explain your answer.

Activity

Working in pairs, study the photograph of the old school classroom opposite. Compare this classroom with your own classroom.

Discussion

What do you know about the history of your own school? Discuss the history of your school with your teacher.

Gathering information about your school

When researching the history of your school, you will need to think about:

- why it was set up and when
- the vision, **mission** and extra-curricular activities
- uniforms, buildings, sports and awards
- the legacy of the school, head teacher, teachers, students
- customs and traditions of the school.

There are many different ways of finding out about the history of your own school. You can start by observing your school buildings and sources of information at your school. Your school library may have information like this:

- primary sources such as photographs that show the school at different times
- copies of old school magazines with photographs and articles about school life during a specific year
- trophies and honour rolls that record the achievements of students over the years.

Schoolchildren during a lesson in Port-au-Prince, Haiti.

Older members of the community can provide interesting information about daily life at school. You can set up interviews with some people. Draw up a questionnaire with questions similar to these:

- Did you attend this school?
- Which subjects did you study?
- Did you do any extra-curricular activities?
- Were you punished if you did not obey rules? How?
- What were your best memories of the school?

Secondary sources such as articles in magazines and newspapers can also provide valuable information about schools. You can search the websites of local newspapers for articles.

Key vocabulary

vision

curriculum (curricula)

uniform

extra-curricular

established

rationale

mission

Project

Working in groups, and then as a class, produce a booklet about the history of your school. To do this you will need to do some careful planning and then work cooperatively. Everyone in the class should make a contribution.

The information that you collect should come from interviews and other primary and secondary sources. You should also compile a bibliography to acknowledge the sources you have used and create a timeline to show the major events in the school's history.

The role and legacy of my school

We are learning to:

- compare our school lives with school lives from different times and places in our country
- appreciate the role and legacy of my school.

School life at different times

Over the years, schools have changed. For example:

- Governments develop new curricula to guide teachers about what should be taught in class.
- Some schools have changed their school uniforms.
- Many schools have improved their structures and built new classrooms, science laboratories, libraries and sports facilities.
- New technology has been brought into classrooms. Teachers and students now use computers, tablets and interactive light boards instead of chalkboards and slates.
- As students, you are encouraged to take a more active role in learning, so there is more discussion and research.
- All children, boys and girls, have access to free education in the Caribbean.

In the past, not everyone had access to schools and education was not compulsory. Children from poor families were often not able to go to school because they had to help their parents at home, and the parents could not afford to pay for school fees and uniforms. More boys received an education than girls.

Exercise

1. In what ways has technology changed how we learn at school?
2. How have classrooms changed in schools over the years? Think about what you use in your classroom to learn.
3. Why do you think the curriculum has changed in the last 50 years? Give an example of a subject in which you learn different content from what your parents learned, for example.
4. Do you think that you receive a good education at your school? How could your education be improved?

The mission of the Trinidad and Tobago Ministry of Education outlined in their Education Policy Paper 2017–2022, is to educate learners:

- to achieve their full potential
- to become productive citizens
- who have the characteristics of resilience, goodwill, honesty, respect, tolerance, integrity, benevolence, civic pride, social justice and community spirit

Discussion

Discuss what it meant to children who did not have free access to good education in the past. What happened to them? What work did they do?

Activity

Write a journal entry in which you reflect on what you have learned about your school and the role your school plays in your community.

The role of your school

Your school helps to educate students such as yourself in your community. It also provides a place where students and their families interact and get to know each other.

The teachers, head teacher, parents and students at the school all have a role to play. For example, the head teacher will provide guidance and vision, the teachers will facilitate and provide good learning experiences for the students, the parents will support and encourage the school and the students will study and learn.

Working together **cooperatively** helps to ensure a good education for the students.

Head Teacher:
responsible for managing the major administrative tasks and supervising all students and teachers

↓

Deputy Head:
works alongside school Head to manage the administrative and educational components of a school

↓

Heads of Department (HOD):
responsible for the running of their department

↓

Teachers:
work alongside the HODs to provide a good learning environment and experience for students to learn in

↓

Students:
study and learn

The legacy of your school

Each generation of teachers and students builds up a **legacy**, which will benefit students in the future. A legacy of academic or sporting success will inspire future generations of students. Students will want to follow in the footsteps of others at the school who have succeeded.

Good academic achievements will help you to get a place at a good university when you leave school. Playing on the first cricket team at your school may help you on the path to a professional career in cricket.

Cricket stars such as Sir Garfield Sobers and Sir Vivian Richards, singer Rihanna, writer Derek Walcott, politician Eric Williams, and many others, have all inspired future generations.

Ex-students can become role models for current students, or donate their time, expertise and money to improve conditions at the school.

Rihanna is one of the most successful pop stars of all time.

Exercise

5. In your own words describe the different roles and responsibilities that people have at school.
6. Why do you think your school is an important part of your community?
7. Have a class discussion with your teacher about the legacy of your school and its role in the community. Then talk about how you can make a contribution to your school both now and in the future.

Key vocabulary

cooperatively

legacy

The life of Ronald Webster

We are learning to:

- examine the life, contribution and legacy of Ronald Webster

The contribution of Ronald Webster

Ronald Webster (1926–2016) was a prominent political figure in Anguilla. He is considered to be the 'Father of the Nation' and the most important person in the history of Anguilla because of the improvements he introduced in governance, infrastructure and the forging of a national identity. He served as Anguilla's Chief Minister from 1976 to 1977 and again from 1980 to 1984.

Ronald Webster is known as the 'Father of the Nation' in Anguilla.

Governance

In 1967, Anguilla declared its independence from the Saint Kitts-Nevis-Anguilla government. Webster had a leading role in the independence of Anguilla. Prior to independence, it had become increasingly clear that the island was being neglected by the administrative authorities in Saint Kitts.

Webster vowed to make Anguilla a more habitable place for its people. In 1967, he led his people in a **revolt** to sever ties with the Associated State of Saint Kitts-Nevis-Anguilla. Following the revolt, a referendum was held on 11 July 1967. The people of Anguilla voted to break away from the Saint Kitts-Nevis-Anguilla government and become a separate colony of Britain.

Finally, and through the persistence of Webster, Britain accepted Anguilla as a British Dependency in 1980.

Infrastructure

Through the leadership of Webster, Anguilla undertook several developmental processes which resulted in a better **infrastructure** for the island. This included paved roads, electricity and running water. The infrastructure of the island had been neglected before the Anguilla Revolution. He was also responsible for the establishment of the social security system in Anguilla.

Exercise

1. Who was Ronald Webster?
2. Why did Anguilla want to remove itself from the Saint Kitts-Nevis-Anguilla government?

Discussion

Have a class discussion about the contribution of Ronald Webster to the development of Anguilla as a nation. What do you think was his most important contribution? Why?

Economic and social development of Anguilla

Once Anguilla had removed itself from the Saint Kitts-Nevis-Anguilla government, Anguilla experienced a complete economic and social change.

The removal of the Saint Kitts government allowed the laying of groundwork for economic take-off and resulted in an improved standard of living for the people of Anguilla. Today, Anguilla has one of the highest standards of living in the Caribbean.

The revolution brought persons from all walks of life together for the common good. His steadfast nature under immense pressure helped to foster a spirit of resilience and self-reliance.

Webster died in December 2016. The Governor of Anguilla, Ms Christina Scott, wrote '*He demonstrated how, through force of character, nations can be formed and grow through peaceful, purposeful actions. That by coming together, and looking to the future with common intent and for the good of all, fairness and opportunity can prevail ... He told me that countries do not develop people, but that people develop countries.*'

Statement from HM Governor's Office in Anguilla on 9 December 2016

In recent years Anguilla has become an upmarket tourist destination, and tourism is one of the mainstays of the economy. Fishing is another important economic activity, and a financial services sector is also being developed.

The flag of Anguilla

Did you know...?

Ronald Webster's birthday, 2 March, is now a public holiday in Anguilla.

Exercise

3. What contribution did Ronald Webster make to the political development of Anguilla?
4. Why do you think Ronald Webster was considered the 'Father of the Nation'?
5. What sectors of industry are important in Anguilla today?
6. What characteristics did Ronald Webster have?
7. Working as a group, create a timeline of the life and achievements of Ronald Webster. Use any primary and secondary sources you can find. Then present your report to the class.

Key vocabulary

revolt

infrastructure

The life of Dame Georgiana Ellen Robinson

We are learning to:

- examine the life, contribution and legacy of Dame Georgiana Ellen Robinson

The contribution of Dame Georgiana Ellen Robinson

Dame Georgiana Ellen (Nellie) Robinson (1880–1972) was prominent in the field of education in Antigua and was a leading figure in the campaign to improve educational opportunities for African-heritage families. She is the only woman to have been awarded the Order of the National Hero in Antigua.

Education

Dame Nellie was born in St John's, Antigua. Nellie was educated in the United States for four years before returning to Antigua, where she attended the Methodist training school Wesleyan Coke College. When that institution closed, she continued her education with the help of a private tutor.

St John's, Antigua - the birthplace of Dame Georgiana Ellen Robinson.

Thomas Oliver Robinson Memorial High School

After Dame Nellie completed her education she thought about how to improve educational opportunities for students of African heritage. Her brother Thomas encouraged her to start her own school and in 1898 she opened the Thomas Oliver Robinson Memorial High School (TOR), in memory of her brother, who had passed away.

Dame Nellie wanted her school to meet the needs of people who could not get into the Anglican-owned secondary schools. Children whose parents were not married could not attend those schools. She knew that people of African heritage were often overlooked, the fees were too high and even if they had the money their parents had to be thought of as influential and part of the island's elite. Dame Nellie wanted to accept all who could afford to pay and then a few others.

Exercise

1. Who was Dame Nellie Robinson?
2. Why did she leave Antigua as a child?
3. What problem did she identify in Antigua and what was her solution?

Discussion

Have a class discussion about the contribution of Dame Georgiana Ellen Robinson to the development of Antigua as a nation. What do you think was her most important contribution? Why?

Development of the TOR

In the early days of the TOR, attempts were made to close the school by people who were opposed to it. Dame Nellie was told that her teachers were not qualified or that the school surroundings were not clean enough.

Despite this opposition, Dame Nellie pressed on and soon her exam pass rate was better than the other schools. As the school's reputation increased, influential parents started moving their children to the TOR because they wanted their children to get the best education available in Antigua. She welcomed them, while still encouraging **scholarships** for poorer families. Soon, her school had children from all parts of society, as well as children from other islands in the Caribbean. Dame Nellie retired as head teacher in 1950, having spent 52 years at the school.

Dame Nellie's other accomplishments included sitting on the Water Preservation Committee from 1912, contributing to the war effort by recruiting young men in 1915 and helping to found the local Girl Guides Association. In the 1950s, when Carnival was introduced to the island she became involved in the planning.

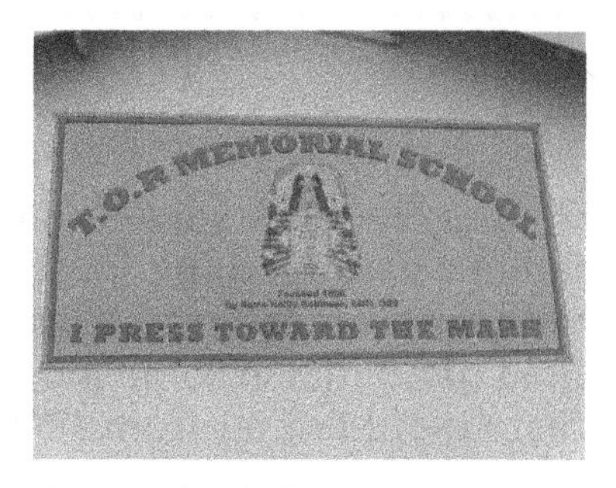

Thomas Oliver Robinson Memorial High School (TOR).

Awards

In 1935, Dame Nellie received a commemorative medal when King George V celebrated Their Majesties' Silver Jubilee. In 1941, she was made an MBE (Member of the British Empire). In 2006, Antigua and Barbuda named Dame Nellie as one of four National Heroes during the 25th anniversary of independence and she was **posthumously** honoured as Dame Companion of The Most Exalted Order of National Hero (DNH). In 2000, she was recognised by the Professional Organization for Women in Antigua (POWA) as 'Woman of the Twentieth Century'.

Research

Research who else has been awarded the Order of the National Hero for Antigua and Barbuda. Choose one person and write a short biography of their life and achievements.

Exercise

4. Why did wealthy parents move their children to the TOR?
5. How did Dame Nellie contribute to the development of education in Antigua and Barbuda?
6. Working as a group, create a timeline of the life and achievements of Dame Nellie. Use any primary and secondary sources you can find. Then present your report to the class.

Key vocabulary

scholarships

posthumously

The life of Sir George F. L. Charles

We are learning to:

- examine the life, contribution and legacy of Sir George F. L. Charles.

The contribution of Sir George F. L. Charles

George Frederick Lawrence Charles (1916–2004) became famous because of his involvement with the rise of the **trade union** movement representing the working class and in the field of politics in Saint Lucia. He also served as the island's first Chief Minister from 1960 to 1964.

As a young boy, Sir George attended St Mary's College, Saint Lucia, where he received his secondary education. Later, while working in Aruba at the Largo Oil and Trading Company, he was exposed to trade union activities, which helped him to understand better the business of the trade union. He returned to Saint Lucia in 1938.

The runway of George F. L. Charles airport.

Trade union activist

In 1944, expansion and renovation works commenced on the Vigie Airport in Saint Lucia. Sir George joined the project as a timekeeper. In 1946, when workers on the project went on strike, Sir George, who had by that time joined the Saint Lucia Workers' Union, represented their interests and brought forward their concerns. This incident resulted in much recognition for his trade union negotiation skills.

In 1946, he became branch Secretary and later, General Secretary to the Union. Sir George encouraged workers to join worker organisations. In 1952, he became President of the Workers Cooperative Union and in 1954 he gained a Certificate of Merit in a Union course at the University of the West Indies. In 1974, Sir George became leader of the Agricultural and General Workers Union. During that time he continued to support the working classes of the island and fought for improved conditions and rights for workers.

Discussion

Have a class discussion on Sir George F. L. Charles' contribution to Saint Lucia. Examine why his contributions were so significant at that particular period in time.

Exercise

1. What roles did Sir George F. L. Charles play in the worker organisations of which he was a member?
2. Where did he gain his trade union experience?
3. Which incident resulted in his gaining recognition among the working class in Saint Lucia?

Political achievements

In addition to being active in the trade union movement, Sir George F. L. Charles contributed to the political landscape of the island. In 1948, while still a trade unionist, he was elected to the Castries Town Board and played an important role in the formation of the island's first political party, The Saint Lucia Labour Party, becoming its first Vice President.

During this time, he called for more rights for the workers of Saint Lucia and for **autonomy** for the island, which was a colony of the United Kingdom at this time. In 1951, elections were held on the island based on **universal suffrage** and Sir George, as leader of his political party, won his seat to the Legislative Council.

As an elected member of the Legislative Council, he was successful in securing legal recognition of the right to paid holidays for workers. In 1952, Sir George became a Justice of the Peace. Then, in 1954, he again won his seat in the government and in 1956 became the first Minister of Education and Social Affairs. In 1960, Sir George became the island's first Chief Minister, serving for four years in that position. He retired from active politics in 1974, but continued to campaign on behalf of the working class in Saint Lucia.

Trade Unions are very important for workers' rights.

Awards

George F. L. Charles was knighted for his contribution to the development of the trade union movement in Saint Lucia and for his contribution to the politics of the island. Today, one of the island's airports and a secondary school bear his name. He died in 2004.

Project

Working in two groups, research the development of the trade union movement in your country. Organise your research into a timeline and present it to your class.

Exercise

4. In which year was Sir George F. L. Charles elected to the Castries Town Board?
5. Which political party did he help to co-found?
6. What were some of the achievements of Sir George as an elected member of the Legislative Council?
7. Working as a group, create a timeline of the life and achievements of Sir George F. L. Charles. Use any primary and secondary sources you can find. Then present your report to the class.

Key vocabulary

trade union

autonomy

universal suffrage

The life of Dame Ruth Nita Barrow

We are learning to:

- examine the life, contribution and legacy of Dame Ruth Nita Barrow.

The contribution of Dame Ruth Nita Barrow

Dame Ruth Nita Barrow (1916–1995) was the first female Governor General of Barbados, from 1990 to 1995. She was dubbed 'The People's Governor General' because her diverse career path influenced so many Barbadians. She was a nurse, an educator, a diplomat, an **activist** and a politician.

Her contributions were especially inspiring because she was able to accomplish so much during an era when it was uncommon for a woman, particularly a Black woman, to attain any influential position in society. Her contributions to Barbados, and to the wider Caribbean, were most notable in the areas of healthcare education, activism and politics.

The flag of Barbados.

Development of healthcare education

Dame Nita made a significant contribution to healthcare in Barbados and the wider Caribbean. She was passionate about improving healthcare in the Caribbean and making quality healthcare accessible to the poor. She believed that the development of the Caribbean region depended largely on the physical well-being of its people.

In 1964, Dame Nita was a health consultant to the World Health Organization (WHO) and an adviser for the Caribbean with the Pan American Health Organization (1963–1975). In this role, she wrote and published many articles on healthcare. Her work resulted in the introduction of the Advanced Nursing Education Programme at the University of the West Indies (UWI) at Mona, Jamaica.

Dame Nita's influence allowed her to take a leading role in advancing healthcare research and policy in Barbados. It can be argued that because of her dedication, Barbados can boast today of having a well-developed healthcare system.

Discussion

Have a class discussion on Dame Nita Barrow's contribution to Barbados and the wider Caribbean. Examine why her contributions were so significant at that particular period in time.

Exercise

1. Who was Dame Ruth Nita Barrow?
2. State the two main social problems Dame Nita spent her life addressing.
3. Explain why Dame Nita believed that quality healthcare was essential for all persons in society.

Activism and politics

Dame Nita came from a family of political activists. Her uncle, Dr Charles Duncan O'Neal (1879–1936), was a founder of the Democratic League of Barbados and was named one of the island's national heroes. He spent much of his life campaigning for equal rights for the poor and in particular the right to have free education, improved housing and civil liberties.

Additionally, her younger brother, Errol Barrow (1920–1987), fought for the independence of Barbados and became the island's first Prime Minister (1966–1976).

Dame Nita was also able to distinguish herself in the political arena. In 1986, she was the only woman on the **Eminent** Persons Group set up to visit South Africa. This group was responsible for investigating **racism** in South Africa. Dame Nita used this opportunity to advocate for equal rights for all Black people.

In 1986 she was appointed Barbadian Ambassador to the United Nations (UN). This paved the way for her appointment as Governor General of Barbados in 1990.

In 1980 she was knighted by Queen Elizabeth II as Dame of St Andrew and Dame Grand Cross of the Most Distinguished Order of St Michael and St George.

Dame Nita used her political influence to advance her beliefs as a feminist and to advocate for the **marginalised** and poor. Over her career, Dame Nita visited more than 80 countries to gather first-hand knowledge of how to provide better social conditions and healthcare for the poor.

She continued to champion their cause, fighting to **eradicate** poverty from their lives, until her death in office in 1995.

Dame Nita Barrow

Research

In Barbados, 28 April each year is National Heroes day. Using the internet, research those Barbadians who have been awarded the national hero honour. Write a brief biography of each one and include any photos that you can find of them.

Exercise

4. What was the name of Dame Nita's relative, who became one of Barbados' national heroes later in life?
5. Explain briefly Dame Nita's role when she visited South Africa in 1986.
6. Explain how Dame Nita used her political influence to advance her beliefs.
7. List three prominent positions she held during her life.
8. Working as a group, create a timeline of the life and achievements of Dame Ruth Nita Barrow. Use any primary and secondary sources you can find. Then present your report to the class.

Key vocabulary

activist

eminent

racism

marginalised

eradicate

The life of Sir Eric Matthew Gairy

We are learning to:

- examine the life, contribution and legacy of Sir Eric Matthew Gairy.

The contribution of Sir Eric Matthew Gairy

Sir Eric Matthew Gairy (1922–1997) was the first Prime Minister of Grenada. He is known as the 'Father of the Nation' having attained **independence** for Grenada on 7 February 1974. Grenada was the first of the Windward Islands to take that bold step.

Trade union activity

In July 1950, Sir Eric formed the Grenada Manual and Mental Workers Union (GMMWU), which would become the nation's most radical **trade union**. It appealed to the neglected peasants, and estate and road workers, especially in rural communities, and within a year it had a membership of 5000.

The flag of Grenada.

The union made eight demands of the Grenada Agricultural Association (an organisation of landowners), including wage increases, holidays with pay and annual sick leave. When these demands were ignored by the Grenada Agricultural Association and the British colonial regime, Gairy called a general strike on 19 February 1951.

It was the first general strike in the island's history and it escalated into a rural **insurrection**. Plantation houses were looted and burned, and crops like cocoa and nutmeg were destroyed. The insurrection was referred to as Sky Red.

On 21 February 1951, Gairy orchestrated a mass demonstration to York House, the seat of Grenada's parliament, where he demanded an audience with the governor. He was arrested, but the insurrection gained strength. The British colonial regime capitulated and Sir Eric gained the demands he made – wage increases, holiday with pay and annual sick leave. Sir Eric had satisfied the needs of the working class.

Project

Working in groups, create a timeline of the life and achievements of Sir Eric Gairy. Use both primary and secondary sources. Make a written or electronic presentation to the class.

Exercise

1. Who was Sir Eric Matthew Gairy?
2. Who were the GMMWU?
3. Explain, in your own words, the role of the GMMWU and Sir Eric in the Sky Red events of 1951.

Social development

In the area of social development Sir Eric engineered an agricultural policy known as 'land for the landless'. Its aim was to encourage poor peasant farmers to engage in agriculture on a larger scale.

He also sought to encourage women to become involved in public life. During his term in office (1951–1979), he appointed women to government positions: two ambassadors, one minister, two parliamentary secretaries and a governor. Grenada became the first country in the Commonwealth to name a female head of state, Dame Hilda Bynoe.

Sir Eric Matthew Gairy

Economic development

Under his leadership, Sir Eric made two important strides towards sustainable economic development. In 1969, he held an event called Expo 69, which was a means of showing off Grenada's manufacturing sector to prospective buyers and showcasing the island as a tourist destination to the world.

In 1976, he signed an agreement to establish the first offshore medical school in the Caribbean. This positioned Grenada to become a focal point in the provision of medical educational services.

The medical school is now a full-fledged university, St George's University (SGU). It offers 43 academic programmes and has a student population of 7500.

SGU is the number one international provider of physicians practising in the United States and contributes 20 per cent to Grenada's **gross domestic product (GDP)** annually.

Discussion

Have a class discussion on what you think was Sir Eric's greatest contribution to Grenada.

Exercise

4. Why was Sir Eric described as the father of the nation?
5. Explain, in your own words, what Sir Eric did to help in the area of social development.
6. In what ways did Sir Eric seek to place women in the public life?
7. What event did Sir Eric organise in 1969 and what was its purpose?
8. In what way did Sir Eric contribute to Grenada by helping to establish the medical school in 1976?

Key vocabulary

independence

trade union

insurrection

gross domestic product (GDP)

Legacies

We are learning to:

- examine the life, contribution and legacy of someone from your country.

The legacy of someone from your country

All countries have historical figures who played a significant role in the development of their country and whose work laid the foundations for the modern countries that we all live in. This can include politicians, teachers, sports personalities or community workers.

In this unit we have looked at the contributions made to their country by Ronald Webster (Anguilla), Dame Georgiana Ellen Robinson (Antigua), Sir George F. L. Charles (Saint Lucia), Dame Ruth Nita Barrow (Barbados) and Sir Eric Matthew Gairy (Grenada).

Their stories show how they have enabled our Caribbean countries to receive recognition from the wider world and to develop self-resilience. Many of them have influenced countless lives in their communities and territories in several ways, including educationally or socially. Many lives were changed for the better.

Marcus Garvey

Some important figures in the modern Caribbean have come from poor and humble beginnings, yet they have managed to leave an indelible mark on life as we know it today in our various countries. Such people often work to change situations in their countries that are negative for most persons, especially the poor and disadvantaged. The result of such contributions is referred to as a **legacy**.

There is a well-known saying that identifies the main purpose of learning about significant people of your country, both past and present. Marcus Garvey of Jamaica said, "A people without a knowledge of their past history, origin and culture is like a tree without roots."

Exercise

1. Explain what you understand by the term 'legacy'.
2. What do you think influences these individuals to try to change certain situations in their country?
3. Research Marcus Garvey. Write a brief report of his achievements.

Project

Working in a group, identify a significant figure from the past that is linked to your country. Create a timeline of his or her achievements.

Explain what you think his or her most important contribution was and why. Use any primary and secondary sources you can find. Then present your report to the class.

Tips:

- Follow the structure of the famous people we have looked at in this unit to see what sort of information you should look for.
- Find out what century they lived in and key dates in their life.
- Note what area they worked in: education, health, and so on.
- Highlight their specific contribution and say how their work changed your community or country.

Some suggestions are given below of someone you could research, but you can choose your own:

- Brian G. J. Canty (Anguilla)
- Curtly Ambrose (Antigua and Barbuda)
- Robert Llewellyn Bradshaw (Saint Kitts)
- Alphonsus 'Arrow' Cassel (Montserrat)
- Bob Marley (Jamaica)
- Jamaica Kincaid (Antigua)
- Lennox Honychurch (Dominica)
- Michele Henderson (Dominica)
- Garfield Sobers (Barbados)
- Jackie Opel (Barbados)
- Clement Payne (Barbados)
- Maurice Bishop (Grenada)
- Keith 'Kayamba' Gumbs (Saint Kitts)
- Sir W. Arthur Lewis (Saint Lucia)
- Joseph Chatoyer (Saint Vincent and the Grenadines)
- Mighty Sparrow (Trinidad and Tobago)
- Calypso Rose (Trinidad and Tobago)
- Truman Bodden (Grand Cayman)
- Rosalie Andre (Nevis)
- Eddie Grant (Guyana)

Eddie Grant

Key vocabulary

legacy

The past and the present

We are learning to:

- identify similarities and differences between the past and the present
- appreciate how people lived in earlier times and how their lives would be different today.

Similarities and differences between the past and the present

There are **similarities** and **differences** between life in the Caribbean in the past and life today. Let us look at a few examples.

Government

Think about the type of government that you have. Today, most Caribbean governments are models of their former colonial owners. They are **democratically** elected. All adults aged 18 years and above can vote for who will represent them in government. In colonial times, the Governor, who was in charge of the country, was appointed by the British monarchy. Our forefathers, therefore, had very little say in how they were governed; today people have more say.

Agricultural worker harvesting crops in Barbados, 1981.

Community life

Some aspects of community life have remained the same. For example, people still celebrate their **traditional** customs during festivals and everyone is encouraged to join in. People are also able to vote in government elections and choose their own leaders to attend to issues that concern their territories. Many people have moved from their traditional communities to urban areas to look for jobs. Their way of life changes when they move.

Transport and travel

People arrived in the Caribbean on ships that took months to arrive. Nowadays, if someone wants to go and visit family and relatives elsewhere in the world they can do so by catching a flight. Cars, buses and aeroplanes provide the main means of transportation today. Donkey-carts, horses and carriages are no longer used. Modern transport is much faster and more efficient than older forms of transport.

Activity

Create a display in your school on the topic of 'the past and present'.

Case study

Farming – past and present

In the past in Barbados, most of the land was used for agricultural purposes. The large sugar-cane plantations existed alongside small-scale vegetable and root crop farming, and pastures with livestock.

Today, the land being used for agriculture in Barbados has declined due to the demand for land for housing and tourism development.

The wide-scale use of pesticides and **fertilisers** is now seen as unhealthy, as there is a feeling that crops may no longer be safe to eat as a result.

Carrying sugar cane to the mill, Spring Hall Estate, St Lucy, Barbados, circa 1890.

Questions

1. Think about your country in the 19th century and compare those times with your life today. Give examples of:
   - **a)** a difference in the way your country was governed
   - **b)** a difference in the way people travelled
   - **c)** a similarity in the way farmers worked
   - **d)** a difference in the education system
   - **e)** a similarity in community life
2. Do you think life is generally better today than it was in the time of your grandparents? Explain your answer and give examples.
3. Pretend that you are a farmer 75 years ago. Write a journal entry about how, in one day on your farm, you would have dealt with your crops.
4. Look for pictures or draw pictures that illustrate the differences between now and then.

Project

Digital storytelling is a short form of digital media production that allows people to share aspects of their life story. People are filmed as they tell their life stories. These films can provide a lot of insight in to the lives of people.

Your teacher will play you a story like this, which you can discuss. Work in groups and make your own digital story about yourselves. You can also include members of your family or community. Take turns to describe interesting parts of your lives on the recording. Play your recordings for others in the class.

Key vocabulary

similarities

differences

democratically

traditional

fertilisers

digital storytelling

Questions

See how well you have understood the topics in this unit.

1. A decade is a period of _____ years.

a) 1000
b) 20
c) 10
d) 50

2. A period of 100 years is called a __________ .

a) century
b) centenary
c) millennium
d) generation

3. Which of these is not a primary source of information?

a) a diary
b) a photograph
c) a textbook
d) a news report about a current event

4. Which of these is a secondary source?

a) a birth certificate
b) a dictionary
c) a radio interview
d) an artefact

5. True or false? Your grandparents are part of your ancestral lineage.

6. Fill in the blanks of what a bibliography shows.

Agard, John: *I Din Do Nuttin, and Other Poems.* Bodley Head, 1983

7. Names four things you can do to trace or find out more about your own life and history. (Hint: sources.)

8. The achievements that are handed down to future generations are referred to as a ________ .

a) legal
b) legacy
c) lineage
d) generation

9. A ________ is a list of sources you have consulted, arranged in alphabetical order.

a) Bible
b) secondary
c) bibliography
d) biography

10. Correct these statements:

a) 1789 is a date in the 17th century.
b) History is the study of the future.
c) Mathematics is a subject in the school calendar.

11. Complete the timeline about Saint Kitts and Nevis:

a) ________ Christopher Columbus spotted Saint Kitts and Nevis.
b) 1538 The first French settlers arrived on ________.
c) ________ The first English settlers arrived on the island.
d) 1783 British rule was finally established with the ________.
e) ________ Slavery was abolished throughout the British Empire.
f) 2005 ________ industry closed down.

12. Give three ways schools have changed over the last 30 years.

13. Explain how you can take an active role in your own education.

14. How have schools in your country changed in the last 50 years? Give two examples.

15. Name two important contributions that Dame Georgiana Ellen Robinson made to the development of education in Antigua and say why you think each was important.

16. Explain the difference between a primary source and a secondary source.

17. Name two important contributions that Sir Eric Gairy made to Grenada and say why you think each was important.

18. Give two reasons why you feel history is important in your life. Explain your answer.

19. Explain how and why you should work cooperatively at school.

Checking your progress

To make good progress in understanding the value and relevance of history/the past, check that you understand these ideas.

- [ ] Explain in your own words the value and relevance of history.
- [ ] Explain what a primary and a secondary source are.
- [ ] Give three examples of a primary and a secondary source.

- [ ] Name four sources where you can find out about your family's history.
- [ ] Name four types of information that you should include in your personal history.
- [ ] Explain why it is important that we appreciate that we are part of a larger community.

- [ ] Name four types of information that you should include when tracing the history of your school.
- [ ] Name four ways that schools have changed today from times past.
- [ ] Explain why it is important that we appreciate the role and legacy of our school in our community.

- [ ] Explain the contribution made by individuals to the Caribbean region.
- [ ] Examine the life, contribution and legacy of someone from your country.
- [ ] Describe the similarities and differences in two areas of life in your country between the past and today.

End-of-term questions

Questions 1–7

See how well you have understood the ideas in Unit 1.

1. For each family type (nuclear, extended, sibling and single parent), write a sentence using the following frames:

   A nuclear family is a good option when ______________.

   An extended family is a good option when ______________.

   A sibling family is a good option when ______________.

   A single parent family is a good option when ______________.

2. **a)** Choose the family type (from nuclear, extended, sibling and single parent) that best describes your family.

   b) Then write a paragraph using this frame:

   The best part of being in a ______________ family is ______________.

   The worst part of being in a ______________ family is ______________.

3. Now choose a family type (from nuclear, extended, sibling and single parent) that is very different from yours. Write another paragraph using this frame:

   I imagine that the best part of being part of a ______________ family is ______________.

   I imagine that the worst part of being in a ______________ family is ______________.

4. How has your family's culture contributed to who you are? Draw a mind map showing how your family has influenced:

   - your religion
   - the foods you know and like
   - your language and style of speaking
   - the festivals and celebrations you take part in

   Add any other ways that your family has contributed to your culture.

5. Describe three factors that contribute to:

   a) good self-esteem

   b) poor self-esteem

6. Sketch a timeline showing the main stages of human development.

7. Which of the following circumstances does not describe a single parent family?

   a) The parents get divorced and the children live with one parent.

   b) The father has died, so the children live with their mother.

   c) The parents are having difficulty, so the children go to live with their aunt, uncle and cousins.

Questions 8–10

See how well you have understood the ideas in Unit 2.

8. Match how a person can be affected by a disease or illness in the workplace with its effects:

a) physical	**i)** friends and community
b) financial	**ii)** money
c) mental	**iii)** the body
d) social	**iv)** the mind

9. In order to prevent diabetes, which foods should you:

a) take out of your diet?

b) include in your diet?

10. Choose one of the following lifestyle diseases: diabetes, lung cancer, heart disease or hypertension.

Research:

a) What causes it?

b) What are the main characteristics and symptoms?

c) How is it possible to prevent it?

d) What are the main treatments?

Write 250 words.

Questions 11–15

See how well you have understood the ideas in Unit 3.

11. Write a journal entry in which you imagine that you live at a time in the past. Describe a day in your life. Give your journal a date.

12. Explain the roles and responsibilities of the head teacher, the parents, the students and the teachers at your school.

13. Give two examples of areas of our lives in which we can see how the present is connected to the past.

14. Make a table in which you give three examples each of primary and secondary sources.

15. "A people without the knowledge of their past history, origin and culture is like a tree without roots." Explain what this means, giving examples from your personal history.

Unit 4: How we govern ourselves

In this unit you will find out

Rules, regulations, rewards and sanctions

- Why rules, regulations, rewards and sanctions are important
  - civic values
  - self-discipline
  - respect for self, others and property
- The consequences of not following rules and regulations
- Rules at home and at school
- Who makes the laws?
  - decision-making
  - consensus
  - conflict
  - compromise

Civic responsibilities, rights and freedom

- Rights, freedom and responsibilities
  - fundamental rights
  - fundamental freedoms
- The Universal Declaration of Human Rights
  - civic responsibilities of the citizens of a country

The concept of humanitarian law

- Why humanitarian law is needed
  - humanitarian law
  - law of armed conflict
  - features of humanitarian law

Humanitarian law – humanitarian perspective

- The characteristics of humanitarian acts
  - protect life and human dignity
- Humanitarian acts in the news

Rules and regulations

We are learning to:

- explain the terms rules, regulations, rewards and sanctions
- understand the importance of rules, regulations, rewards and sanctions.

Rules and regulations

Rules are principles stating how something should be done or how people should behave. There are rules at home and at school. For example, when we play games, we play according to sets of rules.

Regulations are more official and can be enforced in the same way as national laws. Examples are traffic regulations that control the way in which we use roads, and regulations about where we can dump waste materials.

People in authority make rules and regulations. Sometimes people who are affected by the rules and regulations also have a chance to discuss and agree on them.

We have rules at home that are agreed by the family. For example, you may have rules about what time you have to come home and how you address your elders or eat your food, as well as about cleaning your room or helping with chores. Rules help your family to live together harmoniously.

Every school also has rules. These are usually displayed to remind everyone.

Examples of health and safety warning signs.

Exercise

1. Working in groups, read and discuss your school's rules and regulations.
   a) Which are rules and which are regulations?
   b) Why were they made?
   c) Who do you think made each rule or regulation?
2. Look at the list of rules. Working in groups, make a list of five other rules that you have to follow. Each group should choose a different environment, for example, home, school, road, sports club, restaurant, public gardens. Discuss the rules.
   a) Why were they made?
   b) Are they fair?
   c) Do people obey them? Why or why not?

Rules

Speed limit: 60.

No alcohol or drugs are allowed on the school grounds.

Clean up when you have finished.

No fighting.

No dumping.

Respect others.

No talking in the library.

All players to wear white shirts and shorts.

Rewards and sanctions

Rewards are sometimes given to encourage people to obey and follow rules and regulations. At home you may be rewarded if you obey your home rules at all times.

Sanctions are given when people do not follow the rules and regulations. For example, if you do not obey the rules of the road when you drive a car, you may have to pay a fine.

Why are rules and regulations important?

Rules and regulations are made for a reason. Most of these rules are made to protect our safety and to encourage **civic values** to help us live together in harmony. They are designed to help us apply **self-discipline**, so as to **respect** ourselves, others and property.

The table below shows some of the reasons for rules and regulations in certain environments.

Discussion

In groups discuss the importance of rules in different environments.

Environment	We need rules or regulations so that:
Home	• we share the work at home, we keep our homes clean and tidy, we can live in harmony
School	• we keep our school clean, we show respect to others, we are self-disciplined, we work diligently
Library	• we are not distracted when we are trying to work, we look after the resources in the library, we allow others to work
Laboratory	• no one gets hurt, equipment is handled correctly
Beach	• everyone can relax and enjoy themselves, no one gets hurt, the beach is not spoilt
Road	• all road users can use roads safely, the traffic flows

Exercise

1. Write your own definitions of the terms 'rules', 'regulations', 'rewards' and 'sanctions'. Use a dictionary to help you.
2. Read the signs on p. 106 and write your answers to the questions.
   a) Where would you expect to see signs like these?
   b) Why were these rules and regulations drawn up?
   c) Do you think all the rules are necessary?
   d) Would you obey these rules? Explain why or why not.

Key vocabulary

rules
regulations
reward
sanction
civic values
self-discipline
respect

Breaking rules

We are learning to:

- understand the consequences of not following rules and regulations.

The consequences of not following rules and regulations

Rubbish by the side of a road.

Most of us wish we did not have to follow rules, and many of us break rules at some time in our lives. Some people stick gum under a table, or smoke where they are not allowed to. They may get away with it and not receive a sanction.

These actions may be disrespectful to others or to the environment, but they do not immediately threaten the safety of other people. However, breaking rules and regulations can sometimes have serious **consequences**. Look at the examples below.

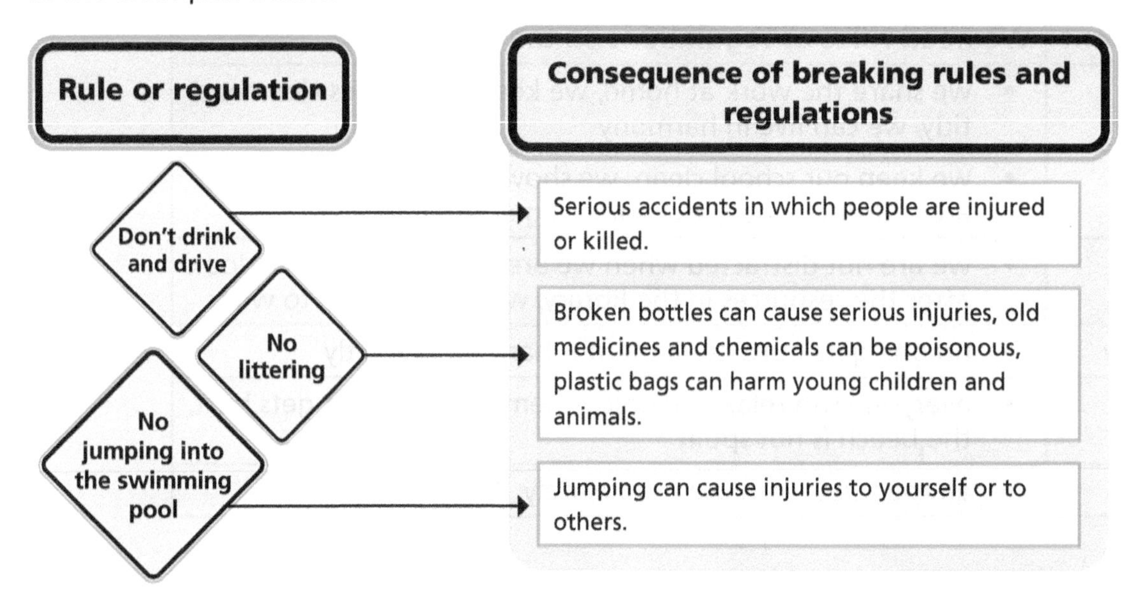

Exercise

1. Look at the photograph at the top of the page and answer the questions.
   a) What rule or regulation is being broken?
   b) Do you think the rule is reasonable? Explain your answer.
   c) Why do you think people are breaking the rule?
   d) What are the consequences? Think about the people who use the road and about safety.
   e) What should the sanction be for breaking this rule? Give a reason for your answer.

Discussion

Discuss this well-known saying in class with your teacher: "Rules are made to be broken!"

Case study

When she was young Mandy found out that she was allergic to nuts. If she ate a nut, she would swell up, go red all over and have trouble breathing. The first time it happened she was rushed to hospital for treatment. The treatment saved her life. After that, Mandy's mother was very careful. No nuts were allowed in the house.

When Mandy grew up, she went to college in another country. She prepared her own food most of the time. One day she bought a packet of prepared chicken. She read the contents list carefully. It did not mention nuts. Mandy knew that there were strict regulations in that country about labelling food, especially food that caused allergies. She warmed up the chicken. About five minutes after she had eaten, she felt her throat tighten and her face start to swell. Fortunately, she got to the hospital in time.

Questions

1. Read the case study again.
   a) What rule did the food producer break?
   b) What were the consequences?
   c) What sanction do you think this producer should receive? Why?
2. Work in groups. Role-play what happens when people do not follow rules in these three scenarios:
   - at home
   - at school
   - any scenario in your country.

   Then create a table like the one below, and list examples of rules in these categories and the consequences of not following them.

Scenario	Rule/regulation	Consequences of not following rule

Activity

Reflect on what you have discussed and learned about rules. Write an essay titled "What happens when people do not follow the rules."

Did you know...?

Rules and regulations about littering are often broken – except in countries like Singapore where there are very severe sanctions for littering.

Key vocabulary

consequences

Rules at home and school

We are learning to:

- explain how rules are made at home and at school.

Rules at home

Rules are made by people to suit certain times and environments. Rules made 100 years ago may no longer be useful and rules that you have at home may not be the same as the rules you have at school.

Many years ago parents or grandparents made **home rules** that the family had to obey. Some of these rules were based on cultural traditions.

A well-mannered family meal.

Children did not question these rules and could be punished if they did not obey them. In some families, children were not allowed to talk at the dinner table and they had to eat everything on their plates. In other families, girls had to serve the men in the family and then eat in the kitchen.

Today, families often sit down together and draw up a list of rules to suit their lives. Everyone can make suggestions and the family discusses why each rule is necessary. For example, the family may decide that everyone should be together for one meal a day and that nobody can watch TV, play games or talk on mobile phones during that time. This allows the family to talk together and share their experiences.

Case study

Table manners are the polite way to behave when you eat a meal with others. Table manners vary in different cultures. For example, some Indian people scoop up food in the fingers of their right hand. In China and Japan, people use chopsticks instead of knives and forks. Here are some rules about eating in a polite way:

- Don't wave your knife or fork around.
- Don't lean on the table.
- Pass around serving dishes and condiments.
- Wait for everyone else to be served before you start eating.
- Never put your knife in your mouth.
- Don't eat noisily, or gulp or slurp drinks.
- Don't eat with your mouth open, or talk and eat at the same time.

Questions

1. Do you follow any of these rules about table manners in your home? Which ones?
2. Do you think table manners are important? Explain your answer.
3. Give one example of how table manners can vary from culture to culture.

Rules at school

School rules set out the rights and responsibilities of students as well as the standards of behaviour the school expects of its students.

School rules tell students and parents what the school considers important. There are rules about how to dress and how to behave towards other students and teachers.

The sports and games that we play at school also have rules. These rules allow the games and sports to be played in a way that is fair and competitive. For example, in cricket there are rules about how you can bowl the ball as well as rules about how many times you can bowl.

School rules have changed over the years. Read these rules from a 19th-century school in the USA.

Old school rules

Pupils must appear at the appointed hours with their hands and faces clean and their hair combed, free from lice and other contagious diseases.

Pupils must neither write, talk, nor whisper to each other during school hours.

Exercise

1. Look at the old school rules opposite. Think of two or three rules you would add to the list.
2. **a)** Why do families need rules?

   b) Why do schools need rules?
3. Read the old school rules again.
   a) Are either of the rules similar in any way to rules that you have at your school?
   b) Which rules would you not expect to see in a modern school? Why?
4. Why do you think rules are important in sport or games? Give an example of a rule from a sport or game that you play and say why it is important.

Activity

1. Working in groups, draw up a list of classroom rules to keep your classroom and school clean and orderly.

   Present your rules to the rest of the class and explain why you drew them up.

   Then display the rules in the class for everyone to read.
2. As a class, suggest one improvement that could be made to your own school rules. You will have to justify your suggestions.

   Then write a letter to the head of the school with your suggestion.

Discussion

Have a class discussion with your teacher about the attitude that students at your school have towards school rules.

Project

Discuss home rules with your family. Draw up a set of rules for your home or revise the list of rules that you already have. You can make up rules about helping in the house, about respecting other family members and about behaviour.

Key vocabulary

home rules

school rules

Who makes the laws?

We are learning to:

- explain the terms law, decision-making, consensus, conflict, compromise
- explain how laws are made in your country
- discuss who has the right to make laws.

Why we have laws

Countries have regulations and **laws**. Laws are a system of rules by which the country is governed. The laws are usually made by the parliament of a country and they are based on the **constitution** of the country.

A constitution is a set of general principles that are drawn up by a country and on which the laws of that country are based. For example, human rights principles, such as equality, may be included in the constitution.

Laws are created after **consultation** with different stakeholders. Once **consensus** or **compromise** has been reached, the law can be used. Laws assist with **decision-making** and the resolution of **conflicts**.

The Honourable Wade Mark, Speaker of the House, seeks to restore order in parliament during the Twenty-Seventh Sitting of the House of Representatives, Port of Spain, Trinidad and Tobago, 28 March 2012.

Who makes the laws?

All member states of the Caribbean Community (CARICOM) are democracies. Their laws are made by members of parliament who have been elected to serve in this role by their citizens. Some laws go through a long process of consultation before they become law. This process is important as it stops authorities from making laws that are not in the interests of our citizens.

When new laws are made or when governments wish to change the constitution, a process of public consultation is necessary so that all citizens have a chance to state their views. This is sometimes done by means of public meetings, or people are invited to submit their views in writing during a certain period of time.

Project

Create a poster showing all the stages of law-making in your country.

How laws are made in CARICOM Countries

Most CARICOM territories have a Governor-General and a parliament with one house – the Legislature. Both are involved in the process of making a law.

Anyone can make a proposal about a new law. For example, a worker may think that it is necessary to forbid something that is happening at work. The worker will report this to their manager, who can bring it to the attention of the government ministry that is responsible for this area or to a parliamentarian.

Most of the time, these proposals are introduced in the parliament. These new ideas are called **bills** when they are officially introduced in parliament.

How a bill becomes a law

A member of parliament introduces the bill.

The bill is made available to all members of parliament and to the public for consideration.

Members of the House debate, **amend** and vote on the bill.

If approved by the House, the bill is sent to the Governor-General for signature. This is called assent.

The Governor-General signs the bill or **vetoes** it. If vetoed, the bill goes back to parliament for further discussion and amendment.

Barbados became a republic on 30 November 2021 and no longer has a Governor-General. The bills are sent to the President for signature.

Exercise

1. Write your own definitions of these words:
   a) laws **b)** conflict **c)** consensus **d)** compromise
2. Role-play a sitting of your country's parliament with both Government and Opposition members to debate a bill on an area that needs attention, for example a bill to deal with littering at school.

   The head teacher can be invited to be the Governor/President of the country to sign the bill to make it law.
3. Working in groups, make a list of all the people whom you think should be consulted if the government proposes to make changes to the education laws.
4. Role-play a consultation between government officials and citizens, in which citizens are invited to give their points of view. Your teacher will help you to choose a related topic.
   When the role-play is completed, reflect on the issues raised during the consultation.

Key vocabulary

laws
constitution
consultation
consensus
compromise
decision-making
conflict
bill
amend
veto

Rights, freedoms and responsibilities

We are learning to:

- explain the terms rights, freedom and civic responsibility
- describe our rights and freedoms as citizens of the Caribbean.

As citizens of our country, we all have rights and freedoms. We also have responsibilities.

Rights and freedoms

A **right** is something to which you are entitled. For example, you have the right to an education. A **freedom** is having the power to do something. So, if you have the right to an education, you must also be allowed the freedom to go to school and study.

Fundamental rights and **fundamental freedoms** are basic rights and freedoms that all human beings have. The right to practise your own religion and the freedom to do this is an example of a fundamental right and freedom.

In Barbados the Constitution states that everyone has the right and freedom to practise their own religion of choice.

Civic responsibility

Your **civic responsibility** is the responsibility you have as a **citizen** of your country. You have the right and freedom to do certain things in your country, but responsibilities go with these rights.

See Unit 4.6 for examples of the civic responsibilities of citizens in the Caribbean.

Exercise

Read the extract from the constitution for Trinidad and Tobago on the opposite page.

1. Write definitions for these terms in your own words:
   a) 'right'
   b) 'freedom'
   c) 'civic responsibility'
2. What do you think 'freedom of movement' means?
3. What is 'freedom of association and assembly'? You may need to ask your teacher for help or do some research for this question.

Research

Choose two of the rights and freedoms from your country's constitution and research what that means to you and your family in everyday life.

Your rights and freedoms

You can find out about all your rights as a citizen by reading the constitution of your country. Here is an extract from the constitution of Trinidad and Tobago:

4. It is hereby recognised and declared that in Trinidad and Tobago there have existed and shall continue to exist, without discrimination by reason of race, origin, colour, religion or sex, the following fundamental human rights and freedoms, namely:

(a) the right of the individual to life, liberty, security of the person and enjoyment of property, and the right not to be deprived thereof except by due process of law;

(b) the right of the individual to equality before the law and the protection of the law;

(c) the right of the individual to respect for his private and family life;

(d) the right of the individual to equality of treatment from any public authority in the exercise of any functions;

(e) the right to join political parties and to express political views;

(f) the right of a parent or guardian to provide a school of his own choice for the education of his child or ward;

(g) freedom of movement;

(h) freedom of conscience and religious belief, and observance;

(i) freedom of thought and expression;

(j) freedom of association and assembly;

(k) freedom of the press.

Activity

Write an essay with the title 'I am proud to be a citizen of my country'.

Exercise

4. Working in groups, brainstorm a list of the rights and freedoms as citizens of your country that you think we should have.
5. Compare your list of rights and freedoms with the list in the extract. Is there anything that you can add to your list?
6. Which of these rights and freedoms do you think are the most important in your lives? Try to rank these rights and freedoms in order of importance.

Key vocabulary

rights

freedom

fundamental right

fundamental freedom

civic responsibility

citizen

Rights and freedoms

We are learning to:

- discuss why some people do not always have rights and freedoms
- describe the civic responsibilities of citizens of your country.

When rights and freedoms are not guaranteed

The Universal Declaration of Human Rights (UDHR) was adopted by the General Assembly of the United Nations in 1948.

The UDHR was created after all the suffering experienced during the World Wars in the first half of the 20th century in an attempt to prevent further suffering. It was the first international statement about human rights and has since been built into the constitutions and laws of most countries around the world.

The Declaration's preamble explains why it was drawn up: to promote basic rights and freedoms for all people. All countries that are members of the United Nations signed the Declaration, and in doing so they agreed to promote respect for human rights.

There are 30 articles in the Declaration. Read the first five articles below and then answer the questions in the exercise.

Discussion

Working in groups, discuss factors that affect rights and freedoms. Why do some people have rights and others not? Can your rights be denied if you live in a democratic state? What course of action can people take when their rights are not respected? Write down your suggested plan of action in the form of a flow diagram.

Article 1: When children are born they are free and each should be treated in the same way. They have reason and conscience and should act towards one another in a friendly manner.

Article 2: Everyone can claim the following rights, despite:

- being a different sex
- having a different skin colour
- speaking a different language
- thinking different things
- believing in another religion
- owning more or less
- being born in another social group
- coming from another country.

It also makes no difference whether the country you live in is independent or not.

Article 3: You have the right to live, and to live in freedom and safety.

Article 4: Nobody has the right to treat you as an enslaved person and you should not enslave anyone.

Article 5: Nobody has the right to torture you.

Unfortunately there are some countries and people who do not respect these rights. In some places, such as Colombia and Uganda, children have been forced to fight in armies. They are denied their basic human rights and freedoms as they are not allowed to go to school and their lives are not safe.

These children are usually unable to take action against this type of abuse, but there are international aid agencies that try to help them.

Voters casting their votes during parliamentary elections on 5 November 2007 in Port of Spain, Trinidad and Tobago. Some people in some countries do not have the right to vote.

Civic responsibility

Your **civic responsibility** is the responsibility you have as a **citizen** of your country. You have the right and freedom to do certain things in your country, but responsibilities go with these rights.

Examples include:

- paying any taxes when they become due
- working with others of different cultural backgrounds, religions or races
- respecting the rights and freedoms of others
- getting involved in what happens in your country, including voting and commenting on laws and bills
- helping wherever you can to make your country a better place to live, such as helping to keep your country clean and helping other people when they need help.

Discussion

Working in groups, discuss what you think are your most important civic responsibilities. Then share your ideas with other groups.

Exercise

1. Why was the Universal Declaration of Human Rights drawn up?
2. Can a Black Asian woman claim the same rights as a White European male? Which article in the Declaration describes this?
3. Why do you think Article 4 was included in the Declaration?
4. Write an essay in which you explain four ways that you can show your civic responsibility. Your essay should have an introduction and a conclusion as well as four short paragraphs of content. The essay should be about 150 words.
5. Working in pairs, find out about places where citizens do not have rights and freedoms. Find two examples. Find out what rights have been denied to these people and why.

Key vocabulary

Universal Declaration of Human Rights (UDHR)

civic responsibility

citizen

Humanitarian law

We are learning to:

- explain the terms humanitarian law and law of armed conflict
- discuss why we need humanitarian law.

What is humanitarian law?

Humanitarian law is an international set of rules that aims to limit the effects of **war** and **armed conflict** on members of the armed forces and on civilians. It *only* applies to situations in which there is armed conflict, and it applies to *all* sides regardless of who started it or who is seen to be right or wrong.

The rules apply to armed conflicts between different states (countries) and between different groups in one state.

The laws were drawn up and have been signed by almost every state in the world including the Caribbean states. Humanitarian laws are accepted as part of the laws by which most states are ruled.

A child in front of her destroyed house in Beirut, Lebanon, in 1986.

Project

Put yourself in the position of someone affected by an armed conflict. Write a journal entry to describe your experience.

Features of humanitarian law

One main feature is to **protect** people who are not taking part in the fighting, including the wounded and prisoners of war. This is to ensure that:

- civilians are not attacked
- soldiers who surrender are not killed or injured
- people who are wounded can be cared for
- medical personnel are protected
- people who are taken prisoner during a war are protected from abuse
- people respect the emblems of the Red Cross, the Red Crescent and the Red Shield so that these organisations can carry out humanitarian work.

Another main feature is to restrict the **methods of warfare** and in particular the types of weapons that are used. Chemical weapons, for example, are banned under humanitarian law.

People who do not respect humanitarian law should be brought to **justice** and punished for their acts. These acts are considered to be 'war crimes' and can be punished in national or international courts of law.

Exercise

1. Complete this sentence:

   Humanitarian law aims to __________ people who are not actively involved in an armed conflict and it also aims to restrict the types of __________ that can be used in warfare.

The need for humanitarian law

4.7

Children are often innocent victims of war. Read this case study about 10-year-old Dima.

Case study

Dima's story

Dima, aged 10, and her family were in a queue of cars waiting to cross the border legally into Lebanon and escape the violence in Syria. A month earlier their home had been destroyed by a rocket.

"We were inside the car waiting for my dad when a rocket fell. I went out with my mother to look for him. There was a lot of dust, I couldn't breathe. My mum was screaming ... people were crying and there was lots of blood."

Her dad had got out to see what the hold-up in the convoy was. Now he lay dead.

Dima's mother and her four siblings were terrified and feared further attacks. They were forced to leave his dead body by the roadside.

They arrived in Lebanon with only the clothes on their backs. Because they have no money, Dima has to look after her siblings whilst her mum works and earns some money.

Questions

1. Discuss why laws are needed to protect people like Dima and her family.
2. Imagine that you met Dima. How do you think you could help her and her family? What would you say to her? What would you do?
3. Write a letter to the United Nations on the experiences of a person like Dima affected by war and conflict. Write 150 words.

Exercise

2. What is a 'war crime'?
3. Does humanitarian law apply when there is a civil war between different groups of people in one country?

Research

Working in pairs, find examples of humanitarian law cases that are in the news at the moment. Your teacher will help you. Find out who has committed crimes against humanity, when these crimes occurred and if the people involved have been punished.

Did you know...?

World Humanitarian Day (every 19 August) is the day on which we pay tribute to all people who have lost their lives in the line of duty and to all those who continue to take risks to relieve the suffering of the less fortunate.

Key vocabulary

humanitarian law

war

armed conflict

protect/protection

methods of warfare

justice

Humanitarian acts

We are learning to:

- explain the term humanitarian act
- identify the characteristics of humanitarian acts.

Terms and concepts

Humanitarian acts can be carried out by individuals or big organisations and can be small or big. They can be done at any time, not just in times of war or conflict.

Some humanitarian acts are likely to involve personal risk. Nurses wearing protective suits escort a man infected with the Ebola virus to a hospital in Monrovia, Liberia, in Africa, 25 August 2014.

Characteristics of humanitarian acts

A humanitarian act is something that you do to help other people. These people may be hungry, sick, injured or in some danger.

- A humanitarian act can protect another person's life or **dignity**, for example, giving medical attention or food to someone to prevent them from dying, or providing someone with a safe place to live.
- A humanitarian act can involve helping or protecting someone you would not normally protect, for example, a person whom you do not know.
- A humanitarian act can involve **personal risk** for the person carrying out the act. Some people who helped with the Ebola crisis in West Africa in 2014 became ill themselves and died from Ebola.

The work of people, such as Mother Teresa, and big organisations, such as Action Against Hunger and Doctors Without Borders, are examples of humanitarian acts that help people in many countries.

We can all show compassion and act in a humanitarian way in our daily lives by caring for people who are ill or injured.

Exercise

1. Explain in your own words what a 'humanitarian act' is.
2. Give one example of a humanitarian act.
3. How could a humanitarian act be dangerous to the person who is carrying out the act?
4. Do your own research on humanitarian acts in your country. Find an example of an organisation that helps people in a humanitarian way. Write a short paragraph in which you explain what the organisation does.

Research

Research the work that is done by two humanitarian organisations, such as Action Against Hunger and Doctors Without Borders. Write an essay of 250 words on each organisation.

Case study

4.8

Mother Teresa

Mother Teresa was born in 1910 in Macedonia. She was a Roman Catholic religious sister and missionary who worked as a teacher in India for many years, before she felt the need to devote herself to caring for the sick and poor in and around Calcutta (now Kolkata), India.

She helped them with basic needs like food and water, and she also helped them to regain their dignity. She did this at personal risk to herself.

In 1950, Mother Teresa founded the Missionaries of Charity, a Roman Catholic religious organisation.

The Missionaries of Charity has grown into a big organisation that today runs hospices and homes for people with HIV/AIDS, leprosy and tuberculosis.

They also provide soup kitchens, medical dispensaries and mobile clinics, as well as children's and family counselling programmes.

The Missionaries of Charity has set up schools and orphanages in many different countries.

In 1979, Mother Teresa received the Nobel Peace Prize for her humanitarian work. She died in 1997.

During her life she helped change the lives of many people in Calcutta and inspired others all over the world to do so as well.

She dedicated her life to helping the poorest people.

Mother Teresa's humanitarian acts have been recognised by countries all over the world.

Questions

1. In which decades did Mother Teresa live and work?
2. Where did Mother Teresa carry out her humanitarian acts?
3. How do you think she put herself at risk by helping the poor people in Calcutta?
4. Name four humanitarian acts that are performed by members of the Missionaries of Charity.
5. Was the work of Mother Teresa recognised? How?

Research

Working in pairs, research the life and work of another person who has performed humanitarian acts. Write a short biography of the life and work of the person you have chosen.

Key vocabulary

humanitarian act

dignity

personal risk

Humanitarian acts in the news

We are learning to:

- find humanitarian acts in the news and in everyday life.

Humanitarian acts in everyday life

Humanitarian acts happen all over the world, all the time. Some of them may be local, such as saving a person from drowning. Others are international, such as helping victims of a hurricane. These are humanitarian acts that we often read about in the news.

International organisations such as the Peace Corps, Doctors Without Borders and Action Against Hunger are often in the news for the humanitarian acts that they perform.

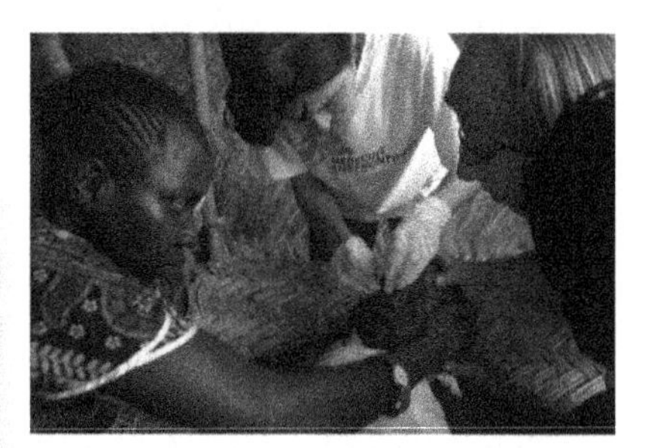

Médecins Sans Frontières help refugees in a camp in Chad, Africa.

The Peace Corps

The Peace Corps is made up of **volunteers** who travel to areas to help with education and better farming skills. The volunteers are not paid to do the work. Their humanitarian acts involve teaching, nursing and community development.

Action Against Hunger

Action Against Hunger works to provide healthy food and water in countries that are experiencing droughts, floods or war, and where people are not able to do this for themselves.

Doctors Without Borders

Doctors Without Borders (called Médecins Sans Frontières, or MSF, in French) provide medical care in places where there is conflict or where there has been a natural disaster. For example, since 2014 doctors and nurses from MSF have been helping West African countries that have experienced an outbreak of Ebola. They also provide vaccinations for children, and medical care for others in need all around the world. The doctors and nurses who work for MSF are all volunteers.

Discussion

What makes people become volunteers, or what prompts a person to perform a humanitarian act? Brainstorm your ideas as a class.

Exercise

1. Name three organisations that are involved in humanitarian acts around the world. In one sentence each, state what each organisation does to help others.
2. Explain what a volunteer is and name two organisations in which volunteers work.

Organisations that help in the Caribbean

A number of humanitarian organisations are active in the Caribbean.

Habitat for Humanity is a non-profit Christian organisation. Its programmes help to eliminate poverty and homelessness in Latin America and parts of the Caribbean, including Trinidad and Tobago, Haiti, the Dominican Republic and Guyana.

The organisation relies heavily on volunteers who give their time to help build houses for people who are homeless. Individuals and businesses also donate money to the organisation.

The Red Cross has branches in many Caribbean countries, with local members and volunteers. Local branches work closely with governments to deliver aid.

The Red Cross helps to educate people on how to prepare for natural disasters such as hurricanes. They also teach people about first aid and how to prevent HIV and AIDS.

The Habitat for Humanity® logo.

Did you know...?

In the Caribbean, the Red Cross has local societies in:

Antigua and Barbuda
Bahamas
Barbados
Belize
Cuba
Dominica
Dominican Republic
Grenada
Guyana
Haiti
Jamaica
Saint Kitts and Nevis
Saint Lucia
Saint Vincent and the Grenadines
Suriname
Trinidad and Tobago

Activity

1. Do your own research on the work of one of the humanitarian organisations you have learned about. Make a short presentation to the class about the organisation.
2. Imagine that you work for an organisation that provides humanitarian help in an area where there is armed conflict. Write an essay which ends '... and I never thought that I would risk my life for this person ...'.
3. Imagine you are working for one of the humanitarian organisations you have learned about and you are helping people who have been in an earthquake. Write a journal entry of your experience in one day. Write 150 words.

Exercise

3. What humanitarian work does Habitat for Humanity do?
4. How do you think you could help a homeless person?
5. Name two ways in which the Red Cross provides humanitarian aid in your country or in a neighbouring country.
6. Would you be willing to volunteer your time to an organisation that does humanitarian work? What would you be willing to do?

Key vocabulary

volunteer

Questions

See how well you have understood the topics in this unit.

1. A __________ is a penalty or punishment for not obeying a rule or law.

a) rule
b) reward
c) sanction
d) compromise

2. Rules are __________ stating how something should be done or how people should behave.

a) principles
b) values
c) rewards
d) sanctions

3. A proposed law that is discussed in parliament is called a __________.

a) rule
b) assent
c) regulation
d) bill

4. All member states of the Caribbean community are democracies. Their laws are made by members of parliament who have been __________ to serve in this role by their citizens.

a) allowed
b) elected
c) chosen
d) selected

5. Complete this sentence: Humanitarian law is a set of international laws which aim to limit the effects of ________.

a) war
b) justice
c) sanctions
d) peace

6. True or false? A volunteer is not paid for the work he or she does.

7. Correct this statement: Your civic responsibility is your duty to protect your country.

8. Write a short definition of the following terms:

a) humanitarian law
b) war
c) armed conflict
d) protect/protection
e) methods of warfare
f) justice

9. Put these steps in order to show how a bill becomes a law.

a) The bill is signed or vetoed.
b) The bill is sent to the Governor-General for signature.
c) Members of the House debate, amend and vote on the bill.
d) A member of parliament introduces the bill.
e) The bill is made available for consideration.

10. Which two of these articles are part of the Declaration of Human Rights?

a) Nobody has the right to enslave you and you should not enslave anyone.
b) People from different cultures do not have the same rights.
c) When children are born, they are free and each should be treated in the same way. They have reason and conscience and should act towards one another in a friendly manner.
d) Nobody has the right to ask you to give them money.

11. Give an example of two rules that you think are essential in any school. Support your answer with reasons.

12. Explain why Mother Teresa was recognised for her humanitarian work.

13. Breaking rules and regulations has consequences. Name one serious and one less serious consequence of breaking a regulation which says: "No littering on the beach."

14. Explain how carrying out a humanitarian act could put your life in danger.

15. Why do you think most people value freedom of thought and expression so highly? What would it be like to live without this freedom? Give an example of something you have read in the news.

16. Imagine that you work for an organisation that provides humanitarian help in areas where there is an armed conflict. Write an essay of about 200 words describing your experiences.

Checking your progress

To make good progress in understanding how we govern ourselves, check that you understand these ideas.

- Explain and use correctly the terms 'rules', 'regulations', 'rewards' and 'sanctions'.
- Describe the consequences of not following rules and regulations. Give two examples.
- Explain the process for how a bill becomes law in your country.

- Explain and use correctly the terms 'rights', 'freedom' and 'civic responsibility'.
- Name five rights that you have as stated in the Universal Declaration of Human Rights (UDHR).
- Explain the purpose of the Universal Declaration of Human Rights (UDHR) and describe one of the articles of the UDHR.

- Explain and use correctly the term 'humanitarian law'.
- Name two features of humanitarian law.
- Explain why there is a need for humanitarian law.

- Explain and use correctly the term 'humanitarian act'.
- Describe the characteristics of a humanitarian act.
- Explain how international organisations give humanitarian help.

Unit 5: Our heritage

In this unit you will find out

Our multi-cultural society

- Our ancestors, culture and cultural background
- How the Caribbean became a multicultural region
  - European settlers
  - African settlers
  - Asian and Syrian settlers
- Aspects of our society – languages, religion and ethnicity
  - Multilingual
  - Multireligious
  - Multiethnic
- The characteristics of our heritage
  - Our cultural heritage
- National identify and patriotism
  - Respect for other cultures
  - Our diverse culture
- Why it is important to preserve our national heritage
  - Co-existence
  - Preservation and conservation
- How we can preserve our cultural heritage
  - Commemorating events
  - Religious festivals
- Restoration of our historical sites

Our multicultural society

We are learning to:

- define and use correctly the terms multicultural, ancestor, cultural background, culture, heritage, cultural heritage.

Ancestors

All countries in the Caribbean embrace many different cultures and people. Every country is a unique and **multicultural** country.

Our **ancestors** are the people from whom we are descended. They are members of our family who lived before us. The ancestors of people who live in your country today come from many different countries.

For example, in Trinidad and Tobago some people are descended from the Amerindians who first lived on the islands. Others are descended from people who went to live there as **immigrants** later on.

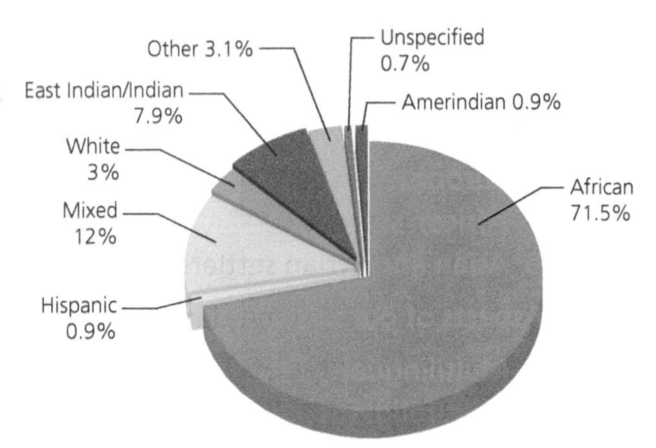

Most people in the Caribbean have East Indian or African cultural backgrounds.

These immigrants came from other Caribbean countries and from Africa, India, China and European countries such as France, Spain, Holland, Britain and Portugal.

Each of these immigrant groups added to the social, religious, ethnic, linguistic and **cultural** landscape of Trinidad and Tobago.

The diverse cultural and religious backgrounds of these groups allow for many festivals and ceremonies throughout the cultural calendar year.

Exercise

1. Read the verse from the calypso on the right. Where did this person's ancestors come from?
2. Compare the ancestor mentioned in this calypso to your own ancestors. Then write a few lines of a calypso about your own ancestors.
3. Make a list of the cultural backgrounds in your country. Which cultural group does your family belong to?
4. Name six countries from which our Caribbean ancestors came. Find these places on a map of the world.

I am the seed of mih father
He is the seed of mih grandfather
Who is the seed of Bahut Ajah?
He came from Calcutta
A stick and bag on he shoulder
He turban and he kapra
So I am part seed of India, India.

from *Jahai Bhai* by Brother Marvin

Culture and cultural background

Culture is the customs, beliefs, arts and technology of a nation or people. **Heritage** is features that belong to the culture of a particular society which were created in the past and have a continuing historical importance to that society. Examples include customs, traditions or languages.

A **cultural background** includes things that a group of people share, such as their religion, language, music, traditions, customs, art and history. Our **cultural heritage** consists of the cultural traditions that we have inherited from past generations.

The culture of people from the Caribbean is therefore rich and **diverse**. People, for example, worship in different ways. Some people are Hindus, while others are Christian or Muslim. Everyone speaks English, but people also speak Chinese, Bhojpuri and Creole.

Some people eat rice, while others use cassava, cou cou or curry. Some listen to music played on the drums; others listen to music played on the sitar. Some celebrate Diwali, while others celebrate Eid al-Fitr or Christmas.

Almost all Caribbean countries have street festivals, for example, Carnival in Trinidad, Crop Over in Barbados and the Moonsplash Festival in Anguilla.

CARIFESTA is a Caribbean-wide event whose aim is to celebrate the people of the region through music, drama, crafts, literature and dance.

Both local events, and region-wide events like CARIFESTA, help create our **national** and **regional** identity.

Dancers at the Crop Over festival in Barbados.

Project

Make a presentation about the cultural backgrounds of the students in your class. First, brainstorm your ideas as a class and decide who will do what. Then, work in groups and do your research. Use a computer to make your presentation. Include photographs or illustrations as well as music.

Exercise

5. In pairs discuss, then write, your own definitions of the terms:

a) multicultural
b) ancestor
c) cultural background
d) culture
e) heritage
f) cultural heritage

6. What is your cultural background? You can begin by answering these questions:

a) Which languages do you speak?
b) Where do you live?
c) Do you have religious beliefs? What are they?
d) Are you a boy or a girl? Does this matter?
e) How old are you?

Key vocabulary

multicultural
ancestors
immigrants
cultural
culture
heritage
cultural background
cultural heritage
diverse
national identity
regional identity

Settlers in the Caribbean (1)

We are learning to:

- explain how the Caribbean became a multicultural society.

The first inhabitants

The Caribbean became a multicultural society through European **colonialism** and **imperialism**, which resulted in people coming from Europe, Africa and Asia to live among the Amerindians who first inhabited the Caribbean.

Amerindians were the first people to inhabit the Caribbean territories. The main tribes were the Tainos, who were part of a group of people called the Arawaks, and the Kalinagos, who were Caribs.

The Tainos and the Kalinagos were farmers. Their main crop was cassava and they also cultivated maize, sweet potatoes and fruits. They used the maize to make beer. They grew cotton to make clothes and bedding. They grew tobacco that they smoked or chewed. The name Tobago comes from the word 'tobacco', which shows how important this crop was.

The Spanish **settlers** arrived in 1492 on Columbus' first voyage. They landed on San Salvador in the Bahamas. When enslaved people from Africa were brought to the Caribbean (as early as 1518), the Amerindians were forced to leave their traditional lands. Most of the Amerindians died from diseases that were brought to these countries by the European settlers. Descendants of these early settlers, known as the Caribs, can be found in Dominica and Guyana.

People in Nevis and other Caribbean territories enjoy the legacy of the Amerindians when they eat cassava bread, farine and warap, and when they drink coffee and cacao. Trinidadians and Tobagonians enjoy the parang music at Christmas, which is a blend of Amerindian and Spanish music.

Christopher Columbus landed in Trinidad in 1498. This picture shows him coming ashore.

Research

Research further the history of your country. Find out about the first European settlers there. Write 250 words on the topic and see if you can find any pictures to go with your writing.

Discussion

In groups, discuss the various settlers who came to your country. Imagine what the journey was like for them. What do you think they found when they got here?

Exercise

1. Who were the first inhabitants of the Caribbean?
2. Which crops did they cultivate? Are these crops still cultivated in your country?
3. How did life change for these people when settlers came to your country?
4. What legacy did the Amerindians leave in your country?

European settlers

Spanish, French and British settlers came to live in the Caribbean from the end of the 15th century. There were also some Dutch and Portuguese settlers. The settlers all came to the Caribbean because European countries at the time wanted to acquire new lands to add to their colonial **empires**.

The first settlers to arrive came from Spain. Spanish explorers sailed into the Caribbean looking for new lands and for gold and silver. Christopher Columbus landed in the Bahamas in 1492. Columbus travelled on to Hispaniola and built a fort which he called 'La Navidad'. He left 39 Spaniards there. The Spanish were more interested in the larger islands of the Caribbean. They used the smaller ones like Dominica and Guadeloupe to obtain water and provisions on their journeys.

The British, French and Dutch came to the Caribbean seeking to claim Caribbean islands. This led to wars which ended with them dividing up the Caribbean between them. In 1627 Saint Christopher (Saint Kitts) was divided between the French and English, the English in the middle and the French on both ends of the island, at Capesterre in the North and Bassetere in the South. The salt ponds on the southeast peninsula were declared common property. The Spanish attacked Saint Kitts and Nevis in 1629.

Saint Christopher and Nevis became very popular for their safe anchorage and supply of fresh water. Nevis became more popular for its valuable stands of timber.

In 1797 British forces captured Trinidad. Trinidad was ruled by the British until 1962, when it became an independent country. The Dutch established themselves in Tobago and used it as a base for their operations to get much-needed salt from neighbouring Venezuela for their herring trade. Saint Vincent was one of the last Lesser Antilles to be settled on by the European settlers. The French and English fought each other for possession of Saint Vincent. The 'Black Caribs', though, resisted the attempts at European settlement. Saint Vincent finally became English in 1783.

After occupying parts of Saint Kitts, the French occupied Dominica in 1632 and Guadeloupe in 1635. The Spanish lost Jamaica to the English in 1655, and in 1644 France took possession of Haiti (the western part of Hispaniola).

1492: Christopher Columbus arrives in the Caribbean.

1492 (December): First Spanish settlement in Caribbean. Fort La Navidad built on Hispaniola.

The English, French and Dutch challenge Spanish supremacy in the Caribbean and they eventually settle on the smaller islands. Spain keeps the larger islands.

17th century: The Dutch establish a base of operations in the Caribbean on Tobago.

1635: The French settle Martinique and Guadeloupe and use them as a base from which to capture other Caribbean islands including Saint Lucia and Grenada.

Exercise

5. Work in four groups. Each group should choose one of the following and find out more about their history in your country and neighbouring countries: Spanish, British, French, Dutch.

   Find out when they arrived and how they influenced the culture and life in your country.

Key vocabulary

colonialism

imperialism

Amerindians

settlers

empire

Settlers in the Caribbean (2)

We are learning to:

- explain how the Caribbean became a multicultural society.

Africans

Most of the African people who moved to the Caribbean were enslaved, and were brought to the islands to provide labour for the sugar plantations.

Millions of Africans were enslaved and were shipped across the Atlantic during the 18th and 19th centuries to work on the sugar plantations and in the sugar factories.

The majority of enslaved African people in the Caribbean arrived between 1700 and 1810, the time period during which Jamaica, Barbados and the Leeward Islands became known for their high levels of sugar production. Sugar was king and Nevis became known as the 'Queen of the Caribees'.

The enslaved African people came from Central and West Africa. They came from the Hausa, Yoruba, Congolese, Igbo and Malinké communities. These people supplied the greatest proportion of the Caribbean population. Between 1702 and 1808, about 840 000 Africans were shipped to Jamaica.

The enslaved African people left a legacy of music and dance and story-telling. Their languages and religions have also had an impact on culture in the Caribbean.

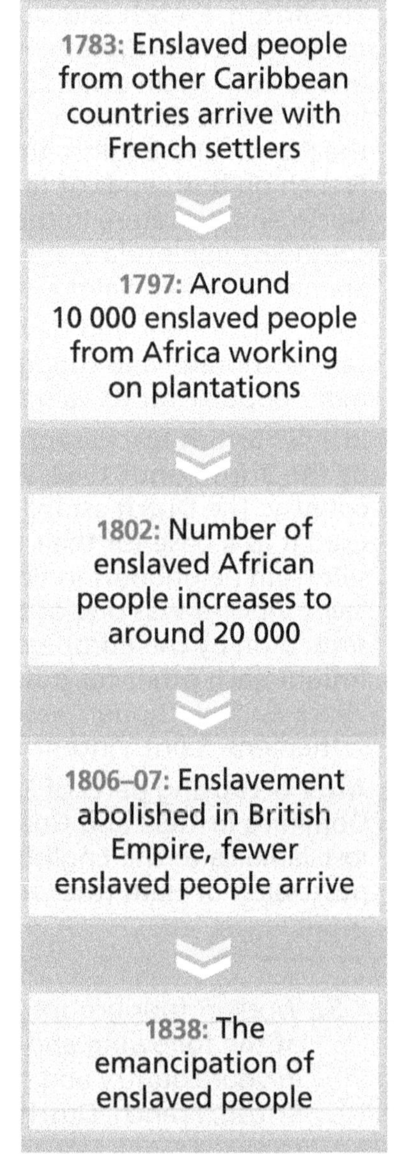

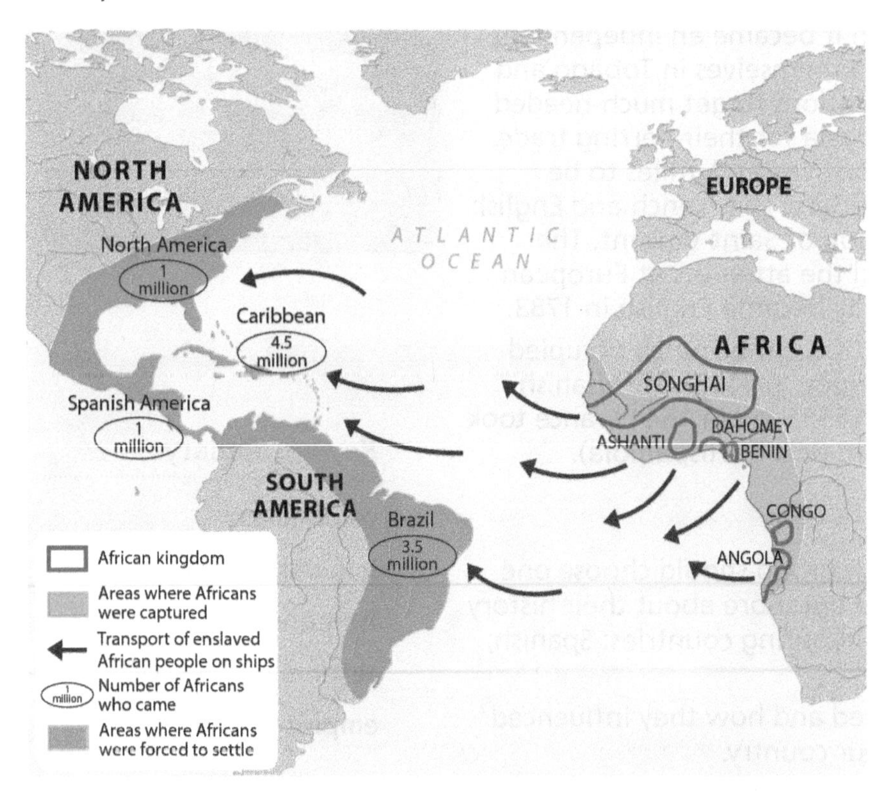

Asians (East Indians and Chinese)

When slavery was abolished in 1838 in the British colonies, most of the enslaved people left the plantations to set up their own small farms and industries. This meant that there were not enough people to work on the big plantations, and this affected the economy of the islands.

Plans were drawn up to bring labourers from India under the indentured labour system. Between 1845 and 1917 East Indians came to larger Caribbean territories, such as Trinidad and Tobago and Guyana, and also to smaller Caribbean territories including Grenada, Saint Vincent, Saint Lucia and Saint Kitts. Most people came from areas in north-eastern India. Most Indian immigrants decided to stay and make the Caribbean their permanent home after they had completed their indenture. They brought their families to the islands, bought land and started their own businesses. Today the descendants of these labourers make up 35–40 per cent of the population of Trinidad and Tobago, a little over 50 per cent of the population in Guyana and about 37 per cent of the population of Suriname. Their cultural legacy is evident in the language, foods, music and festivals of the territories.

Many Chinese people also came to Trinidad, Guyana and Cuba to work on the sugar plantations after the end of enslavement as indentured labourers. The timeline shows the Chinese and Indian immigrations.

1806: First wave of Chinese immigrants arrive from Macao, Penang and Canton (now Guangzhou) to work on the plantations. Only a few stay.

1845: First Indian labourers arrive aboard the ship *Fatel Razack*.

1853–1866: Second wave of Chinese immigrants (about 18 000) arrive from Macao, Hong Kong and Canton under the indentured labour system.

1910–1940s: Third wave of Chinese and Asian immigrants arrive as free migrants.

1917: System of indentured labour comes to an end.

Middle Easterners

The most recent big group of immigrants came from Iraq, Syria, Palestine and Lebanon in the Middle East. Many of them came to Trinidad and Tobago at the beginning of the 20th century. Most of them left their own countries in order to escape religious persecution or economic hardships. Men arrived first and used their business skills to trade goods around the islands. A few reached the shores of the smaller territories such as Dominica and Saint Kitts.

Exercise

1. Look at the map. From which parts of Africa did the Africans come?
2. Why did Africans come to live in the Caribbean?
3. How many East Indians came to live in Trinidad and Tobago under the indentured labour system?
4. Why was the indentured labour system set up?
5. From which places did Chinese immigrants come?
6. Why did the Chinese come to Trinidad and Tobago? Give two reasons.

Activity

Work alone or in pairs and create a painting, a collage or some other type of artwork that reflects the multi-cultural society of your community or island.

Aspects of our society

We are learning to:

- define and use correctly the terms multilingual, multireligious, multiethnic.

The immigrants who came to live in the Caribbean brought with them their own languages, religions and cultural practices, which resulted in a multi-cultural society.

Multilingual

Multilingual means 'speaking many languages'.

In Anguilla, Antigua and Barbuda, Barbados, Dominica, Grenada, Montserrat, Saint Kitts and Nevis, Saint Vincent and Trinidad and Tobago, English is the official language, but many people speak other languages too because of where their ancestors came from.

Multi-religious

The Caribbean is a **multi-religious** region, which means that there are many different religious practices in the region.

People are allowed the freedom to practise their own **religion** and religious beliefs. Catholics, Protestants, Hindus, Muslims, Jewish people and Baha'ists all follow their own religious practices. There are also African traditional religious faiths.

The people who came to live in the Caribbean brought their religious beliefs with them. For example, the Spanish and the French were Catholics, while the British were mainly Protestants and the immigrants from India were mainly Hindu.

Did you know...?

Did you know that the following languages are spoken in these Eastern Caribbean islands?

Anguilla English
Antigua and Barbuda English, Antiguan creole
Barbados English, Bajan
Dominica English, French patois
Grand Cayman English, Spanish, Filipino
Grenada English, French patois
Guyana English, Guyanese Creole, Amerindian languages, Indian languages, Chinese
Montserrat English
Saint Kitts and Nevis English
Saint Lucia English, French patois
Saint Vincent and the Grenadines English, French patois
Trinidad and Tobago English, Caribbean Hindustani, French, Spanish, Chinese

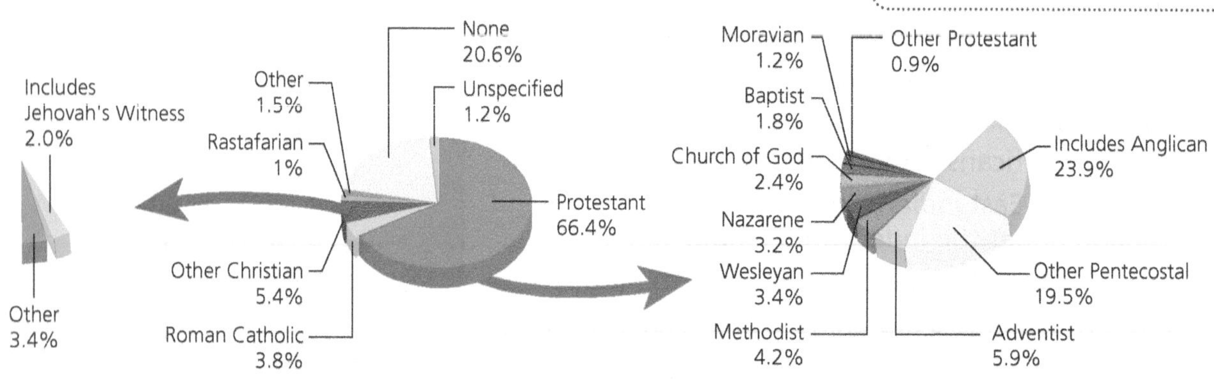

Religions in Barbados (2010).

Multiethnic

An ethnic group is a group of people who have common cultural backgrounds. They belong to an ethnic group because of their ancestors, their language or religion, or because of where they live.

The Caribbean is a **multiethnic** region because there are many different ethnic groups living in the region. Each ethnic group has different cultural traditions. They may eat certain foods or wear certain clothes. They may speak English in a certain way because of the language that they speak at home. Sometimes people of the same ethnic group also look alike.

Research

Work in pairs and do your own research into the different religions that are practised in your own community.

Exercise

1. State if these sentences are true or false. Correct the false statements:
   a) The Caribbean is a multilingual region because everyone speaks English.
   b) The immigrants who came to live in the Caribbean were mainly Catholics.
   c) People in the Caribbean are free to practise whatever religion they choose.
   d) In a multiethnic country everyone looks alike.
   e) The Chinese are an ethnic group living in the Caribbean.
2. Write your own definitions of the terms 'multilingual', 'multireligious', 'multiethnic'.
3. Look at the chart of religions in the Caribbean on page 134. Which of these groups does your family belong to?

Project

Do a survey in your class or school and find out if students know how to say some words in other languages. Choose five words and five languages that are spoken in your country other than English. Draw up a chart to show what you have found out. It might look something like this one.

English Words	Languages				
	French	Spanish	Dutch	Creole	Bhojpuri
Good morning	Bonjour	Buenos dias			

Key vocabulary

multilingual

multireligious

multiethnic

Characteristics of our heritage

We are learning to:

- describe the characteristics (language, religions, traditions, festivals, history) of our cultural heritage.

Our cultural heritage

A **characteristic** is a typical or noticeable quality that someone or something has. For example, people in Trinidad and Tobago speak many different **languages**, including English and Creole. Your country's cultural heritage today is made up of many different things:

- Different languages are spoken, such as English, French, Creole, Arabic and Bhojpuri.
- There are different **religions**, such as Hindu, Islam, Catholic, Protestant, African traditional and Buddhism.
- There are different **traditions** and **festivals**, such as Hosay (Muslim), Diwali (Hindi) and Christmas (Christian).
- There are different types of **cuisine** (food), such as roti and curried mango (Indian), pelau (Spanish) and bamboo shoots and tea (Chinese).
- There are different types of traditional **dress**, such as Indian saris.
- All people in the Caribbean love **music** and dance. We listen to calypso, soca and rumba (all originating from Africa). We enjoy dances like the kuchipudi (Indian) or the lion and ribbon dances (Chinese). African Orisha dance movements are also popular.
- **Folklore** is also different. We hear and tell stories about Anansi (originally from Africa) and Papa Bois (from French Caribbean culture). We also have different **arts and crafts**.
- There are **historical sites** that are part of our cultural heritage, such as Bridgetown and its Garrison (Barbados) and the Brimstone Hill Fortress National Park (Saint Kitts and Nevis), both of which are UNESCO World Heritage Sites.

Diwali celebrations in Port of Spain, Trinidad, 2012.

Research

Research how many different types of music and dance there are in your country. Write 100 words on the topic.

Exercise

1. Give at least one example of cultural heritage that the Caribbean has inherited from each of these groups of people:

   a) Chinese **b)** Indian **c)** African **d)** French **e)** Spanish

2. How many of these characteristics do you have? Count them up and compare with a partner.

Project

Aspects of our culture

Work in groups. You are going to prepare a presentation for a cultural or heritage day at your school. Each group will research and make a presentation about the contribution made by one group of immigrants to the culture of the Caribbean: the Amerindians, the Europeans, the Africans, the East Indians, the Chinese and the Syrians.

Your teacher will help you to choose one of the groups and will organise a field trip to a local museum and library to help you collect information.

Here are some suggestions about steps you could follow or things you could do.

- Discuss how you are going to go about this project. How will you collect information?
- Make a list of categories into which you can organise the information: languages, religion, traditions, music, cuisine (food), dress. Allocate one category to each person in the group.
- Collect information. Make notes as you work. If you find out something interesting about another category, pass on the information to the person in your group who is dealing with that category.
- Collect or draw pictures. Collect real items too (such as clothes or food) and make a display.
- Draft three paragraphs about each category.
- Make posters or a presentation on your computer. Check and edit your presentation.
- Combine the information you have collected into a table. Write the names of the people down the side of the table. Then write short notes about the cultural heritage in categories. For example:

Settlers	Amerindians	Europeans	
Languages		French,	
Religion			
Traditions			
Music			
Cuisine	cassava,		
Dress			

Discussion

In groups, discuss the contributions made by the settlers to our modern society. Collect photographs and make a collage to display all the characteristics discussed.

Key vocabulary

characteristic

languages

religions

traditions

festivals

cuisine

dress

music

folklore

arts and crafts

historical sites

National identity and patriotism

We are learning to:

- define and use correctly the terms national identity and patriotism
- develop an awareness and appreciation for the diverse culture of the Caribbean.

National identity

People from across the Caribbean may have different cultural backgrounds, but we all share a **national identity**, are patriotic and respect the cultures of other people.

National identity is an idea of what it means to belong to a particular country. Often, national identity is carried in particular traditions, culture, language and symbols. For example, most countries have:

- a flag, an anthem, a national **emblem** and national symbols
- a shared history and culture
- a currency (the money used in that country)
- national holidays, customs and traditions.

Patriotism means showing a deep love for, and devotion to, your country. It means taking pride in what your country has achieved and it also means looking after your country and being tolerant and caring of other people who live there.

These are the national symbols of some of the East Caribbean islands:

	National flower	National bird
Anguilla	White Cedar	Zenaida Dove
Antigua and Barbuda	Dagger Log	Magnificent Frigatebird
Barbados	Pride of Barbados	Pelican
Dominica	Carib Wood	Imperial Parrot

Exercise

1. Copy the above table and add in rows with details for Grand Cayman, Grenada, Guyana, Montserrat, Saint Kitts and Nevis, Saint Lucia, Saint Vincent and the Grenadines, and Trinidad and Tobago.
2. Write your own definitions of national identity and patriotism.
3. Which emblems symbolise the national identity of people in your country?
4. Work in groups and make a list of national symbols of **CARICOM** countries (see page 188 for the list of countries) and their national days. Share your ideas with the rest of the class.

Project

Find a topic of your country's cultural history that interests you. Collect pictures of that topic using newspapers, magazines and the internet, and research to help explain why that feature of culture interests you.

Case study

Dominica Creole Day!

Creole Day celebrates the mixture of cultures. It is organised yearly as part of the celebrations leading up to Dominica's Independence Day on 3 November.

On Creole Day,the last Friday in October, most citizens speak in Creole, wear the national dress, and eat traditional and Creole cuisine to show their **patriotism** to Dominica. Schools take part in parades and rallies to help the children develop national pride in the country and learn about the culture.

Questions

1. What does 'Creole' mean?
2. What is the aim of Creole Day in Dominica?
3. Name three ways in which people can show their patriotism.
4. How can you show respect for other cultures in your school and at home?

The national flag of Dominica.

Respect for other cultures

Having **respect** for something or someone can mean admiring them. We respect the achievements of a great sportsperson, for example. But respect also has a more important side to it. Respect means recognising the rights and feelings of other people and not wanting to harm them. We respect other members of our families, our religious leaders and other people. By respecting other people in our community and country we help to create a great country.

Awareness of the diverse culture of the Caribbean

Respecting other people also means being aware of the fact that they have different cultural backgrounds. As you know, the Caribbean has a very **diverse culture** because people have come from many other places to make this region their home. The word 'diverse' means 'different'. So, for example, people with an African cultural background have different ideas and practices from people with a Chinese cultural background. This diversity is something that unifies us and something that we celebrate in the Caribbean. We all take part in festivals that celebrate other cultures. We learn about the beliefs and traditions of others so that we can respect and understand them.

Discussion

Discuss with your teacher what it means to show respect to other people, how you can show respect, and why and when you should show respect.

Key vocabulary

national identity

emblem

patriotism

Caribbean Community and Common Market (CARICOM)

respect

diverse culture

Preserving our heritage

We are learning to:

- define and use correctly the terms peaceful co-existence, conservation and preservation
- explain why it is important to preserve our national heritage.

By respecting other cultures we can live together peacefully in one country. It is therefore important to look after our diverse heritage as well.

Peaceful co-existence

To **co-exist** means to live with other people. For example, we co-exist with people in our own communities and schools. If we live in **peaceful co-existence** we respect each other and we solve problems that arise rather than fighting about them.

Preservation and conservation

If we preserve something, we try to keep it in its original state. So, for example, we can preserve food or we can preserve a building. But we can also preserve a tradition. The terms '**preservation**' and '**conservation**' have similar meanings. If we conserve something, we try to protect something from harm or from being damaged.

This murti (statue or image) of the Hindu deity Hanuman is in Waterloo, Trinidad. It was built to preserve Hindu culture in Trinidad and Tobago.

Case study

Clarence House

Clarence House in Antigua was built in 1783 and was renovated during 1804–1806 for the future King William IV. In later times it became the summer residence of local Governors-General. In the 1990s it was severely damaged by hurricanes, as well as being plagued by termites, and fell into neglect. Its restoration from 2013 to 2016 was guided by the National Parks Authority of Antigua.

Questions

1. How old is Clarence House?
2. Why do you think buildings like Clarence House should be restored?
3. Write your own definitions of 'preservation' and 'conservation'.

Research

Look up the terms 'co-exist', 'preservation' and 'conservation' in a dictionary or on the internet to broaden your understanding of these terms. Then write a short paragraph to explain what each means.

Why do we need to conserve heritage?

Our **cultural heritage** is in the food we eat, the clothes we wear, the music we listen to, the buildings we enjoy and the religions we practise.

It is something we have inherited from the past, that we live with now and that we will pass on to future generations.

Our culture:

- gives us a sense of belonging to a country
- inspires us to carry on traditions
- connects us to other people
- helps us to understand the past
- connects us to the past
- gives us support when we have to face difficult situations
- helps us to understand who we are.

If we do not conserve our heritage, future generations will not understand what it means to be a Caribbean person.

Without this knowledge and understanding of where we come from, people could lose respect for each other, which could result in conflict and unrest in our country.

The Old Court Building in George Town, Grand Cayman, is now the National Museum of Grand Cayman. It has served as a police station, library, school and offices of the Head of State. The building dates back to the 1800s and is Cayman's oldest public building.

Discussion

Have a class discussion about why it is necessary to conserve and preserve our cultural heritage. Your teacher may also invite a speaker to the class to talk about cultural heritage.

Exercise

1. In your own words, explain the terms:

   a) peaceful
   b) co-existence
   c) peaceful co-existence

2. Give two reasons why we need to conserve our cultural heritage.
3. Give one example of what could happen if we did not conserve this heritage.
4. Imagine that you leave your country and you go to live in another country for 10 years. The other country has a different culture.

   What would you miss about your country?

   What would you want to see and do when you returned to this country on a visit?

   Write an essay in which you explain the cultural heritage that you would like to experience on your return to the country.

Key vocabulary

co-exist

peaceful co-existence

preservation

conservation

cultural heritage

Preserving our heritage

We are learning to:

- think about how we can conserve and preserve our cultural heritage.

Commemorating events

We remember and learn to understand our history by commemorating important events. These celebrations help to **conserve** and **preserve** our cultural heritage. For example, we **commemorate** the time when enslaved people were freed and the arrival of our ancestors from other countries.

Study the table below. It provides some information about a few of the festivals held in the Caribbean each year.

Festival	What it commemorates	When it takes place
Emancipation Day	The abolition of slavery and the freeing of all enslaved people in the Caribbean	1 August (public holiday)
Pirates Week Festival	The pirate and buccaneering history of the Cayman Islands	Each year in November
Indian Arrival Day (Guyana)	The arrival of East Indian indentured labourers from India to Guyana on 8 May 1838	5 May (public holiday)
Culturama, Nevis	The cultural heritage of Nevis	Late July to early August each year

Indian Arrival Day is a cultural celebration that takes place each year in May.

Exercise

1. Why is 1 August a public holiday in many Caribbean territories?
2. Do you think that Indian Arrival Day should be a public holiday? Support your answer.
3. What does Pirate Week commemorate?
4. What do you think is celebrated during Nevis Culturama? How is it similar to or different from Carnival celebrations?

Pirate Week Festival takes place each year in May in the Cayman Islands.

Religious festivals

The Caribbean also has several festivals that commemorate events in different religions. The table below summarises some of these events. Religious events do not always take place on exactly the same date every year, because events are based on religious calendars rather than the January to December calendar we use every day in the Caribbean.

Festival	What it commemorates	When it takes place
Easter	In the Christian faith this commemorates the death and resurrection of Christ.	Varies each year, in March or April
Diwali	Diwali is a Hindu festival also called the 'Festival of Lights'. It celebrates the victory of light over darkness.	On Amavasya, that is, the fifteenth night of the dark fortnight of the month of Kartik (October/ November).
Eid al-Fitr	This Muslim holiday, which is also called the 'Feast of Breaking the Fast', is a day on which Muslims are not allowed to fast. It celebrates the end of the 29 or 30 days of dawn-to-sunset fasting during the entire month of Ramadan.	Varies each year, at the end of Ramadan

There are other religious festivals that the Caribbean people share. These include Whit celebrated by Christians, Hosay celebrated by Muslims, Phagwa by Muslims and Ethiopian Christmas by Rastafari.

Exercise

5. Which religion celebrates Diwali? What does Diwali mean?
6. What does Easter commemorate? Is Easter a public holiday in your country?
7. Choose any Caribbean religion. Make a table like the one above with festivals that are celebrated each year.
8. Do you know of any other religion not discussed here? Make a list.

Activity

Work as a class and create a cultural calendar for your classroom. The calendar should have pictures and information about all the main religious and non-religious festivals celebrated by different ethnic groups in the Caribbean.

- Brainstorm a list of festivals.
- Make a list of festivals according to the month in which they take place.
- Decide who will write and collect pictures about each event.

Compile your calendar and display it in the school.

Key vocabulary

conserve

preserve

commemorate

Restoration of historical sites

We are learning to:

- think about how we can conserve and preserve our cultural heritage.

Restoring historical sites

Historical sites are sites that served various political, military, cultural or social purposes in the past. A site can be a house, a military fort, a government building, a factory, a battlefield or a garden, for example.

Historical sites are **social** and **economic assets**. They need to be maintained and restored to their original state if they are to be preserved for future generations.

Restoration of a building involves understanding the significance of a building and then repairing damage caused by use of the building and by the weather.

Restoration sometimes involves removing structures added to the building that are not in keeping with the original style. The grounds around the building also need to be maintained.

Fort George, above Port of Spain in Trinidad, has been preserved for future generations.

Other parts of a site, such as the guns at Fort George in Trinidad, for example, or a library inside a building, need to be preserved as well.

Restoration of a field or a garden requires knowledge of how the area was used in the past. Was it a working farm? Was it a battlefield or the scene of social protest?

Restoration requires expert knowledge. It is expensive and time-consuming. Allowing people to visit historic buildings and making them pay a fee to do so helps to pay for the restoration and conservation of a site.

Did you know...?

The historical site Brimstone Hill on Saint Kitts was built in an effort to recapture Fort Charles on Nevis from the French. The fortress has been restored and preserved.

Exercise

1. Explain what you understand by the term 'restoration'.
2. Why do you think historical sites should be restored?
3. Research a historical site in your country and create a timeline from when it was first established to today. Has it had restoration work done on it?

Case study

Historic Bridgetown and its Garrison

Bridgetown, Barbados, with its natural harbour, was one of the earliest Caribbean seaports. It was also well protected by military outposts along the coast.

It is a well-preserved old town with buildings built in the 17th, 18th and 19th centuries.

The nearby Garrison is a **UNESCO World Heritage Site** military complex with several historic buildings that still have many original features and uses. Its boundary walls are intact and the entrances are in the original locations. The Barbados Defence Force is based there.

Bridgetown's winding roads and alley networks have not changed, nor has the road network at the Garrison. Bridgetown and its Garrison, though, are a popular tourist destination.

Questions

1. Where is Bridgetown located?
2. Explain why you think the old buildings were preserved. What is the value of this site?
3. What do you think had to be done to preserve the Garrison?
4. Do some research on Bridgetown and the Garrison. Find photographs to compare with old and preserved buildings in your country.

The famous red clock tower at the Garrison, Bridgetown, Barbados.

Project

You are going to plan a 'conservation and preservation of our cultural heritage day' at your school.

Step 1. Have a class brainstorm about ways in which you can preserve and conserve your cultural heritage.

Step 2. Identify areas of cultural heritage in your community that you think need conservation.

Step 3. Work in groups. Each group takes one idea from the discussions you have had. Through research on the internet and in the community prepare a presentation in which you explain why these areas need conservation and how they can be conserved. For example, you may identify a place that needs restoring or you may identify a piece of music or a dance that people do not know much about. Your aim should be to educate others about areas that need conservation and preservation and then to explain how this can be achieved.

Step 4. Help to organise a cultural heritage day at your school. Decide how and when you do your presentations.

Did you know...?

In 1751, aged 19, President George Washington of the United States visited Bridgetown. It was the only place he visited outside the United States.

Key vocabulary

social asset

economic asset

restoration

UNESCO World Heritage Site

Questions

See how well you have understood the topics in this unit.

1. A(n) ____________ is someone who lived before us and from whom we are descended.
    - **a)** settler
    - **b)** ancestor
    - **c)** descendent
    - **d)** ancient
2. Someone who speaks more than two languages is ____________ .
    - **a)** bilingual
    - **b)** monolingual
    - **c)** multilingual
    - **d)** multicultural
3. The policy of gaining control over land in another country and exploiting the wealth of that country is called ____________ .
    - **a)** monarchy
    - **b)** settlement
    - **c)** patriotism
    - **d)** colonialism
4. When we ____________ something or someone we remember and show respect.
    - **a)** preserve
    - **b)** commemorate
    - **c)** restore
    - **d)** co-exist
5. When you ____________ something, you maintain it in its original state.
    - **a)** preserve
    - **b)** restore
    - **c)** commemorate
    - **d)** diversify
6. True or false? Our heritage consists of all the buildings that were built by past generations.
7. Name six different aspects of the cultural heritage of the Caribbean.
8. What do these events commemorate?
    - **a)** Pirates Week Festival
    - **b)** Indian Arrival Day
    - **c)** Culturama
    - **d)** Emancipation Day

9. In your own words explain these terms:
   a) cultural heritage
   b) preservation
   c) conservation
   d) peaceful co-existence
10. Name one cultural contribution from each of these peoples who came to settle in the Caribbean:
    a) British
    b) Amerindians
    c) Chinese
    d) Syrians
11. Correct or improve this definition: your national identity is your feeling of patriotism towards your country.
12. Write a definition of the word 'culture' and explain what culture means to you.
13. Name two religious festivals that are celebrated in your community and explain what they are commemorating.
14. Using one historical site as an example, write a paragraph about why the site should be preserved and how this can be done.
15. Complete the table.

Festival	What it commemorates	When it takes place
Emancipation Day		
Pirates Week Festival		
East Indian Arrival Day (Guyana)		
Culturama, Nevis		
Easter		
Diwali		
Eid al-Fitr		

Checking your progress

To make good progress in understanding our multi-cultural society, check that you understand these ideas.

- ☐ Explain and use correctly the terms 'multicultural', 'cultural background' and 'culture'.
- ☐ Name six cultural backgrounds that the Caribbean has.
- ☐ Explain who were the first inhabitants of the Caribbean.

- ☐ Explain and use correctly the terms 'multilingual', 'multireligious' and 'multiethnic'.
- ☐ Name five religious beliefs that people in the Caribbean practise.
- ☐ Explain what makes ethnic groups different from each other.

- ☐ Name five characteristics of our heritage.
- ☐ Describe five characteristics of our cultural heritage.
- ☐ Explain and use correctly the terms 'national identity' and 'patriotism', and describe their features.

- ☐ Explain if there is a difference between conservation and preservation.
- ☐ Explain why it is important to preserve our national heritage.
- ☐ Describe ways we can preserve our cultural heritage.

Unit 6: Religious education

In this unit you will find out

World religions, faith traditions, belief systems

- World religions
  - World religions
  - Religions in the Caribbean
- World faiths: history, practices and impact
  - Christianity
  - Hinduism
  - Islam
  - Judaism and Buddhism
  - Sikhism, Baha'i faith and Confucianism

Beliefs and concepts

- Places of worship
  - Temples, mosques and churches
- Religious symbols
  - The significance of religious symbols
- Religion and the arts
  - The relationship between religion and the arts
- The contribution of religion to the arts
  - Literary and dramatic expression
  - Religious music and dance

World religions

We are learning to:

- explore 'what is religion?'
- identify the main world religions
- define and use correctly the terms religion, belief system, belief and practice.

What is religion?

Religion can be defined as a set of beliefs and practices shared by a group of people. A **belief** is something that you believe to be true about the world. For example, Christians believe that Jesus was the son of God.

A **practice** is something that people do to apply their idea or belief. For example, Buddhists have a practice of sitting meditation. Each religion is different, but most religions have three main characteristics:

- A **belief system**: a set of beliefs or stories that are held by many people, such as how and why we were created, what happens after death and rules or principles about how to lead a good life on Earth.
- Organisation: a religious group is a formal group, with particular rules and specific roles for its leaders.
- Prayer and ritual: most religions offer forms of worship or prayer. They also have their own customs, ceremonies, festivals and other practices and traditions. Followers may gather at a **place of worship**, such as a church or temple.

The main religions

There are 12 main religions: Baha'i, Buddhism, Christianity, Confucianism, Hinduism, Islam, Jainism, Judaism, Shinto, Sikhism, Taoism and Zoroastrianism.

There are also more than a billion people on Earth who consider themselves **secular**, or non-religious. The table shows the popularity of some of the main religions and belief systems.

Exercise

1. Which religion does your family follow?
2. How would you define the terms:

   a) religion **b)** belief system **c)** belief **d)** practice?
3. Do you know people who follow any other religions? If so, which ones?

Activity

Interview someone who practises a different religion or faith from yours. Find out:

a) their main beliefs

b) their weekly practices

c) special annual festivals they celebrate

d) how their religion shapes their everyday life.

Religions in the Caribbean

The Caribbean is a **multireligious** region. The largest religious groups are Protestant **Christians** (including Adventist, Anglican, Baptist, Brethren, Church of God, Congregational, Evangelical, Full Gospel, Methodist, Moravian, Nazarene, Pentecostal, Presbyterian, Seventh Day Adventist, United Church, Wesleyan Holiness), Roman Catholic Christians and **Hindus**; **Muslims** are among the smaller faith groups.

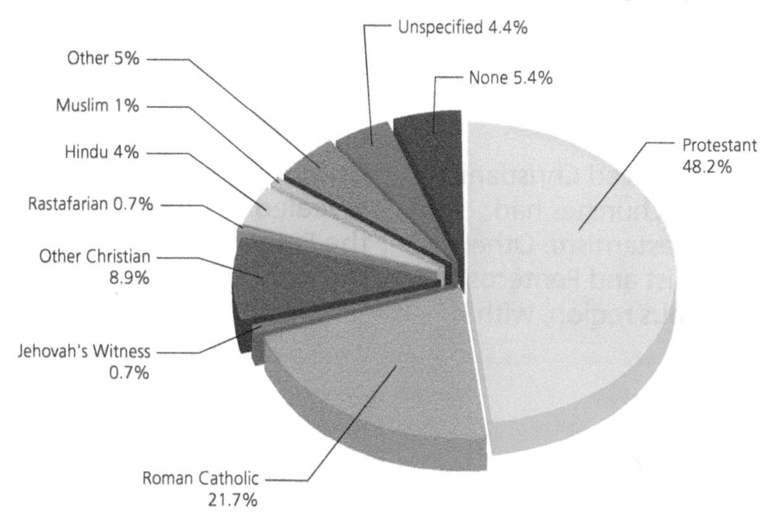

Religions in the Caribbean.

Religion	Number of followers
Christianity	2.2 billion
Islam	1.8 billion
Secular (non-religious)	1.1 billion
Hinduism	1 billion
Chinese traditional religion	394 million
Buddhism	376 million

Religion	Number of followers
Ethnic religions	300 million
African traditional religions	100 million
Sikhism	23 million
Judaism	14 million
Baha'i	7 million
Rastafarianism	600 000

Exercise

4. Which are the five most popular belief systems in the world?
5. You have probably had contact with different religions. Are there any listed in the table that you have not had contact with? List any, and suggest a reason you might not have had contact with them.
6. With which of the religions in the table are you most familiar? Why?
7. List six different types of Christianity found in the Caribbean.

Key vocabulary

religion
belief
practice
belief system
place of worship
secular
multireligious
Christians
Hindus
Muslims

World faiths: Christianity

We are learning to:

- develop an appreciation of the beliefs of Christians
- evaluate the importance of Christian belief systems.

History of Christianity in the Caribbean

Christianity is the world's largest religion. It is based on the life and teachings of Jesus Christ, who was born in the Middle East over 2000 years ago.

From the late 1400s onwards, Europeans introduced Christianity to the Caribbean. By the 1800s, the European Churches had mostly divided between **Catholicism** and **Protestantism**. Other denominations emerged, such as the Methodist and Pentecostal Churches. The Caribbean is now a multireligious region, with many different forms of Christianity.

Did you know...?

Christians believe in one God, and that God is revealed in three ways – the Father, the Son and the Holy Spirit.

Beliefs

The holy book of Christianity is the Bible, which is divided into the Old and New Testaments. The Old Testament is made up of holy writings from before Jesus lived. The New Testament contains stories about Jesus' life.

Christians believe that God the Father sent his Son, Jesus Christ, to heal the relationships between people on Earth. Jesus was **crucified** by the Romans, but his followers believe that he was **resurrected** three days after his death. Christians also believe that Jesus will return to Earth in a Second Coming.

The symbol of Christianity is the cross.

Practices

Jesus' teachings have been interpreted in different ways. However, most Christians share some common practices:

- using the Bible as their main holy book
- meeting to pray or worship in churches
- following Jesus' main teaching of 'love thy neighbour'.

The main Christian holidays are Easter and Christmas.

Did you know...?

The seven Catholic sacraments are: baptism, confirmation, Eucharist, penance, anointing of the sick, ordination and matrimony.

Exercise

1. a) Look at the cross in the picture. In which ways is it similar to or different from other crosses you have seen?

   b) In which places have you seen the Christian symbol of the cross?

Denominations of Christianity

Christianity has divided into different branches of the same religion, known as **denominations**. A denomination has its own particular beliefs and practices. Some of the main denominations are listed below.

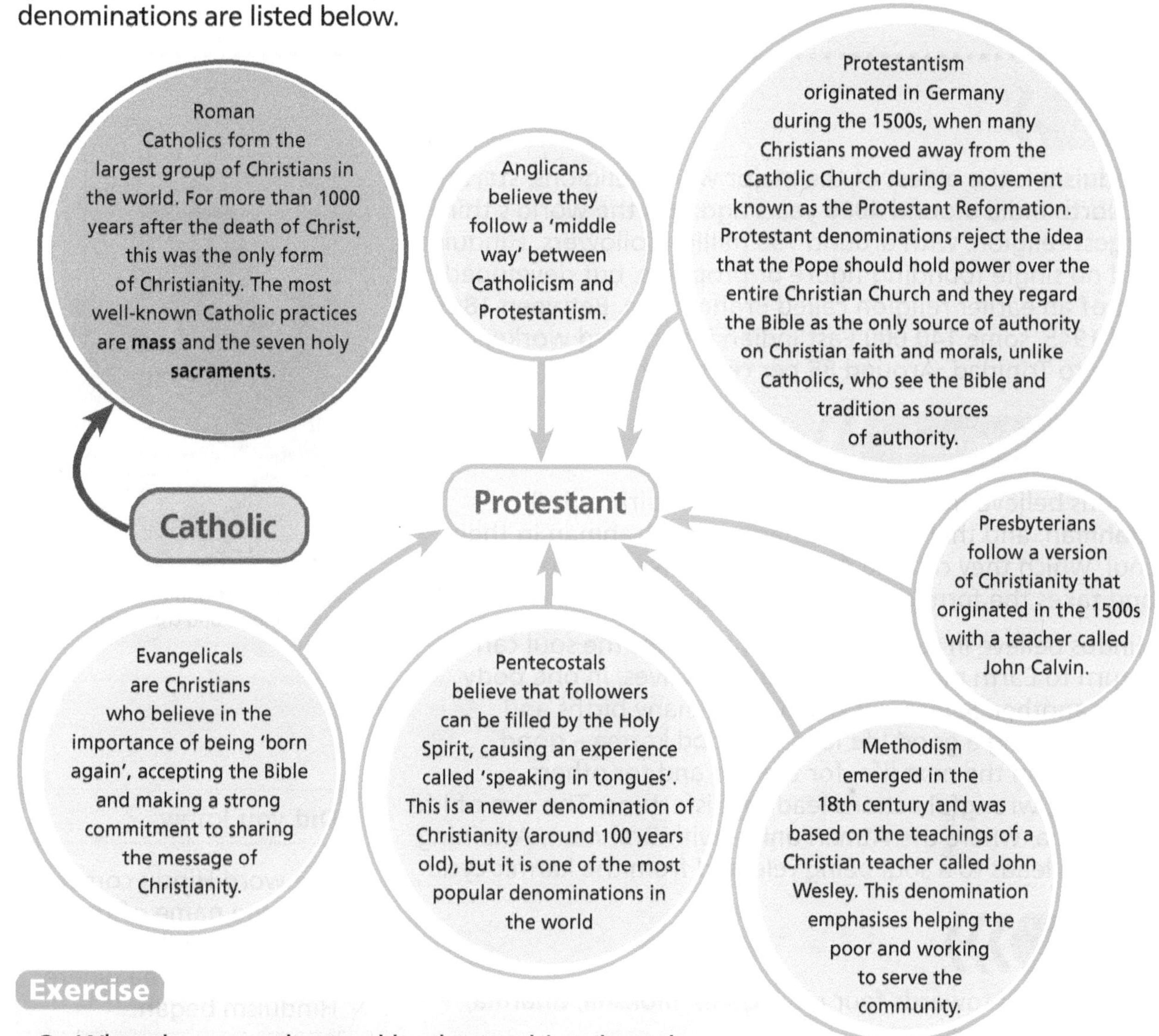

Catholic

Roman Catholics form the largest group of Christians in the world. For more than 1000 years after the death of Christ, this was the only form of Christianity. The most well-known Catholic practices are **mass** and the seven holy **sacraments**.

Protestant

Protestantism originated in Germany during the 1500s, when many Christians moved away from the Catholic Church during a movement known as the Protestant Reformation. Protestant denominations reject the idea that the Pope should hold power over the entire Christian Church and they regard the Bible as the only source of authority on Christian faith and morals, unlike Catholics, who see the Bible and tradition as sources of authority.

Anglicans believe they follow a 'middle way' between Catholicism and Protestantism.

Presbyterians follow a version of Christianity that originated in the 1500s with a teacher called John Calvin.

Evangelicals are Christians who believe in the importance of being 'born again', accepting the Bible and making a strong commitment to sharing the message of Christianity.

Pentecostals believe that followers can be filled by the Holy Spirit, causing an experience called 'speaking in tongues'. This is a newer denomination of Christianity (around 100 years old), but it is one of the most popular denominations in the world

Methodism emerged in the 18th century and was based on the teachings of a Christian teacher called John Wesley. This denomination emphasises helping the poor and working to serve the community.

Exercise

2. What do you understand by the teaching 'love thy neighbour'?
3. You are going to create a portfolio for this topic. Do a timeline of the history of Christianity from the information on these pages.
4. Evaluate in your own words the history, practices and beliefs of Christianity. Add it to your portfolio.

Research

Research one of the different denominations of Christianity. Write 100–150 words about its origins.

Key vocabulary

Catholicism
Protestantism
crucified (crucify)
resurrected
denomination
mass
sacrament

World faiths: Hinduism

We are learning to:

- develop an appreciation of the beliefs of Hindus
- evaluate the importance of Hindu belief systems.

History

Hinduism is the oldest of the major world religions, starting in North India around 4000 years ago. It is the world's third largest religion, with around 750 million followers. Hinduism had no single founding figure or prophets, but developed out of an earlier religion called Brahminism. Between 1845 and 1945, some 140 000 East Indian indentured workers came to Trinidad. Around 85 per cent of them were Hindu.

Brahma, the first God of the Hindu trinity (trimurti) and creator of the universe.

Beliefs and practices

Hindus believe that there is a **universal** spirit called **Brahman**, and that everyone has part of Brahman in their soul, which they call the Atman. This universal soul is eternal and takes the form of many gods and goddesses.

Hindus believe in **reincarnation**. This means the soul can return to Earth many times in different lives, in one body after another. **Samsara** is the cycle of many births and deaths. Living a good life leads to good karma – good fortune – in the next life, for the self and for others. Similarly, wrongful actions lead to misfortune. The aim of life is moksha, where the Atman unites with Brahman. Attaining moksha leads to a soul being released from the karmic cycle.

Did you know...?

The word Hindu comes from the name of the River Indus, which runs through the area where Hinduism began.

Practices

Hindus work towards four main goals: **moksha**, **dharma**, **artha** and **karma**.

- The path to moksha is achieved through spiritual effort and through working selflessly for others.
- Dharma is the set of rules for living a good life.
- Artha is the pursuit of wealth and prosperity in a lawful way.
- Karma is the practice of pure acts, knowledge and devotion in order to reach a higher level of reincarnation in the next life.

Activity

Invite someone from a nearby Hindu temple to visit your class and give a lecture or presentation about the Hindu way of life.

Exercise

1. Why were there no Hindus in Trinidad before the 1840s?

The four paths

6.3

There are four paths to moksha – knowledge, meditation, devotion and yoga. Hindus may choose any of these:

- The path of knowledge (jnana-yoga): studying to attain spiritual knowledge of the relationship between Atman (the soul) and Brahman (the universal soul).
- The path of meditation (dhyana-yoga): freeing the mind of thoughts and emotions so that you can become united with Brahman.
- The path of devotion (bhakti-yoga): worship and devotion to a particular god or goddess. Devotion can be given through actions, words and deeds.
- The path of good works (karma-yoga): living a good life and doing good to others.

The Hindu place of worship is called a **mandir** or Hindu temple. Temples may be dedicated to different gods. Worshippers chant or pray to their chosen gods and goddesses, and make offerings of water, fruit, flowers and incense. Hindus also make a **shrine** for their daily worship at home. This may be a room, a small altar or even a decorated shelf. At the shrine, Hindus make offerings to a **murti**, a holy statue of a god or goddess.

Hindus have several **scriptures**. These include:

- The Vedas: the oldest religious texts in Hinduism. Originally they were not allowed to be written down, so they are known as sruti, 'that which is heard'.
- The Upanishads: part of the Vedas that consider the nature of the soul and reincarnation.
- Smrutis: laws from around 250 BC.
- Ramayana: a long poem about the story of Rama and his wife Sita.
- Puranas: ancient tales about the lives of Hindu saints.

Exercise

2. Evaluate in your own words the history, practices and beliefs of Hinduism. Add it to your portfolio.
3. Which of the four paths do the following represent?
   a) making an offering of fruit and flowers
   b) sitting in quiet meditation
   c) reading the Upanishads
   d) working for charity
4. Create a timeline of the history of Hinduism. Add it to your portfolio.

Guyanese Hindus offer morning prayer in a Lord Vishnu temple in Grove in Georgetown.

Key vocabulary

Hinduism
universal
Brahman
reincarnation
samsara
karma
moksha
dharma
artha
mandir
shrine
murti
scriptures

World faiths: Islam

We are learning to:

- develop an appreciation of the beliefs of Muslims
- evaluate the importance of Muslim belief systems.

History

Islam is one of the fastest-growing religions in the world today.

Muslims believe in a single god, called Allah, who has sent a number of prophets, including Moses, Jesus and Abraham, to teach people his will. They believe that the most recent of the prophets, the Prophet Muhammad, revealed the word of Allah to humanity.

Islam began in Mecca in the Middle East around 1400 years ago and is based on the teachings of the Prophet Muhammad, who was born in AD 570 in the area today known as Saudi Arabia.

There are two types of Muslims: Sunnis and Shiites. Around 90 per cent of Muslims are Sunnis. The Shiites moved away from the Sunnis in AD 632 after the death of the Prophet Muhammad.

The Qur'an is the holy book of Islam.

Beliefs and practices

The holy book of Islam is called the **Qur'an**. It was originally written in Arabic. Muslims believe that the Qur'an is the word of Allah and that every word is sacred. While the Qur'an is being recited aloud, Muslims have to behave with reverence and should not eat, drink or make distracting noises.

There are 114 chapters in the Qur'an. The Qur'an is sometimes divided into 30 parts known as juz'. This makes it easier for Muslims to read the Qur'an during one month. Many Muslims will read more than one juz' every day, especially during **Ramadan**.

Research

One of the most important events in a Muslim's life is the Hajj – a pilgrimage to Mecca. Research the stages of the Hajj. Show your work in a poster or project.

Place of worship

Muslims worship in a **mosque**. Most have a domed roof and a tall tower called a minaret. A man, called a **muezzin**, sings out the call to prayer five times each day from the minaret.

It is mostly men who attend daily prayers at the mosque. Women and men pray separately. There may be a screened-off area in the mosque for women.

There are no pictures or statues in a mosque because Muslims are forbidden to show the Prophet or Allah as human beings. Instead, there are decorative patterns and words from the Qur'an.

Did you know...?

The word Islam means 'submission to the will of Allah'.

Laws of Islam

The practical laws of Islam are the **Sunnah**. Devout Muslims are expected to follow the five 'pillars of Islam', which are:

- the declaration of faith
- prayers five times each day
- giving money to charity
- fasting, especially for the month of Ramadan
- making **Hajj**, a holy pilgrimage to Mecca.

Pilgrims at afternoon prayer on Hajj in Mecca, Saudi Arabia.

Case study

The Muslim year follows the **lunar calendar**. This means that Muslim festivals may fall on different dates each year.

Ramadan is a month-long celebration of the time when Allah revealed the Qur'an to the Prophet Muhammad. To celebrate, Muslims spend Ramadan (the ninth month of the Islamic calendar) in fasting and prayer.

Muslims **fast** each day from sunrise until sunset, so they wake up very early, before the sun rises, in order to have an early meal. Late at night, they may break their fast with a meal called the iftar.

Ramadan comes to an end with the first sighting of the new moon. Once the new moon has appeared, the celebration of **Eid al-Fitr** marks the end of fasting. This three-day celebration is a time when family and friends gather to share food. They also give presents to children and donations to charity.

Question

1. Are the following statements true or false?
   a) The Muslim calendar starts with January and ends with December.
   b) Muslims may not eat or drink anything at all for the whole month of Ramadan.
   c) Eid al-Fitr marks the end of Ramadan.

Key vocabulary

Islam
Qur'an
Ramadan
mosque
muezzin
Sunnah
Hajj
lunar calendar
fast
Eid al-Fitr

Exercise

1. Do a timeline of the history of Islam. Add it to your portfolio.
2. Evaluate in your own words the history, practices and beliefs of Islam. Add this to your portfolio.
3. Name **a)** the Muslim holy book **b)** the Muslim place of worship

World religions: Judaism and Buddhism

We are learning to:

- develop an appreciation of the beliefs of Jewish people and Buddhists
- evaluate the importance of Jewish and Buddhist belief systems.

Judaism: history

Judaism began in the Middle East around 3500 years ago with a prophet called Abraham. Before this time, people worshipped many different gods and goddesses. Abraham believed that he heard the one true God call on him to stop worshipping other idols.

Jewish people believe that there is a single God, who entered into a **covenant** with the Jewish people: in exchange for God's love and protection, they undertake to keep God's laws as set out in the Old Testament.

The Western Wall Plaza and the Dome of the Rock, seen in the background, in Jerusalem, Israel, is a holy place for Jewish people.

Beliefs and practices

Judaism is a very practical religion. Jewish people believe that a person is judged on how they keep the laws and traditions of their faith.

One of the most important Jewish traditions is **Shabbat**, the Sabbath (meaning to rest). It begins at sunset on Friday and ends at sunset the next day. Jewish people hold prayer service followed by a family meal. They do not work on the Sabbath, but spend the day in prayer and with family.

The Jewish holy book is the Torah, a handwritten scroll containing the first five books of the Hebrew Bible. Jewish people believe that God revealed the Torah to Moses on Mount Sinai over 3000 years ago.

Important Jewish festivals are: Pesach, Rosh Hashanah, Yom Kippur and Hanukkah. Jewish people worship in a synagogue or temple.

Exercise

1. Create a timeline of the history of Judaism. Add it to your portfolio.
2. Evaluate in your own words the history, practices and beliefs of Judaism. Add it to your portfolio.

Research

Research the Dome of the Rock. Find out why it is so sacred to both Jews and Muslims.

Buddhism: history

Some belief systems, such as Buddhism, are based on a **philosophy** and do not involve a god.

Buddhism is a way of thinking about and understanding life on Earth based on the teachings of Siddhartha Gautama, who lived around 600 BC. Buddhists believe that Siddhartha attained freedom from suffering, a state called **nirvana**, or **enlightenment**. Buddhists aim to achieve nirvana by practising Buddha's teachings. Many Buddhists are **atheists**.

Beliefs and practices

Buddha taught that everything in life constantly changes, and life contains much suffering. The end to suffering comes from living according to the Middle Way. To live the Middle Way, an individual should neither strive for too much material comfort nor for too much fasting and sacrifice. Buddhists live by the Five Moral Precepts. They may not:

- harm any living thing
- take anything that has not been given freely
- engage in sexual misconduct
- take part in lying or gossip
- take intoxicating substances, such as alcohol or drugs.

An important practice for Buddhists is **meditation**, which can be done in various ways, including:

- sitting quietly, observing the flow of breath in and out
- chanting, singing or contemplating a statue of Buddha
- using a **mandala** or other artwork to focus attention to an invisible centre point
- practising tai chi, yoga, karate or any other martial art.

For many Buddhists, the most important annual festival is Wesak, a celebration of Buddha's life. Buddhists worship in temples and, like Hindus, they may have shrines in their own homes for meditation and acts of devotion.

Exercise

3. Build a timeline and evaluate in your own words the history, practices and beliefs of Buddhism. Add it to your portfolio.
4. Which five things are forbidden to Buddhists?

Siddhartha became known as Buddha, meaning The Enlightened One.

Discussion

Buddhists may also be atheists. How does this differ from other religions?

Key vocabulary

covenant

Shabbat

philosophy

nirvana

enlightenment

atheist

meditation

mandala

Sikh, Baha'i and Confucian faiths

We are learning to:

- develop an appreciation of the beliefs of Sikhism, Baha'i and Confucianism
- evaluate the importance of Sikh, Baha'i and Confucian belief systems.

Sikhism

You have learned about the most popular world religions. Other world religions include people of the Sikh, Baha'i and Confucian faiths.

Sikhism was founded in the 16th century by a leader called Guru Nanak. He taught the importance of leading a life of good actions. Followers seek to do this by:

- keeping God in their hearts and minds at all times
- living honestly and working hard
- treating people fairly and equally
- helping and supporting those in need
- serving others.

Sikhs believe in one God, who has no gender or form, and each person can pray or **meditate** directly to God. Like Hindus, Sikhs believe in the cycle of **karma**, and that each reincarnation depends on one's actions in a previous life.

Sikhs worship at a temple called a Gurdwara. Their holy book is the Guru Grath Sahib. Important Sikh festivals include:

- Diwali: the festival of lights
- Hola Mahalla: a festival where Sikhs watch and participate in martial arts parades, poetry readings and music
- Gurpurbs: celebrations of important dates from the lives of the gurus
- Vaisakhi: the Sikh New Year and celebration of the formation of the Sikh faith.

A modern Sikh family.

Research

Research one of the following festivals:

- Diwali
- Hola Mahalla
- Gurpurbs
- Vaisakhi

Find out what happens during this festival, why it is observed and the significance for people who take part. Add it to your portfolio.

Exercise

1. Research a timeline of the history of Sikhism. Add it to your portfolio. You can do some further research at the library.
2. Evaluate in your own words the history, practices and beliefs of Sikhism.

Baha'i faith

The Baha'i faith was founded in the 1800s in Persia. The first Baha'i to settle in Trinidad arrived in 1956. Today, more than 10 000 people of Baha'i faith live in Trinidad and Tobago.

The Baha'i believe in one god, and emphasise the **unity** of all human beings. Baha'i people believe that there is one good, and that all the major religions share the same message and purpose – to bring human beings together. The Baha'i recognise the prophets of all the major religions, including Abraham, Moses, Jesus, Muhammad, Krishna and Buddha.

Confucianism and Taoism

Confucianism and Taoism are both major religions of China.

Confucianism developed from the teachings of the Chinese philosopher Confucius in the 6th century BC. Confucianism was brought to Trinidad and Tobago by Chinese **immigrants**. It is a **secular** religion, without belief in a god or supreme power. It focuses on how people should behave in their everyday lives, especially in relationship with others. Confucianism encourages **benevolence**, duty, manners, **wisdom** and faithfulness.

Taoism was first recognised as a religious system during the 4th and 3rd centuries BCE. It brings together many other Chinese traditions, and has a close relationship with both Confucianism and Buddhism. The word 'tao' means way or path.

Taoists follow the teachings contained in the Tao Te Ching (also called the Book of Changes). Taoists strive for the 'three treasures': compassion, moderation and humility. Taoist practices include meditation.

Taoism is a religion of unity and opposites; the Yin and Yang. The principle of Yin and Yang sees the world as filled with complementary forces – action and non-action, light and dark, hot and cold, and so on.

Exercise

3. List similarities between the Sikh and Hindu religions.
4. Choose one of the religions discussed on this page. Do some extra research on that religion and create a timeline, history, practices and beliefs for your portfolio.
5. Add to your portfolio a section about your own religion. Do some further research on it (e.g. where else in the world it is followed) and how you follow it.
6. Choose one of the following religions:

   Zoroastrianism; Taoism; Confucianism; Shinto; Jainism.

   Research the religion and present a project showing the main history, beliefs and practices of the religion, as well as its symbols.

Key vocabulary

meditate

karma

unity

immigrants

secular

benevolence

wisdom

Places of worship

We are learning to:

- define and use correctly the term place of worship
- identify places of worship in the Caribbean
- explain the importance of respect in places of worship.

Temples, mosques and churches

A **place of worship** is any building or structure where followers of a particular religion or faith gather to pray, worship or pay respects as part of the practice of their religion or faith. Most religions have their own place of worship.

A Buddhist temple at the pilgrimage site in Mandalay, Burma.

In some religions, natural features also form a place of worship. For example, Baptist Christians may visit rivers and oceans to perform ritual baptisms at certain times of year.

Religion	Place of worship	Main characteristics
Christianity	Church	Large hall; pews or other seating for the congregation; minister stands in front; symbol of cross
Islam	Mosque	Usually has domed structure and minaret (tower); followers take off their shoes inside; no pictures or statues
Hinduism, Sikhism, Buddhism, Taoism	Temple or shrine	May be decorated with gold, bright colours, pictures and statues of gods or goddesses, or of Buddha
Judaism	Synagogue	Special structure at the front where the Torah is kept; rabbi stands in front; congregation may sit or stand

Some activities that may take place at places of worship include meditation, chanting, prayer, ceremonies such as weddings and memorial services, religious study, and community gatherings and activities.

Exercise

1. Define what you understand by 'place of worship'.
2. Research places of worship in your country for as many different religions as you can find. For each one, find out:
   - when it was founded and some details of its history
   - the dates and times of main services
   - any special events held there.

The importance of respect at places of worship

6.7

For all religions, a place of worship is a holy place for people who gather there. It is very important to demonstrate respect in places of worship. You can do this by:

- staying silent or speaking very quietly if allowed
- no eating or drinking (except as part of the rituals)
- no mobile phones; no photographs unless permission has been given
- wearing the required clothing
- adhering to the rules of the building, such as finding out where you may or may not walk or sit.

Activity

Visit some different places of worship. Write a journal entry reflecting on what you noticed and how you felt on your visit.

Case study

Madina Masjid, Bridgetown, Barbados

The Madina Masjid was built in 1957 and was named City Masjid. It was built on land that was purchased with donations from the Muslim community.

In 2000, the Masjid was renamed Madina Masjid. The Madina Masjid is financed by its members and members of the Muslim community.

The activities in the Madina Masjid include:

- prayer five times daily
- readings every Thursday
- lessons of Hadith on the first Saturday of every month
- lessons of the Noble Qur'an on other Saturdays.

Dress: Traditional – men should wear long trousers and long-sleeved shirts. Women should wear dresses or skirts that cover their knees. Shirts should cover the shoulders and arms. Women must wear a headscarf. You must remove your shoes before you enter.

Inside the mosque: As you enter, it is traditional to say 'Assalam o-Alaikum', which means 'Peace be on you'. Stay silent. Women and visitors should remain near the back of the mosque. Spend a moment in quiet meditation. Do not take photographs.

Questions

1. How long has the Madina Masjid been in Bridgetown?
2. Identify three ways you can show your respect when you go inside a mosque. What types of behaviour are disrespectful at a place of worship?
3. Which rules for the mosque are similar to or different from other places of worship you know about?

St John's Cathedral in Antigua, one of the Christian places of worship on the island.

Activity

Design a brochure with information about places of worship in your country. Include information about at least three places of worship.

Key vocabulary

place of worship

Religious symbols

We are learning to:

- identify symbols related to religions, faith traditions and belief systems
- understand the significance of these symbols.

Religious symbols

Most religions have a **symbol** that represents the religion itself. Usually the symbol is a shape or image that has a relationship to the main beliefs or history of the religion.

	The **cross** represents Christ's suffering when he was crucified. Christians believe that Christ died for humanity's sins.
	The most used symbol in the Anglican Church is the cross, seen here in the symbol for the Anglican diocese in Trinidad and Tobago.
ARDENS SED VIRENS	The image of the burning bush is a common symbol for Presbyterian churches. The motto 'Ardens sed Virens' means burning but flourishing.
	The symbol of the cross and flame is used to represent the Methodist Church. It symbolises Christ (the cross) and the Holy Spirit (the flame).
	The fish symbol recalls the miracle of the loaves and fishes, when Jesus took a single fish and a single loaf and used it to feed many people. It is used by Evangelical Christians to represent that they have been born again.
	The symbol of Islam is the **crescent** moon and star. The crescent moon represents the lunar calendar of Allah and the star represents Allah's presence. Muslims are forbidden from worshipping images of Allah.
	The Star of David is the modern symbol for Judaism. It comes from the shield of King David, the king who established Jerusalem as the holy capital of the Jewish people.
	The menorah is a candelabra with seven branches. It reminds Jewish people of the candles used to light the Temple in Jerusalem.

	The hamsa is a symbol of good luck and protection. In Judaism, the hamsa represents the hand of God. In Islam, it is known as the hand of Fatima, daughter of the Prophet Muhammad. The eye in the centre is known as the 'evil eye', a symbol to ward off evil.
	The **Aum**, or **Om**, represents the holy sound used in Hindu meditation and chanting. It is three sounds: a – u – m, which represent three aspects of its meaning: • the three worlds: earth, atmosphere and heaven • the three main Hindu gods: Brahma, Vishnu and Shiva (the **trimurti**) • the three Vedic scriptures: Rig, Yajur and Sama.
	The lotus is a type of water plant. Its roots grow in mud, but the flower floats on water without becoming wet or muddy. In Hinduism, the lotus flower represents living without becoming attached to material things. The lotus has a similar meaning in Buddhism.
	A wheel with eight spokes represents the Eightfold Path, the Buddhist path to enlightenment. At the centre there is often a lotus flower.
	The Khanda is the symbol of Sikhism. Down the centre, it has a double-edged sword, representing divine knowledge. The two sides of the sword represent the division of truth from falsehood. Around the sword is a circle called the Chakar, representing the eternal perfection of God.

Research

In pairs or groups, research one of the following:

- different types of Christian crosses, and what they mean
- different types of lotus flowers from Hindu and Buddhist art
- symbols of any religion of your own choice.

Present your research in a one-page picture with labels.

Activity

Create a brochure or booklet about places of worship and related symbols in your country.

Exercise

1. Why is the cross the symbol of Christianity?
2. Where does the Jewish Star of David come from?
3. What does the star on the symbol of Islam represent?
4. Which flower is an important symbol for Buddhists and Hindus?
5. Which symbol is shared by Muslims and Jewish people?
6. As a class, create a chart using information about symbols of all the world religions, faith traditions and belief systems.

Key vocabulary

symbol

cross

crescent

Aum/Om

trimurti

Religion and the arts

We are learning to:

- appreciate and evaluate the contribution of religion to the arts and describe their relationship
- express views and opinions about religion and art.

What is the relationship between religion and art?

Each religion has many stories and ideas that have provided subject matter for artists. Many religious paintings and sculptures show scenes from the lives of figures such as Moses, Jesus and Buddha.

Art usually has one of three purposes:

- to **entertain**: to provide fun or enjoyment
- to **educate**: to teach the viewer about something
- to **inspire**: to give the viewer a feeling of greater spirituality, awareness or closeness to the divine.

St Peter's Basilica, in Rome, Italy is a church built during the 1500s and 1600s. According to legend, it is built on the burial site of Peter, one of Jesus' 12 apostles.

Religion and art have had a difficult relationship. Some religious leaders (such as the Popes of the Roman Catholic Church) believed that art could be used for evil, and that entertainment could lead to **vices** (sinful or evil actions).

At some points in history, religious people destroyed art that did not show suitable religious themes. Artists then tended to create religious art so that they could continue to paint or draw. So, although some religions destroyed the art of earlier cultures, religion also brought a rich artistic heritage.

In addition, followers have often given money to support their chosen church or temple. Much of this money has been spent on building beautiful places of worship, decorated with paintings and sculptures of religious themes.

Wealthy people, such as royalty and nobility, may become supporters of the **arts** in order to enjoy paintings, sculptures, dance and music. They often request work with religious subject matter in order to gain favour with their gods.

Research

Research famous buildings from a religion of your choice. Draw or paint pictures of the buildings and write a page on how they communicate some of the ideas and practices of the religion.

Discussion

Some forms of Christianity have rejected large, decorated places of worship. Instead, their prayer halls are very simple, without any art. Why do you think they did this? Do you think a place of worship needs to be grand, or can it be simple?

Visual arts

6.9

Visual arts include paintings, drawings and patterns that we look at. Religions that have rich traditions of visual arts include:

- Christianity: paintings, **frescoes** and sculptures depicting the stories of Jesus' life
- Hinduism: brightly coloured sculptures and paintings of the many different gods and goddesses
- Buddhism: statues of the Buddha and pictures depicting his life.

Hajj pilgrimage to Mecca in Saudi Arabia. The picture shows an example of Muslim architecture.

Many Christian paintings show important scenes from the life of Jesus, such as the **Nativity**, the **Temptation of Christ** and the **Last Supper**.

In Islam, it is forbidden to show images of people. Islamic art therefore focuses on strong geometric patterns and **illuminated writing**.

Architecture

Places of worship are designed to give people a feeling of being closer to their God or gods.

Before the invention of modern skyscrapers, temples and cathedrals were the tallest buildings in any city. The cathedrals of the Catholic faith have tall **spires**, high domed ceilings and rich frescoes. Muslim architecture is known for the **domes** and towers of its mosques. Hindu and Buddhist temples have smaller spaces, with many statues and shrines where followers can pray or meditate.

Exercise

1. What are the three purposes of art?
2. Why did some religions destroy much of the art that came before them?
3. What purpose would each of the following pieces of religious art serve?
   a) a painting of a scene from the life of Christ or Buddha
   b) a richly coloured pattern of mosaics in a mosque
4. Which religions do you associate with the following architectural features?
   a) domes and minarets
   b) spires and crosses
   c) temples with statues and shrines

Key vocabulary

entertain
educate
inspire
arts
vice
visual arts
frescoes
Nativity
Temptation of Christ
Last Supper
illuminated writing
spire
dome

The contribution of religion to the arts

We are learning to:

- appreciate and evaluate the contribution of religion to the arts and describe their relationship
- express views and opinions about religion and art.

Literary and dramatic expression

Literary expression includes books and stories. Religious stories form a large part of the literary expression of each culture.

Dramatic expression refers to performances of stories, for example, through theatre and rituals. Often, literature and drama overlap as written stories become the source of plays, theatre and film.

To explore the contribution of religion to our literature and drama, it is necessary to go back to before the main world religions, to the ancient Greeks. They believed in a huge **pantheon** of gods and goddesses who were like humans, except that they had superpowers and were **immortal**.

Greek poets wrote stories about their gods. These are known today as Greek **mythology**. People still use Greek myths in storytelling, literature and films.

The Greeks held festivals in honour of their gods. At these festivals they performed songs, poems and plays.

An ancient Greek writer, Aristotle, wrote a book called *Poetics* in which he set out the structure for a tragedy. This structure has since influenced all the stories, books and films we enjoy today.

Religion	Examples of books or literature
Christianity	Dante Alighieri's *Divine Comedy*; John Bunyan's *Pilgrim's Progress*; the fantasy works of C.S. Lewis and J.R.R. Tolkien
Islam	*1001 Arabian Nights*
Hindu	The Vedas (oldest sacred texts); the Upanishads: 200 books of knowledge and philosophy; *Bhagavad Gita*: a 700-verse scripture on various philosophical matters; the Puranas: a set of stories and allegories

Discussion

If possible, watch a video of one of the following films:

- *Clash of the Titans*
- *Percy and the Lightning Thief.*

Discuss as a class what the movie showed you about Greek mythology. Do you think Greek myths are still interesting to people living in the 21st century? Why, or why not?

Activity

Work in groups. Choose one of the Greek gods or goddesses. Research some of the myths about that figure. Create a dramatisation of the story you researched.

Or

Find videos on the internet of Indian classical dance. Prepare your own example of a classical dance to show your classmates.

Religious music and dance

6.10

Since ancient times people have used dance and music in their spiritual ceremonies and rituals. Drumming, chanting and traditional dance have existed for as long as human society.

Where formal religions have developed, there have been periods where some forms of dance and music were forbidden.

For example, some denominations of Christianity consider dance to be sinful as it was part of pre-Christian pagan rituals.

However, there are many forms of traditional music and dance that have become an important part of religious art forms:

- Christianity:
    - Gregorian chants
    - choral
    - gospel
    - Christian country
    - pop
    - (even) metal music
- Hinduism: classical Indian music and dance
- Buddhism: monks sometimes perform types of dancing and music as part of their religious rituals

Indian classical dance, such as Odissi shown in this picture, is based on sacred dances from hundreds of years ago.

Discussion

Sometimes people want to burn books or artworks that go against their religious beliefs. What do you think of this? Is it OK? What would you say to someone who wanted to do this? Give reasons for your answers.

Exercise

1. Why were some forms of dance and music forbidden?
2. Describe what you notice in the picture of the Indian classical dancers.
    a) Describe their clothing.
    b) Describe the positions of their bodies, especially their hands and feet.
3. For each of the religions that you have covered in your portfolio, add examples to each of them for: art and architecture, **visual arts**, literary and dramatic expression, dance and movement, and music and voice. Try and find one example from your country and one from elsewhere in the world.

Activity

Work in groups. Choose a story from a religion of your choice. Create a booklet re-telling the story, with illustrations. Note, if you choose an Islamic story you may only use patterns, not pictures!

Key vocabulary

pantheon

immortal

mythology

visual arts

Questions

See how well you have understood the topics in this unit.

1. What are the three main characteristics of any religion?
2. Look at the pie chart. What are the three most popular religions in the Caribbean?

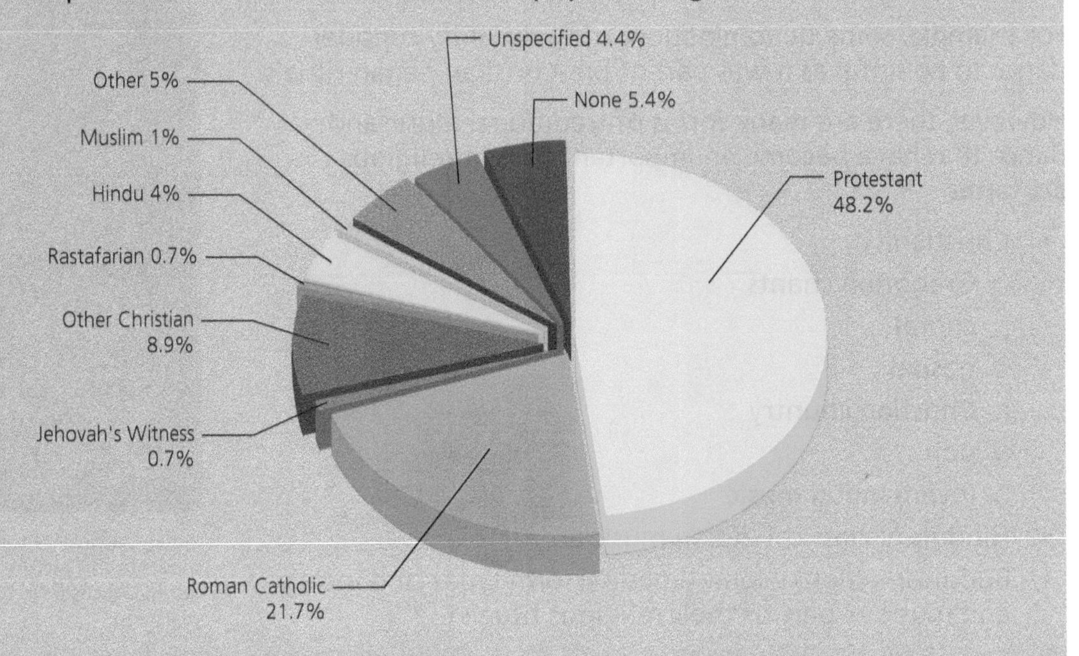

3. What are three popular forms of Protestantism in the Caribbean?
4. Which religion does each of the following belong to?
   a) mass
   b) a Friday night Sabbath meal
   c) a month-long fast
5. The most popular religion in the world is ____________, followed by ____________.
6. List six denominations of Christianity found in the Caribbean.
7. Do a timeline of the history of Hinduism until its arrival in the Caribbean.
8. Which religion is associated with each of the following figures?
   a) the Prophet Muhammad
   b) Moses
   c) Siddhartha Gautama

9. Explain what each of the following symbols represents and which religion it is important to.

a)

b)

c)

10. What does the crescent moon of Islam represent?
11. Explain the relationship between Brahman, Atman and karma. You can draw a diagram to illustrate your answer.
12. Briefly outline the beliefs of the following religions:

    a) Christianity

    b) Hinduism

    c) the Baha'i faith
13. What architectural features can be seen in the following?

    a) Catholic cathedrals

    b) mosques

    c) Hindu and Buddhist temples
14. Explain in your own words, the following terms:

    a) religion

    b) denomination

    c) belief system

    d) secular
15. Explain the main difference between the contributions of Islam and Christianity towards the visual arts.
16. Give two reasons why religion has:

    a) supported the arts

    b) suppressed the arts
17. Research one of the following festivals or rituals:
    - the Jewish festival of Yom Kippur
    - the Jewish festival of Hanukkah

    Create an illustrated poster showing what happens during this festival or ritual, why it is observed and the significance for people who take part.

Checking your progress

To make good progress in understanding religious education, check that you understand these ideas.

- Name the six most popular religions in the world.
- Explain what is meant by the phrase 'belief system'.
- Explain why the Caribbean has so many different religions on our islands.

- Name the denominations of Christianity and outline their beliefs and practices.
- Describe the beliefs and practices of two religions from: Hinduism, Islam, Judaism or Buddhism.
- Explain how the Baha'i and Confucian faiths came to the Caribbean.

- Name the different types of places of worship and the differences between them.
- Explain why it is important to be respectful at places of worship for all faiths.
- Choose three religious symbols and explain what they represent to each faith.

- Describe the relationship between arts and religion.
- Explain how books and stories contribute to the arts and religion.
- Describe how music and dance have contributed to religion.

End-of-term questions

Questions 1–7

See how well you have understood the topics in Unit 4.

1. Explain why rules and regulations are necessary in different environments. Give examples to support your answer.
2. Make a list of four rights and freedoms that you enjoy as a citizen of your country.
3. Write up a list of rules for **a)** home and **b)** school. For each rule explain why the rule should be followed and the consequences of not following the rule.
4. Match these definitions to the words:

   a) laws — **i)** an agreement in which both parties make concessions

   b) conflict — **ii)** agreement

   c) consensus — **iii)** the official rules by which a country is governed

   d) compromise — **iv)** a struggle between two sides with different views
5. Briefly describe the work of an organisation that does humanitarian work.
6. Are human rights always respected? Give an example of an event in which human rights were not respected.
7. Laws are made in a democratic way in your country. Do you agree or disagree with this statement? Explain your answer.

Questions 8–14

See how well you have understood the topics in Unit 5.

8. Explain briefly how the Caribbean became a multicultural society.
9. Why is it important to understand and accept that people have different cultural backgrounds? Write a short paragraph to explain.
10. Write a short essay of six paragraphs in which you mention at least four cultural celebrations that are held in your country or the Caribbean. You should explain why there is a need for these celebrations and what each celebration commemorates.
11. Explain why you think it is important to preserve our cultural heritage. Give at least three examples in your answer of things that you think need to be preserved.
12. Read 5.1.

    a) Draw a pie chart to show the ethnic origins of the students in your class.

    b) Now compare your pie chart with the chart on page 128. Explain what is the same and what is different about the pie charts.
13. Choose a group of people who came to live in your country. Draw a map to show the journeys that these people made in order to reach the islands.
14. Read 5.2 and 5.3. Create a timeline showing:

    a) the first settlers in the Caribbean

    b) European settlers

    c) African settlers

    d) Asian settlers

Questions 15–23

See how well you have understood the topics in Unit 6.

15. Name the religion suggested from the image/symbol below.

16. Name one religious festival linked to this image/symbol.

17. Name one other religious festival celebrated in your country.

18. Select two religions and explain one way in which they are similar and two ways in which they are different. Use the table below:

Religions	One similarity	Two differences
1.	1.	1.
2.		2.

19. You have been recently selected to run a religious youth group. Suggest to young people three ways in which they can become involved in the religious activities of the group.

20. Match each word to its definition:

a) religion	**i)** a set of stories about things
b) belief	**ii)** something that people do to apply a belief
c) practice	**iii)** a system of beliefs and practices
d) belief system	**iv)** something that you believe to be true about the world

21. Hindus believe in a universal soul called __________ . Part of this soul is present in each person, and this individual soul is called __________ . They hope to attain __________ , which means joining with the universal soul.

22. Research one of the following festivals:

- the Buddhist festival of Wesak
- the Sikh festival of Diwali

Create an illustrated poster showing what happens during this festival or ritual, why it is observed and the significance for people who take part.

23. You have created timelines of the history of various religions in this unit. They are:

- Christianity (6.2)
- Hinduism (6.3)
- Islam (6.4)
- Judaism (6.5)
- Buddhism (6.5)
- Sikhism (6.6)

Create one timeline where all of these timelines are combined.

SOCIAL SCIENCES

Unit 7: Caribbean integration and global links

In this unit you will find out

The Caribbean region – our part of the world

- The Caribbean and the rest of the world
  - location of the Caribbean region
- The geography of the Caribbean
  - the natural environment
  - the climate

The Commonwealth Caribbean

- The Commonwealth Caribbean
  - the mother country
  - independent states and dependencies
- Countries of the Commonwealth Caribbean
  - flags of the Commonwealth Caribbean countries
- Physical factors of the Commonwealth Caribbean countries
  - location and climate
  - sea, coastline, freshwater systems
  - forests, mountains and volcanoes
- Social factors of the Commonwealth Caribbean
  - common ancestry
  - languages
  - festivals and sporting events
- Economic factors of the Commonwealth Caribbean
  - agriculture and industry
  - occupations and tourism
- Capitals of the Commonwealth Caribbean countries
- Heads of state and government

The Caribbean and the rest of the world

We are learning to:

- identify the Caribbean region in relation to the rest of the world.

The Caribbean region

The Caribbean region lies near the **continents** of North and South America and near the region that is called Central America.

The Caribbean consists of **island chains** that lie in or around the Caribbean Sea. For example, Cuba, the Cayman Islands, Jamaica, Haiti, the Dominican Republic and Puerto Rico are islands in the chain that is commonly referred to as the Greater Antilles.

The Turks and Caicos Islands are also included in this chain, although they lie in the North Atlantic Ocean and not the Caribbean Sea.

Several **mainland territories** in North and South America, such as Venezuela, are also on the Caribbean Sea and so are considered to be part of the Caribbean.

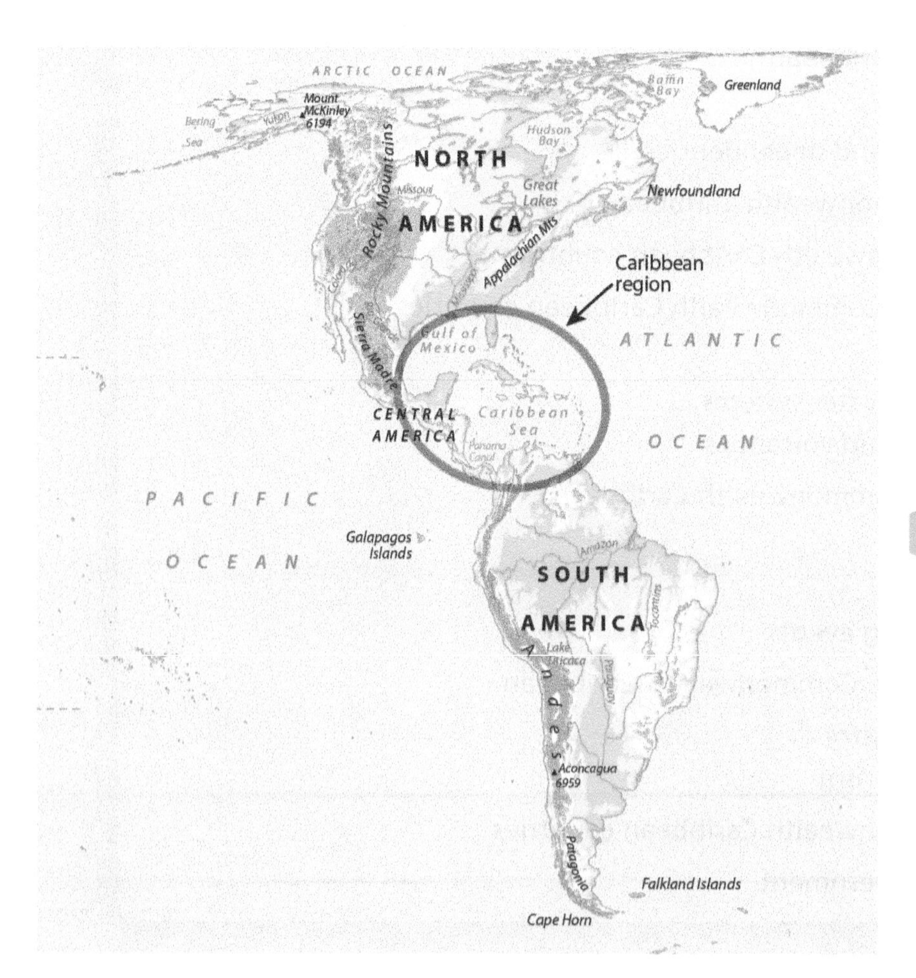

Activity

Your teacher will give you a blank map of the Caribbean. Insert the names of the oceans, seas and chains of islands that you have found. Label your map clearly and neatly. You can also use colours to show the different places on your map.

Exercise

1. Study the maps on these pages and find these places:
   - Atlantic Ocean
   - Pacific Ocean
   - Caribbean Sea
   - North America
   - Central America
   - South America
2. Study the maps and find the following chains of islands:
   - Greater Antilles
   - Leeward Islands
   - Lesser Antilles
   - Windward Islands
3. Find the mainland territories that are part of the Caribbean.

Did you know...?

There are more than 7000 islands in the Caribbean, ranging from big independent nations to small rocky islands that are not inhabited.

Key vocabulary

continents

island chains

mainland territories

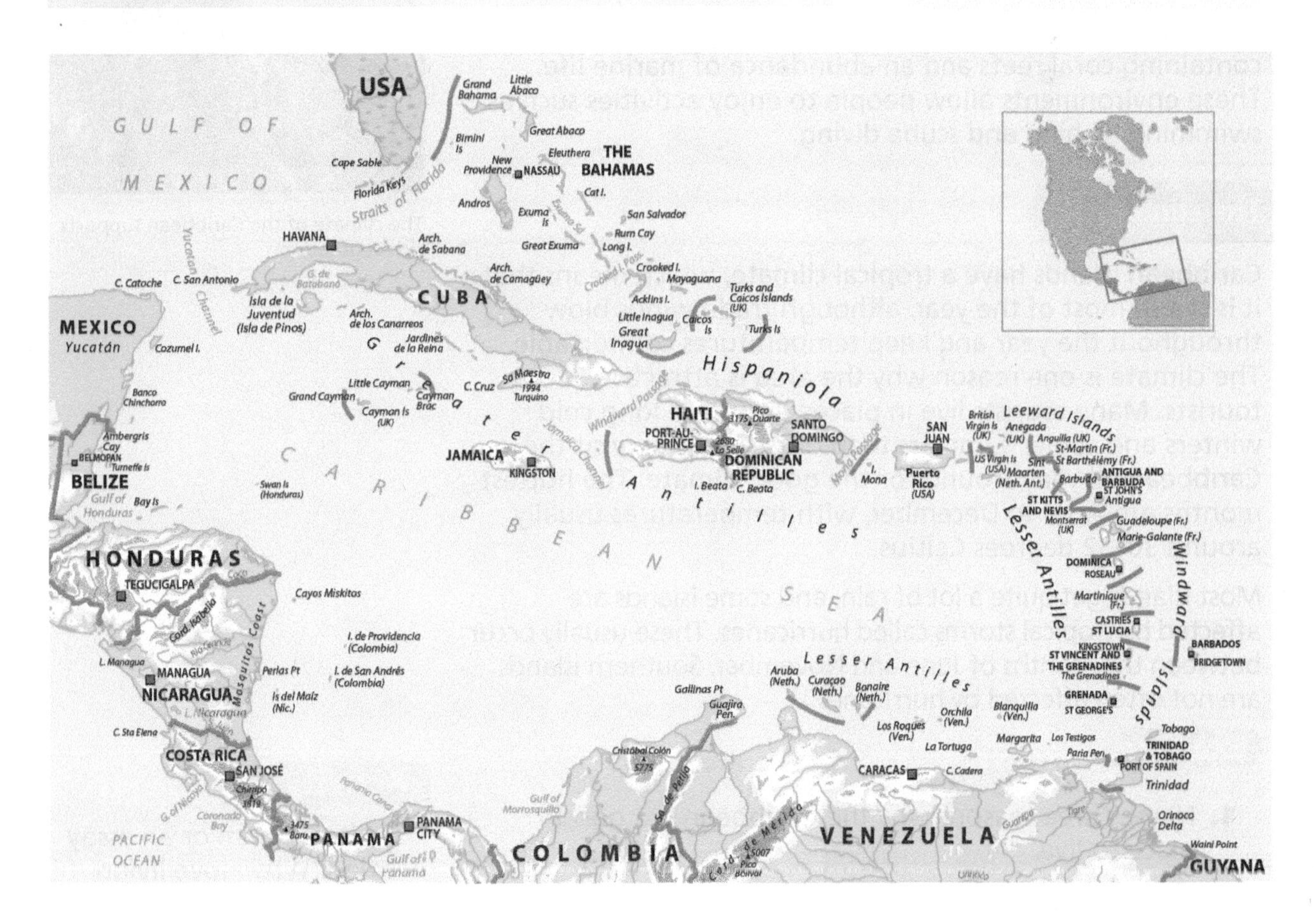

The geography of the Caribbean

We are learning to:

- appreciate the geography of the Caribbean environment
- appreciate the advantages of having a Caribbean climate.

Natural environment

The Caribbean is one of the most beautiful regions of the world, with clear blue oceans, white beaches, and beautiful trees and flowers. This beauty, and the warm and sunny **climate**, make it a very attractive place to live and to visit.

The Caribbean has a varied **natural environment**, from mountains and forests to wetlands and coastlines. There are many species of birds, butterflies and reptiles, as well as different trees, plants and flowers.

Most islands have long beaches surrounded by seas containing coral reefs and an abundance of marine life. These environments allow people to enjoy activities such as swimming, fishing and scuba diving.

The climate of the Caribbean supports rich vegetation.

The climate

Caribbean islands have a tropical climate, which means that it is warm most of the year, although trade winds blow throughout the year and keep temperatures comfortable. The climate is one reason why the area is attractive to tourists. Many tourists live in places that have long cold winters and cooler summers than ours. They can visit the Caribbean all year around for the good climate. The hottest months are April to December, with temperatures usually around 30–32 degrees Celsius.

Most islands get quite a lot of rain, and some islands are affected by tropical storms called hurricanes. These usually occur between the months of June and November. Southern islands are not often affected by hurricanes.

Exercise

1. Name three reasons why the Caribbean is a good place to live.
2. Why are tourists attracted to the Caribbean? Give three reasons.
3. To which types of activity is the climate of the Caribbean particularly suited?

Activity

Write a poem or an essay titled 'Why I love living in the Caribbean region'.

Case study

The Fringe of the Sea

by A. L. Hendricks

Read this poem by a man who lived in Jamaica for many years.

agile:	moving quickly
undulate:	move up and down like waves
saunter:	walk in a slow and relaxed manner
assaying:	testing
consummate:	with great skill
decorous:	polite and in good taste

We do not like to awaken
far from the fringe of the sea,
we who live upon small islands.

We like to rise up early,
quick in the agile mornings
and walk out only little distances
to look down at the water,
to know it is swaying near to us
with songs, and tides, and endless boatways,
and undulate patterns and moods.

We want to be able to saunter beside it
slowpaced in burning sunlight,
bare-armed, barefoot, bareheaded,
and to stoop down by the shallows
sifting the random water
between assaying fingers
like farmers do with soil,

and to think of turquoise mackerel
turning with consummate grace,
sleek and decorous
and elegant in high blue chambers.

We want to be able to walk out into it,
to work in it,
dive and swim and play in it,
to row and sail
and pilot over its sandless highways,
and to hear
its call and murmurs wherever we may be.

All who have lived upon small islands
want to sleep and awaken
close to the fringe of the sea.

From *Under the Moon and Over the Sea – A Collection of Caribbean Poems* published by Walker Books, ISBN 978 1 4963 3448 7.

Questions

1. What did the poet enjoy about living in the Caribbean?
2. What do the words in blue say about what it is like to live in the Caribbean?

This beach in Tobago is typical of the natural environment of the Caribbean that makes it so attractive to inhabitants and visitors.

Discussion

In groups, discuss what you enjoy (or do not enjoy) about living in the Caribbean. Focus on the climate and the natural environment in your discussions.

Key vocabulary

climate

natural environment

The Commonwealth Caribbean

We are learning to:

- explain the terms colony, mother country, independent state, dependencies
- explain what is meant by Commonwealth Caribbean.

Colony and mother country

The islands of the Caribbean have different types of government and many of the islands have kept strong links with former colonial powers. A **colony** is a country or an area that is acquired and controlled by another country, which is called the **mother country**.

Between the 16th and 19th centuries, European powers including Britain, Spain and France established colonies in Asia, Africa and the Americas.

The mother countries exploited the natural resources of the colonies to build up empires and strengthen their own economies. Settlers took land away from the local inhabitants. The Spanish mother country took land from the Amerindians when islands such as Trinidad were Spanish colonies.

A view of Saint Lucia with the Petit Piton in the background.

Independent states and dependencies

Some countries, such as Dominica and Trinidad and Saint Lucia, are **independent states**. They elect their own governments and make their own laws. Other, smaller islands, including Anguilla and the Cayman Islands, are **dependencies** of Britain.

These islands have their own parliaments and they govern themselves, but they are dependent in certain areas. For example, Britain is responsible for the defence of Anguilla, and Queen Elizabeth II is the head of state. British dependencies are called British Overseas Territories.

Did you know...?

The Commonwealth Caribbean is made up of:

Anguilla
Antigua and Barbuda
The Bahamas
Barbados
Belize
British Virgin Islands
Dominica
Grenada
Guyana
Jamaica
Montserrat
Saint Kitts and Nevis
Saint Lucia
Saint Vincent and the Grenadines
Trinidad and Tobago
Turks and Caicos

Exercise

1. Write your own definitions of 'colony', 'mother country', 'independent state' and 'dependencies'. Use a dictionary or the internet to help you.

Research

Read the list of Caribbean states opposite. Do your own research to find out which are independent countries and which are dependencies. Present your answer in the form of a table.

Commonwealth

Commonwealth is a word used to describe a group of countries that work together and help each other. The Commonwealth of Nations, or 'The Commonwealth' as it is usually called, is an association of independent countries that used to form part of the British Empire.

Tourists shopping at a market on a beach in Anguilla.

Commonwealth Caribbean

The **Commonwealth Caribbean** (see page 183 for a list) is a group of English-speaking countries in the Caribbean that used to be part of the British Empire or that are still dependencies of Britain. These countries were referred to as the British West Indies in the past.

The Commonwealth Caribbean countries are very different in size, income, political status and population, but they have close social and political links.

Many of the islands have experienced similar histories. For example, sugar plantations were set up on many of the islands, and enslaved people and indentured labourers were brought in to work on those plantations. When the sugar industry collapsed, the islands had to transform and find other economic activities.

Today, most of the islands have well-developed tourist industries. The people who live in the Commonwealth Caribbean enjoy many common sporting and cultural events.

Did you know...?

The first independent state in the Caribbean was Haiti, which became independent from France in 1804. It is one of the oldest republics in the western hemisphere.

Exercise

1. Complete these sentences:
   a) A ______ is a country or area that is controlled by another country.
   b) _____ countries sent people to settle in the places that they colonised.
   c) Dominica elects its own government and makes its own laws. It is therefore an __________ state.
   d) Anguilla is a British Overseas Territory or a __________ of Britain.
   e) Colonial powers _________ the natural resources of the colonies that they acquired.
2. Write a paragraph in which you explain in your own words what is meant by the term 'Commonwealth Caribbean'.

Key vocabulary

colony

mother country

independent state

dependency

Commonwealth

Commonwealth Caribbean

Countries of the Commonwealth Caribbean

We are learning to:

- identify the countries of the Commonwealth Caribbean
- research the flags of the Commonwealth countries.

The Commonwealth Caribbean

The term Commonwealth Caribbean is used to refer to the independent English-speaking islands and **dependent** and mainland **territories** around the Caribbean Sea. It is made up of the countries listed on the opposite page.

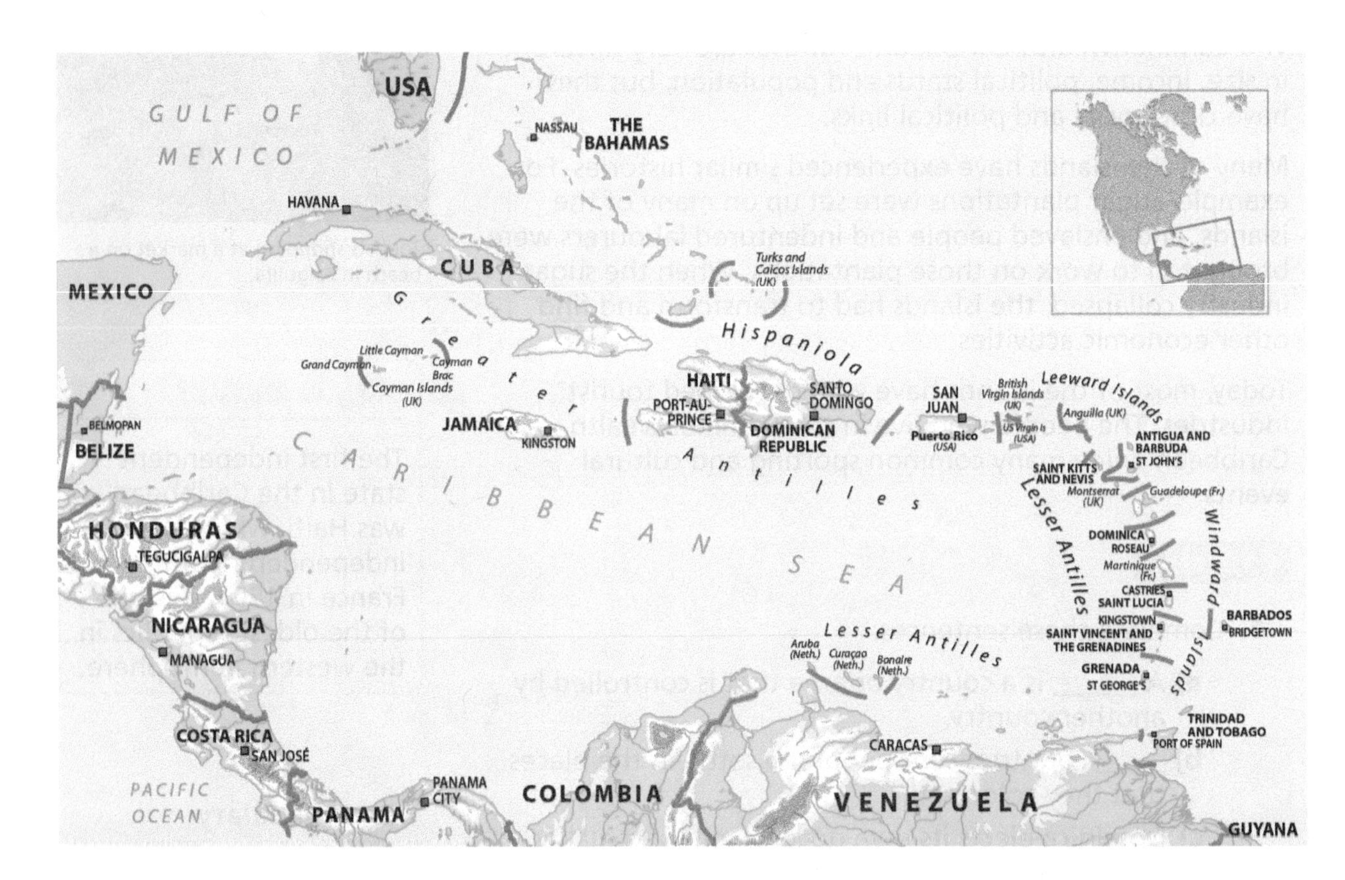

Exercise

1. Find the countries listed on the opposite page on the map above.
2. Are all the countries islands?
3. Of which island chain or mainland is each country a part?
4. Make a map of the Caribbean and use a key to show which countries are part of the Commonwealth Caribbean. Identify also the dependent territories.

Flags of the Commonwealth Caribbean countries and British Overseas Territories

7.4

Each Commonwealth Caribbean country has its own flag. They are shown below.

*Anguilla		*Cayman Islands		Saint Kitts and Nevis	
Antigua and Barbuda		Dominica	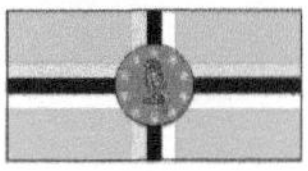	Saint Lucia	
The Bahamas		Grenada		Saint Vincent and the Grenadines	
Barbados		Guyana	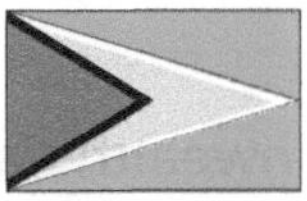	Trinidad and Tobago	
Belize	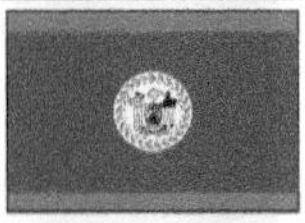	Jamaica	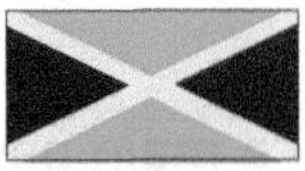	*Turks and Caicos	
*British Virgin Islands		*Montserrat			

*British Overseas Territory

Research

Look at the flags in the table above. Find the flag which belongs to your country and research its history, what the symbols on the flag represent and where in your country it is flown. Write 100–150 words and use cut-out photographs or drawings to illustrate your research.

Exercise

5. Work in pairs. Study the flags in the tables above.

a) Identify the flags of the dependent countries. How do you know they are dependent? Name their mother country.

b) Why do you think many of these countries have the colour blue on their flags? What could the colour represent?

c) Which other colours are commonly used on flags? Do your own research and find out what these colours represent and why they are used.

d) Which flag do you like the best? Give a reason for your answer.

Project

Work in groups.
Create a poster or a PowerPoint presentation of the flags of all the Commonwealth Caribbean countries.

Identify each flag clearly and find some interesting information about some of the flags to add to your presentation. For example, look out for flags that have similar colours or symbols on them and find why these colours and symbols have been used.

Key vocabulary

dependent territory

Physical factors of the Commonwealth Caribbean

We are learning to:

- identify the physical characteristics that link the Commonwealth Caribbean countries
- appreciate the similarities and differences between two countries in the Commonwealth Caribbean.

Many areas of the Caribbean have a similar physical appearance and climate.

Location

The first factor that binds Commonwealth Caribbean countries is their **location**. All the countries are situated in and around the Caribbean Sea.

This area has for a long time been a main passageway for ships moving between different continents. As a result, Caribbean islands were among the first to be colonised.

The geographical location of the islands also makes the islands prone to natural disasters like hurricanes, which cause a lot of damage.

Most islands in the Caribbean have similar uneven coastlines with bays, inlets and beaches.

Climate

All of the islands share a **tropical climate** with average annual temperatures of around 25 degrees Celsius. The amount of rainfall is not the same on all the islands.

The islands to the north tend to be drier than the islands to the south. In countries like Jamaica, the rainfall in the mountainous areas is much higher than in the coastal areas.

Discussion

Why do you think most people in these countries live near the coast?

The sea and coastline

All of the countries border on the Caribbean Sea and some countries, such as the Bahamas, also border on the Atlantic Ocean.

The Caribbean Sea is one of the largest saltwater areas in the world. The temperature of the sea is quite warm and averages between 21 and 30 degrees Celsius during the year.

The coastlines of the countries have similar **physical features** as most have many natural harbours, bays, beaches, mangroves, cays and coral reefs. Most of the people in these countries live near the coast.

Did you know...?

Trinidad and Tobago are the southernmost islands of the Caribbean archipelago, and are geologically an extension of the South American continent.

Freshwater systems

Unlike countries on the mainland continents of North and South America, the islands of the Caribbean have only a few **freshwater** lakes and short rivers. Many of the rivers dry up in summer. Many of the islands have waterfalls.

Forests, mountains and volcanoes

Many of the islands have active volcanoes and ongoing seismic activity, which causes earthquakes. There are active volcanoes on Saint Lucia, Dominica, Grenada, Montserrat and Saint Vincent.

There are big mountain ranges such as the Blue Mountains in Jamaica and the Central Range of mountains in Trinidad. There are also forests such as the Main Ridge Forest in Tobago and the limestone forests of the John Crow Mountains in Jamaica.

There are active volcanoes in the Caribbean – this one erupting is on Montserrat.

Project: Similarities and differences (Part 1)

Work in groups. With the help of your teacher, choose two countries that are part of the Commonwealth Caribbean. You are going to research these countries and compare them to understand what is similar and different in them both. In part 1 of this project, you will compare the physical features of the two countries. Here are some steps that you could follow:

- Brainstorm a list of features to compare.
- Allocate research tasks to each member of the group.
- Complete your research. Make notes and collect pictures.
- Meet as a group and discuss what you have found out.
- Discuss how you will present your information.

Keep your work in a safe place until the next part of the project.

Discussion

What impact do you think the location of the Commonwealth Caribbean countries has had on the history of the countries? Are there similarities?

Exercise

1. Name three physical features that the countries of the Commonwealth Caribbean share.
2. In what ways is the climate similar in the Caribbean countries?
3. In which countries can you see volcanoes?
4. In which countries can you see long mountain ranges and forests? Give examples of each.
5. Do you think the supply of fresh drinking water could be a problem in the Caribbean? Support your answer.

Key vocabulary

location

tropical climate

physical features

freshwater

Social factors of the Commonwealth Caribbean

We are learning to:

- identify the social characteristics that link the Commonwealth Caribbean countries
- appreciate the similarities and differences between two countries in the Commonwealth Caribbean.

The common history of the Commonwealth Caribbean has resulted in many **social links** between the people of these countries.

Common ancestry

Many people in the Caribbean have a common **ancestry**. For example, it is estimated that more than 2.5 million people in the whole Caribbean region have their roots in India.

This is as a result of East Indian people coming to work in the Caribbean sugar plantations as indentured labourers after the abolition of slavery. These workers brought their families to the Caribbean and they played an important part in the economic development of countries in the region.

Countries like Barbados, Saint Kitts, Antigua, Saint Lucia, Dominica and Jamaica had huge sugar plantations and these plantations relied on enslaved people's labour.

The enslaved people came mostly from West Africa. No one knows exactly how many people were brought from Africa to the Americas, but some people estimate that there were as many as 12 million of them. About 40 per cent of these enslaved people came to work in Caribbean countries.

The CARICOM logo consists of two interlocking C's in the form of broken links in a chain, symbolising both unity and the break with the region's colonial past.

Languages

All of the Commonwealth Caribbean countries were formerly part of the British Empire. English has become the official language in all the countries. It is taught in schools and everyone speaks English, although many other languages are also spoken.

Many **immigrant** communities speak their home language among themselves, although they use English for communicating with people outside their communities.

Did you know...?

Organisations like CARICOM promote social and economic links between all the countries in the Caribbean.

Exercise

1. Why are there many different cultural groups in the Caribbean?

Festivals

The **immigrants** who came from India, China, Africa and Europe brought with them festivals and traditions. Many of these continue today and link people across the islands. For example, the East Indians who came to live in Trinidad and Tobago were allowed to practise their Hindu religion and celebrate religious festivals such as Diwali.

People from other cultural groups have been allowed to participate in these festivals too and this has encouraged respect and tolerance between people in the country.

Sporting events

Sporting events are a strong social link between people in the Caribbean. Sportsmen and -women from Commonwealth Caribbean countries compete against each other regularly and also play together in teams against other countries.

The West Indian cricket team, also known as the 'Windies', is a multi-national team made up of players from mostly English-speaking countries of the Caribbean. Athletes from Commonwealth Caribbean countries have shown a great talent for track events such as the 100- and 200-metre running races.

The West Indies celebrate after taking an Australian wicket during a T20 match in Saint Lucia, 27 March 2012.

Project: Similarities and differences (Part 2)

As part 2 of this project, you will compare the social links between the two countries you have chosen. Look at the headings used on these two pages and use them as a starting point for your research.

- Allocate research tasks to each member of the group.
- Make notes, collect pictures and complete your research.
- Meet in groups and discuss what you have found out.
- Discuss how you will present your information.
- Keep your work in a safe place until you are ready to complete the next part of the project.

Discussion

How do you think a language can bind people together? In what ways can it help people get along better? Is it just easier to communicate with each other? Does it make you feel part of the same group?

Exercise

2. What would some citizens of Saint Kitts have in common with some citizens of Trinidad and Tobago today?
3. Pick one the festivals that happens in Trinidad and Tobago. Write a page about the origin of the festival, when it occurs and what happens there.
4. Which major economic development caused the biggest change in the population of the Caribbean?

Key vocabulary

social links

ancestry

immigrant

Economic factors of the Commonwealth Caribbean

We are learning to:

- identify common economic characteristics in the Commonwealth Caribbean countries
- appreciate the similarities and differences between two countries in the Commonwealth Caribbean.

Agricultural activities

Many **economic factors** link the Commonwealth Caribbean countries. Most of the countries are members of a wider association of Caribbean countries, called CARICOM. CARICOM promotes trade between the countries of the Caribbean.

Most Commonwealth Caribbean countries produce sugar cane, tobacco, coffee, cacao, fruits and vegetables. As a result of trade agreements between countries, they can trade **agricultural** products freely between the islands. They also work together to export their crops to other places such as the USA and Europe. Trade therefore binds and links the countries to each other.

Industries

Industries on the islands are wide-ranging and different. Trinidad and Tobago has well-developed petrochemical industries because of the petroleum and **natural gas** resources in the country. Jamaica has **manufacturing** industries such as metals, textiles and paper. Barbados has a **service industry** that includes tourism, and that accounts for most of the country's income.

Occupations

Employment varies from country to country depending on the main economic activity. In some countries most people work in agriculture. In other countries, where tourism is the main source of income, most people are employed in **services**. Citizens of **CARICOM** countries can move around and work in any CARICOM country and this promotes links between them.

Exercise

1. Name the three economic factors that link the Commonwealth Caribbean countries.
2. Name two industries that have developed in Trinidad and Tobago.

Did you know...?

CARICOM has 15 main members:

Antigua and Barbuda

The Bahamas

Barbados

Belize

Dominica

Grenada

Guyana

Haiti

Jamaica

Montserrat

Saint Kitts and Nevis

Saint Lucia

Saint Vincent and the Grenadines

Suriname

Trinidad and Tobago

Did you know...?

Commonwealth Caribbean countries also work together on environmental programmes to protect the region and preserve it for the future.

Case study

Tourism links the countries of the Caribbean. Most countries have well-developed tourist industries. Tourists usually visit more than one country at a time, so they take boats and aeroplanes to move between them. Cruise ships are an important feature of tourism in the Caribbean.

Study this map, which shows the main routes of tourist cruise ships in the Caribbean.

Questions

1. Which Commonwealth Caribbean countries lie on the cruise ship routes?
2. Which Commonwealth Caribbean countries benefit most from tourism?

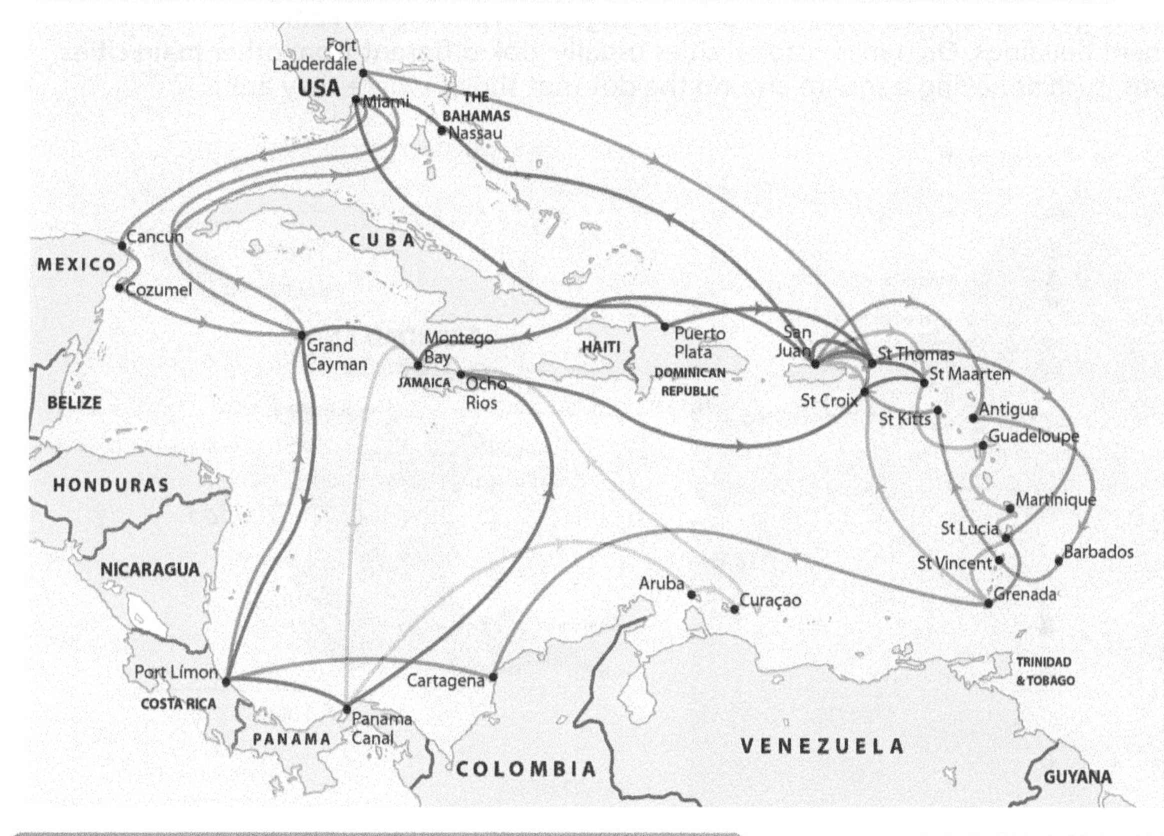

Project: Similarities and differences (Part 3)

Working in your groups, complete your projects by researching and comparing economic factors that are similar and different in the two countries you have chosen. Add this information to the first two parts of the project that you have already completed. Remember to:

- allocate research tasks to each member of the group
- make notes and collect pictures
- discuss what you have found out.

Once your project is complete, present your work to the rest of the class in a group presentation. Display your work in school afterwards for others to read and enjoy.

Key vocabulary

economic factors
agricultural
industries
natural gas
manufacturing
service industry
services
CARICOM

Capitals of the Commonwealth Caribbean (1)

We are learning to:

- identify and find main cities, towns and capitals of Commonwealth Caribbean countries and British Overseas Territories.

Trinidad and Tobago and Guyana

All states have capital cities. A **capital city** is the city from which the government rules a country. The government sits (works) in this city together with the parliament and other government buildings. On a map, capital cities usually look different from other **main cities** and **towns**, such as having a square around the dot that shows where they are.

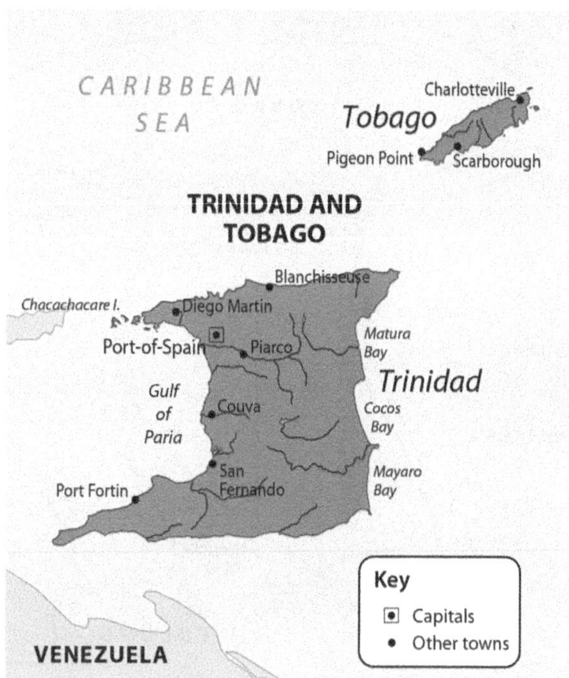

Exercise

1. Work with a partner. Study the maps and find these places:
   a) The capital cities of Trinidad and Tobago and Guyana
   b) The names of two other towns or cities in Trinidad
   c) A town in the north of Tobago
   d) The names of two other towns or cities in Guyana
   e) The name of the sea that surrounds Trinidad and Tobago
2. Your teacher will give you blank maps. Fill in the names of the capital cities and the other main cities and towns you have found on the blank maps.

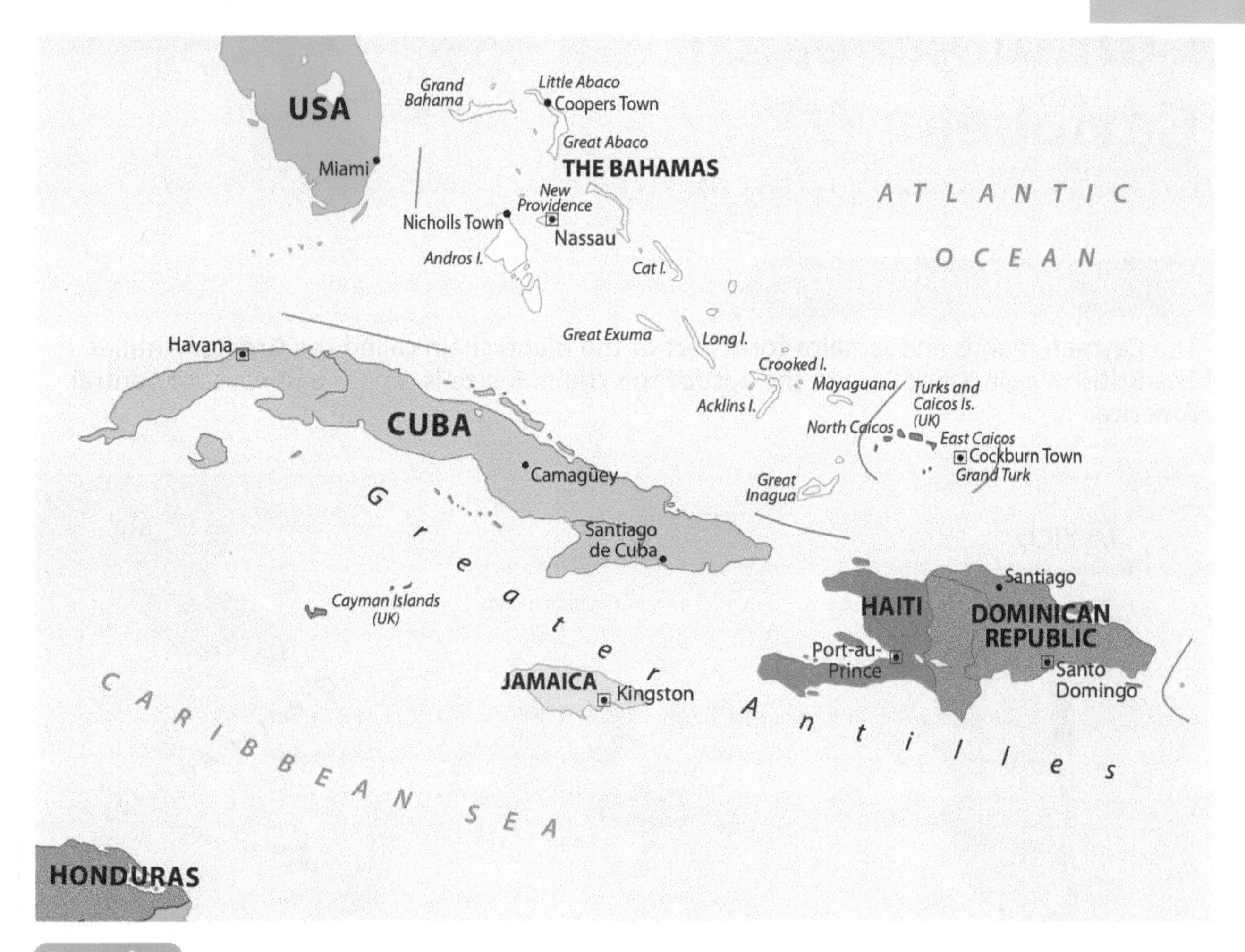

Exercise

3. Work with a partner. Study the map or any other wall map or globe you have in the classroom. Then say if these statements are true or false. Correct the false statements.
   a) Nassau is the capital city of the Bahamas and it is on the island of Grand Bahama.
   b) Cooper's Town is a city on the island of Great Abaco in the Bahamas.
   c) Cockburn Town is the capital of Turks and Caicos. It is on the island of Grand Turk.
   d) Nicholls Town is on the island of Andros in the Bahamas.
   e) The Bahamas is southwest of the United States.
4. Your teacher will give you blank maps. Fill in the names of the capital cities as well as the other main cities and towns you have found on the blank maps.

Key vocabulary

capital city

main city

town

Capitals of the Commonwealth Caribbean (2)

We are learning to:

- identify and find main cities, towns and capitals on a map of Commonwealth Caribbean countries and British Overseas Territories.

Cayman Islands, Jamaica, Belize

The Cayman Islands and Jamaica form part of the island chain called the Greater Antilles. The British Virgin Islands are to the east of this chain. Belize is on the east coast of Central America.

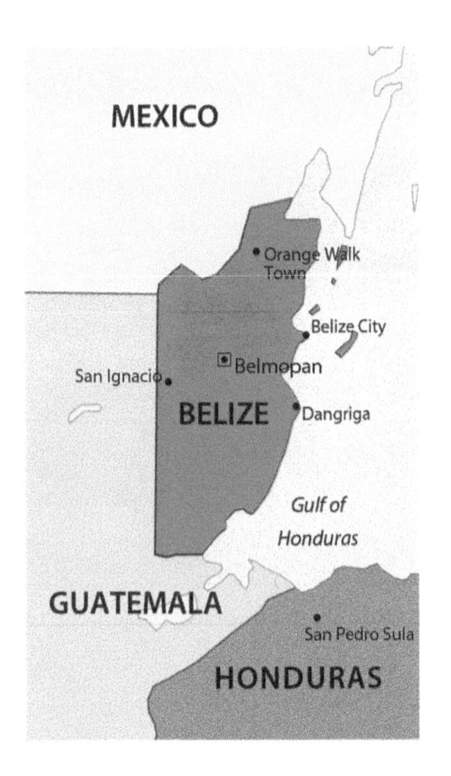

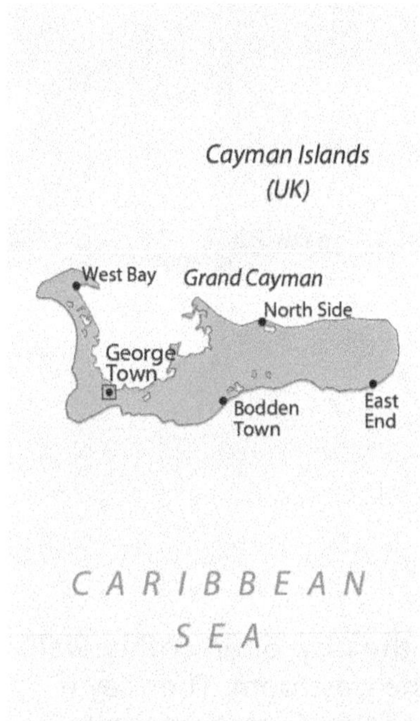

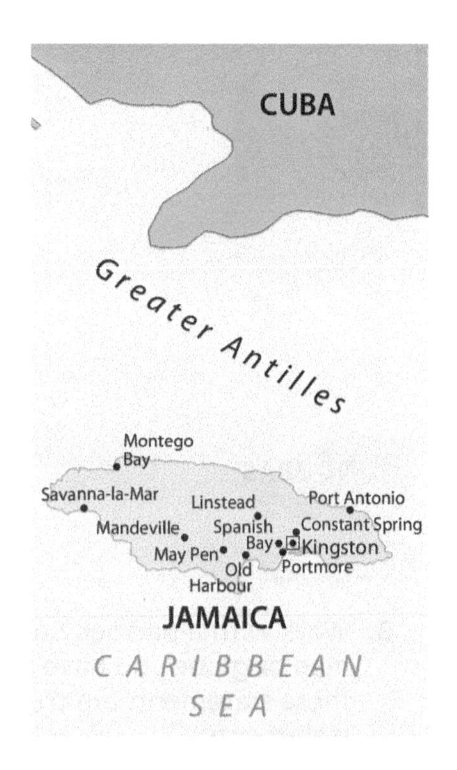

Exercise

1. Work with a partner. Study the maps and find these places:
   a) the capital cities of the Cayman Islands, Jamaica and Belize
   b) the names of two other towns in the Cayman Islands
   c) names of two other countries to the west of Belize
   d) the names of four towns or cities in Jamaica
   e) the name of a town that is on the coast of Belize
2. Your teacher will give you blank maps. Fill in the names of the capital cities as well as the other main cities and towns you have found on the blank maps.

The Leeward Islands

The British Virgin Islands, Anguilla, Dominica, Saint Kitts and Nevis, Antigua and Barbuda, and Montserrat form part of a group of islands often referred to as the Leeward Islands.

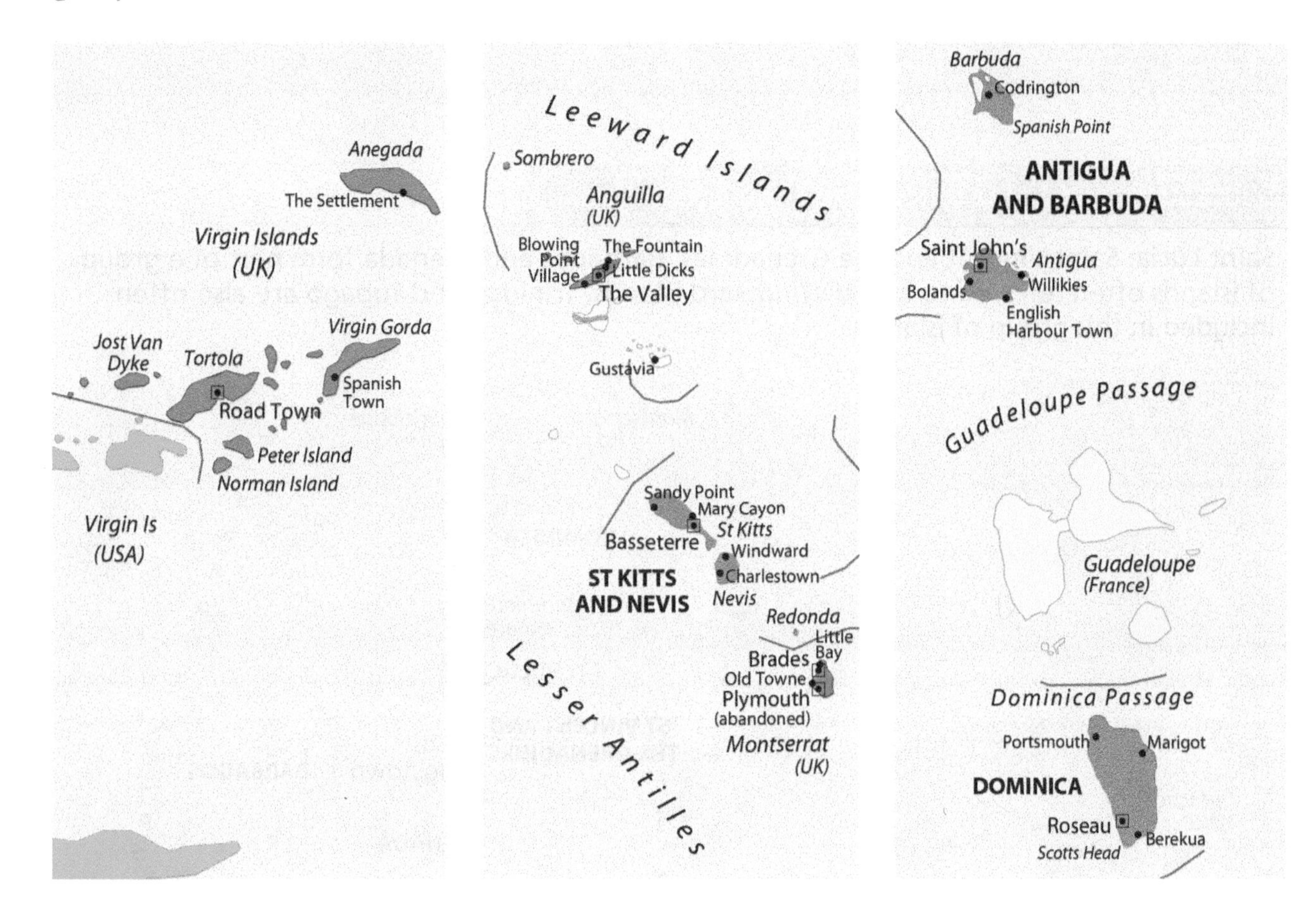

Exercise

3. Work with a partner. Study the map or any other wall map or globe you have in the classroom and then copy and complete this table of information about the maps.

Country	Capital city	Other towns
British Virgin Islands		
		Old Town
	Basseterre	
Anguilla		
Dominica		

4. Your teacher will give you blank maps. Fill in the names of the capital cities as well as the other main cities and towns you have found on the blank maps.

Capitals of the Commonwealth Caribbean (3)

We are learning to:

- identify and find main cities, towns and capitals of Commonwealth Caribbean countries and British Overseas Territories.

Saint Lucia and Saint Vincent and the Grenadines

Saint Lucia, Saint Vincent and the Grenadines, Barbados and Grenada form part of a group of islands often referred to as the Windward Islands. Trinidad and Tobago are also often included in this group of islands.

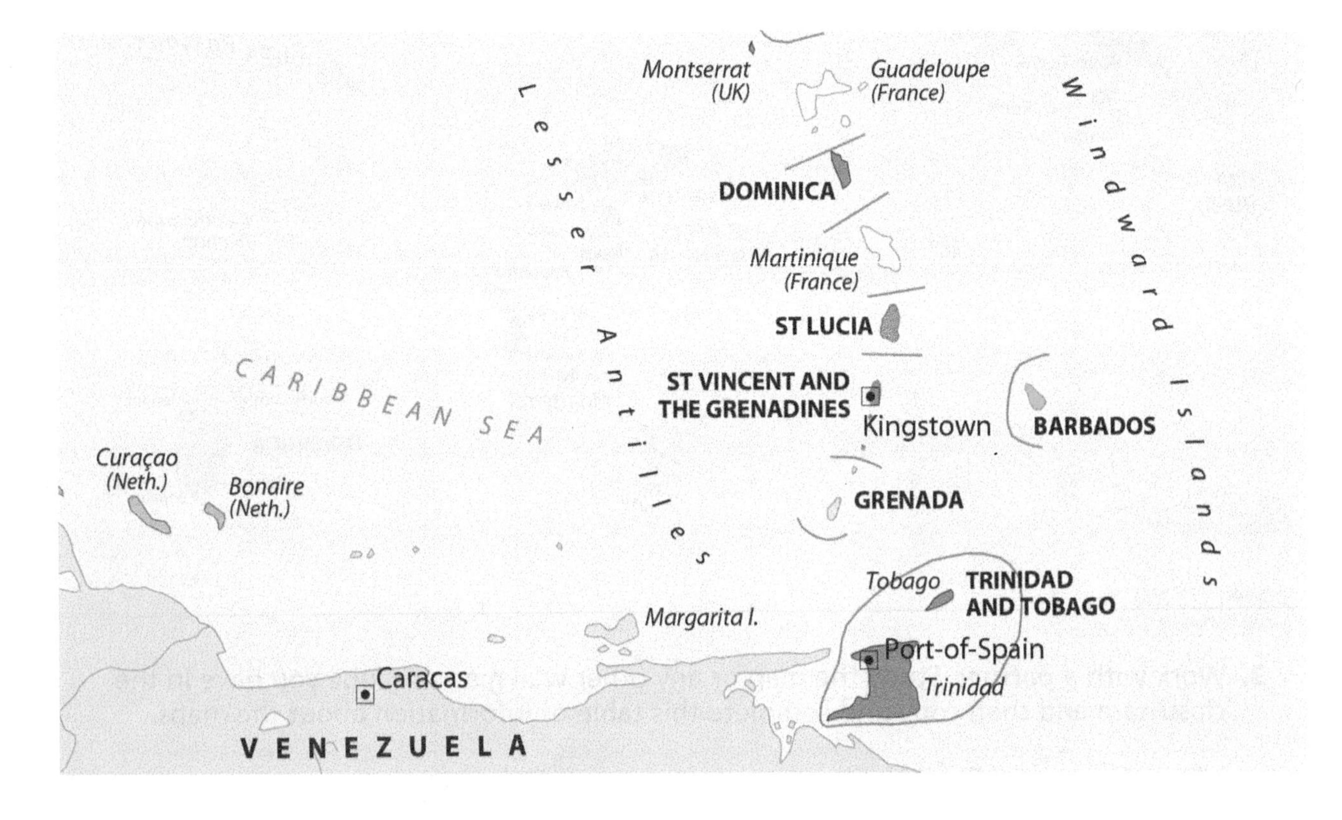

Exercise

1. Work with a partner. Study the maps on both pages or any other wall map or globe you have in the classroom and then complete these sentences.
   a) Saint Lucia and Saint Vincent and the Grenadines are part of a group of islands called the __________.
   b) Saint Vincent and the Grenadines lie to the __________ of Saint Lucia. The capital city is __________.
2. Your teacher will give you blank maps. Fill in the names of the capital cities as well as the other main cities and towns you have found on the blank maps.

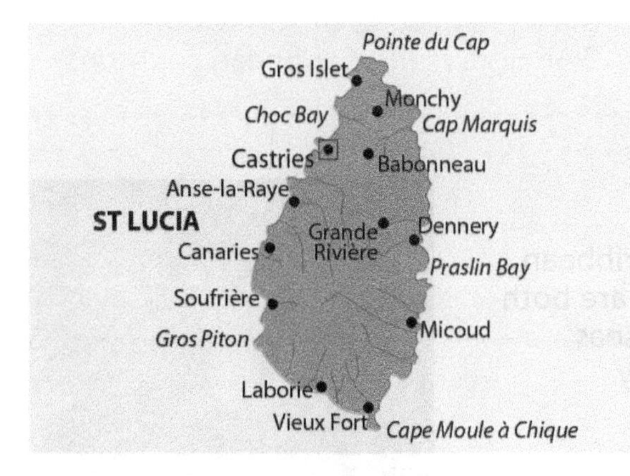

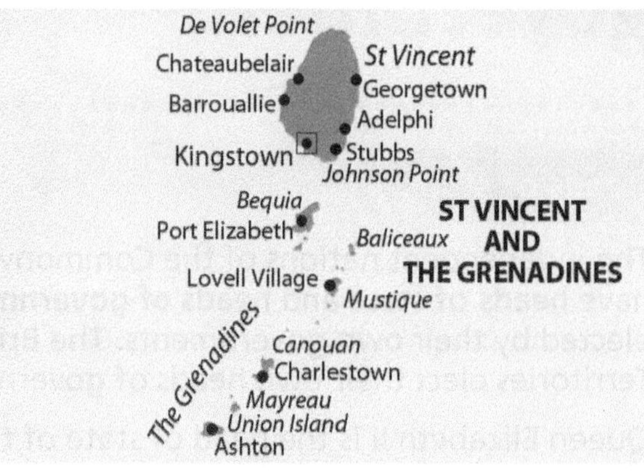

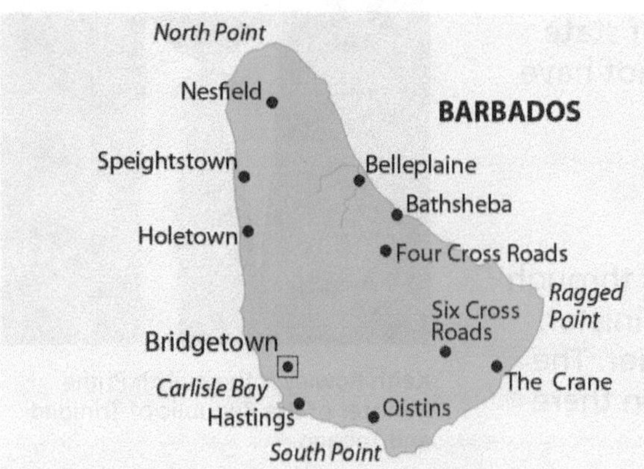

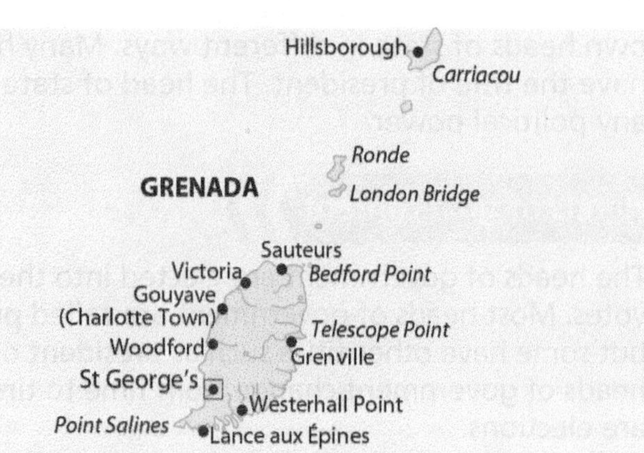

Project

Make a brochure about one of the countries in the Commonwealth Caribbean. Use the information you have already collected and the maps in this book. Collect pictures of the country too. Include a short fact sheet and a short essay about the country in your brochure.

Exercise

3. Work with a partner. Study the maps on both pages or any other wall map or globe you have in the classroom and then complete these sentences:

a) The capital city of Barbados is ____________ and the capital city of Grenada is_______.

b) _____ and ______ are other main cities or towns on Grenada.

c) _____ and ______ are other main cities or towns on Barbados.

d) Barbados lies to the _______ of Saint Vincent and the Grenadines and _______ of Tobago.

Activity

Work alone and write an essay of about 150 words on this topic:

Why is the term Commonwealth Caribbean used?

Explain what the name refers to, which countries are members and what it means to be part of this organisation.

Heads of state and government

We are learning to:

- name the head of government and the head of state of each of the Commonwealth Caribbean countries.

Heads of state

The independent nations of the Commonwealth Caribbean have **heads of state** and **heads of government** who are both elected by their own governments. The British Overseas Territories elect their own heads of government only.

Queen Elizabeth II is the head of state of the British Overseas Territories. The **independent** nations choose their own heads of state in different ways. Many heads of state have the title of president. The head of state does not have any political power.

Keith Rowley is the eighth Prime Minister of the Republic of Trinidad and Tobago.

Heads of government

The heads of government are elected into their roles through votes. Most heads of government are called **prime minister**, but some have other titles such as **president** or **premier**. The heads of government change from time to time when there are elections.

Exercise

1. Work in pairs and ask each other questions about the list of heads of government. For example: Who is the head of government of Saint Lucia? What is his/her name or title? Are there any women who are heads of government?
2. Then research the list of heads of government. Have any of these leaders changed in recent years? Why have they changed?
3. Work in groups. Each member of each group role-plays a head of government of one of the Commonwealth Caribbean states. Role-play a meeting between these leaders. Introduce yourselves and use the knowledge that you have collected about the nations to mention an issue that you would like to discuss at your meeting. For example, you may want to discuss tourism or trade between nations.
4. Work in groups and compile a list of the heads of state of all the Commonwealth Caribbean nations. Your list should include the titles of the heads of state.

Saint Vincent and the Grenadines' Prime Minister Ralph Gonsalves with Pope Francis in 2013.

The head of government and the head of state of each of the Commonwealth Caribbean nations are listed below. Their title and the status of each country is also listed.

Nation	Head of government	Title	Status
Anguilla	Victor Banks	Chief Minister	Dependent territory (UK)
Antigua and Barbuda	Gaston Browne	Prime Minister	Independent
The Bahamas	Hubert Minnis	Prime Minister	Independent
Barbados	Freunde Stuart	Prime Minister	Independent
Belize	Dean Barrow	Prime Minister	Independent
British Virgin Islands	Orlando Smith	Premier	Dependent territory (UK)
Cayman Islands	Aiden McLaughlin	Premier	Dependent territory (UK)
Dominica	Roosevelt Skerrit	Prime Minister	Independent
Grenada	Keith Mitchell	Prime Minister	Independent
Guyana	David Granger	President	Independent/ Mainland Caribbean
Haiti	Jovenel Moïse	President	Principal country and territory
Jamaica	Andrew Holness	Prime Minister	Independent
Montserrat	Donaldson Romeo	Premier	Dependent territory (UK)
Saint Kitts and Nevis	Timothy Harris	Prime Minister	Independent
Saint Lucia	Allen Chastanet	Prime Minister	Independent
Saint Vincent and the Grenadines	Ralph Gonsalves	Prime Minister	Independent
Trinidad and Tobago	Keith Rowley	Prime Minister	Independent
Turks and Caicos	Sharlene Cartwright-Robinson	Premier	Dependent territory (UK)

(Key: Green highlight = CARICOM Member States; Blue = CARICOM Associate Member States)

Key vocabulary

head of state

head of government

independent

prime minister

president

premier

Questions

See how well you have understood the topics in this unit.

1. Identify the Caribbean islands numbered 1–11 on this map.

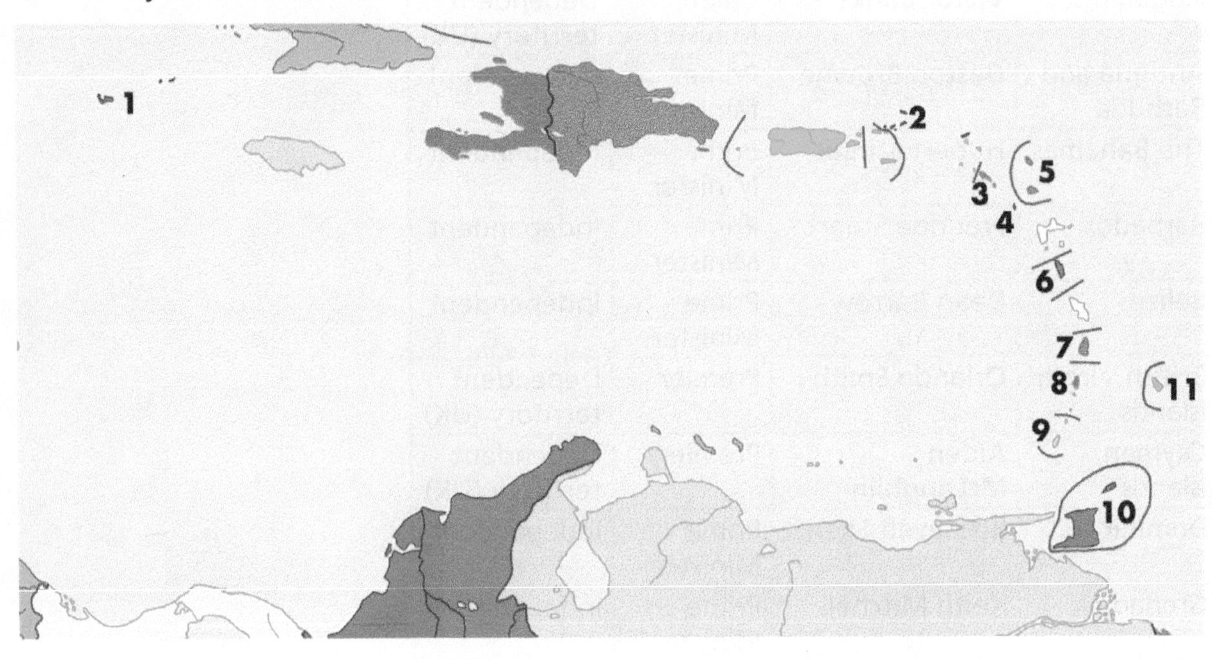

2. The ________ is an association of independent countries that used to form part of the British Empire.
   a) Caribbean
   b) Commonwealth
   c) Commonwealth Caribbean
   d) CARICOM
3. Which two words best describe the climate of the Caribbean?
   a) dry
   b) warm
   c) cold
   d) sunny
4. ________ is one of the most important links between the countries of the Caribbean.
   a) Tax
   c) Language
   b) Industry
   d) Trade
5. True or false? There are active volcanoes on Saint Lucia, Dominica, Grenada and Saint Vincent.

6. Complete this sentence:

   The Greater Antilles is a chain of ________ in the Caribbean.

7. True or false? All the countries in the Caribbean are islands.

8. Why do most people in the Caribbean live near the coast? Give three reasons.

9. Do you agree or disagree with this statement? Explain your answer:

   The natural environment and climate of the Caribbean make it ideal for tourism.

10. Give three reasons why there are links between the Commonwealth Caribbean countries.

11. What is the difference between the independent countries and the dependencies in the Commonwealth Caribbean?

12. Without looking, name as many of the 15 CARICOM members as you can.

13. Name three common economic characteristics that the Commonwealth Caribbean countries share.

14. Explain in your own words, the following terms:

    a) mother country

    b) independent state

    c) Commonwealth Caribbean

15. Name the head of government of your country and explain what that person's role is.

Checking your progress

To make good progress in understanding Caribbean integration and global links, check that you understand these ideas.

Name four island chains in the Caribbean.	Explain why the Caribbean has a climate that makes it a good place to live in and visit.	Explain and use correctly the term 'Commonwealth Caribbean'.
Name all the countries in the Commonwealth Caribbean.	Name five physical factors of the Caribbean Commonwealth.	Choose one of these physical factors and compare them between two Commonwealth Caribbean countries.
Name four social factors of the Caribbean Commonwealth.	Choose one of these social factors and compare them between two Commonwealth Caribbean countries.	Name three economic factors of the Commonwealth Caribbean.
Name the capital city of your country.	Name the capital cities of ten countries in the Commonwealth Caribbean.	Name the heads of state and government of those ten Commonwealth Caribbean countries.

SOCIAL SCIENCES

Unit 8: Our environment

In this unit you will find out

Physical (natural) resources and our environment

- Our physical resources
  - physical and natural resources
- Location of our physical resources
- How our natural resources are used
  - oil and gas
  - agriculture
- How pollution affects our environment
  - positive and negative effects
  - land pollution
  - air pollution
  - water pollution
  - use of fossil fuels
- Care for the environment
  - reduce, reuse, recycle
  - keeping our environment clean and free of litter
  - using our resources wisely

Places and our environment

- Our physical environment
  - oceans, mountains, forests, swamps
- Man-made environments
  - villages, towns, cities
- Significance of environments
  - places of natural interest
  - places of cultural interest
  - sacred sites
  - a sense of place
- Natural disasters
  - droughts and floods
  - landslides, earthquakes and tsunamis
  - hurricanes and tornadoes, volcanoes

Our physical resources

We are learning to:

- define and use correctly the terms physical environment, physical resources and natural resources
- describe the physical resources found in the Caribbean
- explain how our natural resources are used.

Our physical environment and resources

Resources are things that humans use to meet their needs. For example, in early times we used clay to make pots and bowls and then iron to make tools and weapons. Today we use many different resources for many different needs.

Our resources come from our **physical environment**. This is the part of the environment made up of physical factors we can see and use, such as water, soil and mountains. **Natural resources** are things that occur naturally, including:

- air, water and soil
- biological resources such as plants and animals
- raw minerals
- space and land
- wind, geothermal, tidal and solar energy.

Most natural resources are physical resources. **Physical resources** are things we can physically see and touch. In the Caribbean, our main physical resources are oil (petroleum), natural gas, asphalt, bauxite, rivers and forests (for timber).

We can classify resources into two types:

- renewable resources that we can replace or grow back, such as rivers and forests
- non-renewable resources that are difficult or impossible to grow back or replace, such as petroleum and natural gas.

Did you know...?

Some of the physical resources of the East Caribbean islands include:

- **Anguilla** salt, fish
- **Antigua and Barbuda** the islands' location, pleasant climate
- **Barbados** petroleum, fish
- **Dominica** timber, hydropower
- **Grand Cayman** fish, climate
- **Grenada** timber, tropical fruit
- **Guyana** bauxite, gold, diamonds
- **Montserrat** the islands' location
- **Saint Kitts and Nevis** arable land
- **Saint Lucia** forests, sandy beaches, minerals (pumice)
- **Saint Vincent and the Grenadines** hydropower, arable land
- **Trinidad and Tobago** petroleum, natural gas

Exercise

1. Define the following terms:

   a) physical environment b) physical resources
   c) natural resources

2. List six physical resources found in the Caribbean.

How we use petroleum

Petroleum is a fossil fuel mined from deep under the Earth's surface. We rely on petroleum for many uses, including:

- fuel for cars and for large transport, including bunker fuel (for ships), jet fuel and diesel fuel
- synthetic materials such as synthetic rubber (used for car tyres and shoe soles) and synthetic fibres (polyester, nylon and acrylic)
- plastics made from chemicals found in petroleum
- products made from petrochemicals such as paints, make-up, photographic film and some medicines
- pesticides and **fertilisers** used in agriculture.

How we use other natural resources

- Natural gas is also a fossil fuel. It is found in the Earth's crust, usually under the sea. It has many uses including heating, cooling and cooking.
- Asphalt is a type of black, sticky pitch. It is used in the construction of roads.
- Bauxite is a mineral and is principally used to make aluminium, which is used to make cans, cooking utensils, and window and door frames.
- Limestone is an important component of construction materials, including quicklime, slaked lime, cement and limestone slabs. It is also crushed and used to make roads.
- Sand and gravel are used to mix concrete, cement and other building materials.
- Rivers are an important source of fresh water and provide homes for aquatic life, as well as plants and animals that live on river banks.
- Forests are important living **ecosystems**. Trees help to **filter** the air in the atmosphere and provide homes for animals and plants. Mangrove forests help to protect the shoreline from damage during floods and storms and are important breeding areas for many types of fish and sea organisms.

Exercise

3. Name two fossil fuels found in the Caribbean.
4. Describe one use for each of the following resources:

   a) bauxite **b)** asphalt **c)** natural gas
5. Create a documentary or PowerPoint presentation on the main natural resources found in the Caribbean, and some of the important uses of these resources.

Research

In groups, choose one of the following resources to research: petroleum, natural gas, asphalt, gypsum, gravel.

Find out where it is found in the Caribbean, how it is collected and what it is used for.

Trinidad and Tobago has the world's largest deposits of asphalt at the La Brea Pitch lake, near San Fernando, Trinidad.

Key vocabulary

resources

physical environment

physical/natural resources

fertiliser

ecosystems

filter

Locating our natural resources (1)

We are learning to:

- locate where our natural resources can be found – minerals and fossil fuels.

The natural resources in the Caribbean

Geography and climate influence where we find natural resources. Guyana is well known for its gold, diamond, bauxite and, more recently, for large offshore oil deposits. These resources come from many **generations** of plant and animal matter that have built up and become buried. The rock formations of a place, as well as the way that rivers move over the surface of the land, help to create **mineral deposits**.

Did you know...?

Gold and bauxite are two of Guyana's main exports. Other products exported include sugar, alumina, rice, shrimp, molasses, rum and timber.

Location of mineral resources

Minerals are substances found in the Earth's crust. Usually they occur in very small amounts. However, in some places minerals are **concentrated** enough to make it worthwhile to extract them. Minerals such as limestone, gypsum and gravel are obtained by **quarrying** – a way of cutting into rock or ground to obtain stone and other materials. We obtain fossil fuels such as petroleum and natural gas by drilling.

Mineral resources and mining in Guyana

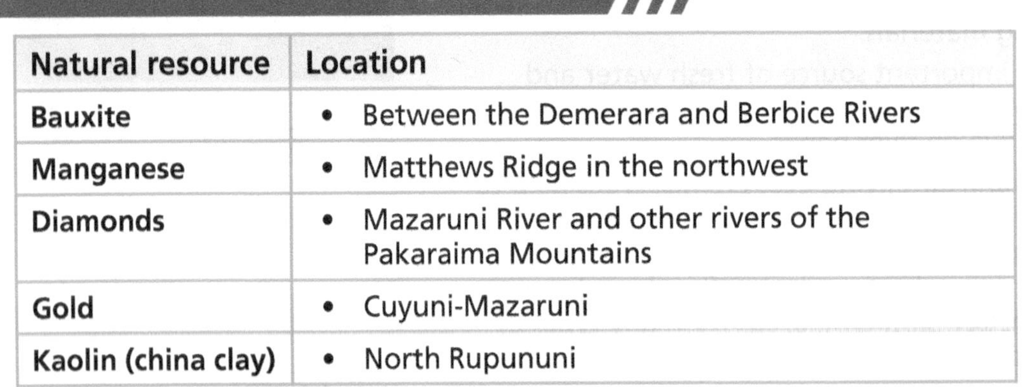

Natural resource	Location
Bauxite	• Between the Demerara and Berbice Rivers
Manganese	• Matthews Ridge in the northwest
Diamonds	• Mazaruni River and other rivers of the Pakaraima Mountains
Gold	• Cuyuni-Mazaruni
Kaolin (china clay)	• North Rupununi

Guyana has many natural resources spread all around the country. Many of the minerals are mined and the raw materials exported. The stone quarries produce aggregates for the local construction market including building sea defences. The map below shows the location of areas where mining is done.

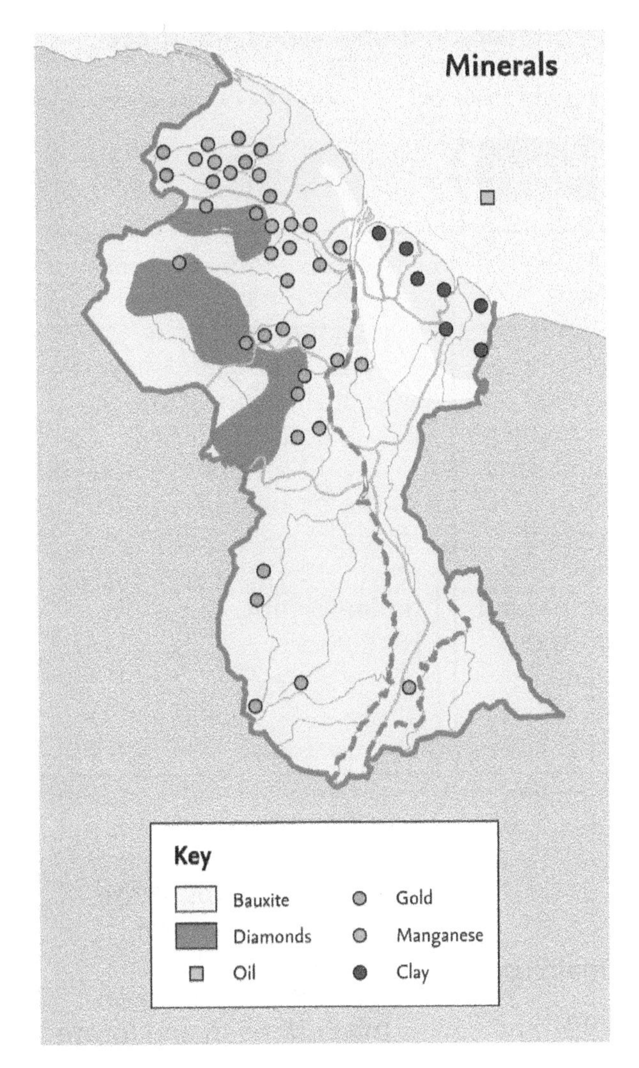

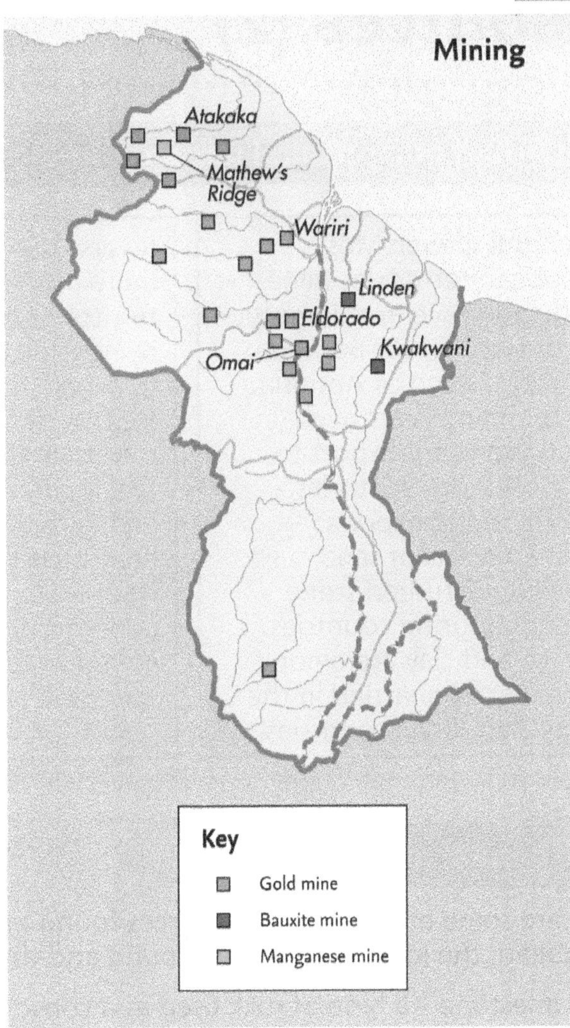

Exercise

1. Trace a blank map of Guyana. Draw the symbols to represent the following resources:

   a) gold **b)** oil **c)** clay **d)** manganese

   e) bauxite **f)** diamonds

2. Using the map above, make a table showing the minerals found in Guyana and their locations.

3. **a)** Which mineral is mostly mined in Guyana?

   b) Which mineral is found mainly around the rivers of Guyana?

   c) What resource is more plentiful along the coast of Guyana? Why do you think this is so?

Key vocabulary

generations

mineral deposits

concentrated

quarrying

Locating our natural resources (2)

We are learning to:

- locate where our natural resources can be found – sand and gravel, rivers, forests.

Locations of other natural resources in the Caribbean

Sand and gravel: Most Caribbean territories mine sand and gravel for domestic use only. However Barbuda, the sister island of Antigua, has for many years been mining sand for export to neighbouring territories. Dominica also exports small amounts of sand, gravel and crushed stone to neighbouring countries. Pumice and clay are among the minerals quarried in the larger Caribbean countries.

Rivers: The larger and more mountainous territories have many rivers which are used to supply them with fresh water. The smaller countries like Saint Kitts and Nevis, Antigua and Barbuda depend heavily on rainfall for fresh water from natural underground storage areas like wells and springs.

Forests: Guyana is one of the Caribbean territories that is famous for its forests. The tropical forests are located in the interior of the South American country. Guyana has one of the highest proportions of forest cover in the world. The forests are an important source of **biodiversity**.

More natural resources

Here are some other natural resources found in the Caribbean, the locations they are found and their main uses:

- Limestone – a type of rock used as a construction material including quicklime, slaked lime, cement and limestone slabs; found in Antigua, Barbados and Trinidad and Tobago
- Pumice – a type of stone found in Dominica, used in concrete blocks, rubber erasers and pet litter
- Silica (silicon) oxide – a type of sand found in Guyana and used in glass-making and in bunkers on golf courses
- Caymanite – a type of rock unique to the Cayman Islands and used in jewellery-making and carvings
- Chromium – a metal found in Tobago, used in industrial processes and for making alloys (metal mixtures that do not rust easily)
- Copper – found in Tobago; an important part of electrical wires.

Activity

Work in groups. Write a list of the natural resources you have studied. Use a map of the Caribbean and locate the territory where each one is found. Write a short description of the mineral including its uses.

Case study

Forest and rivers in Trinidad and Tobago

The maps below show the location of forests and rivers, as well as the main agricultural resources, of Trinidad and Tobago.

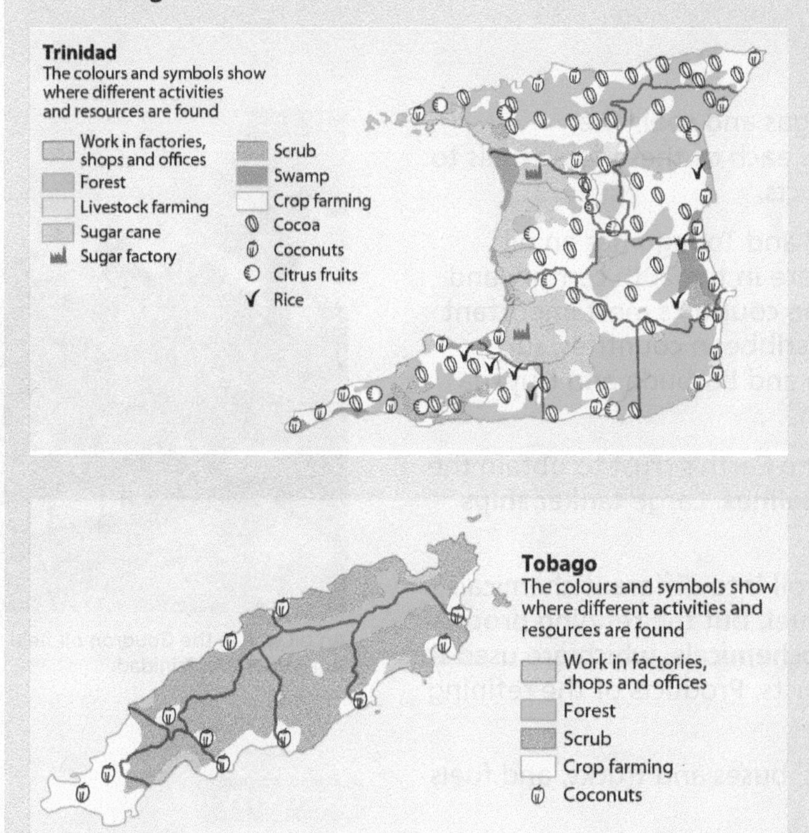

Questions

1. What do the following colours indicate on the maps above?
   a) yellow **b)** orange **c)** green
2. Add to your notebook or folder the symbols that represent:
   a) rice **b)** cocoa
3. **a)** Name four crops farmed in Trinidad.
   b) Which of these crops is also farmed in Tobago?
4. Where are Trinidad's sugar factories located?
5. Which areas in Trinidad are NOT used for farming? Why do you think this is the case?

Activity

Complete a field trip to a place where natural resources are quarried, collected, harvested or mined. Write a reflective journal entry on how our natural resources are used.

Key vocabulary

river

forest

biodiversity

Oil and gas production

We are learning to:

- explain how we use oil and gas.

How we use oil and gas

Fossil fuels include **oil**, natural gas and **coal**. The manufacturing sector processes each of these fossil fuels to produce a wide range of products.

In the Caribbean, only Trinidad and Tobago has an oil industry. Oil was discovered there in the 20th century and oil production is now one of the country's most important industries. Most of the other Caribbean countries, such as Anguilla, Barbados, Antigua and Barbuda and Guyana import oil, fuels and petroleum.

Oil companies drill deep into the Earth's crust to obtain the oil, which they suck up into **pipelines**. Large **tanker ships** carry the oil to **refineries**.

The **refining process** separates oil into different chemicals. Most of the oil is refined into fuel, but the refining process also leaves many residual **petrochemicals**, which are used to produce a huge range of products. Products of the refining process include:

- fuel and diesel oils for cars, buses and trucks, and fuels for ships and aeroplanes
- **gas** used as a fuel for heating and cooking
- **kerosene** used for lighting and heating
- chemical products, such as pesticides and **fertilisers**
- plastics used for toys and other products, synthetic rubber
- lubricating oils and greases used for transport and industrial uses
- bitumen used for road surfacing
- synthetic fibres, such as nylon, acrylic and polyester, used for clothing and other materials
- paints, detergents and cosmetics.

Coal is a type of soft carbon rock that burns easily. Miners dig for coal at coal mines. Most coal is burned at power plants to generate electricity.

Natural gas is used for heating and cooking, generating electricity and as a fuel for vehicles such as cars. It is also used to produce plastics and organic chemicals, including fertilisers.

An oil well in the Goudron oil field, Guayaguayare, Trinidad.

Activity

You know that cars, planes and trains all use fossil fuels, and that their by-products are used in the production of plastics and fertilisers. Make a collage entitled 'Everyday products that involve the use of fossil fuels'.

How oil is refined

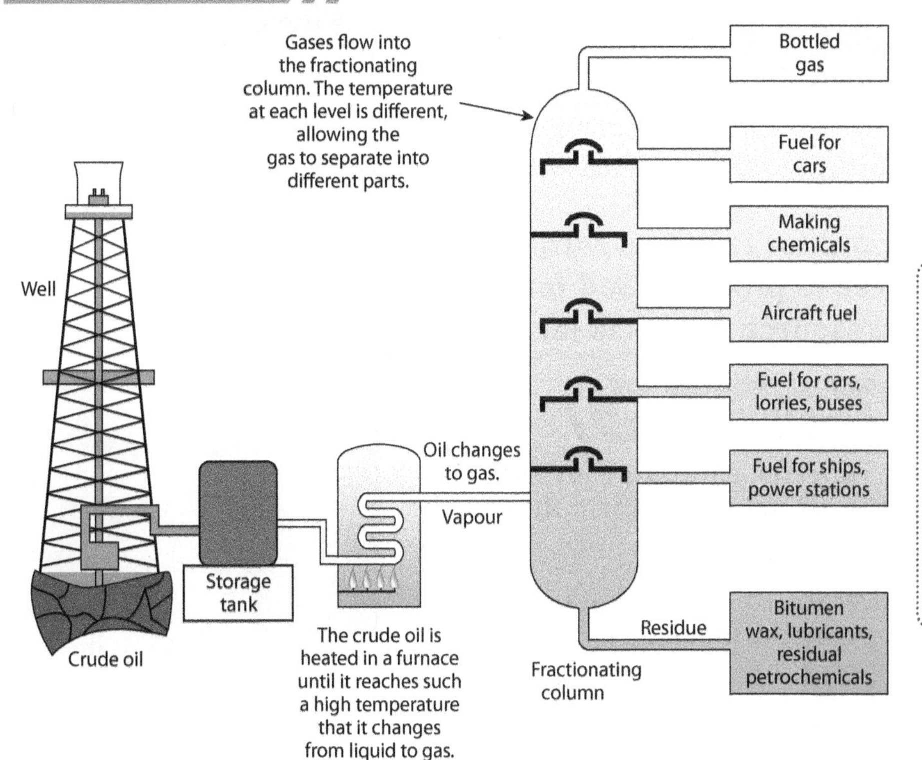

Did you know...?

Natural gas is invisible and has no smell. Gas companies mix it with a very smelly chemical so that it is easy to notice a gas leak. The chemical makes it smell like rotten eggs.

Research

Using the internet, research where your country gets its oil from.

Exercise

Research the different uses of the products of the refining process. Complete a table like the one below, showing the uses of these products. Three rows are left blank for you to add any other products.

Products	Use
Fuel and diesel	
Gas	
Kerosene	
Plastics	
Oil and greases	
Bitumen	
Synthetic fibres	

Key vocabulary

oil
coal
pipelines
tanker ship
refineries
refining process
petrochemicals
gas
kerosene
fertiliser

Agriculture

We are learning to:

- explain how we use agriculture in the Caribbean
- evaluate the positive and negative effects agriculture has on the land.

Agriculture is another word for farming. Farming uses our natural resources to produce food for people to eat. The main resource it uses is land.

Farming makes changes to the environment

Land is a renewable resource. However, agriculture involves many processes that change the natural environment through:

- land clearing
- tilling the soil (turning over the soil to break it up and make it fine enough to grow new seedlings)
- irrigation.

Farmers do many things to **maximise** the yield of their crops. **Yield** is the amount of fruits or vegetables that the farmer harvests per square unit of area. Maximising yield means getting the highest amount of crops possible from the area of land available. In order to increase yield, farmers may:

- use **insecticides** and **pesticides**
- apply chemical fertilisers – these add nutrients to the soil, helping plants to grow faster and produce more fruits or vegetables
- plant a single crop over a large area of land – this is known as **monocropping**.

These techniques all form part of **conventional agriculture** – the type of agriculture used on large farms. However, each of these techniques introduces problems for the natural resources that the farmer uses.

A field of newly planted cassava in Tobago. This is an example of monocropping.

Research

Research one of the following problems caused by conventional farming:

- soil erosion
- agricultural run-off
- **deforestation.**

Draw a labelled picture to show how the problem is caused.

Exercise

1. Name two products that farmers use that come from the oil industry. (You can refer back to the pages on oil production on pages 208–209.)
2. What do you understand by 'monocropping'?
3. In your own words, explain how a farmer can increase the yield of his crops.

Project

Research the crops that are grown in your country. Find a photo of each crop, and add these to your portfolio.

Conventional agriculture – positives and negatives

8.5

Conventional agriculture has several benefits for the farmer.

- Large-scale farming is less work for the farmer; for example, driving a tractor is less work than using a hand plough, and a farmer can irrigate a much larger area with a sprinkler system than with a hand-watering system.
- Cheaper than labour – using technology and chemicals reduces the number of workers the farmer employs.
- Very high yields – chemical fertilisers, insecticides and pesticides allow the farmer to get more crops out of each square unit of land.

Conventional agriculture can also damage the main resource it relies on – the land.

- Clearing land for farming destroys habitats for many animals and plants.
- Monocropping destroys biodiversity and can wipe out many local crop varieties.
- Once crops are harvested, the land is bare. Bare soil easily becomes eroded by wind and rain.
- Insecticides and pesticides pollute the environment.
- Fertilisers run off into the water cycle and can cause unnatural amounts of algae to grow in seas and rivers. This uses up oxygen in the water, causing the death of many aquatic plants and animals.

A farmer using a traditional plough to plant corn in Trinidad.

Activity

Visit a nearby farm or invite a farmer to speak to your class. Find out:

Which crops are farmed there? Does the farmer use any sustainable methods?

Complete a report in response to these questions (of about 250 words).

Solutions – sustainable agriculture practices

There are many ways that farmers around the world are working towards making agriculture more **sustainable**.

- Crop rotation – planting different crops each season helps to **replenish** some of the nutrients in the soil.
- Natural forms of fertiliser instead of chemical fertilisers.
- Using local **varieties** of crops with greater resistance to local pests and diseases than imported varieties.
- Planting different varieties of the same species instead of monocropping, such as several varieties of rice in one paddy, make it more likely they will not be destroyed by a single pest attack.
- **Mulching** prevents water from evaporating so it reduces the need for irrigation.

Discussion

For each of the following resources, discuss why it is important for farming, and how it may be damaged by farming: soil, water, plants.

Key vocabulary

agriculture
maximise
yield
insecticides
pesticides
monocropping
conventional agriculture
deforestation
sustainable
replenish
varieties
mulching

Using our natural resources

We are learning to:

- evaluate the positive and negative effects of using our resources
- explain the causes of global warming and climate change.

Positive effects of using physical resources

The two most important effects of using our natural resources are improvements in people's daily lives and **job creation**.

Fossil fuels provide electricity to light and heat our homes, fuel to power factories, cars, planes and trains, materials for many different products, e.g. plastic, nylon, acrylic and other synthetic materials, fertilisers and chemicals that help our crops, and jobs associated with the mining, refining, transport, manufacturing and processing industries.

A cruise-liner moored in Port of Spain. The cruise-line industry is important in the Caribbean.

Materials such as asphalt, gypsum, limestone, gravel, sand and other materials allow us to construct roads and buildings. Handling these materials creates jobs in the construction and manufacturing industries.

We use land to grow crops for food, and to provide space for housing and other buildings. Land is an important resource to create jobs in the construction and agricultural industries.

Water

- All living things rely on water to live.
- Water is an important solvent. It is used for washing and cleaning, and as a base for many medicines.
- Water is a cooling agent. In industry, water is used to cool down machinery. We also freeze water in order to preserve food.
- Many boats, ships and other vessels travel by sea and by river. In the Caribbean, the cruise-liner industry is an important part of the tourist industry.
- Water provides food – many types of food come from the sea or from rivers. Examples include fish and shellfish. Seaweed is an important source of food as well as medicines.
- Water can also provide power through hydroelectric plants, which generate electric power.

Research

Brainstorm all the ways you use physical resources in one day in your life, from the moment you wake up to the moment you go to bed. Think of all the things you use that are made of or rely on physical resources. Draw a big mind map of all your ideas.

Negative effects of using physical resources

Using physical resources has negative effects too. The main negative effect is damage to the environment.

- Pollution is the introduction of impurities that can damage the land, air or water. At Port of Spain's landfills in Trinidad, where land is used to dispose of waste materials, there are high levels of toxic chemicals in the soil and in the air.
- **Exploitation** means using too much of something and making the resource unavailable for future generations. In Trinidad and Tobago, the current known oil reserves will run out by around 2050.
- Destruction of habitats – mining, quarrying, clearing land and farming all destroy the environment. This damages habitats for other species as well as humans. For example, Chaguaramas, one of the highest mountains in Trinidad and Tobago, has been badly damaged by limestone quarrying at Hermitage Quarry, causing huge amounts of dust and chemicals to be released into the air and into the rivers.
- Damage to sustainable resources – industries such as agriculture involve processes that cause damage to the land so that it cannot grow crops in future.

Two oil tankers collided off Trinidad and Tobago in 1979. This photo shows oil spilling into the ocean from one of the ships.

Global warming and climate change

Burning fossil fuels increases the carbon levels in the atmosphere, which is gradually causing the atmosphere to retain more heat. This causes average temperatures to rise, a process known as **global warming**, which could cause disasters for life on Earth:

- The ice caps at the north and south poles are melting at a fast rate, causing a rise in sea levels.
- Higher sea levels could cause the flooding or disappearance of coastal cities and low-lying islands.
- Changing sea levels cause increases in storms, flooding and tidal waves.
- Increased drought and desertification occur in dry areas.

Discussion

Of all the physical resources you have looked at, which one offers the most positive effects for human life? Which one offers the most negative effects? Discuss your opinions.

Exercise

1. Name two important effects of how we use our physical resources, and give two examples of each.
2. Draw up a table listing two positive and two negative consequences of using our natural resources.
3. Give three reasons why global warming could be disastrous for life on Earth.
4. Why is water so important to us? Give three reasons.

Key vocabulary

job creation

exploitation

global warming

Land pollution

We are learning to:

- describe how land and industrial pollution can have a negative effect on the environment.

Types of land pollution

Land pollution is the **degradation** or destruction of the soil and the Earth's surface. It happens as a result of human activities and the way we use land resources. There are five main types of land pollution.

1. **Deforestation:** the process of clearing land for housing, industry, farming or any other use.

   Consequences: land becomes barren and can never grow back vegetation or support life; surface of land may become dry and cracked; without plant roots to hold land together, **erosion** may occur.
2. **Solid waste:** this includes the organic waste from food, as well as waste materials from packaging. Most waste is dumped in **landfills**. Some sewage systems also dispose of solid waste in landfills.

   Consequences: harmful chemicals leak out from products dumped in landfills; chemicals dissolve into the water in the soil, adding to water pollution; chemicals taken up by food crops may cause illness in people and animals.
3. **Pesticides:** farmers use pesticides on their crops in order to kill pests that destroy or limit crop growth, such as, insecticides to kill insects and herbicides to kill weeds.

   Consequences: pesticides may kill insects or weeds for which they were not intended.
4. **Fertilisers:** Farmers use fertilisers, which are chemicals that make plants grow faster.

   Consequences: both fertilisers and pesticides dissolve into water in the soil, adding to water pollution.
5. **Industrial pollution:** industrial processes are the actions used in factories to produce processed materials and finished goods.

   Consequences: these processes use large quantities of physical resources and release many different chemicals into the environment.

Pollution on a beach in Santo Domingo, Dominican Republic. Toxins from plastic waste can harm marine life.

Project

On pages 214–219 there are six project features for you to complete. Work in groups to complete these projects and compile a report on pollution and its effect on the environment.

Find out more about soil erosion. Draw illustrations showing how soil becomes eroded.

Discussion

Who do you think should be responsible for preventing industrial pollution of the land – government, industry or the community?

Exercise

1. List the five types of land pollution.

The consequences of industrial pollution

8.7

Industrial pollution has the worst consequences for the land:

- The mining industry creates huge holes in the ground. Underground mining can result in the collapse of the Earth over the mined area. Open pit mining creates areas where nothing can grow because of all the dust and debris. Construction and building produce many waste materials such as unused wood, metal, bricks, rubble and plastic.
- Radioactive materials from nuclear power plants are extremely harmful for people and animals. Nuclear waste is usually disposed of underground. These materials go into the water and plants in the area. People and animals may **ingest** them. This may cause birth defects, cancers and many serious illnesses.
- The chemical industry dumps its by-products in land areas; they can cause sickness and death for humans, plants and animals in the area.

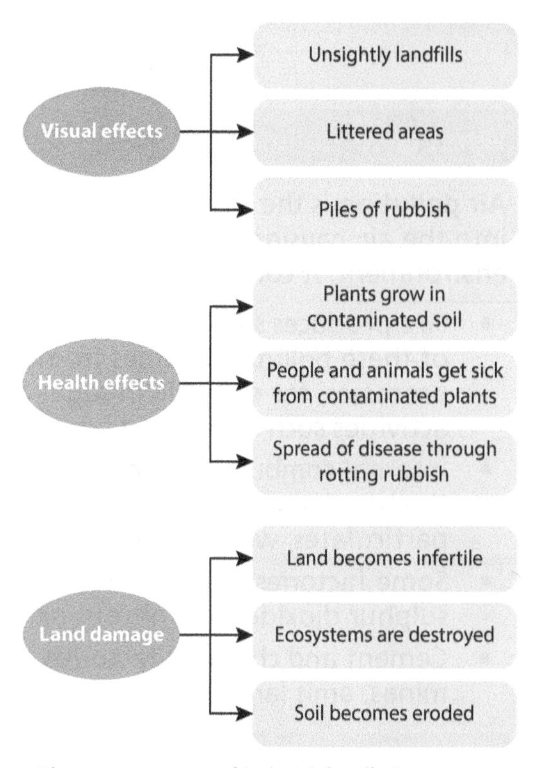

The consequences of industrial pollution.

Solutions to land pollution

- Dumping sites and landfills must be far from human settlements and constructed properly to prevent contamination of the soil and groundwater.
- Farmers should be educated to use organic farming methods, planting a variety of crops and using ecosystems to control pest populations. For example, farmers may use compost rather than chemical fertilisers.
- Communities must stand together to object to industrial pollution when it happens.
- It is important to reduce the number of disposable containers people use. This will reduce the amount of waste in landfills.
- Hazardous materials must not be dumped in the ground.
- Communities should use recycling programmes.

Exercise

2. List two consequences to the environment of land and industrial pollution.
3. Identify which, if any, of these types of land pollution you have noticed where you live.
4. Explain the link between farming, land pollution and water pollution.

Project

In groups, compile a report on the types of pollution and their effects on the environment. Add to your project report.

Key vocabulary

degradation
solid waste
erosion
landfills
industrial pollution
ingest

Air pollution

We are learning to:

- describe how air pollution can have a negative effect on the environment.

What is air pollution?

Air pollution is the addition of solid particles or gases into the air, causing damage to living things and the environment. It comes from many different human activities:

- Fire produces smoke, dust and soot. The main source of these pollutants comes from fire used in industrial processes, for example in sugar cane factories, and from activities such as burning waste materials.
- Internal combustion engines burn petrol. By-products of the burning process include carbon monoxide, lead and particulates, which are released into the air.
- Some factories release gases such as sulphur oxides, sulphur dioxides and nitrous oxides.
- Cement and chemical factories, as well as quarries and mines, emit large quantities of dust into the air.

Industrial air pollution sits side-by-side with the environment. These fishermen in the Caribbean fish, while the air is being polluted nearby.

Effects of air pollution

- Air pollution causes haziness and lower **visibility**.
- People need clean air to breathe. Polluted air can cause many types of illnesses and even death. In cities with heavy **smog**, people have higher rates of lung cancer, chest infections, respiratory diseases and asthma than in rural areas.
- When people breathe carbon monoxide, the chemical lowers the amount of oxygen in the body. This can lead to headaches, dizziness, nausea and even unconsciousness. It can also cause growth problems for unborn babies if the mother inhales the polluted air.
- Sulphur dioxides cause poor growth in plants and can prevent the plants from producing fruit.
- Chemicals in the air can cause materials to rust and **corrode** more quickly than they would in places with clean air.

Project

Research the main greenhouse gases. Draw up a table using the information. Show the name and abbreviation of the gas, a short description of which activities produce the gas and what kinds of problems it produces when it is present in the atmosphere. Add to your project report.

Exercise

1. Describe one natural source of air pollution.
2. Describe two ways that industrial processes cause air pollution.
3. Name three industries that release dust into the air.

The greenhouse effect

The addition of industrial chemicals to the air changes the composition of the atmosphere. Chemicals such as carbon monoxide, sulphur oxides and dioxides create a thick chemical blanket at the top of the Earth's atmosphere, preventing some of the Earth's heat from escaping into space. This produces the **greenhouse effect**, which means the Earth's average temperature is gradually rising.

Solutions for air pollution

Some solutions for air pollution are shown in the mind maps.

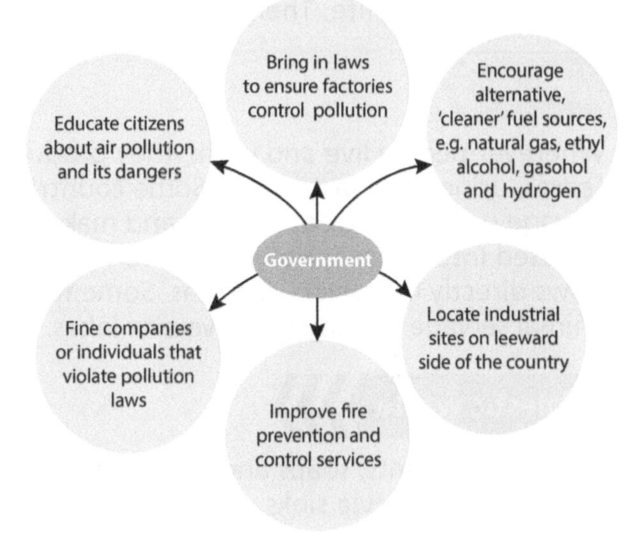

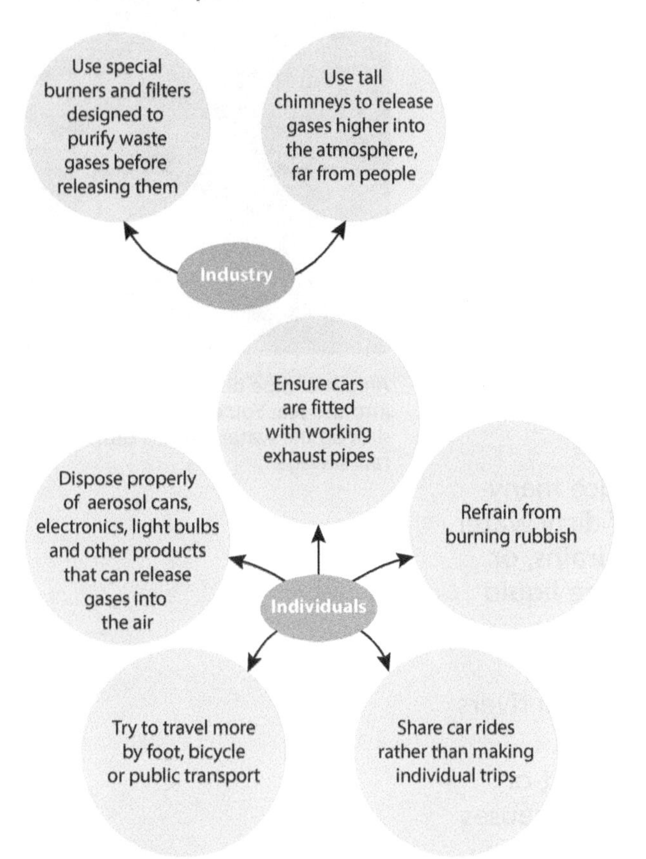

Project

Research the greenhouse effect. Present your information in a diagram showing how the greenhouse effect works. Add to your project report.

Exercise

4. Draw a mind map to show the consequences of air pollution on human health, on plants and on the physical environment.
5. Name three ways in which air pollution can be controlled.
6. Imagine that you live in an area affected by smog. Write a letter to your local councillor with suggestions for ways to improve the situation in the area.

Key vocabulary

air pollution

visibility

smog

corrode

greenhouse effect

Water pollution

We are learning to:

- describe how water pollution can have a negative effect on the environment.

What is water pollution?

Water pollution is the introduction of chemicals and other impurities into a water source, causing damage to human, animal and plant life. There are many different sources.

An outlet pipe discharging raw sewage into the sea. You may be able to see a slick on the water – this is caused by the raw sewage.

Sewage

Wherever people live and work, they produce **sewage** – faeces, urine and wastewater. Some countries have effective sewage systems to treat sewage and make it safe to be released into the sea. However, in some places, raw sewage flows directly into rivers and seas. Some farmers dump animal sewage directly into rivers or lakes.

Domestic waste

All our detergents, soaps and dirty washing water flows into the water system via sinks, drains and pipes. The chemicals and dissolved substances carried in this water travel through water pipes and eventually end up in rivers or seas.

- Industrial waste: factories and industry produce many toxic waste by-products. They may dispose of dirty water from industrial processes by releasing it into drains, or pumping it into rivers or seas. Some of these are liquid chemicals – chemicals that are dissolved in water.
- Fertiliser and pesticides: dissolved chemicals from agriculture run off into the groundwater and into rivers and seas.
- Oil spills: sometimes undersea pipelines may burst or leak, or oil tankers may leak oil into the sea. This causes large areas of heavily polluted seawater.
- Solid waste: waste from industry and domestic use may end up in rivers and seas as a result of littering or improper disposal. Examples of the kind of litter you can find in rivers include old tyres, old appliances, packaging and even dead animals.

Exercise

1. Name three diseases that can be spread by untreated sewage.

Project

Collect photographs of different types of water pollution from the internet. Create a poster showing the effects of pollution on our water supply. Add to your project report.

Consequences of water pollution

- Waterborne illnesses: untreated sewage carries bacteria and viruses, which cause diseases such as cholera, typhoid and hepatitis.
- Toxicity: industrial waste such as lead, mercury and other chemicals that are highly toxic (poisonous) to animals and humans. Mercury, cadmium, arsenic and lead build up in the bodies of people and animals.
- Heavy metals: these can cause many illnesses. People suffer from skin rashes, headaches, fainting, vomiting, diarrhoea, kidney damage and problems with their nervous systems. Pregnant women may suffer miscarriages, or may have babies that are malformed or brain damaged.
- Solid waste: the construction industry releases silt and other solids that cannot dissolve. The particles of these pollutions get suspended in the water, creating conditions that kill many plants and animals.
- Killing marine life: spilt oil cannot dissolve or disperse in water. It sits on the surface preventing light and air from reaching the plants that live in the water. It also coats fish, preventing them from breathing. It gets stuck on the feathers of sea birds, preventing them from flying. Many animals and plants die as a result of oil spills.
- Flooding: solid waste and litter in rivers can cause flooding during the wet season.
- **Acid rain:** chemicals that dissolve into water move into the water cycle, and fall to Earth in rain. They cause acid rain – rain that has high levels of acidity and can damage buildings and other structures.
- **Eutrophication:** detergents and fertilisers carry high concentrations of **nutrients** – nitrates and phosphates that feed plants. These chemicals can cause weeds and algae to grow out of control in dams and rivers. These overgrown plants **deplete** (use up) all the oxygen in the water.

A pond with heavy eutrophication.

Project

Research the consequences of water pollution on the environment. Draw up a table showing the effects and give some local examples that you have found. Add to your project report.

Exercise

2. Name five industrial pollutants and identify five sources of water pollution.
3. Explain two environmental problems caused by oil spills.
4. How does acid rain fall?
5. Which industrial products cause eutrophication?

Key vocabulary

sewage
acid rain
eutrophication
nutrients
deplete

Fossil fuels

We are learning to:

- explain how we use fossil fuels in the Caribbean
- evaluate the advantages and disadvantages of using fossil fuels.

A finite resource

At present, fossil fuels are the cheapest and most convenient form of fuel available to us. However, using fossil fuels has many damaging effects on the environment. They are also a **non-renewable** resource. As they become scarcer, we will need to find alternatives.

Fossil fuels formed over millions of years. However, in just over 200 years, the human population has used up an enormous amount of the planet's coal, gas and oil. Once they are used up, they are gone forever. At present, we extract 4 billion tonnes of crude oil every year. At this rate, our known oil reserves will be finished by the year 2052.

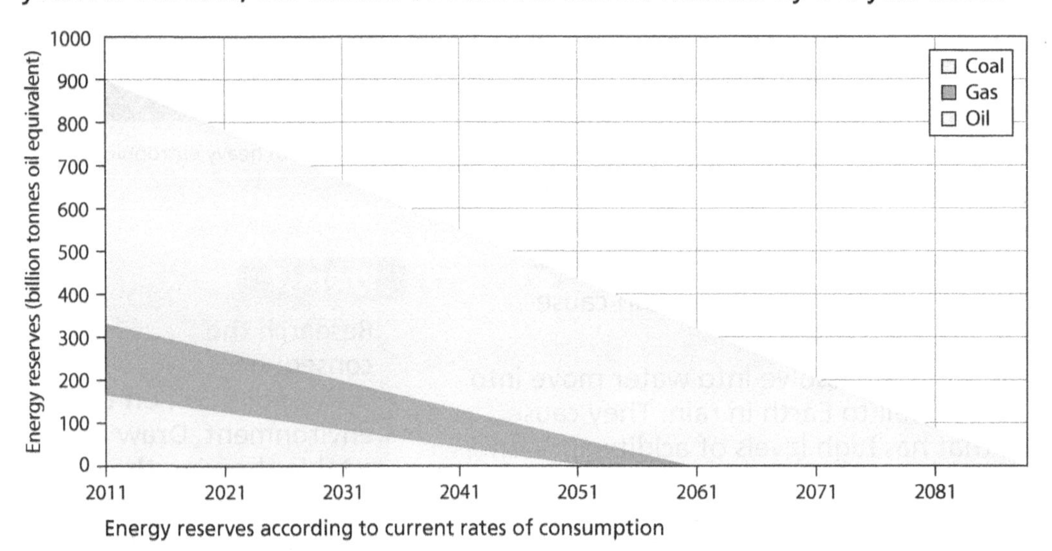

Energy reserves according to current rates of consumption

Exercise

1. What is a non-renewable resource?
2. Look at the graph.
   - **a)** Which fossil fuel will run out first?
   - **b)** Which is the fossil fuel that we have in largest quantities?
   - **c)** When will all our known reserves of fossil fuels run out?
3. Brainstorm all the positive consequences of fossil fuels on people's everyday lives. Think about the ways we work and play, as well as what we use in our everyday lives at home.

Activity

Draw up a table listing eight of the natural or physical resources you have learned about and compare the positive and negative consequences of using each resource.

Advantages of using fossil fuels

Fossil fuels are still our main source of power. They have many advantages:

- They can generate very large amounts of electricity in a single location.
- There are sources of fossil fuels all over the world.
- Burning coal is a very cost-efficient way to produce electricity. Coal is cheap and it burns easily.
- Oil and gas are easy to transport along pipelines.
- Gas power plants are highly efficient. In other words, they produce a lot of power with very little waste.
- It is possible to build power stations almost anywhere.

Disadvantages of using fossil fuels

Fossil fuels produce air, water and land pollution.

- Metal pipelines corrode over time. Broken pipes may leak oil or petrol into surrounding land and water.
- Large waste pits near to oil wells are usually left open. Oil can seep into the groundwater.
- Drilling releases dust into the air, coating nearby crops and causing pollution for animals and humans.
- The flames from burning natural gas give off gaseous **emissions**, which cause air pollution.
- Coal gives off carbon dioxide when it burns, polluting the air. It also gives off sulphur dioxide, polluting the water cycle.
- Coal mining destroys large areas of land.
- Mining is dangerous; miners may suffer accidents, as well as respiratory illnesses.
- Drilling releases chemicals from underground into the groundwater. This becomes known as 'produced water'. This water contains many **heavy metals** such as arsenic, cadmium, mercury, lead, zinc and copper. They are toxic to people and animals.
- As the world's population increases, we consume increasing amounts of fossil fuels. They will therefore run out even earlier than scientists predict.

Exercise

4. List five negative consequences of oil pollution.
5. Describe the effects of the oil spill that you can see in the photo.
6. Which two chemicals are released by burning coal?

Workers remove crude oil that was spilt on a beach in Thailand, 2013.

Activity

Imagine that you are working for an oil company. Create an action plan for:

a) preventing an oil spill

b) responding and assisting in the case of an oil spill or accident.

Discussion

Discuss how your life would change if fossil fuels ran out tomorrow.

Key vocabulary

non-renewable

emissions

heavy metals

Caring for our environment

We are learning to:

- demonstrate ways of caring for the environment: recycling
- explain how the '3 Rs' help to look after our environment.

No single person can stop the damage that humans do to the environment. However, there are ways we can become more responsible in the way we use resources.

The 3 Rs

Consumer culture encourages people to want new things, from technology to clothing. However, the more new things people buy and consume, the more rubbish goes into the Earth's landfills.

Many households still throw all their rubbish into bins, and it ends up in dumps or landfills. The contents of a normal household bin (see opposite) include a large proportion of materials that can be reused or recycled. There are many materials that can be recycled:

- Paper
- Plastics
- Glass
- Aluminium cans
- Used automobile oil
- Tyres
- Iron and steel from old cars and appliances.

There are three principles that can help us make a smaller impact on our environment – the '3 Rs': **reduce, reuse** and **recycle**.

- Reducing starts with buying fewer products and having less 'stuff'. Next, reduce the amount of disposable materials that you use. Many foods are already in packets, so they do not need to be put in bags.
- Reuse products, especially packaging, wherever possible. For example, instead of using disposable cups, food containers and plastic bags, use items that can be reused.
- It is possible to recycle materials such as glass, aluminium, paper and plastic. Find out about recycling programmes in your area, and separate your rubbish into materials for recycling. Fruit and vegetable cuttings can go onto a compost heap.

Activity

Brainstorm ways of how you could reuse or recycle any of these materials: paper, plastics, glass and cans.

Exercise

1. What are the '3 Rs'?

Case study

The Antigua and Barbuda Waste Recycling Corporation (ABWREC) is a non-profit organisation, whose mission statement is 'To assist in bulk waste reduction and the removal of **non-biodegradable** materials from Antigua & Barbuda through recycling'.

Non-biodegradable materials are items that cannot decay or be broken down through natural decay. Examples include plastic products (a water bottle, for example), metal products (a food tin can), rubber (car tyres) and electronics (a computer). ABWREC provides:

- the collection of non-biodegradable materials
- the initial processing and exportation of non-biodegradable materials
- education to the public about recycling
- tours and demonstrations at the recycling faculty
- the distribution of recycling bins
- the short-term loan of recycling bins for special events.

Adapted from: http://www.antiguanice.com/v2/client.php?id=778.

Glass, aluminium, plastic and paper are all recyclable materials.

Research

Do a research project on how materials in your country are recyled. Show your findings on an illustrated poster.

The benefits of the '3 Rs'

Reducing, reusing and recycling have many benefits both for consumers and the environment:

- The consumer saves money by spending less on new goods, especially bags, jars and bottles.
- Less land gets used up for landfills.
- There is less need for waste disposal services, saving money from the national budget; this money can go towards other worthwhile causes.
- Fewer toxic chemicals pollute the water, land and air.
- There is less disease and illness from pollution.
- We save natural resources so that they can be used more sustainably.

Discussion

In groups, discuss the importance of the '3 Rs'.

Exercise

2. What is the mission statement of ABWREC? What do you think this means?
3. What services does ABWREC provide?
4. Give some examples of non-biodegradable materials.
5. Describe the recycling symbol and suggest how the symbol shows its meaning.

Key vocabulary

consumer culture

reduce

reuse

recycle

non-biodegradable

Responsibility for our environment

We are learning to:

- demonstrate ways of caring for the environment.

Keeping our environment free of litter

The food you eat, the way you use energy at home, the amount you travel and the types of products you own and use all make a difference to the environment.

Litter is waste material that gets dropped or left in the environment instead of being disposed of properly.

- Do not drop litter.
- Always find a bin for your waste.
- If you cannot find a bin, collect your litter in a bag and dispose of it properly at home.
- Reuse items such as bottles, jars and tins. Many glass and plastic items can be used for other purposes rather than thrown away.
- Recycle items made from glass, plastic and aluminium.
- Kitchen waste, such as vegetable and fruit peelings, cores and eggshells, can go onto a compost heap to make compost for a garden.
- Items that contain chemicals, such as printer cartridges, batteries and paint, need to be taken to collection points so that they can be disposed of properly.

Did you know...?

Did you know that energy-saver light bulbs use between 25 per cent and 80 per cent less energy than traditional incandescent bulbs? They can last up to 25 times longer than the traditional bulbs too.

Research

Research how to create a compost heap. In groups, create a short video on how to make a compost heap easily and cheaply at home or at school.

Use our resources sensibly!

Use water wisely:

- Take a shower instead of a bath.
- Use a water-saving shower head to use less water during a shower.
- Turn off the water when you brush your teeth.
- Choose **water-wise** plants in your garden – these do not need a lot of water.
- Fix leaky pipes and taps.

Use electricity wisely:

- Turn off appliances and lights when you are not using them.
- Use energy-efficient light bulbs.

Exercise

1. What is litter?
2. Why should each of the following NOT go in a normal bin? Explain what you should do with them instead:

   a) a printer cartridge **b)** vegetable peelings

   c) glass bottles

Travel

Conserve fossil fuels and reduce the amount of air pollution by following these guidelines:

- Do not make unnecessary trips by car or plane.
- Use shared rides and public transport when you can. When possible, ride a bike or walk rather than driving.
- Modern cars need catalytic converters on their exhaust systems to cut down their carbon emissions. Make sure your car's exhaust system is always well maintained.

Food

- Use fruits and vegetables that are in season. This helps to make sure that your produce comes from local producers, without wasting resources.
- Choose meat, fish and vegetables that use sustainable farming methods.
- Do not hunt or eat endangered species such as shark.
- Try eating less meat. The production of meat causes around 20 per cent of the world's greenhouse gases.

Ethical consumerism

People are becoming increasingly aware that all the products they buy and use have an impact on the local and global environment. An **ethical consumer** is someone whose shopping reflects their values and beliefs.

Have you seen any labels on products saying 'free range', 'Fairtrade' or 'organic'? Each of these labels tells us that the company making the product wants the public to know that they are taking care of their impact on the environment.

Buy local, think global

Another principle for ethical consumers is to buy local rather than imported products. By supporting local producers, you can reduce negative consequences for the environment and help to support your country's economy.

Exercise

3. Explain how each of the following can reduce your negative impact on the environment:

   a) sharing transport **b)** eating locally produced fruit
   c) eating less meat
4. List two ways that you can save water and electricity.
5. What do you understand by 'ethical consumerism'?

Activity

In groups, brainstorm an idea to look after the environment in your school or community. It could be a plan to clean up litter or to give advice on the '3 Rs'. Carry out your plan and produce a report, with pictures, of how you carried it out.

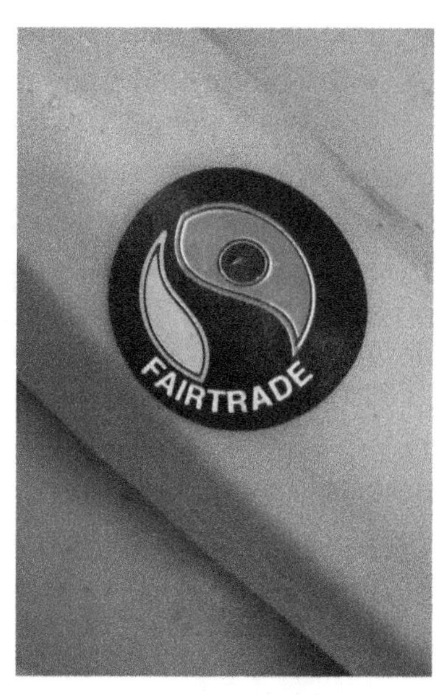

Fairtrade sticker on a banana.

Key vocabulary

litter

water-wise

ethical consumer

Our physical environment

We are learning to:

- define and use correctly the terms physical environment and man-made environment
- identify physical environments in the Caribbean.

The environment

The environment is the world around us. There are two types of environment:

- **physical environment:** this is made up of natural features such as oceans, mountains, forests and swamps. The physical environment, together with the plants, animals and other living organisms in that environment, make up an ecosystem
- **man-made environment:** this is a built environment such as a village, town or city.

A mountain is an example of a natural feature found in the physical environment.

Our physical environment

There are many different types of physical environment on Earth, from the snowy polar caps, to the hot, dry Sahara desert, to deep marine environments miles under the ocean's surface.

The five main environments on Earth are forests, grasslands, deserts, **wetlands** and tundra.

The types of environments found in the Caribbean are outlined below.

Oceans

Saint Kitts and Nevis is made up of two **islands** surrounded on all sides by the Caribbean Sea and the Atlantic Ocean. **Marine** environments surround each of the two islands on all sides. Beaches, coastal areas, coral reefs and deep oceans are all marine environments.

Mountains

Where landforms rise high above sea level, they form **mountains**. Saint Kitts is dominated by three volcanic peaks which run through its centre. Mt Liamuiga is the highest. Nevis is circular with its highest mountain, Nevis Peak, flanked by Round Hill in the north and Saddle Hill in the south.

Activity

Brainstorm all the different kinds of environment you know about. Draw word maps showing these environments and how they relate to each other.

Activities

1. Collect pictures of at least five different environments in the Caribbean.
2. Stick these onto a poster. Next to each picture, give:
   a) the type of environment
   b) names of at least two places where this environment is found

Forests

8.13

Tropical forests are some of the richest environments on Earth as they are home to the greatest variety of plants and animals. A forest is any area of land covered in trees and woody vegetation. There are snowy forests in northern Europe and warm rainforests in central Africa. The forests of the Commonwealth of Dominica are known as tropical rainforests, with a warm climate and large amounts of rainfall.

Key vocabulary

physical environment

man-made environment

wetland

islands

marine

mountains

tropical forest

Wetlands and swamps

Wetlands are a very special type of environment – they form at the meeting point of land and sea. Swamps such as Nariva Swamp and Caroni Swamp in Trinidad are types of wetland. They are important breeding grounds for many types of fish, and they support a rich range of bird and plant life. The mangroves in wetlands help to prevent erosion of land along the coast. Other examples of wetlands in the Caribbean include the Cabrits Wetland and the Indian River Wetlands found in Dominica.

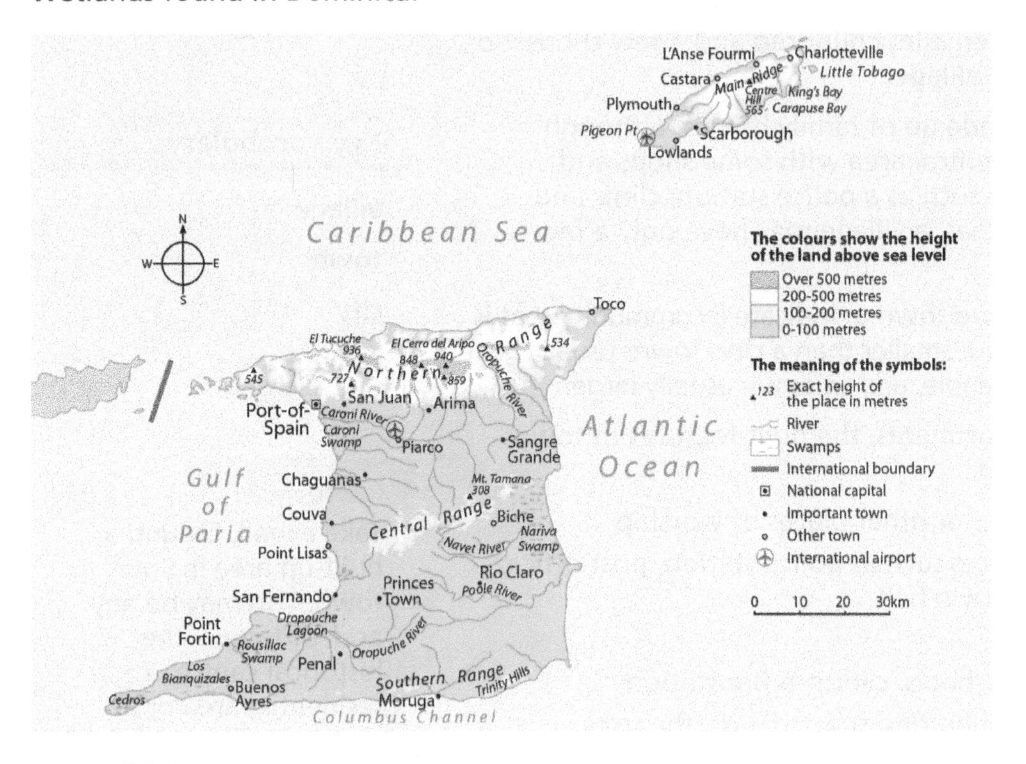

Exercise

1. Look at the map. Create a table of the environments and add names of those found in Dominica. Compare with the environments in your country.
2. Referring to your country, explain the main difference between physical and man-made environments and give two examples of each.
3. Why does the ocean make up such a large part of the Caribbean's physical environment?

Man-made environments

We are learning to:

- identify man-made environments in the Caribbean.

You have learned a lot about the damage caused by human activities, including the building and construction industries. However, designing buildings and other structures is an important part of human life. Without building, we would not have the villages, towns and cities where we live.

An aerial view of Port of Spain, Trinidad.

Villages, towns and cities

Man-made environments are built environments such as villages, towns and cities. Wherever people live, they build their homes as well as public buildings that the community can share. We name communities according to their size. A community of between a few hundred and a few thousand people is known as a **village**.

A village is mostly made up of family homes, although it may have a small central area with some shops and community buildings such as a police station, clinic and church. In farming areas, a village may have only a few tarred roads.

We usually use the word **town** to indicate a community that is larger than a village but smaller than a **city**. Towns usually have fewer than 100 000 people, and cities are usually larger.

Besides houses or apartments, the built features of towns and cities may include:

- churches, temples or other places of worship
- community services such as police station, post office, court building, town hall
- a **cemetery**
- services such as schools, clinics, a fire station
- facilities such as libraries, sports fields, theatres
- businesses, shops and malls
- industrial buildings such as warehouses and factories
- transport infrastructure such as roads, train tracks, bus and train stations, airports, roads and highways and parking areas
- harbour and port facilities.

Key vocabulary

village

town

city

cemetery

Activity

Take a walk around a built-up area in your town. This may be any area of town – the historical centre, a residential area or a cemetery, for example. As you walk, make notes of how the different parts of the built environment make you feel. Write a reflective journal entry about your walk.

Towns and cities in Barbados

8.14

The map below shows the main towns and cities in Barbados.

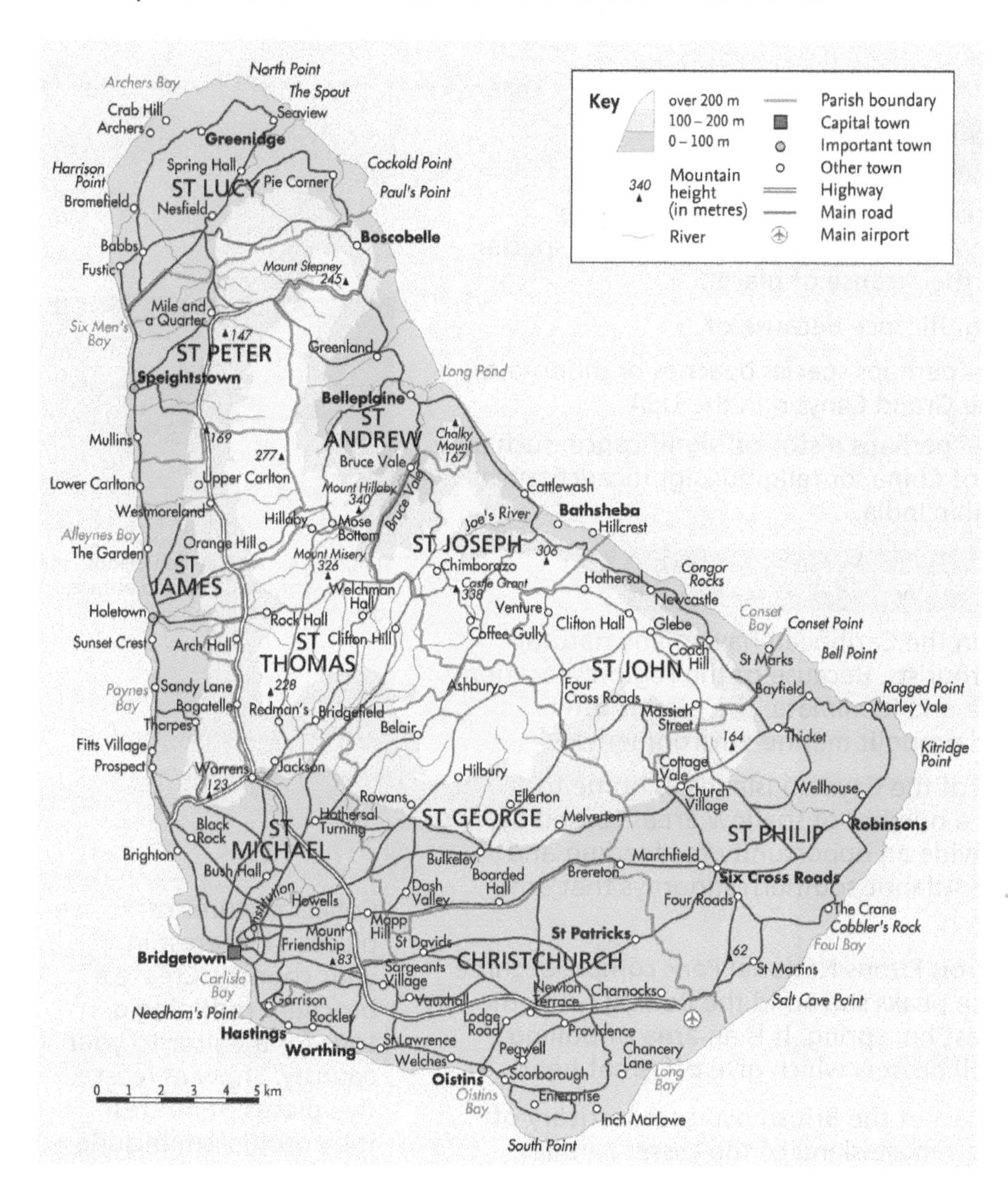

Exercise

1. What is the main difference between a village and a city?
2. Use the map to answer the following questions.
   a) Name three towns that are in the south-western part of the island.
   b) Which two towns are to the north of Mt Hillaby, the highest point in Barbados?
   c) What is the national capital?
   d) Name a town which is in the parish of St Lucy.
   e) Name three towns on the west coast of Barbados, and two towns on the east coast of Barbados.

Places of natural interest

We are learning to:

- understand why some environments in the Caribbean are special and unique to people
- develop a 'sense of place'.

Places of natural interest

Each country has its own places of interest that have characteristics which make those places unique and special. This could be called their '**sense of place**'.

A place may have significance because of:

- natural factors – perhaps special beaches or mountains, for example, the Grand Canyon in the USA
- cultural factors – perhaps historical significance, such as the Great Wall of China, or religious significance, such as the Taj Mahal in India.

Stingray City, the Cayman Islands - the clear seas of the Caribbean attract tourists to the region.

Places of natural interest in the Caribbean

Most of the islands in the Caribbean have many natural factors that attract tourists. Because of the region's location in the Caribbean Sea and its climate, the islands offer beaches, forests and unspoilt marine environments.

Grand Cayman, one of the Cayman Islands, is home to Stingray City. This is a number of shallow areas caused by raised sand that provide an opportunity for feeding and interacting with the Atlantic southern stingrays that are common in the islands.

Dominica's Morne Trois Pitons National Park comprises three volcanic peaks. These peaks surround the Boiling Lake, the world's second-largest hot spring. It is an area of boiling mud ponds and small geysers which give off great heat.

Sombrero Island is part of the British overseas territory of Anguilla, the northernmost island of the Lesser Antilles. There is a lighthouse that marks the shipping lane between the Atlantic Ocean and Caribbean Sea and wildlife such as seabirds and ground lizards.

Exercise

1. What are the two types of factors that give a place significance?
2. Why do most Caribbean countries share similar natural attractions? Suggest two reasons.
3. List at least two natural factors that are unique to your country.

Activity

Collect pictures of places of interest in your country. Create a brochure outlining a tour for a visitor to your country. Show at least five places of interest they could visit. Include information such as directions, opening times, the main points of interest and suggestions for nearby shops and restaurants.

Places of cultural interest in the Caribbean

8.15

The Caribbean is home to many places of interest. Our national heritage is sometimes represented by houses of parliament, national museums, art galleries or even the ruins of old buildings left around our countries.

Examples include, Carr's Bay in the north of Montserrat, which has remnants of a fort with several cannons pointing out to sea in the direction of Redonda. There is also a model version of the War Memorial and Clock Tower that were destroyed by a volcanic eruption in Plymouth. In Nevis there is Hamilton House, which houses the Nevis Island Assembly and the Museum of Nevis History. Fort Charlotte is in Saint Vincent and the Grenadines. It overlooks the capital with most of its cannons pointed inland.

The Caribbean has many places of interest for tourists, including Carr's Bay in Montserrat.

Sacred sites

The **sacred** sites of a country are the places that have special religious or spiritual meaning to its people. Places of worship are one type of sacred site. These also form part of the cultural factors of the country. Cemeteries and burial sites are also places of **significance** as they are the places where our ancestors are buried.

In some Caribbean countries, there are still carvings, sacred ancestral sites and artefacts of **indigenous** peoples. Carib rock drawings can still be seen at Bloody Point in Saint Kitts and at Layou and Yambou in Saint Vincent and the Grenadines.

Descendants of Caribs live on the Carib Reserve in Dominica. They weave baskets and make canoes in the same way as their forefathers. Many Caribbean territories have pieces of Carib pottery in their museums.

Discussion

As a class, discuss the characteristics of a place that make it special or unique. Talk about places in your country first and then the rest of the world.

Activity

Choose a specific historical or religious site that you want to know more about. Interview some elders in your community. Find out how that place looked when they were young, and how people used it. Write a report about the way this place has changed.

Exercise

4. What do you understand by the term 'cultural factors'?
5. Which of the following is not a cultural factor?
   - **a)** a burial site
   - **b)** an old fort
   - **c)** a coral reef
   - **d)** a museum of natural history
   - **e)** a hiking trail

Key vocabulary

sense of place

sacred

significance

indigenous

Natural disasters

We are learning to:

- understand how natural disasters can occur.

Natural disasters

Some places are prone to **natural disasters**, which are caused by natural phenomena such as earthquakes or floods. Because of the geographic location of the Caribbean, we regularly face specific types of natural disaster.

A collapsed part of the Manzanilla/ Mayaro road in Trinidad after flooding in 2014.

Droughts and floods

A **drought** is an extreme water shortage, caused by low rainfall or no rainfall for a long period. Usually droughts occur in areas that have hot, dry weather conditions. Droughts are unusual in the Caribbean, but some places can face droughts when there are hotter and drier conditions.

Floods happen when large amounts of water suddenly rush into areas that are usually dry. Floods may be caused by:

- heavy rainfall and storms, and rivers overflowing their banks
- water being displaced from rivers, lakes, ponds or drains when landslides, solid waste or debris fall into these structures
- high waves, for example as a result of a tsunami or hurricane.

A drought can have many serious effects:

- water shortage for drinking, cooking and irrigation
- loss of crops, lower milk and meat production as cattle may get sick or die
- famine (not enough food for the human population)
- soil erosion caused by wind moving over dry land
- bush fires.

Flooding can have many devastating effects:

- People and animals may drown.
- The water may destroy crops and agricultural areas.
- Buildings and other structures may be damaged or destroyed.
- Waste gets carried into reservoirs, lakes and rivers, polluting freshwater resources.
- Waterborne diseases may spread in areas that have been flooded.
- The water may wash away the top level of the soil, damaging the land.

Exercise

1. Identify two similarities and two differences between flooding and droughts.

Landslides

A **landslide** is a falling mass of soil or rocks that slide down a hill or mountain when rain falls or floodwaters move over the rocks. Landslides can have many damaging effects, including:

- burial of homes, farm areas, animals and even people
- damage to phone lines, roads and paths
- earth and rocks sliding into rivers, displacing water and leading to flooding
- loss of topsoil, leading to barren farmland
- damage or destruction to vegetation and forests.

Did you know...?

In 1997, an earthquake in Cariaco, Venezuela, caused the deaths of 81 people. The Cariaco earthquake could be felt in Trinidad and Tobago.

Earthquakes and tsunamis

Earthquakes usually affect places located on **boundaries** between the plates of land that form the Earth's crust. Deep under the Earth's crust is a layer of semi-molten rock. The movement of this soft rock can cause the plates to move and collide.

A **tsunami** is a giant wave that moves very fast across the surface of the sea, at up to 500 km per hour. When a tsunami reaches the shore, the sea along the coastline gets sucked back into the wave, so the sea seems to disappear before the huge wave hits the coastline. A tsunami is caused by an earthquake under the sea.

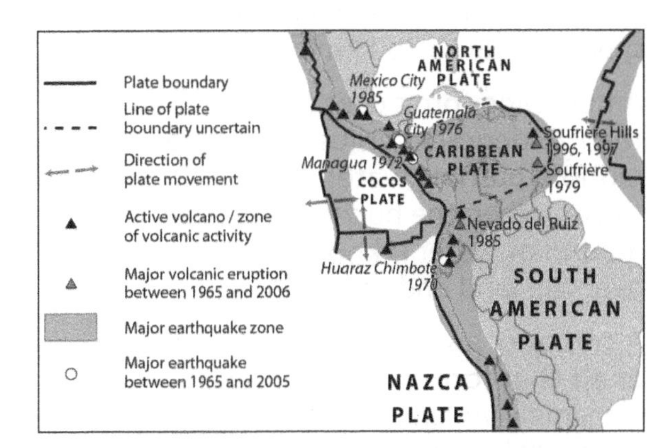

The map above shows the plate boundaries that affect our region.

Exercise

2. Is a flood or drought more likely to occur in your country?
3. Which of the following is true?
   a) Earthquakes can lead to tsunamis.
   b) Tsunamis can lead to earthquakes.

Research

Look at the picture of the Manzanilla/Mayaro road collapse in Trinidad. Research any natural disasters that have occurred in your country in recent years, for example flooding, drought or landslides.

Key vocabulary

natural disasters
drought
flood
landslide
earthquake
(plate) boundaries
tsunami

Hurricanes, tornadoes and volcanoes

We are learning to:

- understand how hurricanes, tornadoes and volcanes can occur.

Hurricanes and tornadoes

In the Caribbean region, the most common natural disasters are those caused by weather conditions such as flooding and high winds. We will now look at more places affected by these kinds of disaster.

A **cyclone** is a tropical storm with a closed, circulating wind pattern. A **hurricane** occurs when a tropical cyclone moves faster than 33 m per second. The area of a hurricane can measure more than 950 km across, and it can move at speeds of up to 300 km per hour.

A hurricane forms over areas of ocean that are warmer than 26 degrees Celsius. Hurricanes move in a spiralling motion, pushing water into a mound at the centre of the storm. When the hurricane reaches the coast, this swirling mound of water is known as a storm surge, which rushes over the land and causes flooding.

A **tornado**, also known as a twister, is a spinning column of air that forms under thunderclouds. Tornadoes can be extremely violent and destructive, with wind speeds of more than 480 km per hour. They can destroy buildings, pull up trees and throw cars and people through the air.

The aftermath of Hurricane Flora, which struck the Caribbean in 1963. This photo shows the damage caused in Haiti.

Activity

Research a famous tornado or hurricane to have struck the Caribbean. Present a project including a description of the disaster and a map showing its movements and the areas affected.

If you choose to research Hurricane Irma or Hurricane Maria, and your island was affected, you could include information about how you and your friends and family were affected, and what your community has done to rebuild the area.

Places in the Caribbean affected by hurricanes and cyclones

The official Atlantic hurricane season is from 1 June to 30 November each year. The south eastern part of the region has the least number of hurricanes, while the south west and north east have the most.

The most violent Atlantic hurricane in history was Hurricane Flora, which took place in September 1963. It passed over the Lesser Antilles, Trinidad and Tobago, the Leeward Antilles, Puerto Rico, Jamaica, Cuba, the Bahamas, Bermuda, and Turks and Caicos, killing some 7000 people in its path.

Exercise

1. What is the difference between a cyclone and a hurricane?
2. During which months of the year are you most likely to experience cyclones in the Caribbean?

Volcanic eruptions

A **volcano** is a type of mountain that has an opening vent leading down into a pool of molten rock deep under the Earth's crust. When pressure builds up underground, the volcano may erupt. Gases and molten rock rise up and spill out of the vent. Smoke, ash and fragments of lava may fly into the air and hot magma and ash flow out of the volcano over nearby land.

Erupting volcanoes may have many destructive effects. They can also cause other natural disasters such as tsunamis, earthquakes, landslides and flooding.

There are three main categories of volcano:

- active: has erupted recently; is able to erupt again
- dormant: has not erupted for a long time, but may be able to erupt again
- extinct: erupted thousands of years ago, but is not able to erupt again.

Lava flows into the sea after the Soufrière Hills volcano eruption in 1997 in Montserrat.

Places in the Caribbean that have volcanoes

Some famous Caribbean places that have volcanoes:

- Dominica: the most famous volcanic areas are the Boiling Lake and Valley of Desolation, which have pools of steaming and bubbling water that release gases and vapours from molten lava below the Earth's crust.
- Grenada: Kick 'em Jenny is an active volcano under the sea around 8 km north of Grenada. It erupted at least 12 times between 1939 and 2001.
- Guadeloupe: La Grande Soufrière last erupted in 1976.
- Montserrat: Soufrière Hills volcano erupted in 1997, destroying the capital city of Plymouth and forcing most of the island's population to flee to safety.
- Saint Lucia: Sulphur Springs is a popular tourist destination where people can drive up to the edge of the volcano and look into the hot springs below.
- Saint Vincent and the Grenadines: La Soufrière volcano is an active volcano that erupted in 1718, 1812, 1902 and 1979.

Activity

Research one of the famous volcanoes in the Caribbean. Write a report with a picture map showing the location of the volcano and interesting facts about it.

Exercise

3. Which is more dangerous: an active or dormant volcano? Give a reason for your answer.
4. In French, 'soufrière' means 'sulphur outlet'. Why do you think so many volcanoes have this word as part of their name?

Key vocabulary

cyclone

hurricane

tornado

volcano

Questions

See how well you have understood the topics in this unit.

1. Copy and complete the table below. List the resources and for each one, tick renewable or non-renewable.

Resource	Renewable	Non-renewable

wood air tide power natural gas soil fresh water
livestock fruit coal gold wind solar energy salt
petrol fish

2. Copy and complete the table. Tick one or more terms that apply to each item.

	Physical environment	Natural environment	Man-made environment	Natural resource
Mountains and rivers				
Apartments and houses				
Sky				
Sunshine				
Ocean waves				
Wetland				
Hotels				

3. For each of the following natural resources, give at least two uses:

a) oil **b)** natural gas **c)** bauxite

4. Unscramble the names of these types of pollution:

a) tatinoesfrode **b)** doils etwas **c)** iistndural

5. Identify two ways that agriculture causes land pollution.

6. Identify two consequences for the land from industrial pollution.

7. Which sources of water pollution are caused mainly by:

a) farmers? **b)** the energy sector? **c)** daily human activities?

8. Name three sustainable agricultural practices.
9. Why are the forests important to the ecosystem?
10. Name three uses of petroleum.
11. Write your own definitions for:
    - **a)** natural environment
    - **b)** physical environment
    - **c)** man-made environment
    - **d)** natural resource
12. Explain why our rivers and forests are important as:
    - **a)** a source of natural resources
    - **b)** a system to protect natural resources
13. Trace a map of the Caribbean from an atlas. Mark on your map four places where natural resources can be found.
14. Do the positive consequences of using our natural resources outweigh the negative consequences? Write an essay in which you outline the main positive and negative consequences of using our natural resources in order to explain your view.
15. **a)** Identify the three main types of pollution.
    b) Choose one type and describe how it can have negative effects on the environment.
16. Suggest an alternative that farmers could use instead of chemical fertiliser.
17. Complete the table by adding at least one physical resource for each country.

Anguilla	
Antigua and Barbuda	
Barbados	
Dominica	
Grand Cayman	
Grenada	
Guyana	
Montserrat	
Saint Kitts and Nevis	
Saint Lucia	
Saint Vincent and the Grenadines	
Trinidad and Tobago	

Checking your progress

To make good progress in understanding our environment, check that you understand these ideas.

- ☐ Name five types of physical or natural resource.
- ☐ Choose three natural resources and explain the different ways we use them in our everyday lives.
- ☐ Explain the different uses we have for oil and gas, and the by-products of oil refining.

- ☐ Identify the different conventional methods of agriculture that farmers use.
- ☐ Explain the advantages and disadvantages of conventional agriculture.
- ☐ Explain how human activities have negative effects on how we use our physical resources.

- ☐ Name three types of pollution.
- ☐ Describe the main problems for each of the pollution types and explain what solutions there are to solve this.
- ☐ Explain the advantages and disadvantages of using fossil fuels and decide whether we should still use them.

- ☐ Name the '3 Rs' that will help us to care for our environment.
- ☐ Explain why sharing a car with your neighbour to work every day will help to save the environment.
- ☐ Explain why the Caribbean region often faces natural disasters.

Unit 9: World geography

In this unit you will find out

World geography: Exploring the world

- What is geography?
  - Human and physical geography
  - Why is it important to study geography?
- The continents and oceans
  - Continents and oceans of the world
- Mountains and deserts
  - Physical features of the continents
- The world's rivers

World geography: Boundaries and borders

- Political maps
  - The purpose of a political map
- The features that define a country
  - Land space
  - System of government
  - National emblems
- Political borders
  - Factors that determine a country's borders
- Our borders
  - Reasons for boundaries: treaties; demarcated boundaries
  - Regional boundaries of Trinidad and Tobago
- Comparing borders
- Creating a new country
  - A fictitious country

What is geography?

We are learning to:

- explain why it is important to study geography.

What is geography?

The word 'geography' comes from the Ancient Greek 'geo-' meaning Earth and 'graphia' meaning writing. In ancient times, geography was mostly about drawing **maps** – pictures of what people thought the surface of the Earth looked like.

In this unit, we will focus on two aspects of geography:

- the relationship between man and his environment (**human geography**)
- the sustainable use of the environment (**physical geography**).

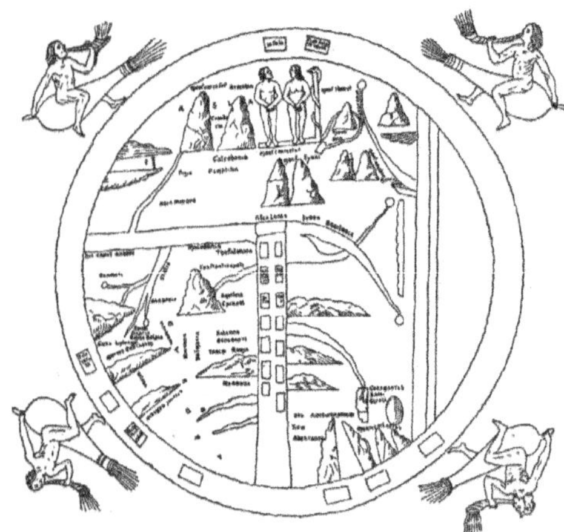

This map is from the 8th century. It shows the world circular but flat, surrounded by a stream of ocean, with four winds represented in the corners.

Human geography

Human geography is the study of how human activity affects or is influenced by the environment.

The environment determines what people can do and create within it, but human activities also affect the environment. For example, we can only create cities close to freshwater resources. However, cities may change the environment and affect the water supply.

Physical geography

Physical geography is the study of the features of the natural environment, such as mountains, rivers, oceans and forests, as well as the processes within our natural environment – for example, the water cycle.

In order to live in a sustainable way on Earth, we need to understand the processes that shaped the planet and continue to affect the climate and the natural environment.

Activity

Using YouTube and SlideShare on the internet, do a search on 'importance of geography'. Find at least two different videos on this topic and watch them as a class. Discuss what you agreed or disagreed with in each video.

Why is it important to study geography?

It is important to study geography for several reasons.

- To understand our natural environment: geography helps us to understand how features such as mountains are formed, and processes such as the water cycle.
- To understand and predict climate and weather: through geography, we can study weather and climate patterns. We can also see how human activities such as industry and air travel affect the world climate.
- To understand cultures: geography helps us to investigate the Earth and the people who live here. We can compare and understand different cultures and religions.
- To develop useful skills: studying geography helps us to develop a range of useful skills such as mapwork, data collection, information and communications technology (ICT) and problem solving.
- To open up a world of careers: geography opens up a number of different careers. This box lists some of the careers in the field of geography.

- Agriculture
- Climatology and meteorology
- Coastal, marine and hydrographic studies
- Community development
- Conservation, heritage and land management
- Environmental and social work
- Hazard assessment and disaster management
- Market research
- Managing natural resources
- Planning, for example urban and social planning
- Population studies
- Tourism
- Geographic information systems

Parlatuvier Bay, Tobago. The study of geography helps us to understand the relationship between humans and their environment.

Exercise

1. What are the two branches of geography called?
2. Write your own definitions of the two branches of geography.
3. Compare the map on the opposite page with a modern map or atlas. How is it different from maps of today?
4. From the list of jobs above, suggest two jobs each from the fields of human and physical geography.
5. Look at the photograph on this page. Suggest what kind of work someone in one of the careers listed might do in an environment like the Caribbean.

Discussion

Have a class discussion about why you think it is important to study geography.

Activity

Use cut-out images from brochures, fliers, newspapers or magazines. Create a collage showing what you have learned about the importance of geography.

Key vocabulary

map

human geography

physical geography

The continents and the oceans

We are learning to:

- name and locate the continents and major oceans on a **globe** and map of the world
- develop research skills using an atlas, websites and other sources.

Continents of the world

The continents make up about 30 per cent of the Earth's surface. The land areas – or **landmasses** – are divided into seven **continents**. The table shows the names of the continents and their approximate area.

Continent	Area (km²)
Africa	30 000 000
Antarctica	14 000 000
Asia	44 000 000
Europe	13 000 000
Oceania	9 000 000
North America	24 500 000
South America	18 000 000

Oceans of the world

Oceans cover about 71 per cent of the Earth's surface and contain about 97 per cent of the Earth's **seas**. There are five oceans on the Earth's surface:

- Pacific Ocean
- Indian Ocean
- Atlantic Ocean, which is divided into the North Atlantic (north of the Equator) and South Atlantic (south of the Equator)
- Arctic Ocean (surrounding the North Pole)
- Southern Ocean (surrounding Antartica).

There are many other smaller seas and oceans on Earth, such as the Caribbean Sea between North and South America.

You can also use a **globe** to explore and locate the oceans and continents of the Earth.

Exercise

1. Look at the world map on the next page.
   - **a)** If you travelled east from the Caribbean, which continent would you eventually reach?
   - **b)** Which continent is directly north of Africa?
   - **c)** Which continent is east of Europe?
2. Write the names of the continents in size order.
3. Name the ocean that is:
   - **a)** between North America and Europe
   - **b)** south of Asia
   - **c)** between Africa and South America
4. Name the ocean that is nearest to the Caribbean.
5. Why do you think you cannot see the islands of the Caribbean on the world map?

Research

Look at different maps of the world on the internet and in an atlas. As a class, discuss the different ways that mapmakers show the world map. Talk about colours, map shape and any other differences you notice.

Comparing the continents

Each continent has its own particular size and shape on the map. However, you may notice similarities and differences. For example, Asia and Europe are wider than they are long. South America, North America and Africa each have a wider area towards the north and a longer 'tail' down towards the south.

Discussion

Discuss any other similarities or differences you notice in the shapes and sizes of the continents.

The World: Continents

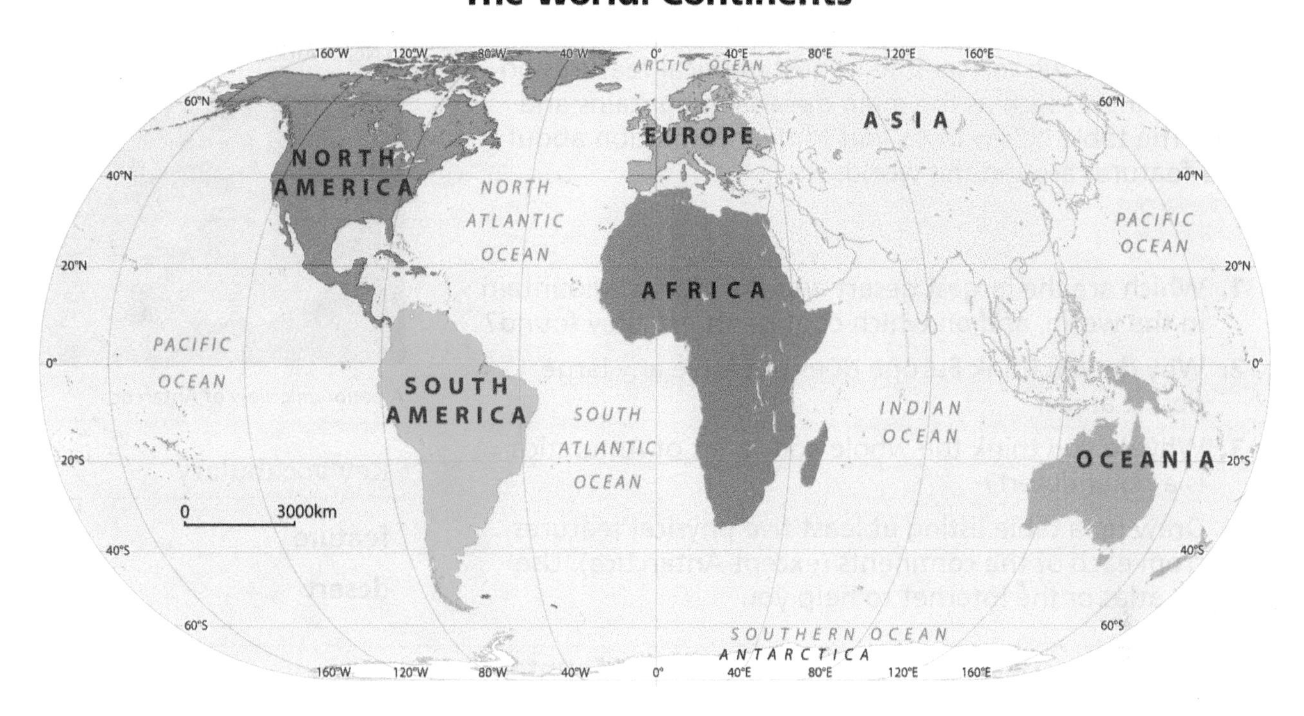

Key vocabulary

landmass
continent
sea
globe

Mountains and deserts

We are learning to:

- name the world's major mountains and deserts
- develop our research skills.

Physical features of the continents

Physical maps show the physical **features** of the land, such as mountains, rivers and seas. On physical maps you can see some of the world's highest mountains and largest deserts.

When we look at a world map, such as the one on the opposite page, we can see the largest physical features on each continent, such as the main **deserts**, mountains and rivers. The table below gives you some information about these features around the world.

A panoramic view of the Sahara desert in North Africa.

A panoramic view of Antarctica.

Exercise

1. Which are the largest desert and the highest mountain in the world, and on which continents are they found?
2. Why do you think Europe does not have any large desert areas?
3. Why do you think the whole continent of Antarctica is a polar desert?
4. Draw up a table listing at least five physical features from each of the continents (except Antarctica). Use an atlas or the internet to help you.

Key vocabulary

feature

desert

Continent	Deserts (area in km²)	Mountain ranges
Asia	Arabian (2 330 000)	Himalayas (3863 km long) Highest peak: Mount Everest (8848 m)
Africa	Sahara (9 400 000)	Highest peak: Mount Kilimanjaro (5895 m)
North America	Great Basin (490 000)	Rocky Mountains (6035 km long) Highest peak: Denali (6190 m)
South America	Patagonia (670 000)	Andes (7242 km long) Highest peak: Aconcagua (6962 m)
Europe		Alps (1200 km long) Caucasus (1100 km long) Highest peak: Mount Elbrus (5642 m)
Australia	Great Victoria Desert (348 750)	Great Dividing Range in Australia (3621 km long)
Antarctica	Antarctica (14 000 000)	Ellsworth Mountains (360 km long) Highest peak: Mount Vinson (4892 m)

The World: Physical Geography

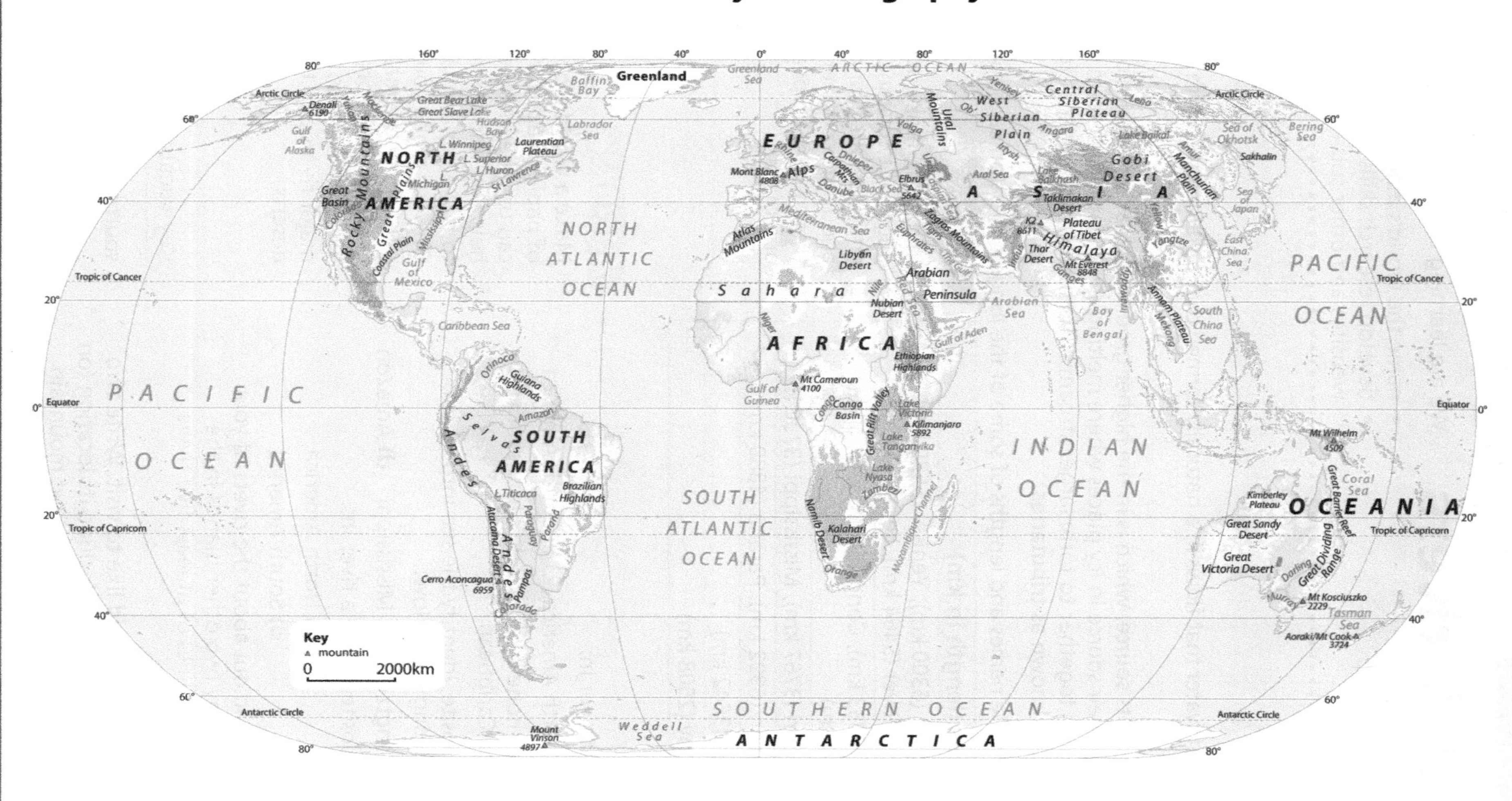

The world's rivers

We are learning to:

- name the world's major rivers
- develop research skills using atlases, websites and other sources.

Rivers of the world

A river is a long body of water that flows in a naturally formed channel along the Earth's surface until it reaches the sea.

A river always begins at its **source**, which is in the higher ground such as mountains or hills. Many rivers have their source in icy places where melting snow gathers to form little streams. The streams join together to form larger streams. The smaller streams that feed into the larger rivers are known as **tributaries**.

The table below shows the names and lengths of some of the longest rivers on each continent.

Continent	Rivers (length in km)
Asia	Yangtze (6300 km), Yenisei (5539 km), Yellow River (5464 km), Lena (4400 km)
Africa	Nile (6853 km), Congo (4700 km), Niger (4200 km)
North America	Missouri (3767 km), Mississippi (3730 km)
South America	Amazon (6992 km), Paraná (4880 km)
Europe	Volga (3642 km)
Australia	Murray (2508 km)

Activity

In groups, make up a jingle of two stanzas entitled 'Our World' about the continents, their mountain peaks and rivers.

Exercise

1. Name the longest river in:
   a) Asia **b)** North America **c)** South America
2. Why do you think none of the world's longest rivers are located in the Caribbean?
3. Use the map opposite. Identify the sea into which each of the following rivers flow:
   a) Nile **b)** Yangtze **c)** Mississippi **d)** Amazon
4. Use the map opposite. Name a river in:
   a) Asia **b)** North America
   c) Africa **d)** South America
5. Use the internet. Find out about the rivers of your country, as well as any two other islands in the Caribbean. Find the names of at least five rivers in each country.
6. Research a country you would like to visit. Write two paragraphs about this country. Include its location (on which continent it is located), the highest mountain peak and the longest river.

Activity

Make a world globe out of papier mâché. You can use the internet to help you find out how to make papier mâché. On your globe you must show the main continents and oceans, mountain ranges, three major rivers and three deserts.

Key vocabulary

source

tributary

The World: Major Rivers

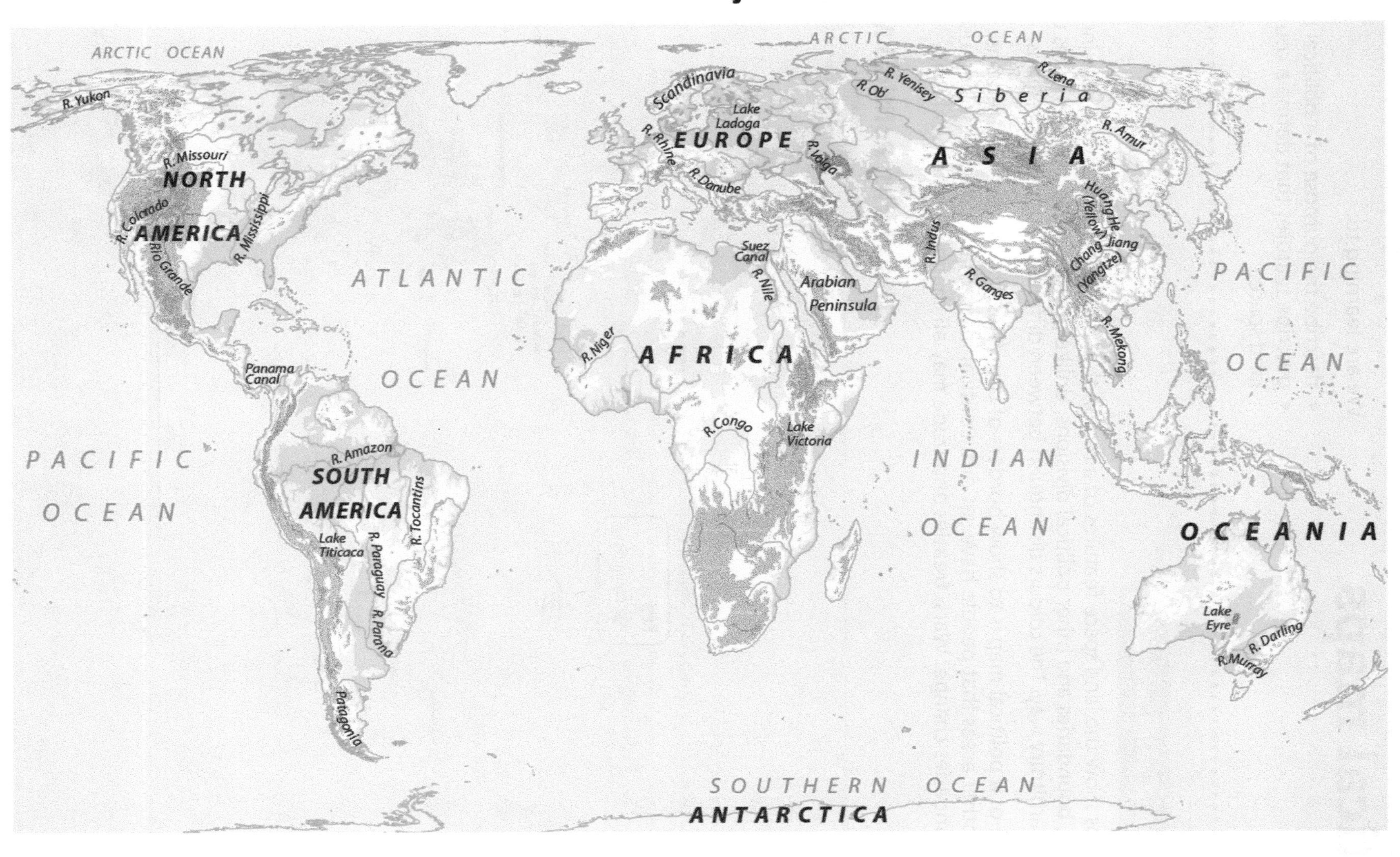

Political maps

We are learning to:

- describe the purpose of a political map
- describe features that define a country: land space.

The purpose of political maps

Political maps show the land space features of a region that people have created. These include towns, cities, **boundaries** and other **political** divisions. Unlike physical maps, political maps use colour in an arbitrary way. The colours distinguish between different countries or regions.

The purpose of a political map is to show borders of countries, states, counties, regions, parishes or other areas that people have set out. Political maps change over time because political boundaries change. Wars, treaties and trade may all change the political map.

The World: Political Map

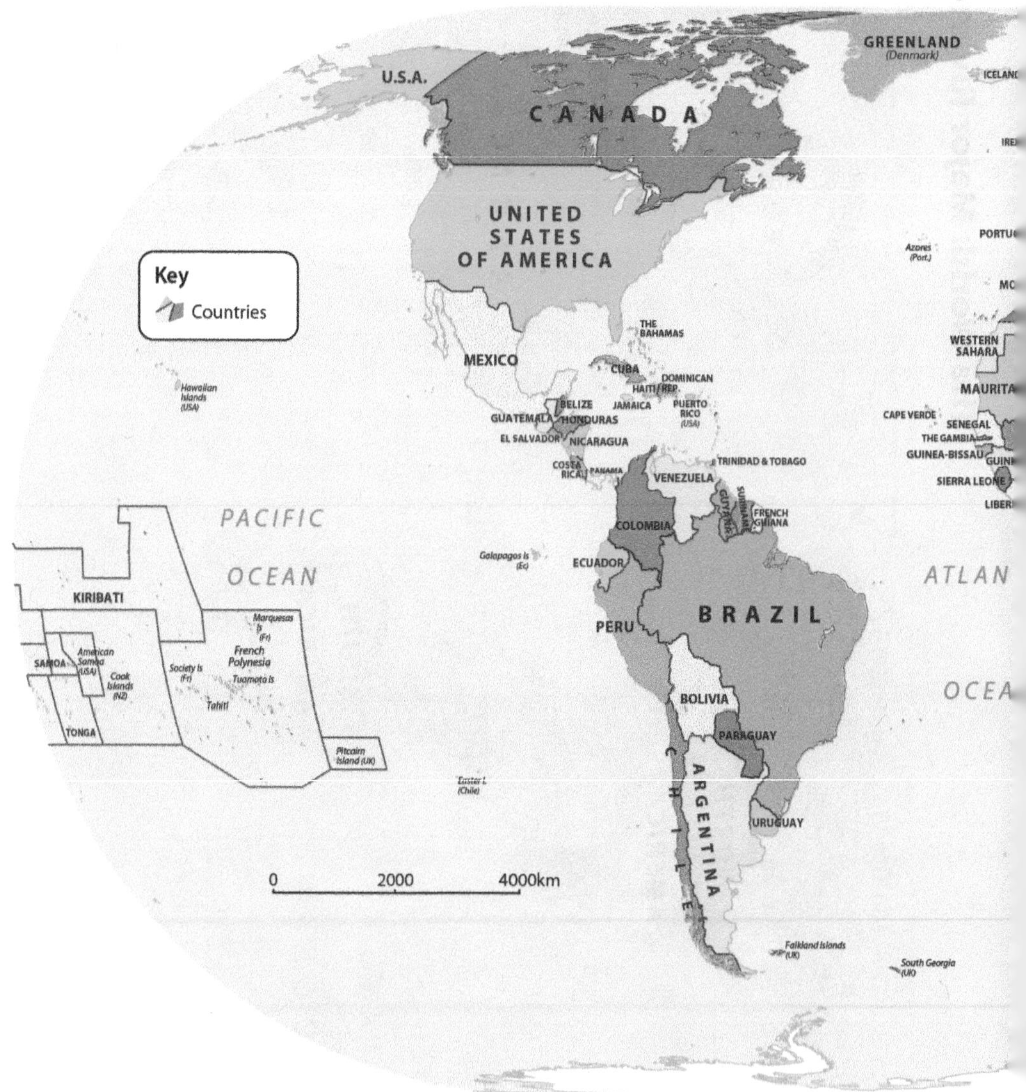

Exercise

Compare the physical map on page 245 with the political map below. Copy and complete this table comparing physical and political maps.

	Physical maps	Political maps
What they show		
How they use colour		
What we use them for		

Key vocabulary

boundaries

political

The features that define a country

We are learning to:

- explain the features that define a country: system of government; national emblems.

Features of a country

There are approximately 195 countries in the world. Each country has its own particular land space and its own particular physical features.

A country is made up of two elements: the land enclosed by its borders and the people who live within its borders. Even though natural features create some of the world's borders, it is important to remember that borders are a human invention.

Governments decide where to separate different countries based on a number of features that make one country different from another. Countries range in size: there are enormous countries, such as Russia, and tiny countries, such as Lesotho and Fiji. However, no matter what its size, a country has several important features, including:

- internationally accepted borders
- people who identify as citizens
- one or more national languages
- a system of government
- a capital town or city.

National identity

Other features of a country relate to its **national identity**. National identity is an idea of what it means to belong to a particular country. Often, national identity is carried in particular traditions, culture, language and symbols. For example, most countries have:

- a flag, an anthem and a national **emblem**
- a shared history and culture
- a currency (the money used in that country)
- national holidays, customs and traditions.

People

In some countries, almost everyone speaks the same language, or follows the same religion, or comes from the same ethnic group. Most countries have a mix of different groups of people. People form groups by **ethnicity**, religion, culture or language.

Activity

There is a CARICOM song, which is the official patriotic song of the Caribbean Community. Here is a selection of the lyrics. In groups, look at the lyrics and decide what they mean.

Celebrating Caricom

[CHORUS] Raise your voices high
Sing of your Caribbean pride
Sing it loud and strong
Feel our hearts beat as one
Celebrate in song
As we rise to heights where we belong
Sound the victory drum
For CARICOM

Activity

Create a poster identifying the national emblems of your country and explain their significance to the people of your country.

The Caribbean: Political Map

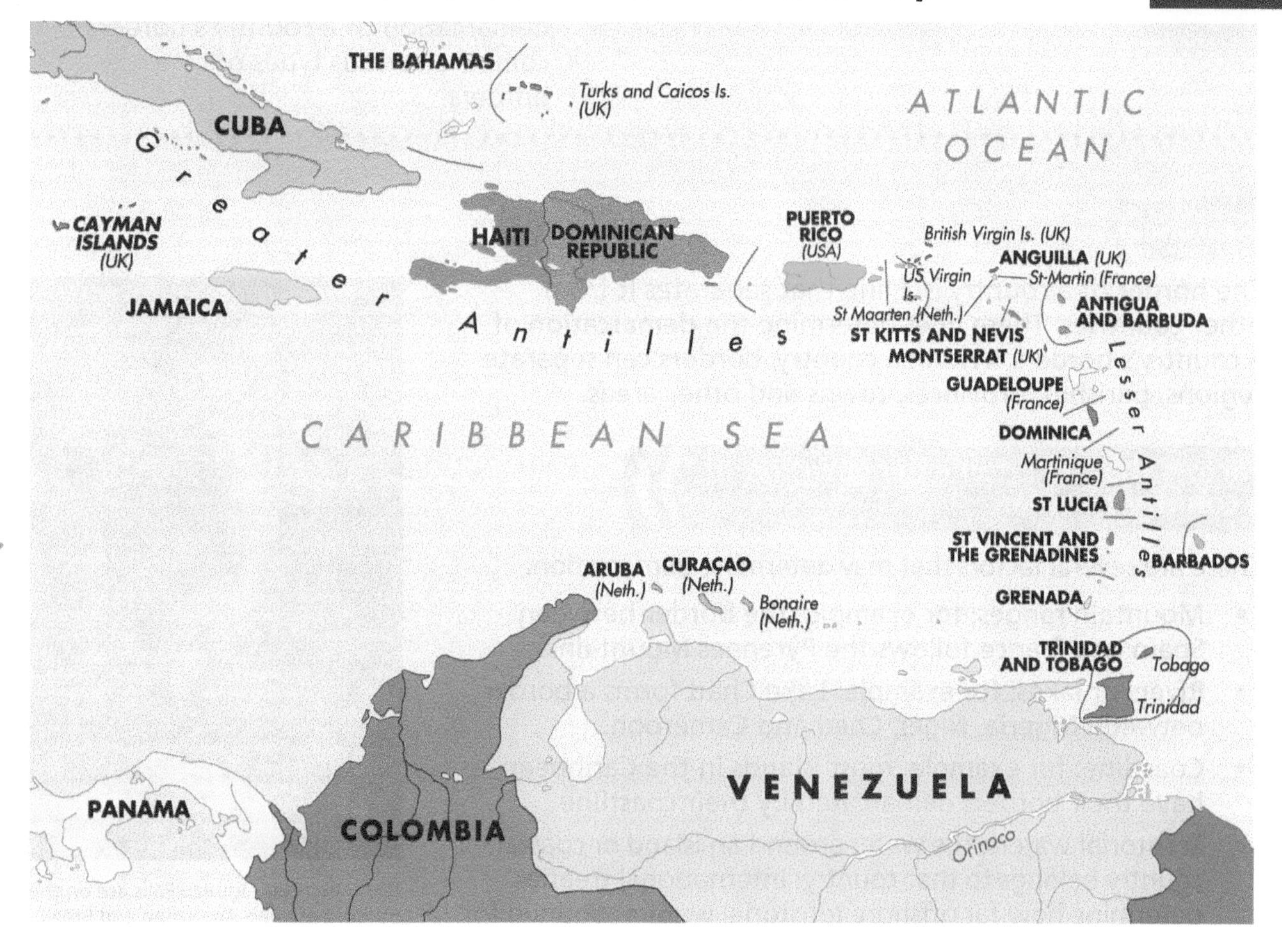

Exercise

1. Use the map above. For each of the following countries, describe its location, size and shape, borders, neighbours and language:
   a) Antigua and Barbuda **b)** Dominica
   c) Trinidad and Tobago **d)** Anguilla
2. What are the two most important elements that make up a country?
3. Choose any world country to research. Draw up a fact file for your country including all the following details: name, continent, population size, official language(s), main religions, main ethnic groups, a picture of the national flag, the name of the national anthem and a picture of one of the national symbols.
4. Choose any five different world countries. Use the internet to research their national emblems. As a class, put together a large world map. Pin the emblems you researched to their corresponding countries.

Did you know...?

China and India are the only countries in the world that have over a billion people.

Key vocabulary

government
national identity
emblem
ethnicity

Political borders

We are learning to:

- examine factors that determine the demarcation of a country's borders
- compare various types of country borders.

Borders

The **border** of a country is a line that separates it from other countries. These lines determine the **demarcation** of a country's borders. Within a country, borders can separate regions, parishes, provinces, towns and other areas.

Factors that determine demarcation of a country's borders

There are several factors that may determine demarcation.

- Mountain ranges: for example, the border between Spain and France follows the Pyrenees Mountains.
- Rivers or lakes: for example, Lake Chad forms a border between Nigeria, Niger, Chad and Cameroon.
- Coastline: for example, most islands in the Caribbean have their borders demarcated by their coastline.
- Territorial waters: the water around an island or coastal country belongs to that country; international treaties determine how far offshore territorial waters continue for.

Mountain ranges, rivers and coastline form **natural boundaries**. Other boundaries are created by political agreements. A **straight-line border** tells you that a country was once under colonial rule. The colonising forces drew lines on the map to mark out their territories.

Most countries share part of their borders with **neighbour states**. The countries of the Caribbean are unusual because most of them are islands, so they do not share borders with other countries.

The spectacular Iguazu Falls are on the border between Argentina and Brazil.

Activity

In pairs, list as many landlocked countries as you can in two minutes. Compare notes with the rest of the class. The pair with the most countries is the winner.

Exercise

1. Give two examples of natural boundaries between countries.
2. What does a straight-line border tell you?
3. What is the function of a border?
4. Compare the types of border used by the following three countries: Trinidad and Tobago; Guyana; Bolivia.
5. Name five factors that determine the demarcation of borders.

Did you know...?

Landlocked countries have no coastline; they may have politically drawn borders, or borders such as rivers or mountains.

Functions of borders

9.7

- Marking out the area that a particular government can control by law – a government may only create and enforce laws within the borders of its country.
- Keeping foreigners out – governments usually keep some control over who is allowed into the country; most countries have border posts where people have to show their passports in order to enter or leave.
- Keeping citizens in – some countries, such as North Korea and Cuba, do not easily give permission for citizens to leave.

Key vocabulary

border

demarcation

natural boundary

straight-line border

neighbour state

landlocked

jurisidiction

Disputed borders

Border disputes arise when people disagree over where a border should lie, or to which country certain land should belong.

Case study

The waters around each country in the Caribbean form an Exclusive Economic Zone (EEZ). This is an area that falls within the legal **jurisdiction** of that country. However, sometimes countries disagree about the boundaries of an EEZ.

In 1990, Venezuela and Trinidad and Tobago signed a maritime boundary treaty. The treaty purported to assign to Trinidad and Tobago ocean territory that Barbados claimed as its own.

In 2006, there was an international court case between Barbados and Trinidad and Tobago concerning the maritime boundaries of Trinidad and Tobago's fishing waters.

The court's ruling and award was issued on 11 April 2006. The boundary was set nearly midway between the land of the two island countries. Although neither country's claimed boundary was adopted by the court, the boundary that was set was closer to that claimed by Trinidad and Tobago.

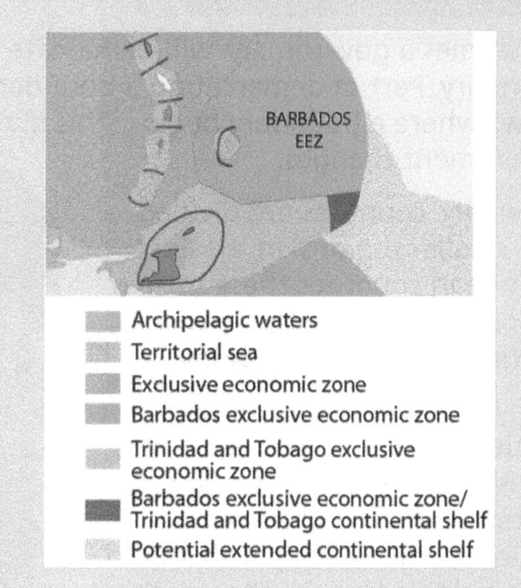

Questions

1. Explain in your own words what an EEZ is for.
2. What are the maritime boundaries of a country determined by?

   a) mountain ranges **b)** rivers

   c) coastlines **d)** territorial waters

   Explain your answer.

Our borders

We are learning to:

- discuss reasons for the borders of the Caribbean countries
- compare types of country borders.

Reasons for boundaries

Boundaries may be set up for different reasons. As you have learned, sometimes a natural feature such as a coastline or river suggests where a boundary lies. However, there are many other reasons boundaries may lie in a particular place. You will look at some of these reasons on this page.

Treaties

A **treaty** is an agreement between two or more regions or countries. There can be treaties which agree land borders or maritime agreements, which establish a specific ocean or sea boundary between two countries (see 9.7).

Demarcating boundaries

Sometimes a government will demarcate a particular boundary. Part of demarcating a boundary is **signage**, which shows where a boundary begins. This may be changed if the government changes.

Internally, countries are divided into smaller regions. In the East Caribbean countries these smaller regions are called either **parishes, districts, regions** or **counties**.

Many Caribbean countries are divided into parishes. The term 'parish' comes from the islands' history under the Church of England, when each parish would have a single church. The parish would be named after the church.

In election times, the parishes, districts or counties, and also the towns and cities, are divided into **wards**.

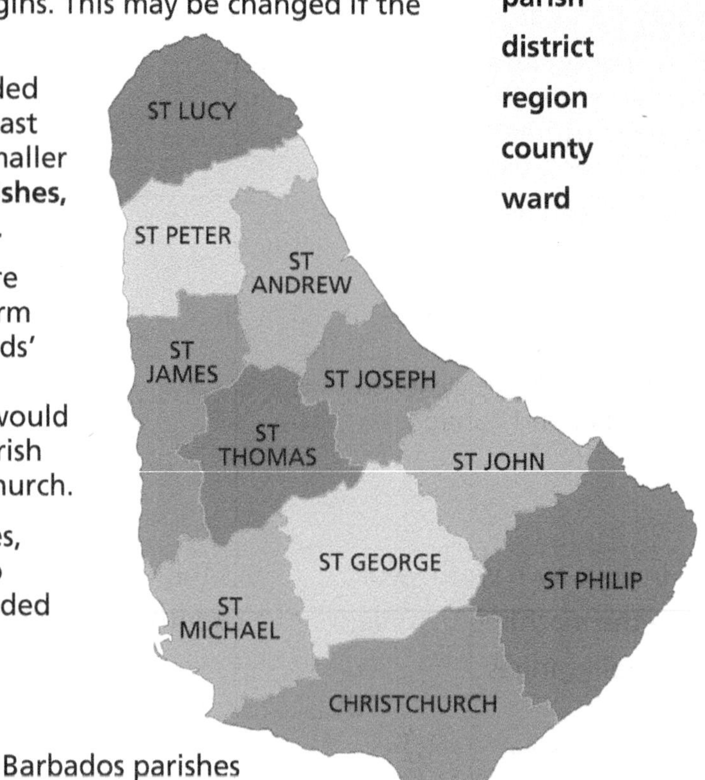

Barbados parishes

Research

Find out about your country's internal divisions, counties or parishes. Draw a map showing them and add in information about key towns and population.

Key vocabulary

treaty

signage

parish

district

region

county

ward

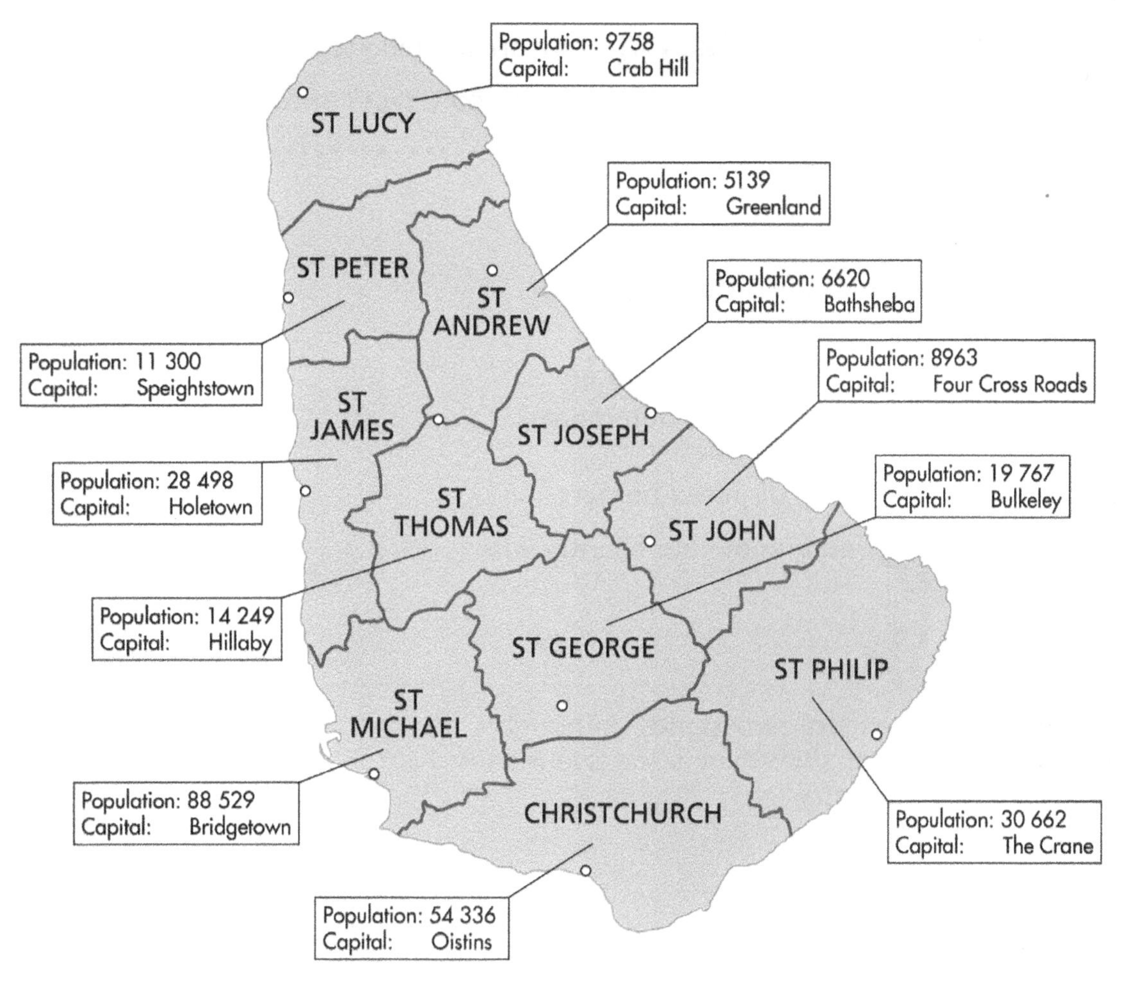

Today, Barbados is divided into 11 regions.

Exercise

1. Name two ways in which a country can be divided up internally and one way in which a country can be separated from another country.
2. What natural feature creates international borders for most of the Caribbean countries?
3. Use the data in the map above. Identify:
   a) 11 parishes
   b) the capitals of Saint Joseph and Saint Michael
   c) the capital of Barbados
   d) the smallest and the largest parish by population
4. Draw a bar graph comparing the populations of all the parishes in Barbados.

Comparing borders

We are learning to:

- compare types of country borders.

Different types of country borders

You have learned about some of the different types of country borders:

- mountain ranges
- rivers
- seas
- coastlines
- territorial waters
- borders determined by treaties
- disputed borders.

Now we will compare the boundaries of your country with other countries in the area.

Saint Kitts and Nevis

Saint Kitts and Nevis is made up of two islands. Although each island is surrounded on all sides by sea, the two islands together make up a single country.

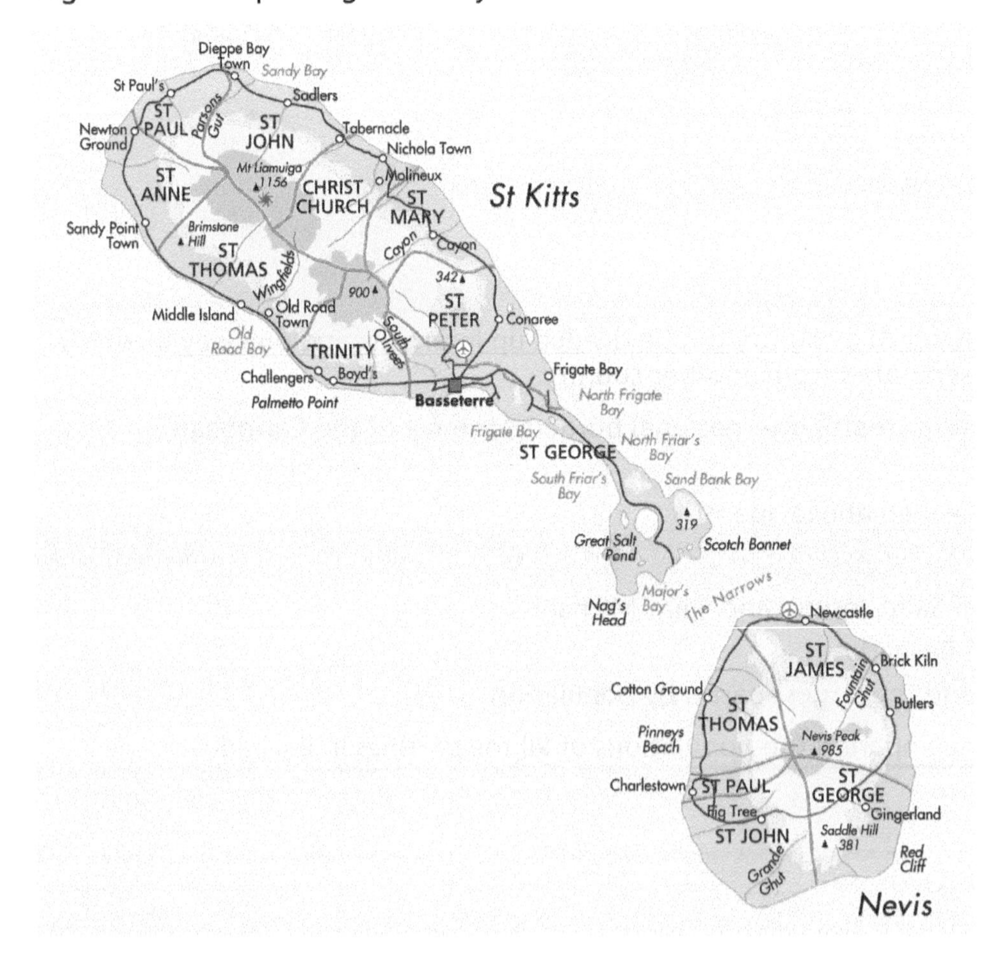

Location of Guyana

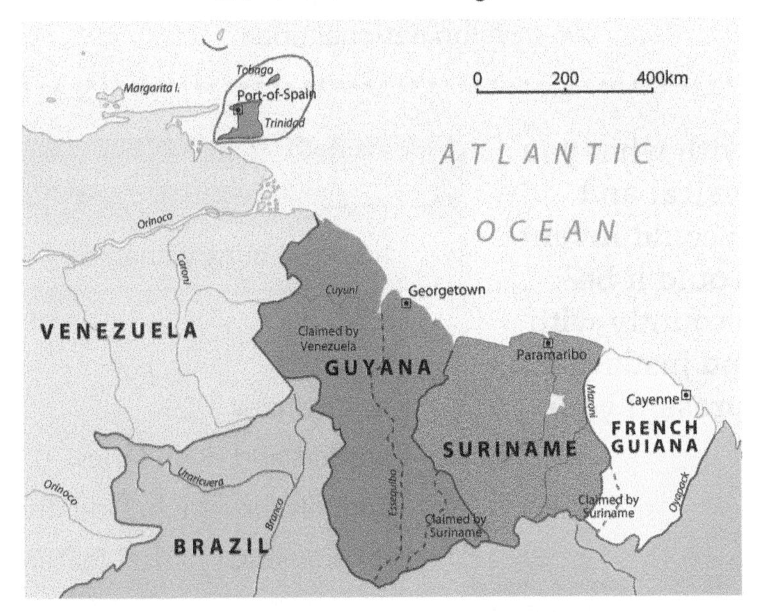

Guyana has part of its border along the coast of the Atlantic Ocean. Inland, it shares borders with three neighbours: Venezuela to the west, Brazil to the south and Suriname to the east.

However, Guyana's neighbours dispute its borders.

The biggest dispute is with Venezuela, which claims almost three quarters of Guyana's land area as well as a large part of its territorial waters.

These are areas that are very rich in oil reserves.

Bolivia

Bolivia is a landlocked country. It has no coastal borders. Its neighbours are Peru, Brazil, Paraguay, Argentina and Chile.

Location of Bolivia

Exercise

1. Match each description below to one of the countries shown on these pages:
   a) landlocked; some borders demarcated by rivers, others by treaties
   b) border partly demarcated by coastline, partly demarcated by treaties with neighbouring countries
   c) border totally demarcated by coastline
2. Name two countries which share borders with Brazil.
3. Trinidad and Tobago share one neighbour country with Guyana.
   a) Which country is their shared neighbour?
   b) What is the difference between Trinidad and Tobago and Guyana in the way they neighbour this country?

Creating a new country

We are learning to:

- create a fictitious country
- make a presentation
- develop national pride.

Now is your time to get creative with what you have learned about countries, physical and political maps and borders. If you could **invent** a country, what type of country would it be? You are going to create a **fictitious** country with all the features discussed below and justification for its boundaries. You will then present your project to your class.

My map should show:

- [ ] title/my country's name
- [ ] scale
- [ ] map key
- [ ] north arrow
- [ ] borders and boundaries
- [ ] symbols for national identity
- [ ] physical and political features
- [ ] capital cities

A fictitious country

'Fictitious' means 'made up'. In your project, you are going to create a fictitious country, with all the features of a real country. You will need to include:

- your country's name
- a physical map
- a political map.

Your physical map should show the main natural features of the country – any rivers, mountains, lakes and deserts, as well as other natural features. Use these features to help you work out the boundaries and borders of the country, as well as any internal boundaries.

Your political map should show boundaries and borders, and the capital city.

Creating national pride

In addition, you will need to create some of the symbols of your country in order to create a national identity. This may include:

- your country's name
- a national animal
- an emblem
- a national anthem.

You may also come up with ideas of events and activities that will help contribute towards national pride.

Guidelines for your project

Your country is made up, but you must give it a location on Earth. Decide on answers to these questions:

- Where is your country located – in which **hemisphere**, and near or on which continent? What is its name?
- Describe the physical geography of your country. Is it a landlocked country within a larger continent? Why does it have the borders it has? Is it a continent of its own, or an island near an existing continent?
- What kind of climate and vegetation does it have? What kinds of weather does your country experience annually? Is it a heavy rainfall area, or dry and temperate? Is it cold and snowy? Does it have deserts or forests? Where are the water sources?
- Which natural resources are found in your country? What are they used for? What is the main energy source?
- What about culture, religion and language? Describe the languages of your made-up country, and any special customs or traditions.
- What political system does the country use? Is it a monarchy, a democracy or a dictatorship? Where is the government located? What is its national emblem?

Once you have answered the questions above, you will be ready to create your country and draw your maps.

Project

Now you are going to create your fictitious country. You need to include maps of your country (physical and political) and you will need to write a commentary explaining why you chose the various features and boundaries for your country. Use the information on these pages to help you.

When you have finished your project, show it to a partner and then answer the following questions.

Exercise

1. Answer the following questions about your partner's project.
   a) What is the country name?
   b) What is the climate like?
   c) What is the population size?
   d) What are the main natural resources?
2. Identify similarities and differences between your country and your partner's.
3. Write a reflective journal entry on the creation of your fictitious country.

Discussion

Discuss what contributes towards national pride. As a class, brainstorm activities and events that help develop the national pride of a country.

Key vocabulary

invent

fictitious

hemisphere

Questions

See how well you have understood the topics in this unit.

1. Name the five oceans and seven continents that are on the Earth's surface.
2. List six different physical features you might see on a physical map and briefly explain what each one means.
3. Copy and complete. Fill in the names of the continents in the correct columns of the table.

In northern hemisphere	In southern hemisphere	In both hemispheres

4. List three ways that a political map is different from a physical map.
5. Identify two famous rivers on each of the following continents:
   a) Asia
   b) Europe
   c) North America
   d) Africa
6. Research and identify, name or draw the following features of your country:
   a) anthem
   b) capital city
   c) flag
   d) national emblem
7. Look at the map on page 245. Identify the continents where the following lakes are:
   a) Lake Superior
   b) Lake Victoria
   c) Lake Titicaca
   d) Lake Baikal
8. Name the three largest islands in the Caribbean.

9. Name the countries numbered 1 to 11 on this map.

10. For each of the following countries, name the capital city:

a) Dominica
b) Guyana
c) Saint Kitts and Nevis
d) Saint Lucia
e) Saint Vincent and the Grenadines

11. Explain in one paragraph what geography is and why it is important to study it.

12. Is it possible to make an accurate map of the world on a single flat piece of paper? Give reasons for your answer.

13. Suggest three factors that can determine the borders of a country.

14. Give examples of three different types of country borders, and explain which type you have in your country.

15. Sketch a map of your country showing the boundaries and names of all the regional corporations.

16. If someone asked you "Where is the Caribbean?" how would you answer them? Include the location in relation to continents and seas and the main island groupings.

Checking your progress

To make good progress in understanding world geography, check that you understand these ideas.

- [ ] Name the two branches of geography.
- [ ] Name five jobs or careers that studying geography can lead to.
- [ ] Give three reasons why it is important that we study geography.
- [ ] Name the five oceans and seven continents on the Earth's surface.
- [ ] Name two physical features of each of the continents.
- [ ] Explain what a political map is.
- [ ] Name five features of a country that help to define it.
- [ ] Explain the difference between a political map and a political border.
- [ ] Explain the reasons for boundaries.
- [ ] Name five different types of natural borders.
- [ ] Explain the different functions of the borders that belong to a country.
- [ ] Explain the differences between the borders of countries.

Unit 10: The world around us

In this unit, you will find out

World geography: Locating places

- Longitude and latitude
  - Purpose of longitude and latitude
- History of longitude and latitude
  - Inventors of longitude and latitude

The Caribbean region

- Locating the Caribbean
  - Location of the Caribbean in relation to the rest of the world
- Caribbean territories
- Caribbean region and integration
  - Geography of the region
- Integration movements
  - CARIFTA, CARICOM, CSME

Building map skills: conventional signs

- What is a map and what are basic map features?
- Observing, using and drawing maps

Building map skills: map scale

- Types of map scale (ratio, linear, scale)
- Working with map scales and measuring distance
- Using map scales; scaling up and down

Building map skills: cardinal points

- The eight cardinal points

Building map skills: locating places

- Finding places on a map
  - Easting and northing grid lines
- Maps of today

Longitude and latitude

We are learning to:

- describe the characteristics and purpose of lines of longitude and latitude
- locate places and give locations using longitude and latitude.

Characteristics of lines of latitude

Lines of latitude are imaginary lines that run horizontally from east to west. Latitude is measured in degrees (°) north or south of the Equator. The North Pole is at 90° north and the South Pole is at 90° south. There are 180 lines of latitude. The main lines of latitude you will notice on maps are:

- the Tropic of Cancer (23.5°N)
- the Tropic of Capricorn (23.5°S)
- the Arctic Circle (66.5°N)
- the Antarctic Circle (66.5°S)
- the North Pole (90°N)
- the South Pole (90°S).

The Equator is at 0° – this line divides the Earth into the northern and southern **hemispheres**.

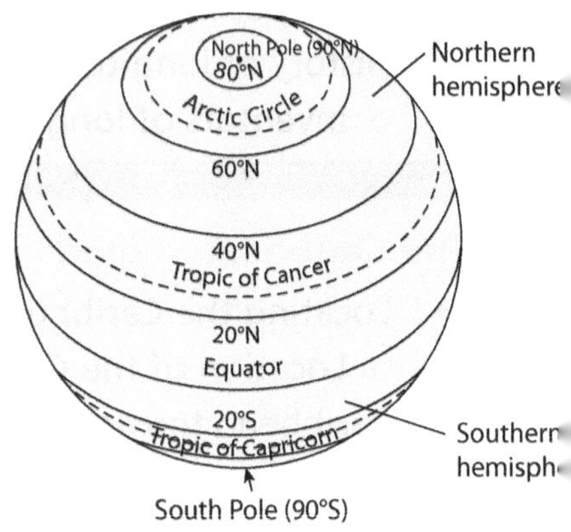

Lines of latitude.

Characteristics of lines of longitude

Lines of longitude are imaginary lines that run vertically from north to south. They are measured in degrees.

The most important line of longitude is the **prime meridian** (0°). This is also known as the Greenwich Meridian, because it runs through the Greenwich Observatory in Britain. Exactly halfway round the Earth from the Greenwich Meridian is the International Date Line, at 180°. The eastern and western hemispheres are situated to the east and west of the prime meridian.

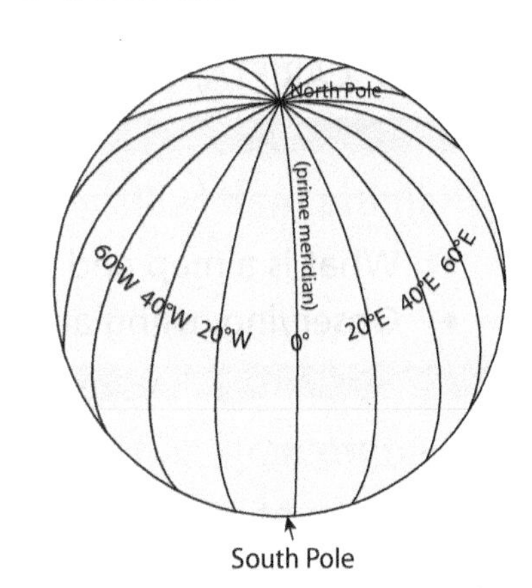

Lines of longitude.

On the map to the right, you can see that Cayo Coco's latitude is halfway between 22°N and 23°N. Its longitude is halfway between 78°W and 79°W. We can write its position as 22.5°N, 78.5°W.

Discussion

In pairs discuss the purpose of lines of latitude and longitude, and identify two characteristics of both.

Purpose of longitude and latitude

Remember, lines of longitude and latitude do not exist in real life. They are tools that help people locate places on maps and describe positions.

Look up Dominica in an atlas. Next to the name of Dominica, you will see the page number, followed by a grid reference and then the coordinates (15°25'N 61°20'W). The coordinates for Dominica tell you that it is situated 15 degrees and 25 minutes north of the Equator and 61 degrees 20 minutes west of the Greenwich Meridian.

The table shows you the longitude and latitude of cities in the Caribbean, as well as some of the major cities of the world.

City	Coordinates
Basseterre, Saint Kitts and Nevis:	17°17'50" N 62°43'14" W
St George's, Grenada:	12°3'10" N 61°45'11" W
New York, USA:	40°46'23" N 73°58'21" W
Paris, France:	48°51'17" N 2°20'50" E
Cape Town, South Africa:	33°55'18" S 18°25'14" E
Sydney, Australia:	33°51'43" S 151°12'37"E
Beijing, China:	39°54'59" N 116°23'49" E

The International Date Line

In 1884, delegates attended the International Meridian Conference in the USA to work out an international prime meridian. They agreed on the Greenwich Meridian.

Fortunately, this meant that the 180° meridian (exactly opposite the 0° meridian) mostly passed over water. This line is known as the International Date Line (IDL).

When it is Monday to the left of the IDL, it is Sunday to the right of the IDL. People who cross the line from east to west skip forward by one day. People who cross the line from west to east go back a day.

Exercise

1. Name the line of latitude that is:
   a) furthest to the north and south of the Equator
   b) at 23°S and at 23°N
2. Lines of longitude are given in degrees east or west of the Greenwich Meridian. Is the International Date Line 180°W or 180°E of the Greenwich Meridian? Explain your answer.
3. Complete the following sentences:
   a) Saint Lucia is situated ___________ of the Equator and _________ of the Greenwich Meridian.
   b) Belize is situated ___________ of the Equator and _________ of the Greenwich Meridian.
4. Look at the cities in the table above. Which city/cities:
   a) are in the southern hemisphere?
   b) is furthest north?
   c) is furthest east?
   d) is closest to the Equator?

Activity

On a globe of the world, find the Equator, the Tropic of Cancer and the Tropic of Capricorn. Also identify the Greenwich Meridian and the International Date Line. For each line, identify two countries that have that line passing through them.

Key vocabulary

line of latitude

hemisphere

line of longitude

prime meridian

History of longitude and latitude

We are learning to:

- appreciate the work of inventors of latitude and longitude.

Latitude

For thousands of years, people have used the skies to help with navigation.

The Phoenicians were part of an ancient civilisation in the Middle East. They were known for exploring the world by boat. As long ago as 600 BC, the Phoenicians used the sun and stars to work out their latitude. The Polynesians also used the movement of the stars to work out their latitude.

The ancient Greeks started using grid lines to show latitude and longitude. This was a suggestion by Greek astronomer Hipparchus around 300 BC. Hipparchus also found a way to locate places on Earth by observing the positions of the sun, moon and stars.

Around 225 BC, Eratosthenes, a Greek mathematician and astronomer, measured the circumference of the Earth (the distance around the Earth) by calculating the distance between Alexandria in northern Egypt and Syene in southern Egypt. Once he worked this out, he was able to work out the circumference of the Earth.

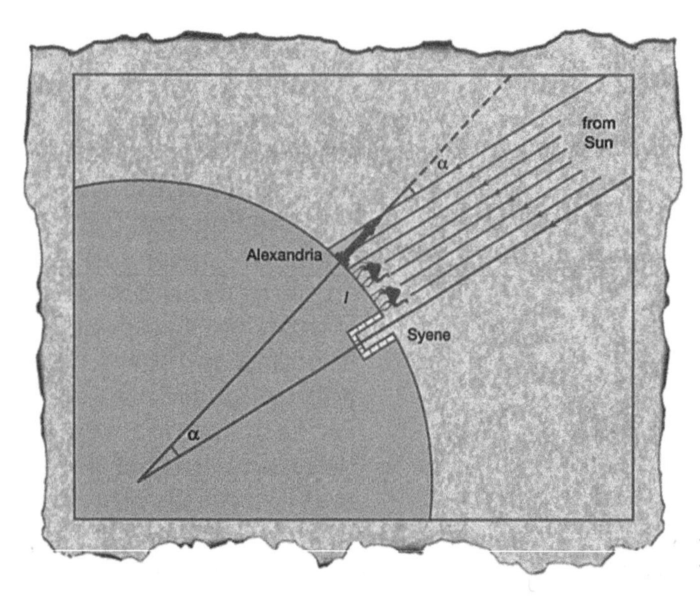

Eratosthenes' knowledge of the sun's position and the distance between two points enabled him to calculate the Earth's circumference.

This discovery helped the Greeks to draw maps, as they then were able to find their latitude easily using trigonometry and the positions of the sun, moon and stars.

Ancient scholars also made many mistakes in their ideas and writings about geography. The Roman scholar Ptolemy believed that the circumference of the Earth was shorter than it actually is. As a result, Christopher Columbus made the mistake of believing he could reach Asia by sailing west from Europe.

The longitude problem

Up until the 18th century, there was no internationally accepted system for calculating longitude. This was a problem for sailors because as soon as they set sail they were 'at sea', an expression that came to mean 'lost'.

Scientists had problems working out how far they had travelled from east to west. It was easier to calculate latitude because they could work out the length of the day, the height of the sun or the distance of the stars above the horizon.

Early mariners used a 'dead reckoning'. They threw a log overboard at the bow (front) and timed how long it took for the log to pass the stern (back) of the ship. They would use this to work out how fast they were travelling, and from that calculation work out how far they had travelled. However, this was very inaccurate because the boat's speed could easily increase or decrease.

In 1707, five British naval ships got lost in heavy fog. Because there was no system of longitude, they miscalculated where they were and 2000 sailors died as a result. In response to this, in 1714, the English parliament offered a prize of £20 000 to anyone who could solve the longitude problem.

One solution was to measure the time at sea and to measure the time on a clock at another place and compare the difference between the two clocks.

However, this was not simple. Clocks at this time operated using metal **pendulums**. A pendulum swings around wildly during storms at sea and metal expands and contracts with changes in temperature, which affected how they worked.

A clockmaker called John Harrison eventually won the prize, after many years of work.

Today, **Global Positioning Systems (GPS)** using satellites have made it possible to identify coordinates from anywhere on Earth.

Exercise

1. Name three ancient civilisations that learned to navigate using the sun, moon and stars.
2. Name two ancient Greeks whose discoveries helped navigators to find their latitude position.
3. Why was it easier to work out latitude than longitude?
4. Create a jingle about the history of latitude and longitude.
5. Create a timeline about the history of longitude and latitude. Add photos from the internet.

Research

Work in groups. Each group chooses and using the internet researches one of the following navigation instruments:

- back staff
- kamal
- astrolabe
- octant
- sextant
- quadrant
- bearing compass
- magnetic compass
- ring dial.

As a class, make a timeline with pictures of the different navigational instruments at the correct places, showing when they were invented or used.

Activity

In groups, create a jingle of two stanzas using the names of the people who created longitude and latitude.
(Tip: Eratosthenes and John Harrison.)

Key vocabulary

pendulum

Global Positioning System (GPS)

Locating the Caribbean

We are learning to:

- locate the Caribbean on a world map
- identify the location of the Caribbean and your country using lines of latitude and longitude.

Locating the Caribbean

To find the Caribbean on a world map:

- First find the continents of North America and South America.
- Look at the narrow strip of land that joins the two continents.
- To the east you will see the Gulf of Mexico and the Caribbean Sea.
- The Caribbean region is located in and around the Caribbean Sea.

Activity

Your teacher will hand out blank maps of the Caribbean. Insert the Tropic of Cancer, the Caribbean territories and their capitals, and the surrounding bodies of water.

The Caribbean: Political Map

Locating your country on the world map

For example, Trinidad and Tobago is made up of two **islands** to the east of the Caribbean Sea and to the north of Venezuela. The country is located between latitudes 10°N and 12°N and between longitudes 60°W and 63°W.

Activity

Follow the steps for locating Trinidad and Tobago to find your own country's longitudes and latitudes.

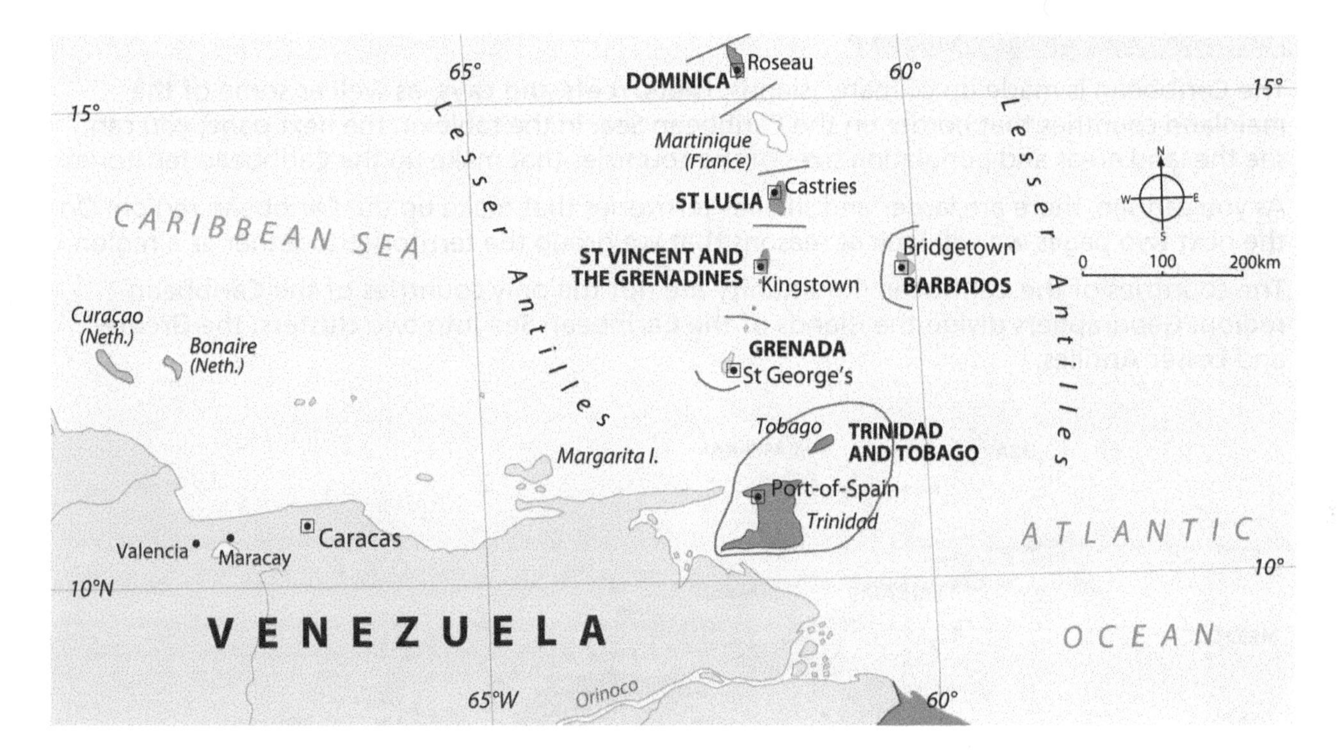

Exercise

1. Copy and complete.
   a) The Caribbean region is located in the ____ Sea.
   b) To the east of the Caribbean is the ____________.
   c) Many Caribbean territories have the ___ Sea on their southern coast and the ___ Ocean on their northern coast.
2. For each of the following territories, find the territory's capital city on the map. Describe where it is located – to the east, west, north or south of the island or territory.
   a) Barbados b) Saint Lucia c) Saint Vincent
3. Name Trinidad and Tobago's nearest neighbours:
   a) in the Caribbean Sea
   b) on the mainland of South America

Discussion

The countries of the Caribbean are considered part of North America although some are closer to South America. Why? Do you agree that this should be the case?

Key vocabulary

islands

Caribbean territories

We are learning to:

- name and locate Caribbean territories, their capitals, seas and oceans on maps of the Caribbean
- compare sizes of Caribbean territories.

Territories of the Caribbean

The Caribbean is made up of many islands, **islets, reefs** and **cays**, as well as some of the **mainland** countries that border on the Caribbean Sea. In the table on the next page, you can see the land areas and population sizes of the countries that make up the Caribbean territories.

As you can see, there are larger and smaller territories that make up the Caribbean region. On the next two pages we will look at reasons that we group the territories together as a region.

The countries of the Caribbean Community are not the only countries of the Caribbean region. Geographers divide the islands of the Caribbean Sea into two clusters: the Greater and Lesser Antilles.

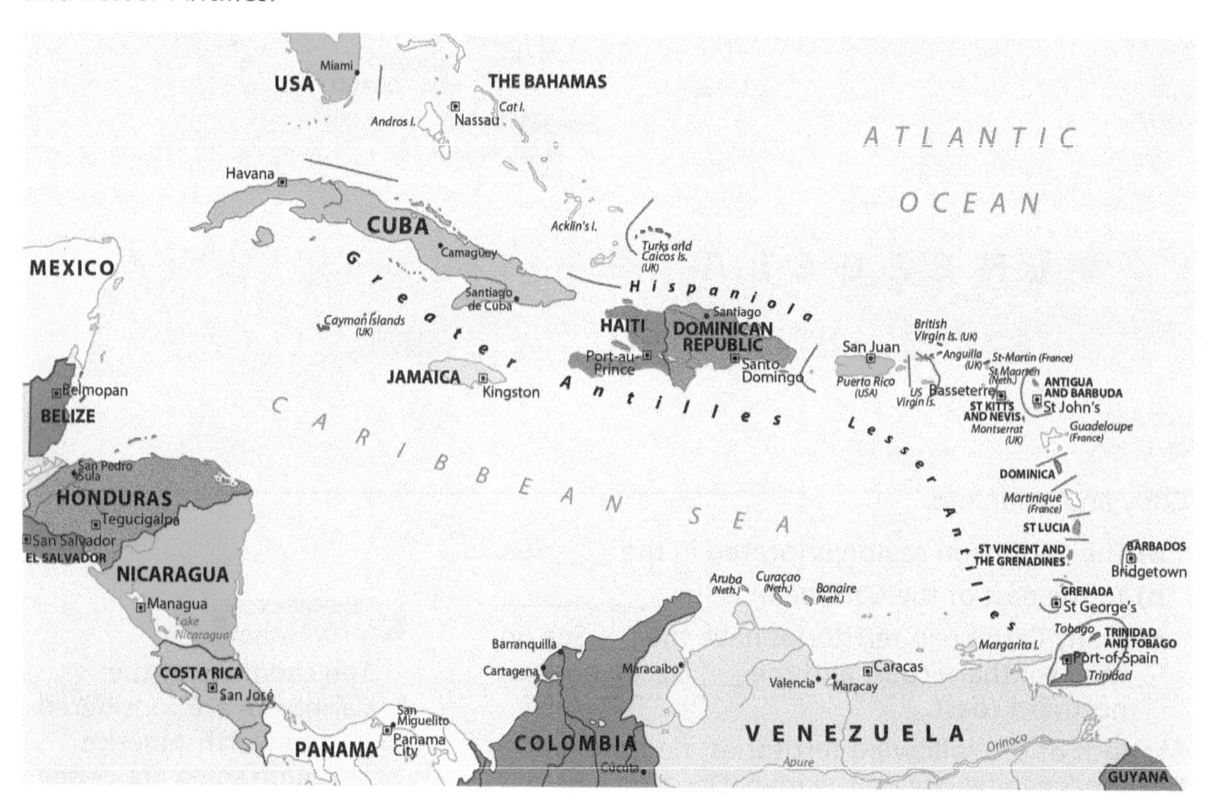

Exercise

1. Identify the three largest islands in the Caribbean.
2. a) Which has the greater number of islands – the Greater or Lesser Antilles?

   b) Which has the greater landmass – the Greater or Lesser Antilles?

Research

Research the sizes and capitals of the non-sovereign states of the Caribbean (states that are governed by other countries).

Territory	Area (km²)	Population size
Anguilla	91	16 752
Antigua and Barbuda	442	92 436
The Bahamas	13 878	324 597
Barbados	430	290 604
Cuba	105 806	11 252 000
Dominica	751	73 607
Dominican Republic	48 442	9 980 000
Grand Cayman	264	57 268
Grenada	344	110 694
Guyana	214 970	735 222
Haiti	27 750	10 110 019
Jamaica	10 991	2 950 210
Montserrat	102	5267
Puerto Rico	9104	3 508 000
Saint Kitts and Nevis	261	51 936
Saint Lucia	616	163 922
Saint Vincent and the Grenadines	389	102 627
Suriname	163 821	579 633
Trinidad and Tobago	5128	1 222 363

Did you know...?

The Puerto Rico Trench to the north of Puerto Rico is the deepest point in the Atlantic Ocean.

The Antilles

The Greater Antilles is made up of five islands – Cuba, the Cayman Islands, Hispaniola (Dominican Republic and Haiti), Puerto Rico and Jamaica. The Greater Antilles makes up more than 90 per cent of the land area of the West Indies. These islands are also home to more than 90 per cent of the population of the West Indies.

The Lesser Antilles is made up of eight independent countries – Antigua and Barbuda; Barbados; Dominica; Grenada; Saint Kitts and Nevis; Saint Lucia; Saint Vincent and the Grenadines; Trinidad and Tobago – as well as 16 other non-sovereign states and territories. The islands of the Lesser Antilles are divided into: **Windward** Islands in the south, **Leeward** Islands in the north, Leeward Antilles in the west.

Activity

Create a map of the Caribbean for your classroom wall on a large sheet of poster card. On each territory, label it with its name, size and population.

Exercise

3. Identify five countries in the Lesser Antilles and name their capital cities.
4. Which cluster of islands has the greater number of small islands – the Greater or Lesser Antilles?
5. Name three of the Leeward Islands and three of the Windward Islands.

Key vocabulary

islet

reef

cay

mainland

windward

leeward

Reasons for Caribbean integration

We are learning to:

- examine reasons for the existence of the Caribbean as a region
- suggest ways of strengthening Caribbean integration.

Reasons for Caribbean integration

Sometimes countries from an area join together to cooperate as a group. This is known as **regional integration**. Each territory in the Caribbean is very small, with limited resources and a tiny population in comparison to its more powerful neighbours in North and South America. There are several reasons that the territories of this region have agreed to cooperate as a unified region:

- geography of the region
- common history
- integration movements including sporting and economic agreements.

This picture was taken at Pigeon Point, Tobago. Most islands in the Caribbean have similar coastal vegetation because of the location of the Caribbean region.

Geography of the region

Compared with their larger neighbours, the territories of the Caribbean need to join together in order to represent a larger collection of people. They share the same geographic location and many of the same geographical features:

- island geography – large areas of coastline as a result of being surrounded on all sides by the sea
- tropical rainforests – most of the territories have tropical climates with tropical rainforest vegetation and diverse species of plants and animals
- hazards such as storms, hurricanes and earthquakes.

The many small islands each face the challenge of limited resources, as well as vulnerability to natural disasters. By working together as a region, the territories of the Caribbean are better able to manage the challenges of their geographical resources.

Exercise

1. Which of the following types of habitat are most commonly found in the Caribbean region?

   a) desert **b)** mountains **c)** beach

2. In your own words define 'regional integration' and explain how it works in the Caribbean.

Activity

Write a reflective journal entry titled 'I love living in the Caribbean'. Highlight at least three aspects of the Caribbean region that you love.

Common history and culture

The countries of the Caribbean share many similarities such as history, language and culture. The effects of globalisation have affected the islands of the Caribbean in similar ways, and many of the islands share similar social problems.

Because of these similarities, the countries of the Caribbean benefit from joining together as a single region.

For example, the most popular sport in the Caribbean is cricket. The British originally brought the game to the Caribbean under colonial rule. The earliest cricket matches took place in the early 1800s, among officers of the British **military**.

Cricket became a symbol of the Caribbean people's struggle to be free of colonisation. In the early days cricket clubs were White-only, and enslaved people were not allowed to take part. Black players were forced to found their own clubs. This changed as inter-island competitions became more frequently organised. The competitions brought together people of all backgrounds from each island as they shared the desire to see their home island win.

Brian Lara, known as The Prince of Port of Spain, seen here breaking the world test batting record when he scored 400 runs for West Indies against England at the Recreation Ground, Antigua, 12 April 2004.

The West Indies cricket team from 1933.

As Caribbean society became more democratic and **integrated**, the West Indian cricket team became a reflection of that integration. The Caribbean produces many highly talented cricket players, which helps improve national pride.

Exercise

3. The Caribbean region is situated near the Tropic of Cancer. Suggest four ways that this affects the geography of the region.
4. Why do you think cricket is so popular in the Caribbean?
5. At first, cricket was a game for the colonial 'masters' and enslaved people were not allowed to play. What changed this?
6. Explain what you understand by regional integration in sport.

Discussion

Discuss why the sizes of the Caribbean territories make it important for them to cooperate as a single region.

Key vocabulary

regional integration

military

integrated

Integration movements

We are learning to:

- examine Caribbean integration movements
- suggest ways of strengthening Caribbean integration.

Examples of integration movements

As a region, Caribbean countries stand together as a stronger group, which helps them negotiate with richer, more powerful countries. Any formal agreement or strategy to bring the area together is known as an **integration movement**.

Regional integration increases the **cooperation** among the islands, and allows each island to add its strengths and resources to those of the group while benefiting from the strengths and resources of others.

Regional cricket team

Cricket is the most popular sport in the Caribbean. Other countries around the world have a team to represent a single country. However, because the Caribbean is made up of so many small territories, the countries of the Caribbean put together a team that represents the best players from that group of territories in the region. Although each territory has its own domestic team that competes in regional competitions, the West Indies regional team represents the whole Caribbean region in international matches.

Activity

Use the cooperative strategy 'Think, Pair and Share' to suggest ways of strengthening Caribbean integration.

Federation

The West Indies Federation was a political grouping that existed between January 1958 and May 1962. Several Caribbean islands, including Trinidad and Tobago, Jamaica, Barbados and several other islands from the eastern side of the Caribbean, came together to join the Federation. The aim of the Federation was to achieve independence from Britain, as a single, self-governing state. However, the Federation was dissolved in 1962.

The flag of the West Indies Federation (1958–1962).

Free trade and globalisation

The term **globalisation** comes from a process in which the world becomes more connected, where people, goods and information can move quickly and easily between different countries all over the globe.

One aspect of globalisation is free trade. This is the removal of quotas, taxes and other laws so that people can do business and move goods and services easily between different countries. Free trade has advantages and disadvantages:

- Member states can get a larger variety of goods and services available within the Caribbean – it is possible to import and export goods, services and labour very easily.
- It can also damage local economies as overseas businesses may be able to supply very cheap goods and services, and local people may be unable to compete.

CARIFTA, CARICOM and CSME

The Caribbean Free Trade Association (CARIFTA) was founded by four Caribbean states in December 1965. The aim was to unite the economies of the member states, give them a greater presence in the global market and encourage development in the region by:

- increasing trade – encouraging the buying and selling of goods between member states
- diversifying trade – increasing the variety of goods and services available
- liberalising trade – removing tariffs and quotas in the area
- ensuring fair trade – setting up fair rules for members to follow that would protect smaller industries.

In 1973, CARIFTA became the Caribbean Community (CARICOM). The CARICOM Single Market and Economy (CSME) is a development strategy that integrates the economies of CARICOM member states.

Joined together as a region, the Caribbean forms a much bigger market economy, allowing the region to compete in the international market more effectively. It also provides a larger market of consumers for each island's goods and services.

The Caribbean Community (CARICOM) emblem.

Activity

Create a scrapbook to show at least three reasons for the existence of the Caribbean as a region.

Exercise

1. Explain what you understand by 'regional integration'.
2. List the organisations founded to foster regional integration.
3. List six reasons for the integration of the Caribbean region.

Key vocabulary

integrated movement

cooperation

globalisation

What is a map?

We are learning to:

- define and use correctly the terms map, cartography and cartographer
- explain the role of a cartographer
- identify basic map features
- explain the uses of maps.

Uses of maps

What is a map? A **map** is a diagram that shows a particular place on Earth, usually on a flat surface. It may show the whole or part of an area. When you look at a map, you have to imagine you are looking at the ground from directly above it in the air. This is called a **bird's-eye view**. If the map is showing a room or building, this view is called the **floor plan**.

The purpose of a map is to show the relationship between specific features that are represented on the map. A map is usually much smaller than the area it represents, so it is impossible to show every feature of a real place on a map. For this reason, different types of map show different information. For example:

- Political maps show the shapes of countries and their main cities.
- Physical maps show natural features such as mountains, rivers, lakes and deserts.
- Road maps show the roads in an area.
- Tourist maps show tourist destinations, hotels and other places of interest for tourists.
- Resources maps show where particular natural resources occur, or where particular kinds of industry take place. **Cartography** is the study of maps, and the art of drawing maps. A **cartographer** is someone who plans and draws maps as their profession.

Activity

Trace a map outline of your country. Use symbols to fill in the main mountains, rivers and cities on each island. Draw a key or legend.

Activity

Create a map of a local area, such as your school or community and show basic map features using the symbols on the next page.

Exercise

1. Match each type of map to the closest description.

Type of map	What it might show
a) physical	**i)** oil fields, crops grown
b) road map	**ii)** borders, capital cities
c) resources map	**iii)** streets, roads, highways
d) political map	**iv)** rivers, lakes, mountains

Features of maps

Maps follow **conventions**. A convention is the usual way of doing something. In mapping, the main conventions are:

- a title – tells you what the map shows
- a map **scale** – shows the relationship between the size of the map and the size of the area in real life
- a **legend**, or **key** – shows what each symbol represents
- symbols – give information about real objects
- a direction arrow that points north
- a border for the map.

Discussion

What is a cartographer's job and why is it important? How do symbols make it easier for cartographers to show things on maps?

Trinidad and Tobago

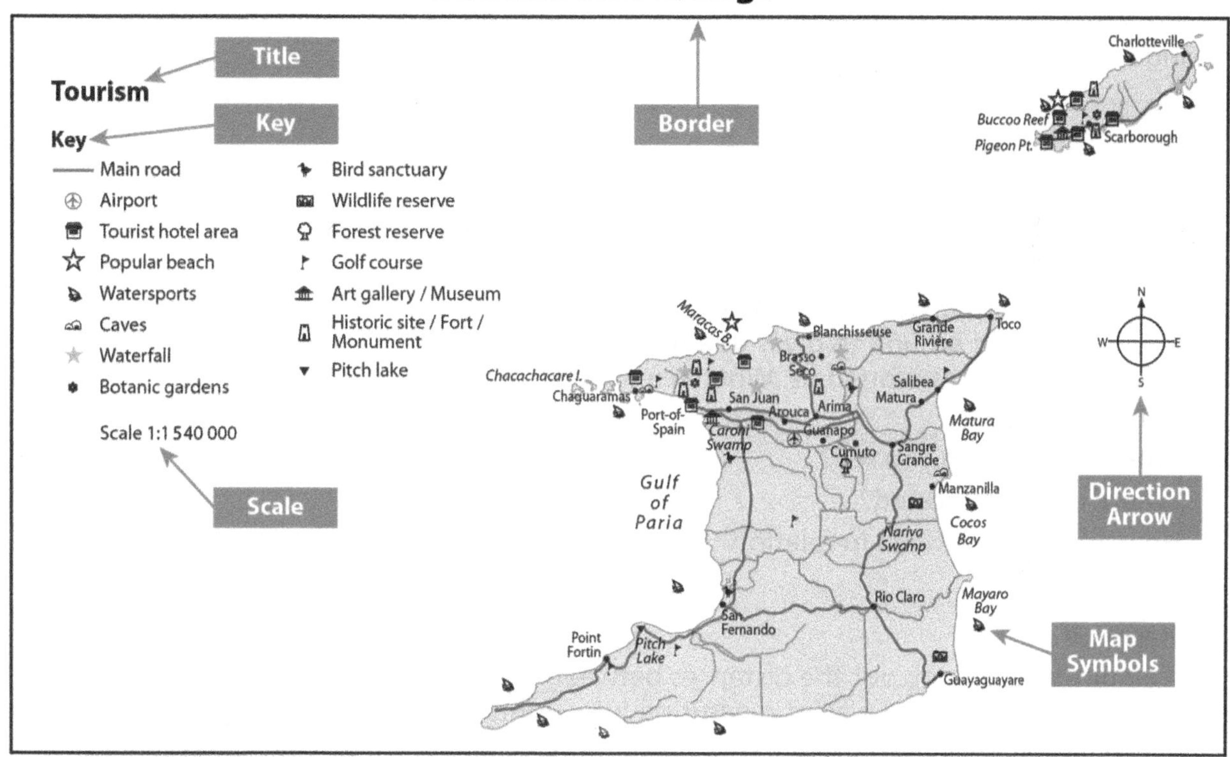

Exercise

2. Write one example of something represented on the map using the colour blue.
3. Write two examples of things represented by shapes on a map.
4. Draw the symbol for a:
   a) golf course **b)** bird sanctuary
   c) art gallery/museum **d)** airport
5. Describe four different ways we use maps.

Key vocabulary

map
bird's-eye view
floor plan
cartography
cartographer
convention
legend/key
scale

Observing and drawing maps

We are learning to:

- sketch and draw maps
- develop skills in observing geographic features
- explore the immediate environment
- build competence in ICT
- extract relevant information from images.

Placing features on a map

In order to draw maps, you need to know how to place the main map features. Remember that they are title, scale, key, use of symbols, north arrow and a map border. If a map is missing any of these features, it is an incomplete map.

Observing geographic features

If you take a walk around your community, you will observe many features, both natural and built. Roads, buildings, trees, hills and other features all form part of your environment.

Observation is another word for looking and noticing. Observing the world around us gives us a good idea of the **location** of the features around us. When we observe our environment, we ask:

- What features can you see?
- Where are they located?
- How are they arranged in relation to each other?

Measuring

It can be difficult to work out the distances between different features. A useful way of measuring is by using **paces**. A pace is a long step. Usually we use one pace to equal approximately one metre. You can pace out your classroom or school grounds to work out the approximate distances between places.

Exercise

1. What do you understand by 'observation'?
2. Why is observation the first step in drawing maps?
3. Work in groups. Find out the dimensions of your classroom. You can measure using paces (large steps), or by using a metre rule, tape measure or any other instrument. Use your measurements to make a sketch of the classroom.

Activity

Work in groups. Each group chooses a particular part of your neighbourhood.

a) Use a digital camera or the camera from a smartphone. Take reference pictures of the area.

b) Use the reference pictures to help you draw a sketch of the area.

c) Present your sketch and photographs in a neat, labelled wall display.

Representing your environment

There are a range of techniques you can use to represent your observations – drawn sketches, diagrams drawn on a computer, videos, photographs and spoken or written descriptions.

When you walk around your neighbourhood, you can use sketches, videos, snapshots and written notes to help you jot down what you see and how the features are arranged in relation to each other.

There are many different kinds of computer software you can use to help you make maps. Some examples are quikmaps.com and scribblemaps.com.

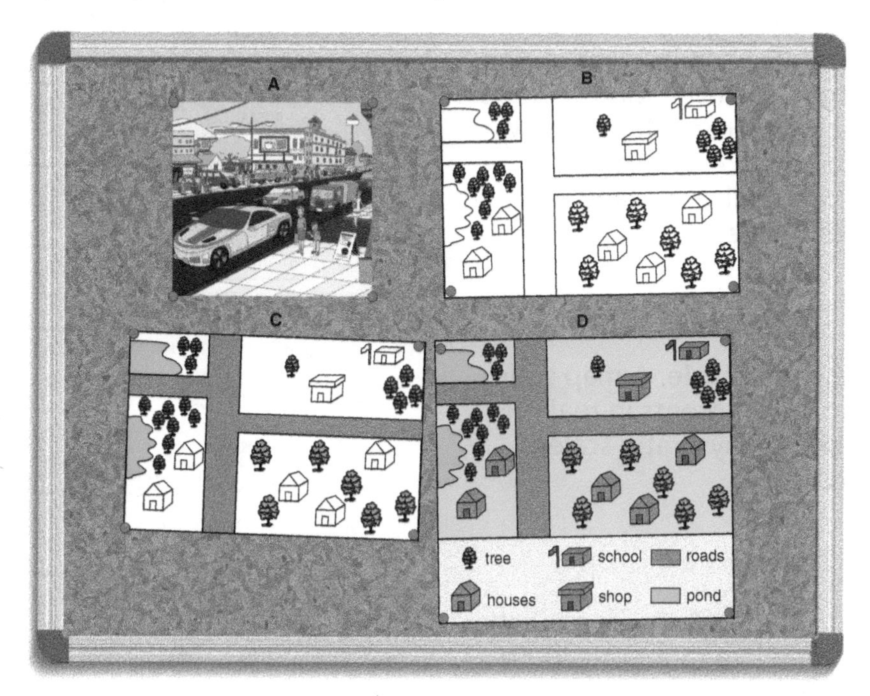

Exercise

4. List the main features you would need to show in a map of:

   a) the inside of your classroom **b)** your school grounds **c)** your street

5. Look at the pictures above. Match each description below with one of the pictures:

   rough sketch   photograph
   computer drawing   neat hand drawing

6. How can photographs help you make a map of your neighbourhood?

Activity

In groups, collect at least five different kinds of maps. You can use atlases, city road maps, tourist maps and any other maps you can find.

a) Do any of the maps NOT use the basic map features?

b) Are there any maps that do not show north? How do you know where north lies on these maps?

c) Note any differences in the symbols used on each map.

d) What other differences do you notice?

Project

Use a computer to generate a diagram of one of the following:

a) your school grounds

b) your house and the surrounding buildings in your street

c) any area of your choice in your neighbourhood.

Key vocabulary

observation

location

pace

Types of map scale

We are learning to:

- distinguish between large scale and small scale
- identify the types of scale.

Scaling up, scaling down

A map is a reduced (or scaled down) representation of a place in the real world. Accurate maps are drawn **to scale**. That means that each unit you measure on a map represents a certain number of units on the ground. There are different ways of writing map scales.

Look at the three maps to the right. Each map takes up the same amount of space on the page. However, Map C shows the whole of the Caribbean region, whereas Map B shows a more detailed part of this region: the Lesser Antilles; and Map A shows a higher level of detail: the island of Dominica. Each map has a different scale.

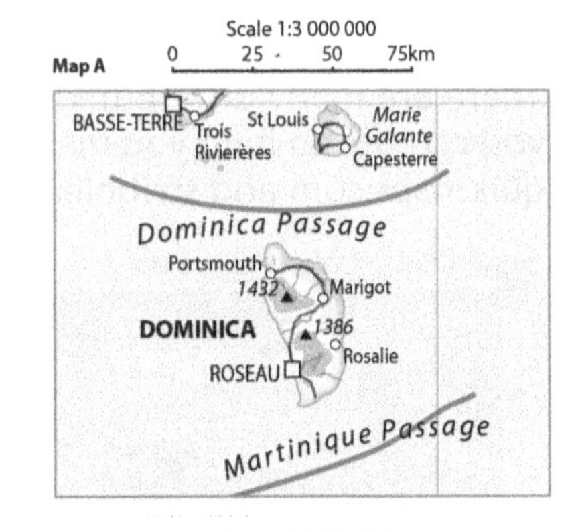

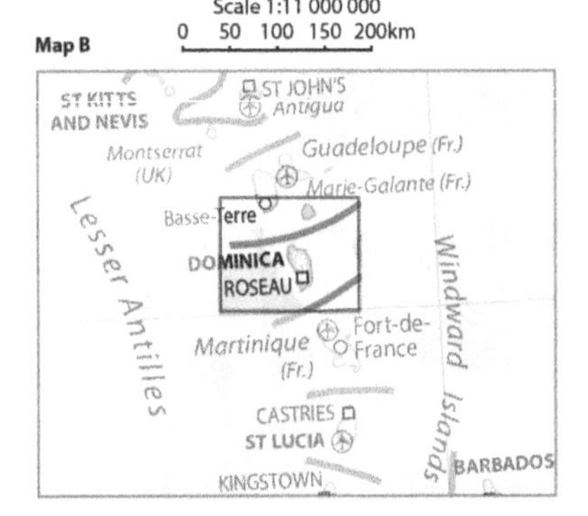

Types of scale

Above each map, you can read the **map scale**. A map scale tells you what each unit on the map represents in real life. We can show a map scale in different ways: ratio scales, linear scales and scale statements.

Ratio scale

Look at Map A. The **ratio scale** is 1: 3 000 000. This is a number ratio. It is important to remember that in a ratio scale, both the numbers refer to the same unit of measurement. 1 cm on the map is equivalent to 3 000 000 units on the ground. If we measure a distance of 1 cm on the map, we have to multiply by 3 000 000 to see what it represents in real life:

1 cm × 3 000 000 = 3 000 000 cm

There are 100 000 cm in 1 km. So, to work out this distance in km, divide by 100 000. 3 000 000 ÷ 100 000 = 30. 1 cm on the map shows 30 km on the ground.

Exercise

1. Write the number scale for each of the three maps on this page, and then write in words what the scale means.

   Map A 1:_____ 1 unit on the map represents ___ units on the ground.

Linear scale

Under the number scale, you can see a **linear scale**. A linear scale makes it easier to work out the relationship between a unit on the page and distances in real life. The linear scale shows you the real-life distance represented by each centimetre on the map.

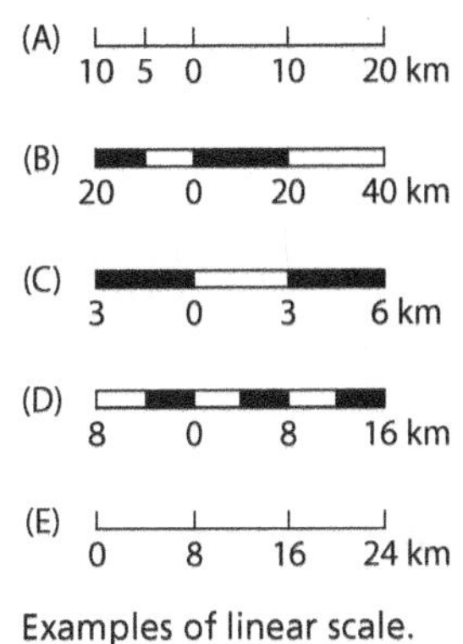

Examples of linear scale.

A scale statement

Sometimes scale is expressed as a **scale statement**, for example: 1 cm = 25 km. This is not a ratio scale, because the units are not both in the same unit of measure. It tells you the relationship between units on the map and units in real life.

The larger the scale of a map, the more detail it shows in real life. So, Map A is the largest scale of the three maps here. Map C is the smallest scale map.

Exercise

Map B 1: ____ 1 unit on the map represents ___ units on the ground.

Map C 1: ____ 1 unit on the map represents ___ units on the ground.

2. In pairs, work out how to complete these rules about scale:

   a) Larger scale maps represent (more/less) detail than smaller scale maps.

   b) The higher the number of units each unit on the map represents in real life, the (larger/smaller) the scale of the map.

3. Look at the following maps in an atlas. Write down the scale of each one as a number scale:

   a) the world

   b) Africa

   c) the Caribbean

4. Work in pairs. Choose one of the maps. Measure the distance between two cities on the map. Calculate the distance in kilometres using the scale.

5. Go back to the measurements you took of your classroom (see page 278). Draw a scale map of your classroom. Show the positions of the doors and windows, as well as at least one item of furniture. Show your scale on your classroom map.

Discussion

The distances on maps do not always give us an idea of how long it takes to travel between two places. Discuss some of the reasons for this.

Key vocabulary

to scale

map scale

ratio scale

linear scale

scale statement

Working with map scales

We are learning to:

- measure the distance between two places using the linear scale.

Measuring distance between two places

There are 100 000 cm in 1 km. There are 100 cm in 1 m.

Let's say that you want to work out the distance between Point A and Point B in your country. On the map, the distance is about 2 cm.

- Multiply by the map scale: 2 cm × 600 000 = 1 200 000 cm.
- Now we need to divide by 100 000 in order to work out the distance in km: 1 200 000 ÷ 100 000 = 12 km.

  2 cm on the map represents 12 km on the ground.
- To work out a distance in km, you can measure the distance in cm on the map, and use this formula:

$$1 \times s/100\,000$$

If a map scale is 1: s, where s represents the number scale.

Activity

You will need: a ruler, an atlas.

a) Find a map of Africa in your atlas.

b) Measure the length of the continent. Calculate it in km.

c) Measure the width across the continent at its widest point. Calculate it in km.

d) What do you notice?

Exercise

1. What is the number scale of the map opposite?

2. Copy and complete: 1 cm on the map represents ______ in real life.

3. Use the map to work out the distance between the following places:

a) Dominica and Grenada

b) Port of Spain, Trinidad and San Juan, Puerto Rico

c) Barbados and Saint Lucia

4. Name five countries that are within 500 km of Saint Lucia.

5. The map opposite is not very useful if you want to work out distances within Montserrat.

a) Why not?

b) Would you need a map with a larger or smaller scale? Explain your answer.

Activity

Use an atlas of the Caribbean and compare maps of five different countries.

a) Write the names of the five countries and the map scale of each.

b) Which country is shown at the largest scale?

c) Why do you think the countries are shown at different scales?

The Eastern Caribbean

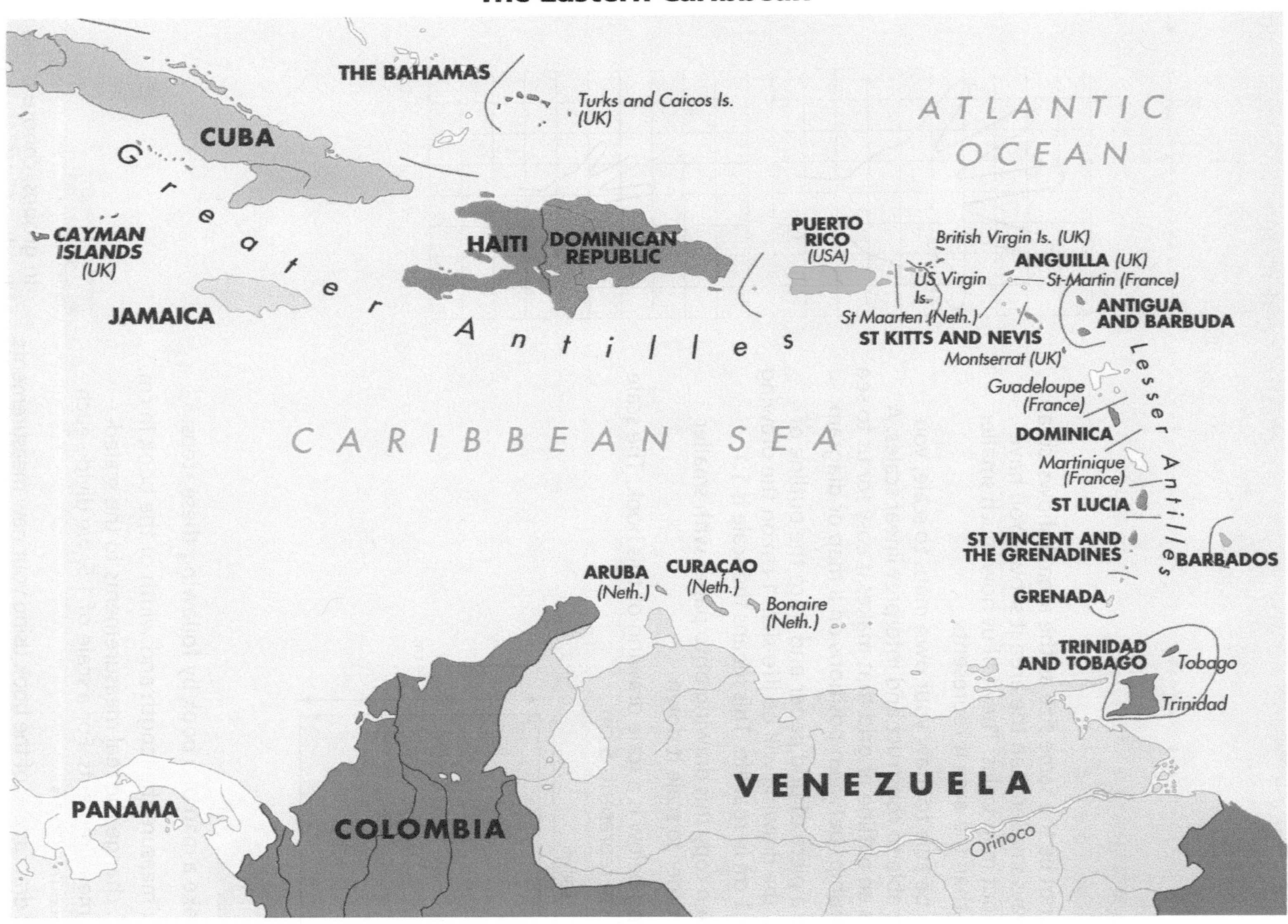

Using map scales

We are learning to:

- construct and interpret linear scales on a map
- use templates of maps.

Scaling up or down

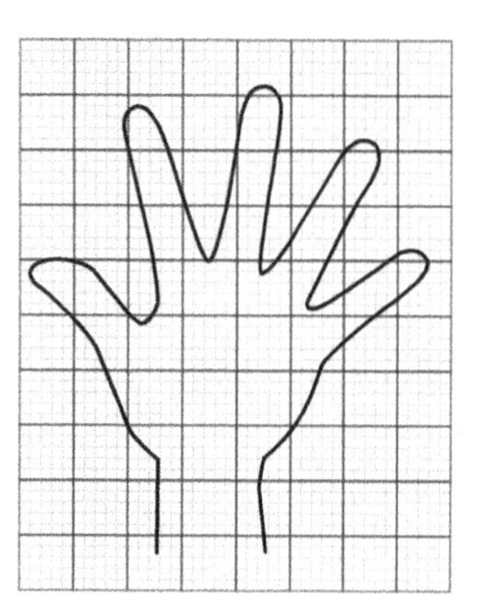

A map cannot be the same size as the area it shows. so a map is always smaller than the area it shows. You have learned about map scales. They tell us how much smaller the map is than the area it represents.

In order to be able to draw your own maps to scale, you need to be able to construct and interpret linear scales. A **template** is an outline or grid that makes it easy for us to see the relationships between positions on a map or diagram.

If you take a piece of grid paper and trace the outline of your hand, the drawing will be life-size. 1 cm on the drawing represents 1 cm in real life. This means the scale is 1:1.

You can then copy this drawing onto paper with smaller squares in order to scale it down.

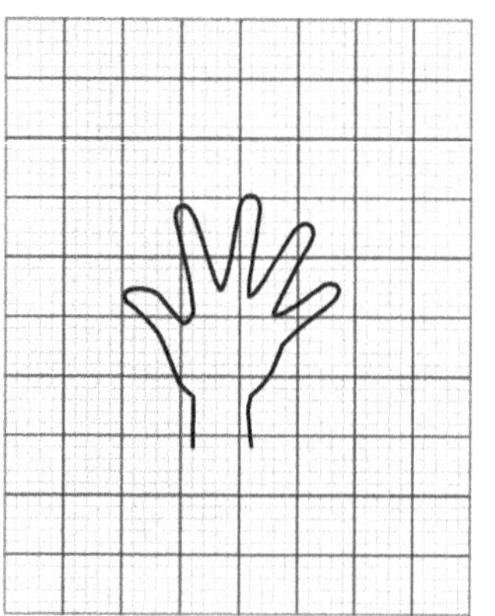

The drawing below is a scale drawing of this book. The scale is 1:5, or 1 cm represents 5 cm.

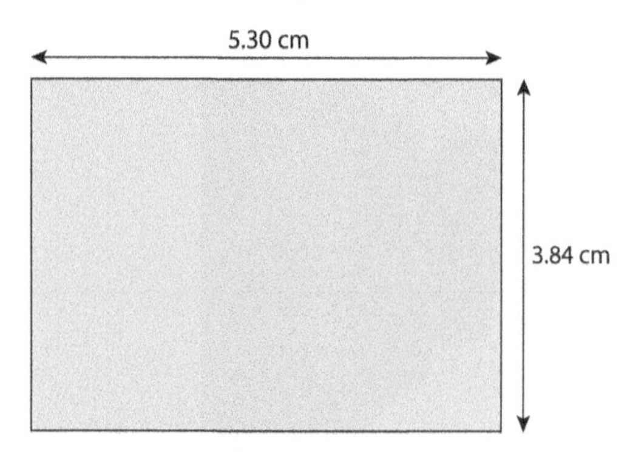

Map templates

You can make a map of a book by following these steps:

- Step 1: measure the length and width of the book in cm.
- Step 2: change the real measurements to the scaled-down measurements. For a scale of 1:5, we divide each measurement by 5.
- Step 3: draw a map of the book using your new measurements. Remember to write the scale under your book.

Here is a map of a classroom, using a scale of 1:100. The students measured the length and width of the classroom in metres. They also showed the door, windows, board and desks.

Activity

In groups, choose three books of different sizes. Draw maps of your books using a number scale of 1:5.

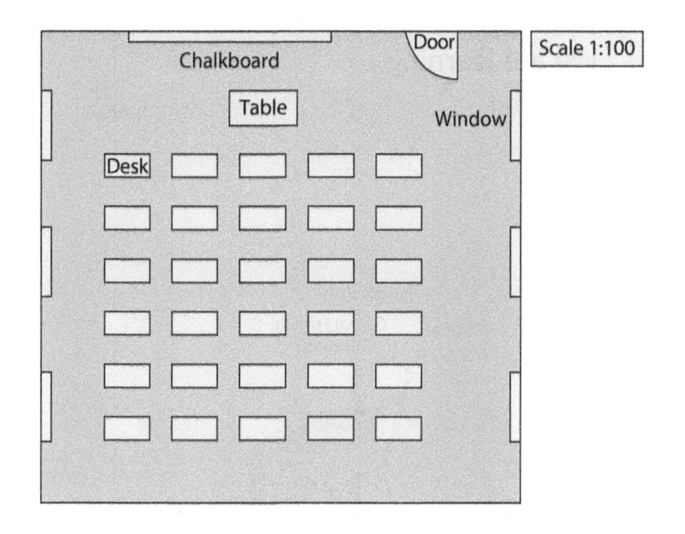

Activity

Work in groups. Make your own classroom map similar to the one in the picture. Use a scale of 1:100. Measure the length and width of the classroom in metres, using a ruler or tape measure. Also measure the door, windows, board and desks or tables.

The following outline of Trinidad and Tobago is drawn at a scale of 1:2 093 000.

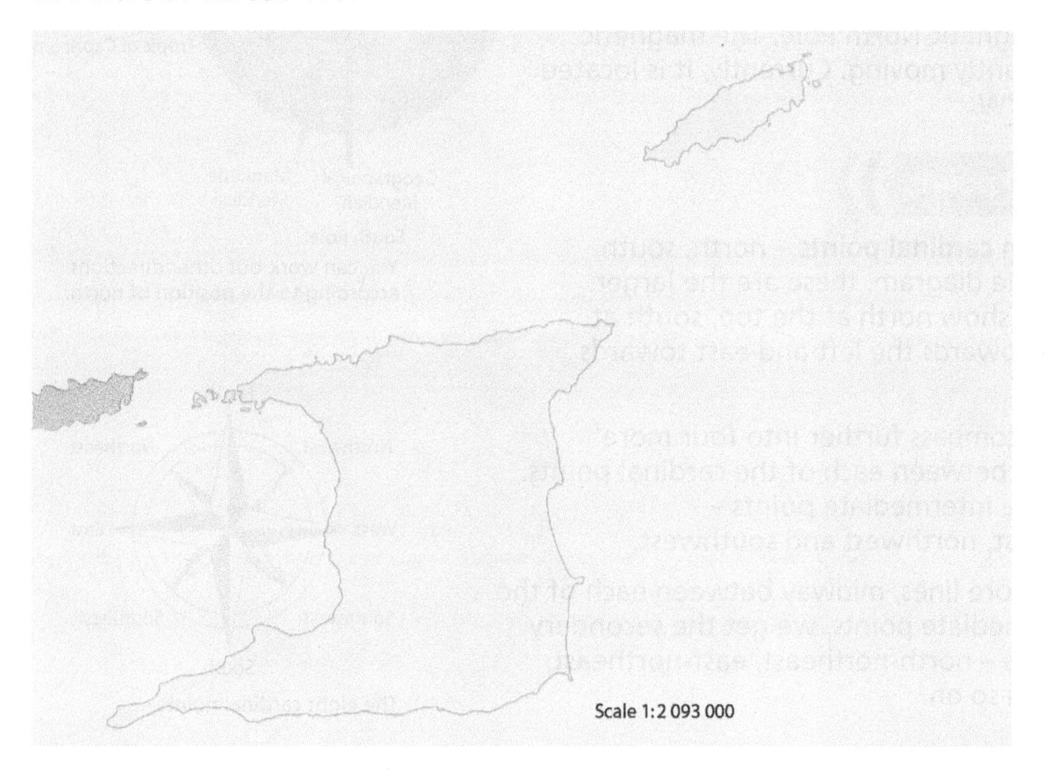

Exercise

1. What do you understand by:

   a) scaling up? **b)** scaling down?

2. Describe how you would scale the above map up to draw it at a scale of 1:600 000. Use grid paper to do this.

3. Choose another island from your atlas.

   a) Identify the scale.

   b) Draw it at a smaller scale on grid paper.

Key vocabulary

template

Cardinal points

We are learning to:

- use the cardinal points to give and follow directions
- identify eight cardinal points.

Magnetic north and true north

On any map, when you see an arrow pointing towards the letter N it is showing the direction of north. It is known as the north point. A **compass** is an instrument used to show direction. The pointer always shows the direction of north.

When you hold a magnetic compass, the arrow always pulls in the direction of **magnetic north**. This is the direction of the magnetic North Pole. The magnetic North Pole is constantly moving. Currently, it is located at about 86°N, 160°W.

North Pole
Magnetic Meridian
Geographical Meridian
Tropic of Cancer
Equator
Tropic of Capricorn
Geographical Meridian
Magnetic Meridian
South Pole

You can work out other directions according to the position of north.

The eight cardinal points

There are four main **cardinal points** – north, south, east and west. In the diagram, these are the larger arrows. We usually show north at the top, south at the bottom, west towards the left and east towards the right.

We can divide the compass further into four more directions, midway between each of the cardinal points. These are called the intermediate points – northeast, southeast, northwest and southwest.

If we draw eight more lines, midway between each of the cardinal and intermediate points, we get the secondary intermediate points – north-northeast, east-northeast, east-southeast, and so on.

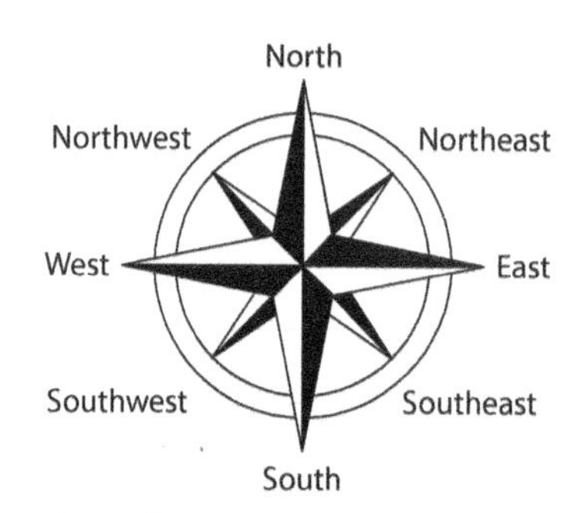

The eight cardinal points.

Exercise

1. Name the:
   a) four cardinal points
   b) four intermediate points
   c) eight secondary intermediate points
2. Find a map of Africa in your atlas. Copy the table and fill in three countries that belong to each region of the African continent. Explain to a friend how you decided where each region was.

Region	Countries
North Africa	
Southern Africa	
East Africa	
West Africa	

Make your own direction finder. Cut out a small square of clear plastic. Draw a diagram of the sixteen-point compass rose on the plastic. Use your direction finder to help you work out the direction on the map below:

a) from Old Road Town to Basseterre **b)** from Cotton Ground to Brick Kiln **c)** from Cayon to Frigate Bay

Key vocabulary

compass

magnetic north

cardinal points

Saint Kitts and Nevis

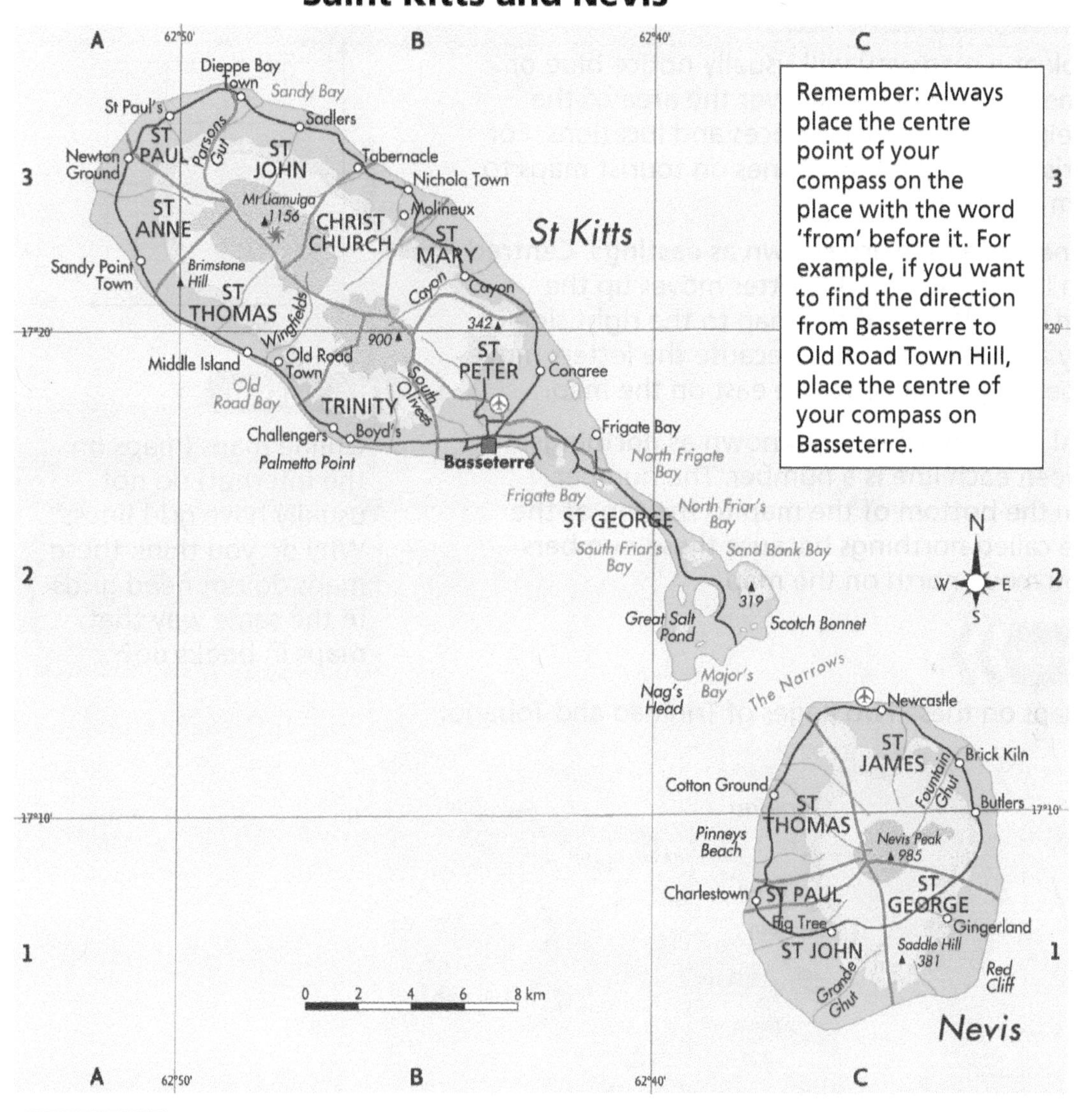

Remember: Always place the centre point of your compass on the place with the word 'from' before it. For example, if you want to find the direction from Basseterre to Old Road Town Hill, place the centre of your compass on Basseterre.

Exercise

3. Look at a Caribbean map. Identify an island:

a) towards the north and **b)** south of the Caribbean

4. Look at a world map. Identify continents:

a) in the northern and southern hemisphere and

b) in both hemispheres

Finding places on a map

We are learning to:

- distinguish between easting and northing grid lines
- explain the purpose of **grid squares** and grid lines
- give grid references.

Easting and northing grid lines

When you look at a map, you will usually notice blue or brown **grid lines** that form blocks over the area of the map. These help us to find exact places and locations. For example, tourists can use the grid lines on tourist maps to find a museum or beach.

The vertical lines on a map are known as **eastings**. Centred between each line is a letter. The letter moves up the alphabet from the left side of the map to the right side of the map. They are called eastings because the letters move up the alphabet as you move to the east on the map.

The horizontal lines on a map are known as **northings**. Centred between each line is a number. The number increases from the bottom of the map to the top of the map. They are called northings because these numbers increase as you move north on the map.

Northings

Eastings

Discussion

Online maps (maps on the internet) do not usually have grid lines. Why do you think these maps do not need grids in the same way that maps in books do?

Using grid lines

Look at the maps on these two pages of Trinidad and Tobago:

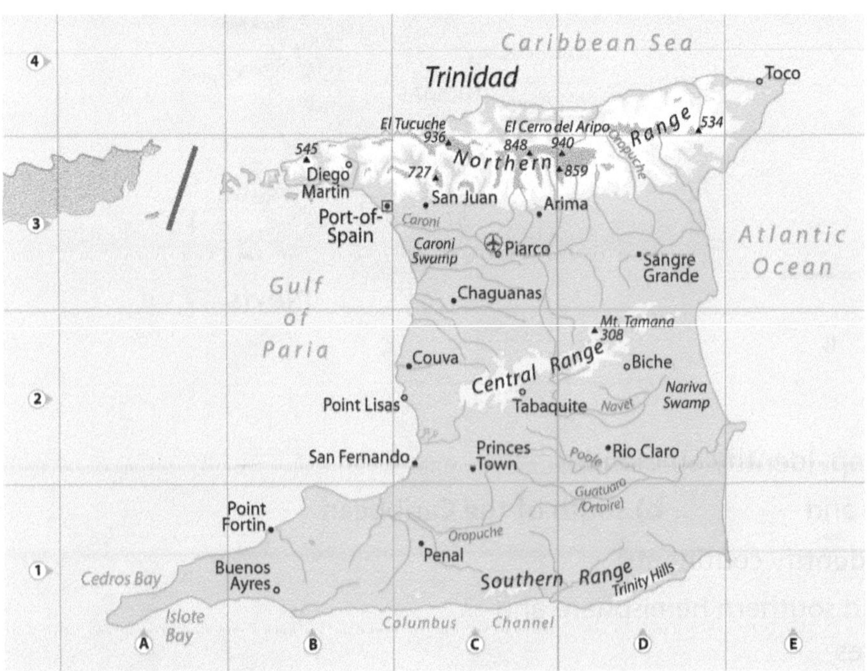

Imagine that you want to find Piarco on the Trinidad map, but you cannot remember where it is. You could spend a long time looking for the name on the map, and you may find it after a while. Or you could look up Piarco in the index at the back of the atlas. You would find the following **grid reference**:

Piarco C3

Find the letter C along the bottom of the map, and place your finger in that block. Now find the number 3 along the left side of the map, and place another finger in the block numbered 3. Move the two fingers along the grid lines until they meet. This locates block C3. Look carefully inside the block. Can you find Piarco?

Key vocabulary

grid lines

northings

eastings

grid (or grid square)

grid reference

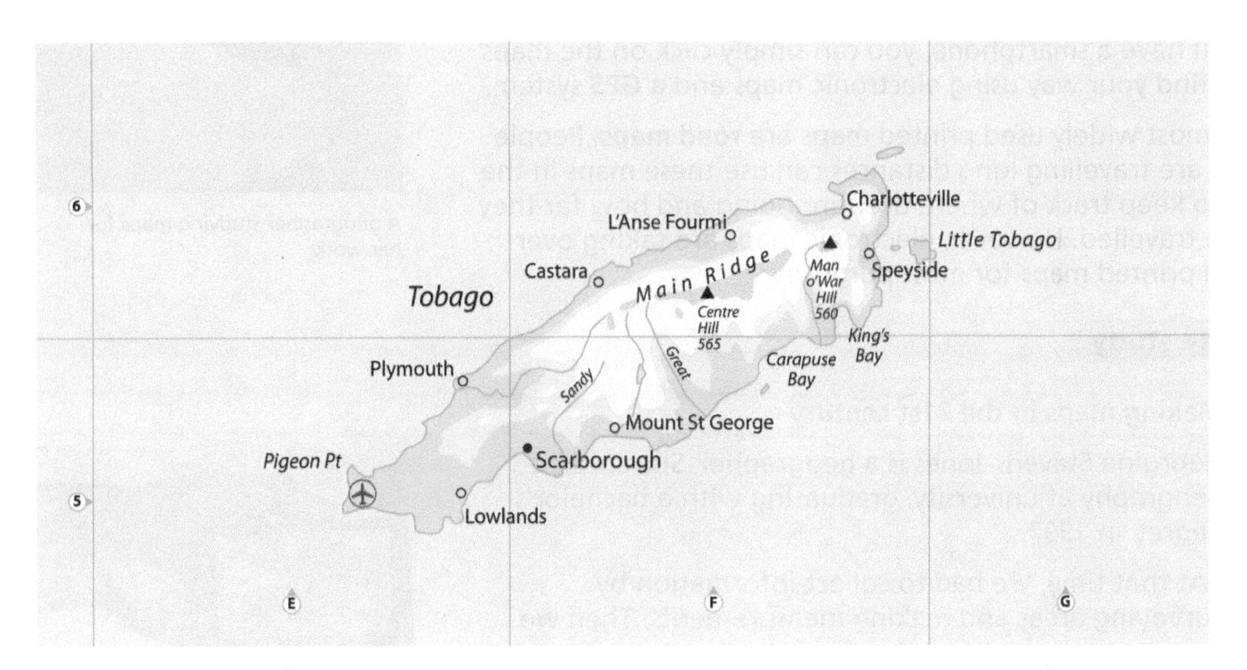

Exercise

1. What are the two kinds of grid lines shown on maps?
2. Why do we use these lines on maps?
3. **a)** Name the swamp found at D2.
   b) Name two bays found in A1.
   c) Name two towns found in F6.
4. Write down the grid references for:
   a) the Northern Range mountains
   b) the Central Range mountains
   c) Mt Tamana
5. Draw a grid like this one. Now choose any three of the blocks. Draw a different shape in each block. Have a partner write the grid references for each of your shapes.

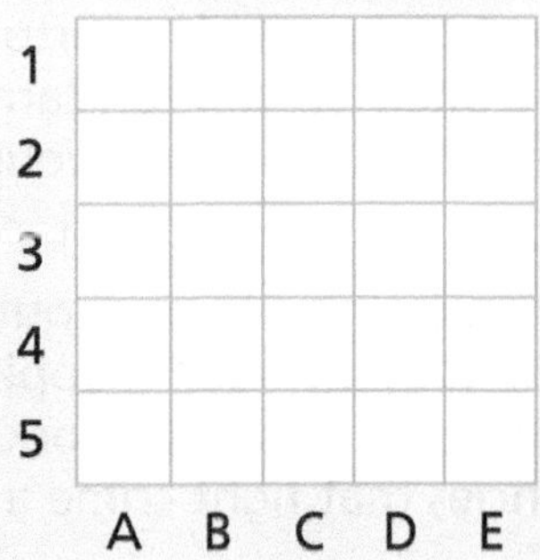

Maps of today

We are learning to:

- describe recent developments in uses of maps
- compare maps of today with those of 20 years ago
- develop research skills.

Using maps to get around

The maps we use today are very different from the charts that explorers used in the past. Think about what you do when you need to go to a new address, or if you get lost. If you have a smartphone, you can simply click on the maps and find your way using electronic maps and a **GPS** system.

The most widely used printed maps are **road maps**. People who are travelling long distances can use these maps in the car to keep track of where they are going and how far they have travelled. However, electronic maps are taking over from printed maps for most purposes.

A geographer studying maps for her work.

Case study

Making maps in the 21st century

Georgina Stevens-Jones is a geographer. She studied geography at university, graduating with a bachelor's degree in 1997.

"At that time, we had to collect information by **surveying** areas and making measurements. Then we drew maps by hand on sheets of clear **acetate**. We carefully layered the sheets, and took photographs to create the final map. Nobody does that anymore. Today you would just use a GPS!

"A map was something printed on paper. You folded it up and carried it with you. If the information became out-of-date, you had to look for a newer one and throw away the old one.

"Today, people just update their smartphones and computers via the internet. You can carry a world map, to any degree of detail, with you in your pocket."

After Ms Stevens-Jones graduated, she worked with social services organisations to map outbreaks of tuberculosis. Later jobs included mapping ecosystems. Many of her fellow students now work for national intelligence agencies that fight crime and terrorism.

GPS can give accurate, up-to-date information.

Did you know...?

The USA had more than 400 000 people employed in the mapping industry in 2010. Researchers predicted that this industry would grow by 35 per cent to employ 550 000 people by 2020.

"Traditionally, geographers studied the natural environment and its relationship with human society. Cartographers focused on creating and drawing maps. This has changed since the 1990s. A new field, called **Geographical Information Systems (GIS)** has emerged. This combines the fields of cartography and geography."

Ms Stevens-Jones says that geography opens up a world of fascinating career fields. Some of her fellow students have done the following kinds of work:

- built models of the Earth using GPS, in order to draw maps
- studied volcanic activity to predict future eruptions
- studied earthquake patterns
- used photographs and other digital images to create 3D models of places
- carried out environmental impact assessments to discover whether buildings and developments are sustainable for the environment
- studied outbreaks of diseases in different environments.

Activity

Work in groups. Use a mapping application on a computer, such as Google Maps.

a) Find a map of the whole of your country.

b) Zoom in to find the location of your school.

c) Find the locations of each group member's home.

d) On your own, get the directions from school to your house. Then get the directions using the online map. What differences did you notice?

Exercise

1. Copy and complete the table to show ways that maps have changed since the 1990s.

	Before 1990s	Today
How cartographers collect information		
How maps get drawn		
How people store or carry the maps		
How we update the information		
Any other differences		

2. Why do you think people still use road maps?

3. Unscramble the names of the different fields of study:

a) ohpyregag

b) cragharptoy

Discussion

What are the benefits of new technology for students of geography?

Key vocabulary

GPS (Global Positioning System)

road map

surveying

acetate

GIS (Global Information Systems)

Questions

See how well you have understood the topics in this unit.

1. What do we use lines of longitude and latitude for?
2. Look at this map scale and complete the sentences about it. 1:10 000
   a) 1 cm on the map represents _____ in real life.
   b) If the distance between two places is 25 km, the distance between the places on the map will be _____.
3. Give three examples of what you might use a map for.
4. Name the following lines:
   a) the line of latitude that divides the Earth into two equal hemispheres
   b) the line of longitude that runs along 0°
5. Identify the tropic to which each point refers:
   a) the tropic that passes through Australia and Chile
   b) the tropic closest to the Caribbean region
6. Identify five features that are missing from the map (hint: see 10.7).

7. Trace the map onto a piece of paper. Place each of the missing features onto the map. (Hint: the scale is: 1 cm represents 12 km. You will need to make up a title.)

8. What happened on the following dates to aid regional integration?

   a) 1958
   b) 1962
   c) 1965
   d) 1973

9. Copy and complete:

   The purpose of a map is to show the ________ between specific ________ on the map.

10. Draw a compass rose showing the eight cardinal points.

11. Draw a rough map of either of the two islands of your country, showing main mountains, rivers and wetlands. Draw a map key and include a north pointer.

12. Use a world map.

    a) What is the scale of the map?
    b) Would a larger map of the Caribbean have a larger or smaller scale?

13. Each set of coordinates tells you the position of a city somewhere in the world. Work out on which continent it is located and then use your atlas to help you identify the city.

    a) 33°56′S 18°28′E
    b) 40°45′N 73°57′W

14. Explain three main differences between the maps we use today and those of the past.

15. Explain what you understand by 'regional integration' and why it is important.

16. Work out the rule for naming directions and fill in the missing words:

    Always start with ________ or ________ first, for example, northwest, northeast, southwest or southeast. For the secondary intermediate points, start with the closest ________ point first, then refer to the closest ________ point. For example, north-north-west is the point between ________ and ________.

cardinal	intermediate	north	northwest	north	south

17. Choose one of the organisations dedicated to regional integration. Find out which states belong to the organisation and what its main aims are.

18. Locate your country on three different maps:

    a) a world globe
    b) a map in an atlas
    c) online

    In your journal, explain how you found your country on each map. Choose from the following: index; contents page; lines of longitude and latitude; online search engine; looking at continents and seas.

Checking your progress

To make good progress in understanding the world around us, check that you understand these ideas.

- ☐ Name the characteristics of longitude and latitude.
- ☐ Explain the purpose of lines of longitude and latitude.
- ☐ Give an overview of how longitude and latitude were discovered.

- ☐ Explain the four steps that you would need to take to find the Caribbean on a world map.
- ☐ Name the five largest territories in the Caribbean.
- ☐ Give three reasons why the territories in the Caribbean work together as a unified region.

- ☐ Name five different types of maps.
- ☐ Name the five features, or conventions, that a map should always have.
- ☐ Explain the difference between a political map and a physical map.

- ☐ Explain why maps have scales.
- ☐ Name three different types of scale used on maps.
- ☐ Name the eight secondary intermediate points on a compass.

End-of-term questions

Questions 1–3

See how well you have understood the topics in unit 7.

1. Identify four common factors that bind the Commonwealth Caribbean and explain how the factors bind the countries.
2. Make a list of 10 countries that are members of Commonwealth Caribbean.
3. Identify the following flags of Caribbean countries.

Questions 4–7

See how well you have understood the topics in unit 8.

4. Write ten tips for caring for the environment.
5. Your school is hosting some students from abroad for an interschool exchange programme. Your class receives the task of planning a tour of significant places in your country. Choose a place that you would like to propose for the tour. Write your proposal, including these details:

   Name of place:

   Type of attraction or site:

   Why it is significant/worth visiting:

   Directions:
6. Identify each type of natural disaster:
   a) a very fast, spinning wind
   b) hot liquid rock from underground explodes through a hole in the Earth's crust
   c) heavy rainfalls cause too much water to rush over the Earth's surface
   d) plates of the Earth's crust collide
7. Which natural disasters are mostly likely to affect:
   a) a mountainous area
   b) a coastal area
   c) a place located on the boundary between two plates of the Earth's crust

Questions 8–11

See how well you have understood the topics in unit 9.

8. Describe what each term means, and draw what it might look like on a map:
   a) compass rose **b)** line scale **c)** number scale **d)** border
9. Using an atlas, look up the geographical coordinates for the following countries:
   a) Anguilla **b)** Saint Kitts and Nevis **c)** Guyana
10. Explain what we mean by lines of longitude and latitude, and give three examples of each.
11. Trace the following world map. Fill in the names of the seven continents and five oceans.

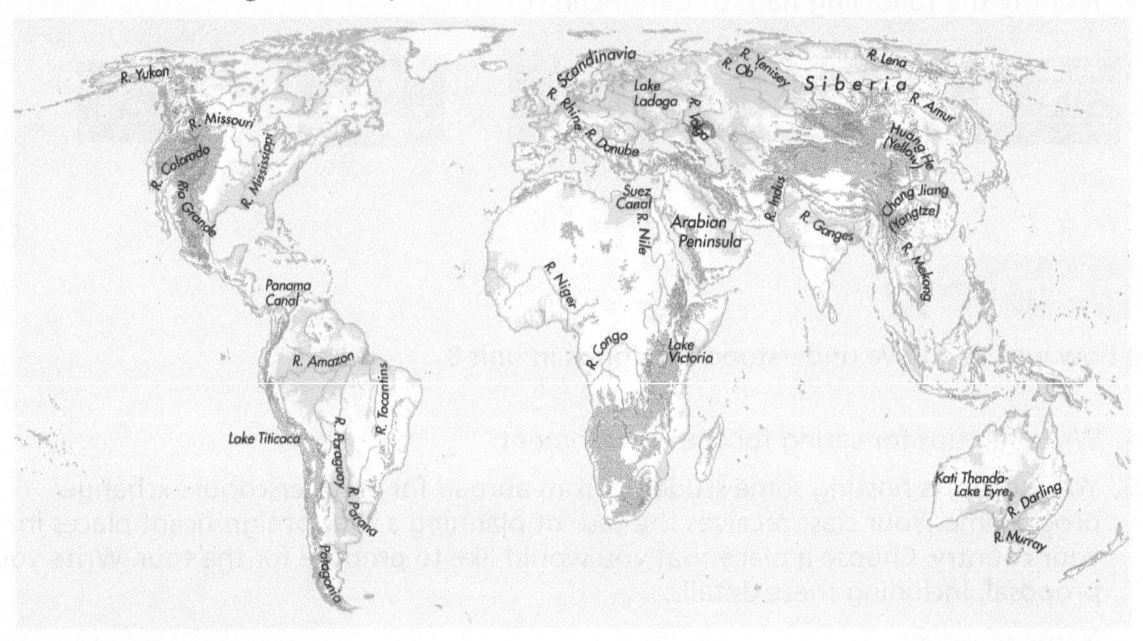

Questions 12–13

See how well you have understood the topics in unit 10.

12. Research the history of the West Indies Federation and write an essay of about 250 words on its members, its aim and history.
13. Copy in your exercise book and add the mapping conventions to this illustration.

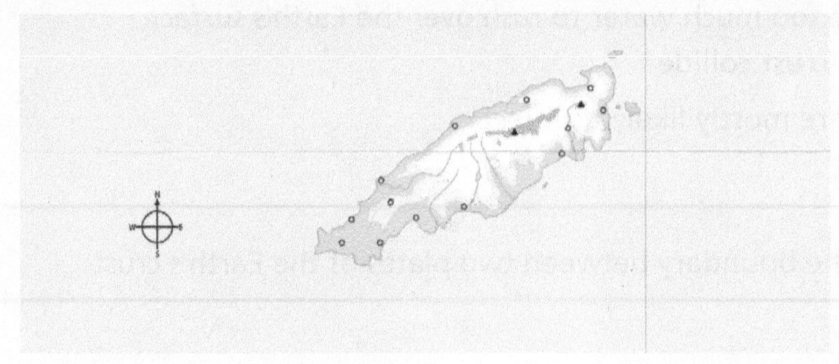

Glossary

ability something one is able to do, for example the ability to read or tie one's shoelaces

acetate a type of clear plastic

acid rain rain that contains high levels of acidic compounds that can corrode buildings

activist someone who campaigns to bring about political or social changes

adolescence the period in which a child changes to become an adult

adulthood the period from about 18 years onwards, when a person is fully grown

ageing getting older

agricultural/agriculture economic activities related to farming

agricultural practices methods used in agriculture to provide safe and healthy food products

air pollution the introduction of gases or fine particles into the air, causing contamination of the air

amend change and improve

Amerindians indigenous people who lived in the Caribbean before us

ancestral lineage parents, grandparents, great grandparents, great-great grandparents and so on

ancestor/ancestry the family you come from, especially their ethnicity or cultural origins

appreciate give value to

appreciation a sense of valuing something and seeing its worth

armed conflict a fight or battle in which weapons are used

art usually refers to visual art, such as paintings, drawings and sculptures

arts creative endeavours including visual art, literature, music, dance and drama

artha the Hindu pursuit of wealth and prosperity in a lawful way

arts and crafts decorative handicraft and design

aspect one side of something, for example of yourselves (physical, social, ethical, intellectual or emotional)

atheist a person who does not believe in God or gods

attitude a feeling or opinion about something or someone

Aum/Om the symbol of Hinduism, and also the sound used in meditation

aunts and uncles your parents' brothers and sisters and their spouses

autonomy the control of a country, government or group by itself rather than by someone else

balanced diet the correct types and amount of food

belief something that you believe to be true about the world

belief system a set of stories about things, such as how and why we were created and what happens after death

benevolence kindness and helpfulness

bibliography a list of the sources (usually secondary sources) that you consulted when doing research

bill a proposed law that is discussed in a parliament

biodiversity the great range of living plants and animals that live as part of an ecosystem

biological function having children

bird's-eye view a view from directly above the ground

blood ties a connection based on common ancestry, such as having one or more shared parents

body mass index (BMI) a ratio that tells you your weight in relation to your height

border edge of a country, or a line separating two countries or regions

boundaries outlines; dividing lines; lines that enclose a given area

Brahman the supreme spirit in Hinduism

breadwinner the person who earns the main income for a family or household

bullying using one's greater power to force someone else to do something or to feel powerless

capital anything that an economy needs so that it is possible to produce goods and services

capital city the urban area where the government is based

cardinal points the main points of direction: south, north, east, west, southeast, northeast, southwest and northwest

Caribbean Community and Common Market (CARICOM) an organisation of 15 Caribbean nations and dependencies, established in 1973

Catholicism the original organised form of Christianity, which remained unchanged for over 1000 years

cartographer someone who plans and draws maps

cartography the study of maps and drawing maps

cay a low island composed mainly of coral or sand

cemetery a place where the dead are buried

century a period of 100 years

change a process of becoming different from what you were before

characteristic a feature or quality that others can use to define someone or something

childhood the period of human life from one year to about 12 years

children from birth to 18 years, a person is considered a child

Christians/Christianity people who believe in the teachings of Jesus Christ

citizen a member of a country who has certain rights and must perform certain duties towards that country

city a large human settlement of more than 100 000 people

civic responsibility your duties to your country

civic values values which help people to live better and safer lives

climate the weather conditions in an area

coal a soft black carbon rock that burns easily and is a major fuel

co-exist live peacefully with others

colony a country that is controlled and often exploited by another country

colonialism gaining control over land in another country and exploiting the wealth of the other country

commemorate when we remember and show respect for someone or something, perhaps with a celebration

common-law marriage a couple who live together as husband and wife without getting married

Commonwealth association of independent countries that used to form part of the British Empire

Commonwealth Caribbean group of English-speaking countries in the Caribbean that used to be part of the British Empire or that are still dependencies of Britain (see page 180 for a list)

community the people with whom you live and work

compass instrument used for identifying direction

composition what something is made up of, or the proportions of its elements

compromise an agreement in which both parties make concessions (allowances)

concentrated occurring in large amounts per square unit of area

conflict a serious struggle between two sides with differing needs, views or interests

conflict resolution to find a peaceful solution to disagreements

consensus agreement

consequences the result or effect of something

conservation/conserve protecting, restoring and preserving

constitution a set of principles on which the laws of a country are based

consultation giving people an opportunity to discuss an issue

consumer culture the culture of buying new products or valuing things that are new

continent one of seven major landmasses on Earth

convention the usual way of doing something

conventional agriculture a method of growing edible plants using fertilisers, insecticides and pesticides

cooperation working together

cooperatively working helpfully with others

corrode become weaker and break down

county a territorial division within a country, forming the main unit for local administration

courtship the art of seeking the love of someone with intent to marry

covenant an agreement between two or more people

creativity a person's capacity to use their imagination to come up with original or new ideas and solutions

crescent a curved shape representing one of the phases of the moon

cross a symbol made of a long vertical line with a short horizontal line crossing it near the top, representing Christianity

crucified (crucify) put to death by nailing to a cross

cuisine a style or manner of cooking

culture the customs, beliefs, arts and technology of a nation or people

cultural the customs, traditions and beliefs of a society

cultural background the beliefs and traditions that a group of people share

cultural/educational function skills acquired within a family that contribute to a child's education

cultural heritage the cultural traditions that we have inherited from past generations

curriculum (curricula) the syllabus; the subjects you learn about at school

customs behaviour that has been established for a long time

cyclone a violent tropical storm or wind where the air moves very fast in a circular pattern

decade a period of 10 years

decision-making the process of reaching decisions, especially in a large organisation or in government

deforestation the removal of trees and vegetation to create open spaces for human activities

degradation where the beauty or quality of something is destroyed or spoiled

demarcation a border that shows how a country is divided

democratically government of the people, by the people, for the people, through their elected representatives

denomination a group having a distinctive interpretation of Christianity

dependency a country that is dependent on a mother country for certain aspects of its governance

dependent territory a territory that does not possess full independence, but remains outside the controlling state's integral area

deplete to use up or finish

deposits places where minerals are found

desert a sandy or stony area on the Earth's surface that gets less than 25 cm of rainfall per year

dharma the Hindu set of rules for living a good life

diet the food and drink consumed by a person; can also be an eating plan to live a healthier lifestyle

differences specific instances of being unalike

digital storytelling being filmed as you tell your story

dignity the need and right to honour and respect

district an area of a town or country

diverse having variety and differences

diverse culture different cultural backgrounds living together

documents formal written information

dome a rounded structure over a circular base, forming the roof of a building

dress complete style of clothing or costume

drought an extreme water shortage caused by low rainfall or no rainfall for a long period

earthquake a sudden shockwave caused by the movements of plates at plate boundaries

eastings vertical lines running from north to south on a map

economic asset something which has an economic value with an individual, company or country

economic development improving a country's standard of living

economic factors factors which relate to trade, industry, occupations and wealth

economic function bringing in income to fulfil basic needs for food, shelter, security and clothing

economy wealth and resources of a country

ecosystems interconnected systems of living organisms and the features of their environment

educate to teach a particular lesson or demonstrate information or an idea

educational function skills acquired that form part of a child's education

education the teaching of knowledge, ideas, opinions, beliefs and skills

Eid al-Fitr a three-day celebration for Muslims to mark the end of Ramadan

emblem an object that symbolises a quality, type, group, etc.

eminent well known

emissions gases that are given off during a chemical process

employee someone who is paid to work for someone else

employer a person or organisation that employs people

emotions strong feelings such as love or anger, or strong feelings in general

emotional to do with feelings

emotional changes changes that affect how a person feels and thinks

emotional function to provide for the emotional needs of a family's members

empire people and lands ruled by a single person or country

enlightenment in Buddhism, a state of full understanding and knowledge of all things

entertain to give pleasure or enjoyment

environment the world around you

equality the right of different groups of people to have a similar social position and receive the same treatment

eradicate get rid of

erosion where soil is gradually being damaged and removed by the waves, rain or wind

established to set up or to start up

ethical to do with values, morals and principles of right and wrong

ethics what is morally right and wrong

ethical consumer someone who selects which products they buy based on ethical values, such as organic production or fair trade

ethnicity a grouping based on shared ancestry; people with shared ethnicity are known as ethnic groups

eutrophication a form of water pollution when fertilisers run into lakes and rivers

exercise physical activity that helps to make our bodies strong and healthy

exploitation the overuse of something

extended family a larger family, with additional family members besides the nuclear family

extra-curricular a subject not normally part of the usual school or college courses

family group of people who may live together and are related by blood, marriage or another union

family tree a tree-like diagram that shows the structure of a family

fast a period in which people abstain from eating or drinking

feature a geographical landform or part of the environment, such as a mountain or river

fertilisers chemicals that promote fast plant growth

festival a day or period set aside for celebration or feasting

fictitious made up; not real

filter clean by passing through a device such as a mesh

flood large amounts of water suddenly rushing into areas that are usually dry

floor plan a view of a building's layout from directly above

folklore the unwritten literature of a people as expressed in folk tales, proverbs, riddles, songs, etc.

forest an area thickly covered with trees and shrubs

forgiveness to let go of any grudge or hard feelings you may hold against a person for past actions

freedom the power to act and speak as you choose

frescoes durable wall-paintings using watercolours on wet plaster

freshwater water that is not salty

fundamental freedom basic freedom

fundamental right basic right

future something that may or will occur

gas a substance in a form (such as air) that is neither liquid nor solid

gender being male or female

gene units of hereditary information, in sequences of proteins in your cells, inherited from your parents

genealogical related to the history of the past and present members of a family or families

generation the set of members of population living at a particular time

genitals the organs of sexual reproduction

globalisation a process of making the world more connected, with goods, services and people moving and communicating easily and fast between all parts of the world

Global Information System (GIS) a system of information which combines cartography and geography

Global Positioning System (GPS) a navigation system that provides data about time and location

global warming a gradual increase in world temperatures caused by gases, such as carbon dioxide, that stop heat escaping into space

globe a map of the world in the shape of a ball attached to a support frame

goods material objects that people can see or touch, and which they can buy

government the system by which a state or community is governed

grandparents the parents of your parents

greenhouse effect an increase in the amount of carbon dioxide and other gases in the atmosphere that scientists believe to be the cause of the warming of the Earth

grid a network of lines that cross to form blocks

grid lines vertical and horizontal lines over a map

grid reference a pair of letters and numbers that show the position of a place on a grid

gross domestic product (GDP) the total value of goods produced and services provided in a country during one year

Hajj Muslim pilgrimage to Mecca, which takes place approximately two months after Ramadan

head of government an elected political leader, usually the prime minister but sometimes the president

head of state the head of the country, who performs mostly ceremonial duties; for example, a monarch or a president

health physical, mental and social well-being; absence of illness or injury

health care the provision of medical services such as clinics, hospitals and pharmacies

health concerns any issues that affect people's health in a particular place

health indicators data measures that indicate how healthy or unhealthy a population is

healthy response response that leads to understanding and resolution

heavy metals metals that build up in the bodies of living organisms

hemisphere one half of a sphere or globe

heredity the passing on of characteristics from one generation to the next, through the genes

heritage features that belong to the culture of a society that were created in the past and have a historical importance to that society

highly skilled having training or qualifications in a particular field

high self-esteem the knowledge and understanding that one is worthy of love and appreciation, and capable of achieving one's goals

Hindus/Hinduism belief that there is a universal soul called Brahman; this universal soul can take the form of many gods and goddesses

historical sites places and buildings associated with a specific point in time

history an account of events that have happened in the past.

home rules rules made and followed by families

hormone a substance in the body that regulates specific types of growth, development or activity in the body

human capital the types of capital that are made up of people and their skills, abilities, talent and knowledge, e.g. management, training, employees

human geography the relationship between humans and their environment

humanitarian act an act which helps a person in need

humanitarian law international laws that aim to limit the effects of war

human resource development educating and training the workforce

human resources employees, workers or personnel and their various skills and abilities

hurricane intense tropical cyclone that moves faster than 33 metres per second

identity the way you think about yourself, the way the world sees you and the characteristics that define you

illuminated writing decoration in colours, gold or silver used on some manuscripts or printed works

immigrant a person who has moved to a different country to live there permanently

immortal able to live forever

immune system the system that helps the body fight diseases and infections

imperialism a policy of expanding a country into other lands through the use of force if necessary

impressionable easily influenced; easily learning from what happens around them

independence being able to do things without assistance or direction; self-government or self-rule

independent where a nation, country or state exercises self-government

independent state a country that elects its own rulers and governs itself without interference from another country

indigenous originally present in a place; living there naturally; not imported from another place

individual one; a single person or being (rather than a group)

individual differences the specific differences between individuals

individuality the qualities that make a person different from others

industrial work related to factories and production

industrial pollution pollution on land, in water and in air from industrial factories releasing pollution

industries economic activities, or sections of economic activities such as tourism or manufacturing

infant mortality rate (IMR) number of children per 1000 that die before the age of one

infancy the first year of human life

infrastructure the basic facilities of a country, which allow it to function, such as roads, power and communication networks

ingest to take food or liquid into the body

innovation a new way of doing something, especially involving technology

insecticides chemicals that kill insects

inspire to give a particular feeling of being moved, influenced or guided

insurrection revolt or uprising

integrated joined together or working cooperatively as a single unit

integrated movement a formal agreement or strategy to bring an area together (in this case Caribbean countries)

intellectual to do with thinking and reasoning

invent to create or make up

Islam means 'submission to the will of Allah'; Muslims believe in a single god, called Allah

islands landforms surrounded on all sides by water

island chain a chain or cluster of islands

islet a small island

job creation the process of creating opportunities for people to work

jurisdiction the authority that an official organisation has to make legal decisions

justice fair treatment and punishment when laws are broken

karma the Hindu practice of pure acts, knowledge and devotion in order to reach a higher level of incarnation in the next life

kerosene a liquid mixture manufactured from oil used as an aircraft fuel, in domestic heaters and as a solvent

kinship the most basic form of human relationship, based on blood ties or unions such as marriage or adoption

knowledge understanding a subject by experience or studying

labour the work that people do to provide goods and services

landfills large open pits or holes used to store waste

landlocked enclosed on all sides by land

landmass a large body of land, such as a continent

landslide a falling mass of soil or rocks that slides down a slope such as a hill or mountains

language spoken sounds and written symbols to communicate

Last Supper Christ's final meal with his apostles

laws the official rules by which a country is governed

leeward towards the side sheltered from the wind

legacy something handed down to future generations, or received from an ancestor or predecessor

legend/key a list of what each symbol represents on a diagram or chart

life expectancy how long people are expected to live, on average, in a country

lifestyle diseases diseases that may be caused by the way people live

linear scale a scale expressed showing a line distance and what that distance represents in real life

line of latitude an imaginary line that runs horizontally around the globe

line of longitude an imaginary line that runs vertically around the globe

litter rubbish such as paper, plastic, bottles or tins that are left in an open or public place; littering is the act of dropping this type of rubbish in public

location a site or position

loss of productivity decrease in the amount of work that human resources can get done

low self-esteem the feeling that one is unworthy of love and appreciation, and incapable of achieving one's goals

lunar calendar a calendar based on the cycles of the moon

magnetic north the direction in which a compass needle points, which moves slightly over time because of the position of the Earth's axis

main city important or big urban area

mainland a continuous stretch of land that makes up the main part of a country or territory

mainland territories in the Caribbean these are territories on the mainland and include Belize, Suriname, Guyana and French Guiana.

mandala in Buddhism or Hinduism, an object of various designs symbolising the universe, usually circular

mandir name for a Hindu temple

man-made environment surroundings formed by structures made by people

manufacturing the business of making goods in large quantities in a factory

manufacturing practices standards that manufacturers have to meet in the production of their goods, so that they are of high quality to the customer and do not pose any risk

map a picture that shows an area of the Earth as seen from above, showing either physical or political features

map scale the relationship between distances on a map and the corresponding distances in real life

marginalised made to feel alone and isolated

marine relating to the sea, or to an environment that is mostly salt water

marriage a legally or formally recognised union of two people

mass a prayer service involving the holy Eucharist, in which Catholics eat a wafer, and perhaps sip wine, in a ritual sharing in the body and blood of Christ

maternal care care available to pregnant mothers and mothers who have recently given birth

maximise to get the highest results or the most out of something

mediation a process in which a third person assists two conflicting people to reach a resolution

meditation/meditate practice of noticing and allowing thoughts and emotions to pass through the mind

mentorship having a colleague appointed as someone to advise and oversee your progress

methods of warfare the type of weapons that are used in war

military relating to soldiers or armed forces

mineral deposits concentrations of minerals in the Earth's crust

mission the aims and purpose of an organisation

moksha the Hindu goal of becoming one with Brahma, and release from the cycle of reincarnation

monocropping planting a single crop variety over a large area of land

mosque Muslim place of worship

mother country a country that has colonies or dependencies

mountains landforms that rise high above sea level

muezzin man who sings the Muslim call to prayer, usually from a minaret in the mosque

mulching a layer of organic matter, such as wood chips or other plant matter, that breaks down gradually and feeds the soil

multicultural/multiculturalism consisting of many cultures

multiethnic from many different cultural backgrounds

multilingual speaking more than two different languages

multireligious having many different religious practices

murti a Hindu holy statue of a god or goddess

music an art form consisting of sequences of sounds in time, characteristic of a particular people, culture or tradition

Muslims followers of the religion of Islam

mythology a body or collection of myths or stories belonging to a people and addressing their origin, history, deities, ancestors and heroes

nation group of people who share a history; also used to describe people of a particular country

nation building contributing to the economic growth and social improvement of the country

national identity a sense of who you are and that you are part of a country

Nativity Christ's birth

natural boundary a boundary formed by a natural feature such as a coastline

natural disasters damaging natural phenomena such as earthquakes or floods

natural environment natural areas (not the built environment)

natural gas a gaseous mixture consisting mainly of methane trapped below ground; used extensively as a fuel

natural resources resources that occur naturally, such as water, wind, soil, plants, animals and minerals

neighbour state a country that is adjacent to another country, or shares its borders

nephews and nieces your siblings' children

next of kin your closest living relatives

nirvana in Buddhism, a state of full understanding and knowledge of all things; escape from suffering

non-biodegradable items that cannot decay or be broken down through natural decay

non-renewable something that we cannot grow more of or replenish; it will run out

northings horizontal lines running from west to east on a map

nuclear family a mother, father and their children living together in one household

nutrients organic compounds that help plants and micro-organisms to grow

observation careful looking

oestrogen hormone responsible for the development of female sex characteristics

oil liquid fossil fuel

on-the-job training training that a worker gets while they are working

oral source where information is passed on by the spoken word

origins where you come from

pace a long step, usually about a metre in distance

pantheon all the gods of a people considered as a group

parents mothers and fathers, responsible for taking care of their children

parish a village or town which has its own church

past events that happened before the present time

patriotism a feeling of strong support and love for your country

peaceful co-existence communities living together peacefully, without conflict and with mutual respect

pendulum a device used to regulate a clockwork mechanism, mounted so that it can swing freely under the influence of gravity

personal history the history of the people from whom you are descended (your ancestors) and the people to whom you are related

personality the type of person you are, shown by the way you behave, act, feel or think

personal qualities characteristics or **traits** that make you who you are

personal risk danger to yourself

pesticides chemicals that kill insects, weeds and fungi that damage crops

petrochemicals any substance obtained from petroleum or natural gas

philosophy the use of reason to understand the nature of the world and existence

physical able to be seen or touched

physical capital any types of capital that you can see, hold or touch, e.g. cash, machinery, natural resources

physical changes changes that affect the physical shape, size or functioning of the body

physical environment natural surroundings, made up of features such as oceans, mountains, forests and wetlands

physical features natural features like mountains, lakes and the sea

physical geography features of the natural environment, such as mountains, rivers, oceans and forests, as well as the processes within the natural environment

physical resources resources that we can see and touch, such as oil, minerals and forests

pipeline long length of pipe laid over the ground or underground to enable transfer of e.g. various forms of fuel

place of birth where you were born

place of worship a place where people gather to pray and meditate

plate boundaries where the plates of land that form the Earth's crust meet

political relating to the public affairs of a country, or to the power structures that control one or more countries

population pyramid a graph that shows the age and sex distribution of a population

posthumously something that happens after a person has died, which is related to something they did while alive; for example, someone might receive an award posthumously

practice something that people do to apply their idea or belief

premier an elected leader, like a prime minister

present something that exists or is happening now

preservation/preserve maintaining an original state

president can be an elected political leader or a head of state

primary (preventive) healthcare to prevent a disease or illness before we catch it

primary source a document or object created at the time

prime meridian the imaginary line running from the North Pole to the South Pole running through Greenwich in England and north 0° longitude

prime minister an elected leader of the government who has political power

principles basic ideas or rules that explain or control how something happens or works

production the process of growing or making goods to be sold

productive capable of producing goods and services that have monetary or exchange value

protect/protection keep safe or free from injury

Protestantism a branch of Christianity that protested against some of the traditions of the Catholic Church; all later denominations come from Protestantism

puberty the period of physical development during which adolescents begin to develop sexually until they are capable of sexual reproduction

quality a measure of excellence; how excellent something is

quality of life the level of health, comfort and happiness that an individual or group enjoys

quantity number; how many of something there is

Qur'an the Muslim holy book

quarrying the process of cutting or digging into stone or land to obtain minerals

racism the incorrect belief that people of some races are inferior to others

Ramadan a month-long fast during which Muslims have no food or drink during the day

rationale the reasons or intentions for someone to do something

ratio scale a scale expressed as a number ratio or fraction, e.g. 1:100 means 1 cm on the map represents 100 cm, or 1 m, in real life

reconstituted family a family in which one or more parents have children from previous relationships

recycle to process a material into a new material; for example, we can recycle old broken glass to make fresh glass

reduce make or use less of something

reef a ridge of sharp coral, rock or sand just below the sea's surface

refining process where crude oil is processed into more useful products

refineries a factory where oil gets converted into other chemicals

region part of a country, which is not its capital or its surrounding area, or a collection of countries

regional identity a sense of who you are and that you belong to a part of a country or a group of countries

regional integration the joining together or working together of countries that are close together, in order to make them economically and politically more powerful

regulations a set of official instructions issued by authorities

reincarnation the belief that one will be reborn in a different body (plant or animal)

relationships the way people are connected to each other

religion a system of beliefs and practices shared by a group of people

replenish to put back or make more of

resolve/resolution to come to an agreement

resource anything natural or physical that people can use to improve their standard of living or create wealth

respect due regard for someone or something

responsibility a duty; something you are accountable for

responsibilities the things we are expected to do as part of our **role**

restoration repairing and renovating so that something is brought back to its original state

resurrect bring back to life

reuse to use something again

revolt when a group of people try to change the political system of a country by force

reward something which recognises an achievement

rights moral principles or norms that describe certain standards of human behaviour.

risk a situation that can involve danger, harm or loss

river a body of water that runs over the land from a source above sea level (e.g. in a mountain) towards the sea

role a pattern of behaviour that comes from your position in the family

rules a set of instructions which prescribe how you should act or behave

sacrament the giving of spiritual grace to those taking part in a Catholic ceremony

sacred very holy; having religious significance

samsara the cycle of births and deaths that a Hindu soul goes through

sanction a penalty or punishment for not obeying a rule or law

scale a drawing or object that has been reduced or enlarged from its original size

scale statement scale expressed in a statement; for example, 1 cm = 1000 km

scholarship money provided by an organisation to help a student pay for school or university

school rules rules made and followed at school

scriptures holy writings or books

sea large area of salty water that covers most of the Earth's surface

secondary (curative) healthcare care given to patients to cure them of their disease or illness

secondary source a document created after an event took place

secular non-religious; not following a religion

self-discipline to make yourself do things when you don't want to

self-esteem how much you like and value yourself, how much you appreciate your personal worth

semi-skilled having some training in using tools or machinery

senescence the condition of becoming gradually weaker with old age

sense of place characteristics that make a place special or unique

service activities that people provide in an economy, e.g. teaching, plumbing, tourism or banking

service industry an industry that provides a service for people, but does not produce finished goods or products

settler someone who comes to live in a country

sewage human faeces, urine and wastewater from laundry and washing

sexual attraction the feeling of wanting to be sexually closer or more intimate with another person

sexual feelings warm, excited feelings in the body as a result of sex hormones

Shabbat the Jewish Sabbath day, which begins at sunset on Friday and ends at sunset the next day

shrine a place for prayers and religious offerings, usually with pictures or statues of religious symbols

sibling household a household in which the parents are absent, so the older brothers and sisters take care of younger siblings

siblings children born to the same parents

signage sign that tells you, for example, the name of the village, town, region, country that you are in

significance importance; meaning

similarities things that are the same in some ways

single parent family one parent living with his or her children

skill a specific learned or developed ability, e.g. driving a car

skilled having some training in a particular field

skills (variety) a range of abilities to perform a specific task or a number of different skill types which contribute to a country's economic development

skills development a process in which a country, economy or firm provides education and training for its workers so that they can improve their existing skills and develop new ones

skills enhancement improvement of existing skills

smog thick hazy fog caused by pollutants in the air

sociable when people like to meet and spend time with each other

social to do with relationships and society

social asset something which belongs to everyone (or the whole of society), such as a historical site

social environment the world made up of the people around an individual, including the home, love and affection of family, relationships with family, friends, peers and acquaintances

social function the family teaching its children to learn how to interact and communicate with others and how to form relationships

social links links between people such as language and common ancestry

social skills how we communicate and interact with each other, both verbally and non-verbally, through gestures, body language and our personal appearance

solid waste garbage or rubbish in solid form rather than in liquid or gas form

source (history) documents and written texts where we learn about history

source (geography) the place where a river starts, usually in a mountain or hill

spire a tall, thin cone or pyramid, usually on top of a church tower

standard of living the degree of wealth and material comfort that a person or community enjoys

straight-line border a border that is drawn in a straight line, usually as a result of being a man-made border originating on a map rather than originating from a real physical feature, e.g. a river

strategy a plan of action

succession training training up an employee to prepare them for promotion

Sunnah the practical laws of Islam

survey/surveying an examination and record of an area of land, in order to create an accurate plan or description

sustainable something that can be continued without destroying the resources that make it possible

symbol a picture or sign that represents a particular meaning

talent a special natural ability that makes a person particularly good at something

tanker ship ships that carry oil or natural gas

template an outline or grid

Temptation of Christ Jesus' 40-day fast in the desert after being baptised, during which Satan visits to tempt him

testosterone hormone responsible for the development of male sex characteristics

tolerance acceptance of views, beliefs or behaviours that are different from one's own

tornado rotating column of air that forms under a thundercloud

to scale uniformly reduced or enlarged; showing the relationships in proportion to real life

town urban area of up to 100 000 people, smaller than a city

trade union an organisation for workers which represents their rights at work

traditional following the customs or ways of behaving that have continued in a group of people or society for a long time without changing

traditions beliefs, behaviours and actions that people hand down from one generation to the next

trait a feature or quality distinguishing a particular person or thing

treaty an agreement between two or more regions or countries

tributary a stream that feeds into a larger river

trimurti in Hinduism the trimurti are the three main aspects of Brahman and are made up of the gods Vishnu, Brahma and Shiva

tropical climate warm temperatures all year round, specifically in the areas surrounding the equator

tsunami a giant wave that moves very fast across the surface of the sea

tuition assistance a process whereby an employer pays for the employee's further training

unhealthy response response that leads to further conflict

uniform set of clothes for the members of an organisation, such as schoolchildren or scouts

union joining together of two people to form a family

unique the only one of its kind; unlike any other

unity being joined together or in agreement

universal affecting everyone or everything

Universal Declaration of Human Rights (UDHR) declaration of human rights by countries that are members of the United Nations

universal suffrage the right for all adults to vote in an election

unskilled not having any specific skills

varieties genetic differences between individuals of a particular species

veto reject, not to approve

vice sin or evil

village a settlement of between a few hundred and a few thousand people

visibility how far it is possible to see

vision planning for the future in an imaginative and creative way

visiting relationship a long-term partnership where the partners do not live together, but one visits the other from time to time

visual arts something creative you can see or look at

volcano land formation that opens with a vent to molten lava in the Earth's crust below; it may be active, dormant or extinct

volunteer someone who chooses to work or help but is not paid for the work he or she does

war armed conflict between people

ward a smaller division within a county, usually used for voting purposes

water-wise efficient in its use of water

wealth in economic development terms, the amount of money or possessions that a country has

wetland a land environment that is regularly soaked with water, where the land connects with a river or sea

windward into the wind; on the side facing into the wind

wisdom to use knowledge and experience to make good judgements

work cooperatively working helpfully with others

yield the amount that can be harvested per square unit of land

Index

Acknowledgements

The publishers wish to thank the following for permission to reproduce photographs. Every effort has been made to trace copyright holders and to obtain their permission for the use of copyright materials. The publishers will gladly receive any information enabling them to rectify any error or omission at the first opportunity.

p8: John Birdsall/Alamy; p10: Age fotostock/Alamy; p11: Bob Krist/Corbis; p13: Vladimir Wrangel/Shutterstock; p15: John Birdsall/Rex Features; p17: Eye Ubiquitous/Alamy; p22: Stephanie Rabemiafara/Getty Images; p27: James Quine/Alamy; p28: Monkey Business Images/Shutterstock; p31: Chris Rout/Alamy; p35: Wolfgang Kaehler/Getty Images; p40: David sanger photography/Alamy; p41: Hola Images/Getty Images; p42: National Film Board of Canada / contributor/Getty Images; p45: MaRoDee Photography/Alamy; p50: WIN-Initiative/Neleman/Getty Images; p54: Eye Ubiquitous/Getty Images; p56: LatitudeStock - Ian Brierley/Getty Images; p57: LatitudeStock/Alamy; p58 (T): Ellen Rooney/Getty Images; p58 (B): Bank of Nevis Ltd; p59: Allstar Picture Library/Alamy; p61: Janine Wiedel Photolibrary/Alamy; p62: Richard Wareham Fotografi e/Alamy; p63: Custom Medical Stock Photo/Alamy; p64: Terry Harris/Alamy; p65: Anthony Asael/Getty Images; p67: Ian Patrick/Alamy; p68: Michael Ventura/Alamy; p74 (T): Archive Farms/Getty Images; p74 (B): Fox Photos/Stringer/Getty Images p76: Hulton Archive/Stringer/Getty Images; p77: Steven Wright/Shutterstock; p78: Fredrick Kippe/Alamy; p81: Harvey Meston/Archive Photos/Getty Images; p82: Samir Hussein/Getty Images; p83: Sean Sprague/Alamy Stock Photo; p85: Bryan Bedder/Getty Images; p86: Bettmann/Getty Images; p87: Railway fx/Shutterstock; p88: AR Photo/Alamy p89: Ray James Spencer; p90: ATGImages/Shutterstock; p91: chrisdorney/Shutterstock; p92: University of the West Indies; p93: Peter Probst / Alamy; p94: Niyazz/Alamy Stock Photo; p95: Keystone Pictures USA/Alamy Stock Photo; p96: Everett Collection Historical/Alamy Stock Photo; p97:Dpa picture alliance/Alamy Stock Photo; p98: Wolfgang Kaehler/Getty Images, p99; Hulton Archive/Stringer/Getty Images; p106: Northallertonman/Shutterstock;P108: Vilainecrevette/Alamy; p110: Age Fotostock/Alamy; p112:Kerwynw/Demotix/Corbis; p114: Danita Delimont/Alamy;p117: Pedro Rey/stringer/Getty Images; p118: Megapress/Alamy; p120: Zoom Dosso/stringer/Getty Images; p121: Allstar Picture Library/Alamy; p122: Horizons WWP/Alamy; p129: Eye Ubiquitous/Getty Images; p130: 2d Alan King/Alamy; p136: Sean Drakes/Getty Images; p139: Wolfgang Kaehler/Getty Images; p140: MJ Photography/Alamy; p141: Joymsk140/Shutterstock; p142 (T): Salim October/Shutterstock; p142 (B): meunierd/Shutterstock; p144: Paul Thompson Images/Alamy; p145: Filip Fuxa/Shutterstock;; p152: Marbury/Shutterstock; p154: Heritage Images/Corbis; p155: PRAKASH SINGH/AFP/Getty Images; p156: Vehbi Koca/Alamy; p157: Art Directors & TRIP/Alamy; p158: Robert Harding World Imagery/Alamy; p159: Myimagefi les/Alamy; p160: Jupiterimages/Getty Images; p161: Grzegorz knec/Alamy; p162: Robert Harding World Imagery/Alamy; p163: M. Sobreira/Alamy; p166: Janis Lacis/Shutterstock; p167: Images & Stories/Alamy; p169: Deepu Sg/Alamy; p178: Stockolio/Alamy; p179: Steve Murray/Alamy; p180: philippe giraud/Getty Images; p181: Sunpix Travel/Alamy; p184: John Warburton-Lee Photography/Alamy; p185: Westend61 GmbH/Alamy; p186: Jiri Flogel/Shutterstock; p187: Jim Watson/Getty Images; p196 (T): Dan Kitwood/Getty Images (B): Tiziana Fabi/Getty Images; p203: Robert Harding World Imagery/Alamy; P208: Sean Potter/Alamy; p210: Tony Boydon/Alamy; p211: Bill Bachmann/Getty Images; p212: LatitudeStock/ Alamy; p213: Francois LOCHON/Getty Images; p214: Tommy Trenchard/Alamy; p216: Raul Touzon/Getty Images; p218: Pix/Alamy; p219: Photoshot Holdings Ltd/Alamy; p221: Karnt Thassanaphak/Shutterstock; p223: EdBockStock/Alamy; p225: Cm studio/Alamy; p226: Sean Pavone/Alamy Stock Photo; p228: Bob Krist/Corbis; p230: ImageBROKER/Alamy Stock Photo; p231: Andrew Woodley/Alamy Stock Photo; p232: Andrea De Silva/REUTERS; p234: Omikron/Science Photo Library; p235: Justin Kase z12z/Alamy; p240: Ivy Close Images/Alamy; p241: ImageBROKER/Alamy; p242: John P Kelly/Getty Images; pp244 (T): Incamerastock/Alamy; pp244 (B): Blickwinkel/Alamy;; p252: Marcelo Rudini/Alamy; p266: Universal Images Group Limited/Alamy; p272: David Noton Photography/Alamy; p273 (L): Central Press/Stringer/Getty Images; p273 (R): Rob Griffi th/AP Photo; p274: Yuiyui/Alamy; p275: Panachai Cherdchucheep/Shutterstock; p290 (T): Senarb Commercial/Alamy; p290 (B): D. Hurst/Alamy